New Strategies for Educational Fund Raising

Edited by
Michael J. Worth

Foreword by
Vance T. Peterson

AMERICAN COUNCIL ON EDUCATION
PRAEGER
Series on Higher Education

Library of Congress Cataloging-in-Publication Data

New strategies for educational fund raising / [edited by] Michael J. Worth ; foreword by Vance T. Peterson.
     p. cm.—(American Council on Education/Praeger series on higher education)
     Sequel to: Educational fund raising. 1993.
     Includes bibliographical references and index.
     ISBN 1–57356–518–0 (alk. paper)
     1. Educational fund raising—United States.   2. Universities and colleges—United States—Finance.   I. Title: New strategies for educational fund raising.
II. Title: Educational fundraising.   III. Worth, Michael J.   IV. Educational fund raising.
     LB2336 .N49 2002
     379.1'3—dc21   2002066890

Formerly ACE/Oryx Press Series on Higher Education

British Library Cataloguing in Publication Data is available.

Library of Congress Catalog Card Number: 2002066890
ISBN: 1–57356–518–0

First published in 2002

Praeger Publishers, 88 Post Road West, Westport, CT 06881
An imprint of Greenwood Publishing Group, Inc.
www.praeger.com

Printed in the United States of America

The paper used in this book complies with the
Permanent Paper Standard issued by the National
Information Standards Organization (Z39.48–1984).

10 9 8 7 6 5 4 3 2 1

This book is dedicated to the memory of my parents

Joseph Henry Worth, Jr.
1909–1956

Meta Christine Worth
1910–1980

Contents

Foreword

T he 1990s were a decade of unprecedented economic growth and
new records in philanthropic support of higher education. At
the same time, while colleges, universities, and schools were setting and achieving higher goals, the competition for support intensified.
Organizations that previously had not been engaged in fund raising entered the arena, and what had been primarily an activity of U.S. educational institutions became an international phenomenon. The early
years of a new decade—indeed, a new century—have seen a slowing in
economic growth, but the needs of higher education have continued to
grow unabated in the United States and throughout the world. In addition to competition for philanthropic support, education now must
work to establish its continuing importance and priority in the public
consciousness in an environment consumed by concern with international security. The challenges confronting institutional advancement
professionals thus call for even greater skills and levels of dedication.

Michael Worth's 1993 book, *Educational Fund Raising: Principles and
Practice*, defined the field of educational fund raising, or development,
for the 1990s, bringing together for the first time in a comprehensive
volume both the wisdom of practitioners and the findings of emerging
research in the field. It was among the best-selling books in history on
educational fund raising and came to be used as a textbook in many of
the growing number of university courses on the topic. A decade later,
this current volume extends that earlier work with new and revised
material suited to the new fund-raising environment. It will be as im-

portant as the previous volume was as a resource to advancement professionals, campus CEOs, and scholars interested in educational advancement. It reflects the changes of the past decade: the expansion of the fund-raising arena to engage new constituencies and the entire globe, the impact of technology on advancement practice, and the increasing importance of sound management of the advancement program, which now commands substantial resources on many campuses. This volume also reaffirms some of the basic principles that are still relevant, emphasizing that fund raising remains a blend of art and science and that the development of relationships between individuals and their institutions, by identifying shared values, still lies at the heart of it.

What also comes through clearly from the words of various authors is the extent to which advancement has become an important focus for the entire campus, including boards, CEOs, deans, and chief financial officers. Institutional advancement professionals take the lead in developing advancement strategy and programs, but board members are setting clear standards for planning and for measuring the effectiveness of fund raising, presidents and school heads are devoting increasing portions of their time to cultivating and soliciting donors, and chief financial officers and fund raisers are working more closely together as philanthropy becomes a critical source of capital for achieving institutional goals. This is likely to become an even greater reality in the years ahead, requiring that advancement officers play an even larger role in the overall leadership of colleges, universities, and schools, with a continuing increase in the number of them who become CEOs.

To meet their greater responsibilities in this new era, institutional advancement officers will need to go beyond the application of their already considerable professional skills in order to maintain a broad perspective on the trends and issues confronting their profession and all of higher education, to understand and work comfortably in an environment of increasing diversity, to always think in a businesslike manner while continuing to emphasize the central importance of human emotions, values, and relationships in philanthropy, and to be innovative and flexible in responding to changing technology and market forces.

In view of its practitioners' expanding roles and responsibilities, the advancement profession itself needs to be continuously engaged in self-examination and renewal. It must assure that the profession is clearly defined, that its techniques reflect the growing body of knowledge based on basic and applied research, and that advancement offices can account for the resources they expend to produce results, while adhering to the highest ethical standards. *New Strategies for Educational Fund Raising* engages all of these subjects and thus makes an important contribution to our knowledge and perspective at a critical juncture in the history of the advancement profession.

Vance T. Peterson
President, Council for Advancement and Support of Education

Preface

I served as general editor of *Educational Fund Raising: Principles and Practice*, which was published by the American Council on Education and Oryx Press in 1993. In the Preface to that book, I said that it was intended to replace Francis Pray's 1981 *Handbook of Educational Fund Raising*, which had become obsolete in view of the dramatic changes that had affected the field in the intervening decade. But, by the end of the 1990s, it became clear that the word "obsolete" might now be directed toward my own work, as the changes since 1993 had been even greater than those of the decade before. That recognition was the genesis of this current volume.

This book is entitled *New Strategies for Educational Fund Raising* because the environment for educational fund raising has changed, and fund raisers must indeed adopt new strategies and adapt old ones to meet new opportunities and challenges. In Abraham Lincoln's words, "As we begin anew, we must think anew."

While this volume may correctly be described as a "sequel" to the 1993 book, it clearly is not a "revised edition" of that work. Some of the authors from that earlier book are again included here to address the same topics, but their chapters have been updated and revised to reflect the changes of the intervening years. Other chapters cover the same topics, but are addressed in this book by new authors, some of whom replace 1993 contributors who may have subsequently retired, left the profession, or moved on to new responsibilities and are no longer specialized in the subject of their earlier writing. Perhaps the most revealing aspect of changes to the fund-raising environment over the past decade is how some chapters in this book discuss concepts that did not even exist as a part of our professional lexicon a decade ago—for example principal gifts and benchmarking. Others, including those in the section of the book entitled Traditions of Giving, discuss changes in American society and the world that were not prominent in the minds of educational fund raisers a decade ago, but which may present the most significant realities affecting development work in the decades ahead.

In the Preface to *Educational Fund Raising: Principles and Practice*, I said that fund raising was "a blend of science and art . . . still a profession taught by relating experience more than by presenting formulas and graphs." In the past decade, the field has gained a larger body of knowledge, and the "science" of related disciplines, such as marketing, have come to be more commonly applied. But, I still think that fund raising is a combination of science and art. There is more science in the use of information and communication technology. The use of financial instruments in the planning of gifts has become far more sophisticated. And, fund raising has borrowed from the tested techniques of business to improve the management of its programs and the measurement of their effectiveness. But, the essence of the work—the cultivation of relationships between individuals and institutions—is still primarily an art. The chapters in this book reflect that continued blend of the science and art of fund raising.

As I said in 1993, the field of fund raising still stands somewhere between astrology and astronomy in its intellectual rigor. However, the increasing interest of academic researchers in fund raising as a field of study is a healthy development of recent years, and it is reflected in this volume. Some chapters in this book are written by full-time academics who have focused their scholarly work on fund raising and philanthropy, and who have added immeasurably to our practitioner-based insights. Indeed, in 2001, I joined their ranks as Professor of Nonprofit Management at The George Washington University, after thirty years as a practicing development officer.

Like all books that include the works of multiple authors, the style is not entirely consistent from chapter to chapter, despite the best efforts of the editor. There is occasional redundancy, since the chapter subjects overlap somewhat. I allowed some redundancy to remain because I thought the points were essential anchors for more than one discussion. Some chapters concern sophisticated topics and may be stimulating reading for even seasoned professionals. Others are essentially introductory, appropriate overviews for new or aspiring development officers, but, I believe, never harmful as refreshers for even the most seasoned practitioners.

The chapter authors represented herein, both practitioners and academics, are among the most accomplished and respected authorities in their fields. It has been an honor and a privilege for me to have worked with them in producing this volume. I take full responsibility for its weaknesses. They justly deserve the credit for its strengths.

Michael J. Worth
Washington, D.C.

Acknowledgments

This book is in many ways a tribute to my long association with Jim Murray, retired Vice President of the American Council on Education, who helped to guide me in editing the 1993 *Educational Fund Raising: Principles and Practice* and whose advice was again important at the initiation of this volume. I am grateful to Jim for the professional and personal friendship we have enjoyed over the years. I express thanks to Teresa Crawford, my former Executive Assistant at The George Washington University, for her help with editing and to Lisa Barton Kranz, my former student at George Washington, who offered helpful comments on drafts of the Introduction and Conclusion. I am grateful to Professor Kathryn Newcomer, Chair of the Department of Public Administration at George Washington, for her wonderful support in my transition to full-time faculty status, which coincided with my work on this book. I have worked with six presidents or chancellors in the course of a thirty-year development career and have learned something about fund raising—and leadership—from each of them. I am grateful for the lessons learned from Francis J. Michelini, J. Stuart Dooling, Robert L. Gluckstern, John B. Slaughter, Lloyd H. Elliott, and Stephen Joel Trachtenberg. Most of all, I thank the distinguished authors who have contributed their work and wisdom to make this volume possible.

Contributors

John Abrahams is Director of Research and Information at the Council for Advancement and Support of Education in Washington, D.C.

Matthew J. Beem is a Fellow at the Midwest Center for Nonprofit Leadership at the University of Missouri–Kansas City and Executive Vice President of Hartsook & Associates in Independence, Missouri.

Ruth Constantine is Vice President for Finance at Smith College in Northampton, Massachusetts.

Jon S. Dellandrea is Vice-President and Chief Advancement Officer at the University of Toronto in Toronto, Ontario, Canada.

David R. Dunlop is a consultant and speaker. He is the former Director of Capital Projects at Cornell University in Ithaca, New York.

Gail Ferris is Executive Director of Alumni/Development Services at The George Washington University in Washington, D.C.

Karin Lee George is Vice President for Advancement at Smith College in Northampton, Massachusetts.

Bruce R. Hopkins is Of Counsel to the law firm of Polsinelli, Shalton & Welte in Kansas City, Missouri.

Patricia King Jackson is Assistant Head of School for Development and Alumni Relations at Sidwell Friends School in Washington, D.C.

Marianne Jordan is Director of Corporate and Foundation Relations at Bowdoin College in Brunswick, Maine.

Andrea Kaminski is Director of Development at the Meriter Foundation in Madison, Wisconsin. She was Vice President for Research and Programs at the Women's Philanthropy Institute in Madison, Wisconsin, when she wrote this chapter.

Kathleen S. Kelly is Professor of Communication and Public Relations at the University of Louisiana at Lafayette in Lafayette, Louisiana, where she holds the Hubert J. Bourgeois Research Professorship.

Peter K. Kimball is Director of Gift Planning at Harvard University in Cambridge, Massachusetts.

Susan K. Kubik is Vice President for Institutional Advancement at Northampton Community College in Bethlehem, Pennsylvania.

James M. Langley is Vice Chancellor for External Relations at the University of California–San Diego in San Diego, California.

Robert R. Lindgren is Vice President for Development and Alumni Relations at The Johns Hopkins Institutions in Baltimore, Maryland.

William P. McGoldrick is a partner in the consulting firm of Washburn & McGoldrick in Latham, New York. He was previously Vice President for Institute Relations at Rensselaer Polytechnic Institute in Troy, New York.

Judith E. Nichols is an independent fund-raising and marketing consultant in Portland, Oregon.

Scott G. Nichols is Dean for Development at the Harvard Law School in Cambridge, Massachusetts.

Sara L. Patton is Vice President for Development at the College of Wooster in Wooster, Ohio.

Vance T. Peterson is President of the Council for Advancement and Support of Education in Washington, DC.

Paul A. Robell is Vice President for Development and Alumni Affairs at the University of Florida in Gainesville, Florida.

Ronald E. Sapp is a consultant. He retired as Director of Planned Giving at The Johns Hopkins Institutions in Baltimore, Maryland.

Joanne B. Scanlan is Senior Vice President, Professional Development, at the Council on Foundations in Washington, D.C.

Fritz W. Schroeder is Executive Director for Annual, Regional, and Alumni Programs at The Johns Hopkins University in Baltimore, Maryland.

Jake B. Schrum is President of Southwestern University in Georgetown, Texas.

Frank D. Schubert is Executive Director of Resource Development for Principal Gifts at the University of Texas at Austin in Austin, Texas.

Adel S. Sedra is Vice-President and Provost at the University of Toronto in Toronto, Ontario, Canada.

Eric Siegel is Director of Prospect Management and Research at Claremont Graduate University in Claremont, California.

Curtis R. Simic is President of the Indiana University Foundation in Bloomington, Indiana.

Linda G. Steckley is Associate Dean for External Relations at the Duke University School of Law in Durham, North Carolina.

Eugene R. Tempel is Executive Director of the Center on Philanthropy at Indiana University in Indianapolis, Indiana.

James M. Theisen is Director of Development at Philips Exeter Academy in Exeter, New Hampshire.

Charles H. Webb is Vice President for University Development at Michigan State University in East Lansing, Michigan.

Roger L. Williams is Associate Vice Chancellor for University Relations at the University of Arkansas in Fayetteville, Arkansas.

D. Chris Withers is Vice President for Advancement at the University of Richmond in Richmond, Virginia.

Michael J. Worth is Professor of Nonprofit Management at The George Washington University in Washington, D.C. He was Vice President for Development and Alumni Affairs at The George Washington University from 1983 to 2001.

Introduction: New Strategies for a New Age

Michael J. Worth

> When we talk about the new economy, we're talking about a world in which people work with their brains instead of their hands. A world in which communications technology creates global competition. . . . A world in which innovation is more important than mass production. A world in which investment buys new concepts or the means to create them, rather than new machines. A world in which rapid change is a constant. A world at least as different from what came before it as the industrial age was from its agricultural predecessor. A world so different its emergence can only be described as a revolution.[1]
>
> —*Encyclopedia of the New Economy*

I sometimes think about change in the context of my own grandmother's life, which began in 1884 and continued for ninety-eight years, encompassing the introduction of electricity, the automobile, the radio, the telephone, television, space travel, and the computer. She lived through two world wars, a depression, and enormous changes in family life. She was born in a time of transition, from the agricultural age, in which most people worked on farms, to the industrial age, in which most people's jobs were in places such as factories and mines. She lived to the edge of yet another new age, the information age, in which those alive today are likely to live the balance of their years.

Her father and her husband were coal miners. As in most industrial age jobs, they worked with their hands. Most people working during the industrial age held jobs in which they either made or extracted *things*. One could watch coal miners work and know what they were doing. There also was no question about the purpose of their efforts. Coal was used to power factories and railroads and to heat homes. The relationship between what the miners produced and people's daily lives was evident. Theirs was "real work," and my grandmother understood quite well what it was her father and her husband did for a living.

Her son, my father, became a department store manager. I am not certain that my grandmother knew exactly what he did in the course of a working day—management is somewhat more abstract than mining coal—but she knew that a manager was "the boss," a concept consistent with the industrial model, so she had at least a point of reference. In addition, the environment of a department store was familiar to her; she knew the nature of what was done there, even if she may not have understood the specific responsibilities of individual employees.

But, when I accepted my first position as a college development officer, it was clear to me that my grandmother did not completely understand my role. She had never been to college, but she knew it to be a good thing and was proud that her grandson worked on a campus, where she assumed most people employed were professors. But, when I offered the simplest description of my responsibilities as "raising money," I think I caused her some concern about whether I had found a legitimate job. When one of my cousins married a consultant, my grandmother asked me what he did, and I simplified again, saying, "He gives advice." Her skeptical expression told me that she was concerned about whether he had a job at all! Within the span of her lifetime, the world had moved from an agricultural society to an industrial economy to the beginning of the information age, in which ideas—even advice—could be regarded as products.

Throughout most of my grandmother's life, change occurred gradually enough that she could adapt to it. The transition to commercial jet aircraft occurred in the 1960s, more than fifty years after the Wright Brothers' first flight. Today, change occurs much more rapidly, challenging people's ability to keep pace. Personal computers became generally available only in the 1980s and the Internet in the 1990s, yet both already have undergone several generations of development and have become pervasive in our lives. Broadband may soon make today's modems seem as antique as the small black-and-white television screens I remember from my own youth. Some say that the PC itself is almost obsolete and that Internet "appliances" soon will integrate electronic communications even further into our daily routines.

The next quarter-century's changes may equal or exceed all of those in my grandmother's entire long life. Colleges and universities are not insulated from change in society, and all of them will be affected, as will those who make their lives on the campus, including development officers. Those who are in the midst of their development careers today must be able to respond to change quickly and confidently if they are to remain effective, even survive, in their jobs. The nature and definition of the development officer's job is changing. It is being shaped by new needs, priorities, and pressures facing educational institutions and the nation. It may in years ahead become as different from what it was when some professionals began their development careers as a consultant's work is from the task of a coal miner just a century ago.

FOUR POWERFUL FORCES

There are four powerful "forces of change" that are having the greatest impact on higher education fund raising and philanthropy, and that will continue to drive change in the coming decades: demographics, technology, globalization, and what I call the "dominance of market thinking."

Demographics

The population of the United States is growing more diverse by race, national origin, culture, language, and perspective. Student bodies, and eventually alumni bodies, will include many individuals whose backgrounds and experiences may be quite different from those who have traditionally attended higher education institutions. Alumni in the future may have different priorities, respond to different messages, and hold different expectations of their alma maters than did those of the past.

The average age of Americans, indeed of people around the world, is increasing. Individuals age eighty-five and above are the fastest growing segment of the population. The much-heralded intergenerational transfer of wealth holds enormous potential for philanthropy and will influence the style and substance of fund-raising programs.

There have been significant changes in the demographics of wealth that may influence patterns of giving. For example, as a result of vigorous economic growth in the past two decades and the arrival of global capitalism, the distribution of wealth has become more concentrated, both in the United States and around the world. This shift may account at least in part for the increased reliance on very large gifts from relatively few donors.

Technology

Exploding advancements in technology and the promise of broader, faster access to the Web are creating new opportunities for colleges and universities to recruit students, communicate with their alumni and donors, and even offer courses and programs to people who never visit the campus. Information and communications technology already has been incorporated in college and university fund-raising programs and promises to change the practice even more in the years ahead.

But, the growth of the virtual world also poses challenges to traditional institutions. Access to information offers more choices and makes people less dependent on any particular institution as a source of education, entertainment, or social connection. It is now possible to engage in continuing dialogues with friends and associates with common interests who are situated anywhere in the world. Not constrained by geography, or even by language—the computer will translate—people are free to join any group they find to be of interest, not just those that happen to be close to home. As John Naisbitt says, "E-mail is a tribe maker. Electronics makes us more tribal at the same time it globalizes us."[2] As people associate themselves with smaller and smaller tribes, defined by narrow common interests and shared virtual experiences, there are obvious implications for colleges and universities, traditionally among the most important "tribe makers" in our society.

At the same time, the advancement of technology and global communication also may create some backlash, a greater need for connection to communities of shared experience. Such needs may serve to increase even more the bonds to a college or university that is able to capture the power of technology in order to continue a relationship with its graduates throughout their lives. But, these are choppy waters and it will take both skill and planning to navigate higher education institutions safely through.

Globalization

Higher education and philanthropy have become international enterprises. Distance learning technology promises to create an even more vigorous international marketplace for education as geographic separation becomes less of an impediment to communication. As higher education has become more international in scope, with increasing exchanges of students, professors, materials, and ideas across the globe, the fund-raising arena has expanded as well. American higher education institutions are seeking support from donors throughout the world. At the same time, faced with reductions in traditional government support, colleges and universities in many nations are emulating the American model in seeking philanthropic support from their own domestic sources and from donors in the United States. This globalization is increasing both competition and the need for cross-cultural communication and understanding.

Dominance of Market Thinking

I use the phrase "dominance of market thinking" to encompass several related trends, reflected in the adoption of market values and a business vocabulary in virtually all aspects of our society, including higher education. The dominance of market thinking is manifested in reliance on competition to determine value, the linking of reward with performance, the measurement of performance in quantitative (usually financial) terms, and an enthusiasm for entrepreneurial initiative. Many observers have noted the "corporatization" of higher education, which increasingly applies concepts of business in setting goals and evaluating results. In this environment, some donors also see their colleges and universities in new ways. Many expect to play a much greater role in setting the institution's agenda than did their predecessors a generation ago, and view philanthropy as a form of "investment," expecting a measureable "return" in the form of improved institutional performance. As discussed further in this book's Conclusion, on some campuses the distinction between traditional fund raising and business activity is becoming blurred, potentially changing the role of college and university development officers and the relationship between fund raising and other administrative functions of the institution. The emphasis on accountability and performance measurement is altering the way in which development officers are evaluated and rewarded for their efforts. This shift may eventually change the way they understand and perform their jobs.

Although separated here for purposes of discussion, these four powerful forces of change are not independent of one another, and it is not always simple to identify cause and effect. For example, communication technology has made globalization possible. In turn, it is globalization that has increased economic competition, heightening the focus on the market value of education and everything else. Many have observed that communication technology also played a vital role in the fall of communism and the opening up of global capitalism. But, it seems likely that demographics were relevant, too, with the rise of a new generation less familiar with and committed to the ideological struggles of the past. In a world as complex as this one, any analysis of trends and forces of change is inevitably somewhat messy, the boundaries ill-defined.

These four forces of change are of particular relevance for fund raising because they influence the perspectives and attitudes that people hold, the way in which they communicate with each other, how they define themselves as members of groups, and how they relate to the institutions in their lives. These are variables that are central to philanthropy, especially in higher education.

What all the forces have in common—and the condition toward which they all lead—is greater competition, among higher education institutions themselves and between higher education and other non-profit organizations that also seek philanthropic support. As discussed in Chapter 1 of this book, competition is not a new concept in American higher education. What is new is its intensity, its international scope, the speed with which competitive decisions need to be made and implemented, and how quickly their consequences are realized.

NEW STRATEGIES FOR A NEW AGE

The four forces of change are reflected in this volume in two ways. First, some of the chapter topics are related specifically to one or another of them. For example, the chapters in Part VI (Traditions of Giving) specifically address the implications of an increasingly diverse society and of globalization. The impact of technology is explicitly acknowledged in the chapter on development information systems and the new "businesslike" environment is evident in the chapter on benchmarking, accountability, and measuring performance.

But, the four forces also are woven throughout all the chapters, even those that discuss traditional fund-raising topics. There is almost no aspect of fund raising and philanthropy that has not been affected by the need to respond to today's new environment. For example, technology has changed annual giving programs and the practice of prospect research. The chapters on those subjects reflect the impact. Global competition and the dominance of market thinking have changed corporate giving, and the chapter on that topic captures the new realities. Perhaps most significantly, the new environment is even evident in the changing ways in which the development officer's work is defined, measured, and rewarded—new approaches that are discussed by several authors. This change increases even more the need to consider both development as a profession and its ethical dimensions, topics addressed in two chapters of this book.

In the Conclusion, some issues and perspectives reflecting the four forces of change will be discussed, and final thoughts expressed there will reflect optimism about the future of higher education and philanthropy. There are enormous challenges facing higher education, and threats to the future of philanthropy will be identified throughout this book. To be successful, colleges and universities will need to pursue new strategies for fund raising, embracing new techniques and adapting old principles to a new time and different circumstances.

But, surely, in an age when ideas are more valuable than machines and people are the ultimate resource, there will be an important place for institutions devoted to the advancement of knowledge and the development of human minds. And, the impulse for philanthropy has endured many centuries of our history. It has its roots in fundamental human aspirations and desires. People still are altruistic, and most want to do the right thing. People still give money to people and to causes in which they believe. Success in fund raising is still built on trust, earned in sustained relationships over the long term. The more things change, the more at least some things stay the same. I think my grandmother would have understood—and agreed.

NOTES

1. John Browning and Spencer Reiss, *Encyclopedia of the New Economy* (reprinted from *Wired Magazine*, March 1998), 1.

2. John Naisbitt, *Global Paradox* (New York: William Morrow and Company, 1994), 23.

PART I

The Development Function

The following chapters establish the context within which educational fund raising occurs, providing a solid overview of the elements of the development program. Although these chapters may be of greater interest to those who are new to the field than to veterans, the material also offers some points worthy of consideration by senior development professionals.

Chapter 1 places educational fund raising, or development, in the broader context of institutional advancement and attempts to clarify the definitions of these terms. The establishment of common definitions is one criterion of a profession. The fields of institutional advancement and educational fund raising have yet to achieve such commonality, and although the discussion in Chapter 1 does not resolve that problem, it does offer some important distinctions.

One need not be a dictionary buff to be concerned with definitions, since they reflect broader concepts that affect the way we think about and do our jobs. While this book focuses on educational fund raising, it is essential for the development officer to understand that he or she is a member of a professional institutional advancement team, and that the institution's success depends upon coordination and integration of the various advancement specialties. This understanding is so important to the strength of colleges and universities that it offers an appropriate place to begin the discussion.

Chapter 2 provides an overview that may be particularly helpful to the beginner. It defines the landscape of educational fund raising and how the various elements covered in the balance of the book relate to each other in an integrated whole. While introductory, it offers some principles concerning the allocation of effort and resources that may be helpful reminders to even experienced professionals.

Chapter 3 places contemporary educational fund raising in the context of history. It is not a history of philanthropy, a subject with which fund raisers also should be familiar, but rather a brief history of organized educational fund raising in the United States and the evolution of the professional field in which most readers of this book likely work, or plan to work. It is perhaps important to all of us, as professionals as well as individuals, to have some sense of our heritage. Such understanding affects how we view ourselves and our roles, and ultimately, how we perform. Chapter 3 attempts, however briefly, to provide that perspective.

CHAPTER 1

Defining Institutional Advancement, Development, and Fund Raising

Michael J. Worth

The American system of higher education is admired around the world, both for its quality and diversity. No other nation sends such a significant percentage of its population to college, and none offers such a wide range of institutions and programs to meet individual needs and ambitions. Despite criticisms that are sometimes directed toward them, America's colleges and universities are regarded as models by many institutions elsewhere around the globe.

Many nations are undergoing a dramatic transition in their higher education systems. Previously reliant almost entirely on their governments, colleges and universities in many countries now face declining government funding and are being encouraged to develop alternative sources of support. At the same time, strengthening higher education is viewed as a critical national strategy for growth in a global economy based on information technology. In this time of change, many nations are seeking to emulate higher education in the United States, especially with regard to the development of philanthropic support. The success of American higher education is deeply rooted in the nation's history and culture. Institutions in other parts of the world exist in very different environments, but they may find it useful to understand the roots of American practices in order to determine how or whether they may be adapted to their own situations.

Steven Muller describes the historical traditions that influenced the development of American higher education. The earliest colleges were often sponsored by churches, and the principle of separation between church and state kept them independent of government interference. The "commercial character" of American society emphasized the practical value of higher education to the individual and did not treat it as a public benefit to be provided by the government. And, American culture emphasized individual initiative in the public interest and a limited role for government.[1] As a result of these historical traditions, the American higher education system developed in a way that provides its colleges and universities with considerable autonomy.

In the United States, colleges and universities never have been agencies of the federal government. The responsibility for higher education has been left primarily to private initiative and state government. As Muller notes, the first colleges in the United States were private and were sustained at least in part through voluntary contributions. Although many also received help from state governments, they remained independent of government control and thus firmly established a tradition of independence early in the nation's history.

When state universities were created in the United States in the nineteenth and twentieth centuries, their governance structures were designed on the model of the existing private institutions. Their boards of regents or trustees, while usually politically appointed, insulate public colleges and universities from direct control by the state government and provide them with the freedom to compete with other institutions, both public and private, in the quest for students, resources, and status.

It is this element of *competition* among institutions that historically has most distinguished American higher education from the systems of other nations and that largely accounts for its quality. As in the commercial arena, competition among colleges and universities creates a desire to grow and improve, promoting excellence. In recent decades, as federal student aid has come to favor loans over scholarships and as students have come to view higher education from the perspective of "consumers," the competition among all institutions, public and private, has become even more intense.

In seeking to adopt American practices, colleges and universities in many parts of the world face significant challenges related to their unique histories, traditions, and governance structures. In other nations, most colleges and universities still are owned, operated, and principally funded by the national government. Others are owned by private individuals, much like proprietary institutions in the United States. Many universities are governed by their faculties, with presidents, chancellors, or rectors being elected by faculty vote. This is in contrast to the American model of lay governance, in which presidents are appointed by and accountable to boards of trustees or regents, drawn from the business and political communities outside of the academic world. As will be discussed in other chapters of this book, these differences in governance and leadership have considerable implications for the practice of institutional advancement.

Although a growing endeavor in higher education throughout the world, the concept of institutional advancement as a management function of higher education institutions is of American origin, and colleges and universities in the United States are still among its most sophisticated practitioners. As Muller explains, the rise of institutional advancement programs in American colleges and universities is directly related to their diversity and competitive nature:

> The function of institutional advancement in American institutions of higher education is to enable each individual college or university to do well in a competitive environment and to assist the whole sector of higher education to compete effectively for available resources. In a nation that contains such an enormous variety of institutions, each college and university needs to develop and pursue its own distinct strategy for the acquisition of resources. It does so within a society where no effective national policy governs the matter and in which the public policies of the different states, regions, or localities vary significantly. It is primarily the individual institution, rather than the government, that is responsible for its own well being and even survival.[2]

As colleges and universities in other nations seek to develop institutional advancement programs based on the American model, they will need to go beyond merely adopting the techniques of advancement practice. They also will need to examine their basic structures of governance, redefine their relationships with government, and work to nurture the traditions on which American-style advancement programs have been built. This likely will be accomplished only in the context of a much broader transformation of their entire political and economic systems, which is well underway in some nations.

A. Westley Rowland offers an expansive definition of institutional advancement as "all activities and programs undertaken by an institution to develop understanding and support from all its constituencies in order to achieve its goals in securing such resources as students, faculty, and dollars."[3] The activities and programs that generally fall under the institutional advancement banner include alumni relations, internal and external communications, public relations, fund raising, and government relations. Enrollment management is a concept that includes not only student recruitment but also the strategic packaging of financial aid to attract applicants and various programs for retaining currently enrolled students. This discipline sometimes has been regarded as a component of institutional advancement and at other times has been viewed as a related but distinct field.

Writing in 2000, Peter Buchanan suggests that the definition of advancement may be changing again; indeed that advancement itself may be evolving into the new concept of integrated marketing. Noting its similarity to Rowland's definition of institutional advancement, he cites Larry Lauer's description of integrated marketing:

> coordinating the planning of initiatives with the participation of all the areas of the institution that have a stake in its success. Its aim is to mobilize the total institution. It is a total organizational approach that stresses everyone's responsibility to help advance the institution's goals and objectives.[4]

Not only is the definition of institutional advancement itself ever changing, but the vocabulary used to describe its constituent parts is often inconsistent and confusing. This book is concerned with one important component of institutional advancement: educational fund raising. This function includes all the programs and activities by which the college or university seeks gifts and grants from private sources to support its programs and to build long-term strength through improvements to its facilities and additions to its endowment.

The term "development" is usually used interchangeably with "fund raising." On most campuses, and in many other organizations, the office responsible for fund raising is called the development office and the professionals who work there are called development officers. The senior executive in this area is often the vice president or director of development. Some institutions have a "vice president for development and alumni relations" or a "vice president for advancement," these titles suggesting that this officer's responsibilities encompass a broader portfolio. Peter Buchanan speculates that there may be an emerging trend toward the appointment of senior campus officers for integrated marketing, but he acknowledges few examples as of 2000.[5] As Roger Williams notes in Chapter 26 of this book, there has been some trend at research universities since the 1990s to separate the functions of fund raising and communications, with each reporting directly to the president or through two different vice presidents. However, whatever the specific organizational arrangement, it does not alter the *concept* of institutional advancement, which stresses the interrelatedness of its component functions.

In recent years another new term—"total resource development"— has also come to be used on some American campuses. This concept encompasses all efforts to obtain financial resources, through fund raising, entrepreneurial ventures, partnerships, and various other activities. The full dimensions of total resource development have yet to be defined at the time of this writing, but it is discussed further in the Conclusion of this book.

Although others have claimed credit for introducing the term, Robert L. Stuhr says that "development" was first used at Northwestern University in the 1920s and originally had a meaning not too different from today's definition of "institutional advancement." Stuhr describes the birth of the term and the concept as follows:

> The period just after the First World War was a time of decision for Northwestern. . . . The University had to decide whether to remain what it was or to become a great university in the modern sense. It chose the latter course.
>
> Although the first step in this new direction was the launching of a bold campaign to create a skyscraper metropolitan campus to house the professional schools, the people behind the undertaking realized that greatness would never result from this short-term project alone. They realized that the decision to move forward carried with it an indefinite commitment to the future.
>
> A special department of the university was created to serve in meeting this commitment. . . . Somewhere in the course of discussions and committee meetings, the phrase "Department of Development" was coined.[6]

Stuhr defined the objectives of a development program in a way that resembles Rowland's later definition of institutional advancement. Stuhr's objectives included building acceptance for the institution (alumni and public relations), providing the kind and quality of students the institution wants (enrollment management), and obtaining financial support (fund raising). Over the years, however, the meaning of "development" gradually narrowed and the term came to be used synonymously with "fund raising." The term "institutional advancement" became the accepted designation for the broader objectives mentioned by Stuhr.

This book follows the most common contemporary practice; that is, the terms "development" and "fund raising" are used interchangeably and "institutional advancement" is used for the broader effort discussed above. However, it is worthwhile to make a distinction between development and fund raising, at least in concept if not in everyday usage.

Development is a sophisticated *process* that includes several steps or stages. It begins with the institution's academic plan, from which specific financial needs and fund-raising goals are derived. It proceeds to the identification of likely prospects for gifts to support those needs. This step involves using sophisticated research methods and other means, discussed later in this volume, first to identify those financially capable of making gifts and then to learn their particular interests and match them with the institution's needs.

Once development officers identify donor prospects, they must establish programs to cultivate the prospects' interest in the institution and its specific plans and needs. To be effective, this cultivation must include more than just social contact and providing information. It requires *involving* donor prospects in the institution's planning in a sincere, substantive, and intellectually challenging way, helping to build their identity with, and commitment to, the institution's goals. This involvement is neither superficial nor manipulative. Successful cultivation means giving prospective donors a real and meaningful voice in institutional planning and decision making, while at the same time protecting the institution's rightful freedom and autonomy. Maintaining this balance requires that both the donors and the institutional leaders have a sophisticated understanding of higher education and its traditions.

Only when these initial steps in the development process have been achieved is the institution ready for fund raising, which in its narrowest sense means solicitation, or simply "asking for gifts." After the gift has been made, there is yet another step in the development process: stewardship. Stewardship includes faithfully and competently carrying out the purposes of the gift and continuing to communicate with the donor regarding the impact of that gift on the achievement of institutional goals. Stewardship is itself an element of cultivation for the next gift, making the development process truly a cycle, in which the donor's involvement and relationship with the institution expands and deepens over time.

Ideally, through this process the development officer can help bring together the donor's most cherished philanthropic aspirations with the highest goals of the college or university. When this occurs, the gift becomes an enriching and rewarding experience for both parties—a far cry from the opportunistic image the term "fund raising" sometimes brings to the minds of the uninformed.

In this concept of development, fund raising is but one aspect of a complex process involving the institution, its hopes and goals, and the aspirations of its benefactors. Fund raising is episodic; development is continuous. Fund raising is focused on a particular objective or set of goals; development is a generic and long-term commitment to the financial and physical growth of the institution. Successful fund raising requires a specific set of interpersonal and communicative skills; development requires a broader understanding of the institution and its mission as well as patience, judgment, and sensitivity in building relationships over the long haul. A "fund raiser" is an individual skillful in soliciting gifts; a "development officer" may be a fund raiser, but he or she is also a strategist and manager of the entire development process.

These conceptual distinctions are important. Without them, those who work in development too often fall into simplistic misunderstandings of their own roles, and institutions appoint development officers with unrealistic expectations of what the job should and must entail. Failure to understand development as distinct from (and more complex than) merely fund raising deprives development professionals of the respect and regard their considerable skills deserve. As Thomas Broce writes,

> Fund raising as a professional process is best understood when considered in the broader process "development." The latter term encompasses the entire operation from goal identification to gift solicitation. Fund raising should not be confused with "tin cupping." Almost anyone can get token donations. High school band members can sell candy to buy new uniforms. What we are dealing with is the professional process involved in securing significant support.[7]

Again, the terms "development" and "fund raising" are used interchangeably throughout this book, and "institutional advancement" is used for the broader concept of which they are a part. That is the most common everyday practice, and an effort to continually distinguish these terms would simply complicate the reader's task. The terms "integrated marketing" and "total resource development" are not used in any substantial way in this volume; the definitions of these term are still evolving at the time of this writing, and the focus of this book is on fund raising. However, there is a continuing need to clarify the meaning and the relationships of institutional advancement, development, fund raising, and the more recent concepts of integrated marketing and total resource development. Such clarity is important to enhance understanding and appreciation of the development function in our colleges and universities and to gain appropriate professional recognition for those who manage it.

As Robert Payton observes, "Properly understood, fund raising rises to its rightful role as institutional development. The development function integrates with the academic objectives of the institution. It is as honorable and useful and important as any other function in achieving institutional purposes."[8] Echoing Payton, Frank H.T. Rhodes adds that fund raising is "neither an optional extra nor a distraction from the core business of the university. The core business of a university is learning, in its most expansive sense. Fund raising is an exercise in extended learning, an effort to create wider familiarity and a greater support for the most basic activity of our society."[9]

NOTES

1. Steven Muller, "The Definition and Philosophy of Institutional Advancement," in *Handbook of Institutional Advancement*, 2nd edition, ed. A. Westley Rowland (San Francisco: Jossey-Bass, 1986), 2–3.

2. Ibid., 4.

3. Rowland, *Handbook of Institutional Advancement*, xiii.

4. Peter McE. Buchanan, "The Evolution of Advancement in the 21st Century," in *Handbook of Institutional Advancement*, 3rd edition, ed. Peter McE. Buchanan (Washington, DC: Council for Advancement and Support of Education, 2000), 67.

5. Ibid.

6. Robert L. Stuhr, ed., *On Development* (Chicago: GonserGerberTinkerStuhr, 1977), 3–4.

7. Thomas E. Broce, *Fund Raising: The Guide to Raising Money from Private Sources* (Norman: University of Oklahoma Press, 1979), 27.

8. Robert L. Payton, "The Ethics and Values of Fund Raising," in *The President and Fund Raising*, ed. James L. Fisher and Gary H. Quehl (New York: American Council on Education/Macmillan, 1989), 35.

9. Frank H.T. Rhodes, "Introduction," in *Successful Fund Raising for Higher Education*, ed. Frank H.T. Rhodes (Phoenix, AZ: Oryx Press/American Council on Education, 1997), xxiii.

CHAPTER 2

Elements of the Development Program

Michael J. Worth

T o speak of an institution's fund-raising "program" in the singular
is to oversimplify the reality. Development offices manage a variety of programs, each having somewhat different objectives and
each using a particular set of fund-raising tools and techniques.

These various fund-raising programs can look quite different. The excitement and bustle of a phone center contacting alumni for gifts to the
annual fund bears little resemblance to the patient, quiet conversation
of a planned giving officer working with a donor's tax adviser. The foundation support specialist sitting at a PC crafting a detailed proposal is
engaged in work quite different from that of a major gifts officer rushing
to catch a plane on the way to visit a donor prospect. But these apparently diverse efforts must relate to each other and to the institution's
particular needs and circumstances.

This chapter provides a brief overview of the elements of a development program. Later chapters discuss each of these elements in greater
detail. While the information in this chapter may seem basic to the
experienced development officer, newcomers may find it a useful framework for the more focused chapters that follow.

THE FUND-RAISING PYRAMID

The development program can be represented by a pyramid, as shown
in figure 2.1. The base of the pyramid is the institution's *total constituency*, including all those individuals and organizations that might logi-

Figure 2.1
The Fund-Raising Pyramid

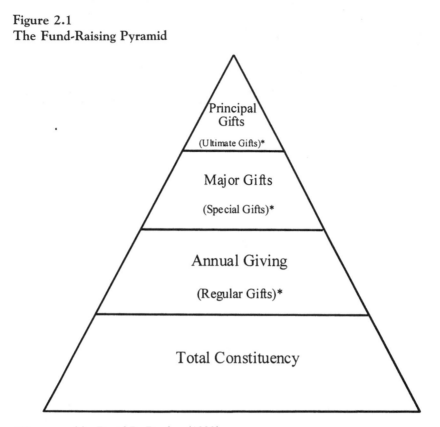

Principal
Gifts

(Ultimate Gifts)*

Major Gifts

(Special Gifts)*

Annual Giving

(Regular Gifts)*

Total Constituency

*Terms used by David R. Dunlop (1993)

cally be interested in providing support. The constituency of most colleges and universities includes alumni, faculty and staff, parents of students, corporations, foundations, "friends," and other individuals and groups. In universities with medical centers, patients served by an affiliated hospital or faculty practice also would be members of the institution's constituency.

Some observers argue that today's donors respond more to ideas and opportunities than to institutional loyalties, and that the institution's constituency thus extends beyond traditional groups to all individuals who may have interests related to its programs. However, the prevailing view remains that those with some natural linkage to the institution, such as parents and alumni, comprise its most obvious and promising constituents.

Some percentage of this constituency supports the "annual giving" program, providing gifts to support the institution's current operating budget. Individuals who participate in annual giving may also be prospects for higher levels of support.

A smaller percentage of donors make "major gifts," usually toward important capital needs of the college or university, such as facilities or endowment. There is no uniform standard for what constitutes a "major" gift. The definition must be relative to the institution and the capacity of its constituency. Some may consider a gift of $10,000 to be major for them, while others may define it as $50,000, $100,000, or more.

A relative few individuals reach the top of the giving pyramid and make what have come to be called "principal gifts." A principal gift is of such magnitude that it has a significant impact on the institution, or at least one of its programs or departments. The definition of a principal gift is also relative, but the $5,000,000 or $10,000,000 level is sometimes a defining point. In the 1990s and early 2000s, some institutions have received gifts of more than $100,000,000. Some refer to these as "mega gifts," but no standardized terminology has developed. Such gifts are large principal gifts.

The pyramid depicted in figure 2.1 also shows another set of terms at each level: "regular," "special," and "ultimate" gifts. These are terms introduced by David Dunlop in his earlier writings.[1] He also explains them in Chapter 8 of this book.

Dunlop's terms take the perspective of the donor. They do not necessarily relate to the terms "annual, major, and principal," defined by the level or amount of gifts, although in many cases there is a correspondence. According to Dunlop, a regular gift is one made on a "regular," usually annual, basis, to support the current operating budget of the institution. A "special gift," as the term implies, is made to meet some nonrecurring need of the institution, such as construction of a new building. Many special gifts are large enough to be considered major gifts. Dunlop defines an "ultimate gift" as the largest gift of which the individual is capable, in essence the gift of a lifetime. An individual's ultimate gift might not be large enough to be considered a principal gift from the perspective of the college or university, but many principal gifts likely are ultimate gifts from the perspective of those who give them.

Some writers and practitioners tend not to make a clear distinction between "ultimate gifts" and "principal gifts," but rather use the terms synonymously. While the two may coincide in many actual situations, there is a distinction in the terms, as explained above.

Some major and many ultimate gifts are "planned gifts." These are long-term commitments established with any of a wide range of financial planning techniques—and are thus arranged in light of the individual's overall financial and estate considerations. Some argue that all major gifts are "planned," as contrasted with "unplanned," but the term is most commonly used to mean gifts made by will or through some type of life-income arrangement. The college or university gains access to the gift only after the death of the donor or some other beneficiary. Such gifts used to be called "deferred gifts," and some still make a distinction between gifts that are "outright" and those that are "deferred," the latter received after the death of the donor or another individual. But the term "planned" has generally replaced "deferred" to refer to all gifts that are a part of the donor's financial and estate plan and mature after an individual's death. For simplicity, this book generally uses the word in that way.

Planned giving is not depicted here as a separate element of the fund-raising pyramid. It is more properly viewed as a tool that is used with increasing frequency in major and principal gift fund raising. Some institutions feel that the relationship between major gifts and planned gifts is so strong that they organize their programs to combine both specialties, for example, by establishing an "Office of Major and Planned Gifts." Others continue to see them as somewhat distinct and maintain separate but coordinated programs and staffs for raising major gifts and planned gifts. Similarly, some larger colleges and universities have separate staffs and offices with responsibility for principal gift fund raising. However, in most institutions, principal gift programs are a part of the major gift function or are handled directly by the chief advancement officer.

Planned giving has become an increasingly important area of fund raising in the past decade, reflecting growth of wealth in the form of appreciated property and the aging of the population. Such gifts grew at an astonishing rate of 40.5 percent annually between 1993 and 1997, coinciding with a strong stock market.[2] Development officers who specialize in planned giving have grown in number and in the sophistication of their skills. Moreover, at least some knowledge of planned giving is an essential skill for any development officer who works with individual donors.

The shape of the fund-raising pyramid represents the number of donors participating in each category, which declines with each successively higher level. But if the pyramid were drawn to represent dollars resulting from gifts at each level it would be inverted, that is, upside down with the broad part at the top and the narrow part at the bottom. An old fund-raising axiom stated that 80 percent of the dollars comes from 20 percent of the donors. More recent literature has revised this to say that 90 percent of the dollars comes from 10 percent of the donors, and some say there is a need the need to revise the formula further (perhaps to 95 percent or more from 5 percent or fewer), reflecting the increasing dependence of colleges and universities on larger and larger gifts from relatively few, very major donors.

Some observe that the pyramid has become "steeper" in recent years because of the increased impact of a few very large gifts at the top.[3] Others, such as Judith Nichols in Chapter 14 of this book, argue that changing demographics and lifestyles have made the fund-raising pyramid obsolete. However, most practitioners still subscribe to its usefulness, at least as a conceptual tool.

Comprehensive development programs aggressively solicit all constituencies and at all levels of the fund-raising pyramid. But the most successful are those that focus on the higher levels of the pyramid, on those major gifts and principal gifts that will produce the largest share of overall support and that have the greatest potential impact on the institution.

CAMPAIGNS

Among the most visible of today's educational fund-raising efforts are the major comprehensive campaigns, many having goals in the hundreds of millions or billions of dollars and extending over a period of five years or longer.

In earlier decades, colleges and universities mounted "capital campaigns" to raise money for specific facilities or endowment needs. Ongoing annual giving and planned gift programs were often run concurrently with, but separately from, the capital campaign. Although institutions still sometimes undertake traditional capital campaigns for specific purposes, in the 1970s, 1980s, and 1990s it became increasingly common practice to combine goals for annual, capital, and planned giving under an overall "comprehensive campaign" umbrella.

By the 1990s, campaigns became a subject of debate within the development profession, with some arguing that lack of common accounting and varied campaign lengths were making comparisons among institutions difficult and undermining the credibility of goals. The Council for Advancement and Support of Education (CASE) responded by publishing the CASE Campaign Standards in 1994, intended to standardize the reporting of campaign results. Today, there is debate within the development profession about whether campaigns are still appropriate and effective strategies at all in an era when major gift fund raising has become a continuous process at many colleges and universities. Some of these issues are considered further in Part IV of this book.

The campaign itself does not appear in the fund-raising pyramid; it is more accurately described as a fund-raising strategy than as a distinct element of the development program. Today's comprehensive campaigns are designed to enhance the visibility of the institution's needs and increase the urgency for all types and levels of support.

ADVANCEMENT SERVICES

Some aspects of a development program remain behind the scenes, carried out by development professionals who may never contact a donor or ask for a gift. The "back room" functions of research, records, gift administration, and information systems management have become increasingly important as development programs have become more comprehensive and intense. Today's development offices include highly specialized, skilled professionals in all of these "support" areas, which are often subsumed under the overall term of "advancement services." Perhaps no aspect of fund raising has been as changed by the explosion of technology over the past decade. Today's development offices include positions for computer programmers, network managers, and other specialists with highly technical skills. Public university foundations, which have responsibility for the management of gift funds as well as for fund raising, also employ professionals trained in managing investment funds. In most private institutions, these responsibilities are in separate offices and the investment professionals are not a part of the development office staff.

Research is essential to identify those individuals who have the capacity and interest to provide major gifts so that development officers can focus their attention on the best prospects. Because the best prospects for new gifts are often past donors, programs that provide careful stewardship and provide donors with timely information on the impact of their gifts also can pay significant dividends in continued support.

Until the past decade, stewardship was a neglected activity in many development programs. Too many donors made gifts only to hear nothing from the institution until the next solicitation. Stewardship should be a responsibility of all development officers who have continuing relationships with donors. But, many development offices also have specialized staff to help manage and monitor stewardship activity, assisting development officers with such tasks as the preparation of reports and the planning of events.

Systematizing and regularizing communication with donors about their past gifts is more than good fund-raising practice. It should be viewed as part of the responsibility that development officers and their institutions incur when they accept a gift for some purpose. This is a dual responsibility, which includes careful efforts to use the gift as the donor intended as well as keeping the donor informed. Continuing attention to stewardship can improve not only fund-raising performance but also the sense of trust and confidence upon which the donor's relationship to an institution must be built.

THE FUND-RAISING TOOLBOX

The fund-raising techniques employed at any particular time depend upon the level of the anticipated gift and the nature of the prospective donor. Annual giving programs, which focus on relatively small gifts from a large number of donors, rely on the devices of mass communication, such as the mail and the telephone. Modern annual giving programs are as much science as art, using the latest in computer systems and marketing technology. The Internet has become an increasingly important tool, and it is clear that its role will continue to grow as access becomes ever more pervasive and more and more donors become accustomed to online transactions. Many institutions provide the opportunity to make a gift via their websites, and an increasing number employ e-mail in soliciting gifts. The most successful annual giving programs also use personal solicitation, some involving organized cadres of volunteers managed by an annual giving professional.

Annual giving programs often emphasize "the numbers," aiming for increases in revenues and donor participation. Some annual giving programs downplay specific needs, focusing instead on unrestricted general support. In contrast, the solicitation of a major gift is more art than science. It is almost always face-to-face and requires a commitment to the long-term process of communication, education, and relationship building. Few major gifts are unrestricted or directed to current operating needs. They usually are designated for a specific endowment or facility, reflecting the interests and experiences of the donors. The effective major gift solicitor is therefore well prepared with a knowledge of both the institution's programs and the prospect. Gifts involving some aspect of planned giving demand that the development officer be expert in not only the art of fund raising but also the science of financial, tax, and estate planning.

FOUNDATION AND CORPORATE SUPPORT

Foundation and corporate donors may participate at any level of the pyramid, although obviously they do not make planned gifts. In practice, while local businesses may support the annual fund, few large corporations or foundations participate in annual giving programs except through employee matching gift programs.

Foundations and corporations also tend to be reluctant to make major gifts to endowment, preferring instead to support specific programs or projects. That is because they are generally less interested in the welfare of a particular institution than they are in how that institution can help advance their own broader philanthropic goals. While individual donors may have an emotional commitment to the college or university and wish to support it for its own sake, most corporations and foundations are committed first to their particular areas of interest. For corporations, these interests often relate to the firm's business—for instance, computer engineering. Foundation interests usually reflect the concerns of the founding donor or the foundation's traditional mission—say, saving the environment.

During the 1990s, corporate giving became even more focused on areas related to business interests. Many corporate giving officers are required to demonstrate that the company's giving program in fact has a measurable impact and contributes to the bottom line of profit. Many relationships between corporations and universities have become complex, involving research and training partnerships, cause-related marketing and sponsorships, and other arrangements quite distinct from philanthropy. Over the past decade, many foundations have shifted their priorities away from higher education toward elementary and secondary education and toward organizations that serve children, the environment, and other social concerns.

Fund raising from corporations and foundations requires a sophisticated understanding of the institution's educational and research strengths, and solicitations often include a written proposal that relates the institution's program to the donor's interests. Because many corporations and foundations establish detailed procedures and deadlines for requests for support, corporate and foundation solicitation requires highly specialized fund-raising skills and knowledge.

The increasing focus of corporate and foundation giving has blurred the line between fund raising and "grantsmanship." Debates have arisen on some campuses as to which activities properly belong to the development office and which should be handled by a separate office of sponsored research or sponsored programs. Many partnerships and joint ventures blur the line between what is a gift and what is a business relationship. Some involve elements of both philanthropy and business, while others are purely business relationships. Other relationships may include contracts between corporations and higher education institutions for the training of company employees. Because contacts between the corporation and the campus may be many and varied, a development officer working in this area must have a wide knowledge and understanding of the institution's academic and research strengths.

Recognizing the growing complexity of relationships between the campus and the business world, some institutions have reorganized their corporate relations programs such that professionals in this area report jointly to the chief development officer and another campus officer, for example the provost. Such a structure acknowledges the close link between academic programs and the interests of these donors, and the need for the institution to present a coordinated and consistent approach to companies that may be their donors as well as their partners and their "customers."

THE FUND-RAISING LIFE CYCLE

An old theory in biology proposed that the development of an individual organism reflects the stages in evolution of the species to which it belongs. For example, early in its development, the human embryo has features that resemble gills, which evoke an image of the early forms of life from which we all descend. The growth of other features—and eventually consciousness—come later in the development of the individual fetus, echoing the appearance of these features in the evolutionary history of the human species.

Although this theory has been discredited as a principle of biological science, the concept nevertheless provides a convenient model for analysis of the fund-raising pyramid depicted in figure 2.1. The growth of an individual donor's giving relationship to an institution parallels the evolution of the institution's overall fund-raising program. Most individuals begin their support of a college or university through participation in the annual fund. As their interest and financial means increase over the years, they may make major gifts in support of particular purposes or campaigns. And in the end, they may designate the institution in their wills to receive the substantial fruits of a lifetime's work.

An institution with a new development program might well follow the same pattern, beginning with an annual giving program, in order to identify those among its total constituency who have the ability and proclivity to give. Only when the annual giving program has produced a sufficient group of such individuals would the institution begin to consider seeking major gifts from them. And only after these individuals have had the time to develop deeper feelings for the institution would the college introduce a planned giving program to address their estate planning needs.

Robert Stuhr recommends this step-at-a-time approach:

> If an institution is to have a well-rounded program, it is not nec-
> essary that it immediately build up an enormous development staff
> and start going in all directions at once. Instead, the institution
> should decide what is required to have a complete program, and
> then move toward its development in an orderly fashion. Each in-
> stitution can grow into its program, just as has been the case with
> the field of development itself.[4]

Some argue that the process described above is outdated in light of the new wealth rapidly acquired by young technology entrepreneurs during the 1990s and their philosophy of giving. This group of "new philanthropists" may find unrestricted support to an annual giving program to be of little interest and may begin their giving careers well up the pyramid, responding to exciting opportunities for philanthropic "investment." Some say that younger donors make decisions quickly, without prolonged involvement and cultivation by the institution. They are said to respond more to ideas and to have less loyalty to particular institutions, thus making traditional linkages less important. However, most practitioners continue to advocate building relationships over the long term, in respect of the life cycle of the individual's giving, especially when a principal or ultimate gift is the eventual goal.

DESIGNING THE FUND-RAISING PROGRAM

As explained above, the most successful development programs are those that emphasize principal and major gifts, because the few donors at the top of the pyramid provide the largest portion of total support. However, the overall design of the institution's development program should reflect its particular characteristics and needs as well as the realities of its constituency. Despite its desire for major gifts, a young institution with most of its alumni under age fifty might find it futile to invest all of its resources in a sophisticated planned giving program while ignoring the annual fund. At the same time, a venerable college or university that put all its efforts into the annual fund would deprive itself of those resources most likely to make a long-term difference in its strength and security.

A small liberal arts college located in a rural setting far from corporate offices and with little research activity among its faculty might be wise to downplay efforts with national corporations and foundations. This does not mean that it should totally ignore these sources, but rather that it should allocate proportionately less effort toward them than it directs toward alumni, parents, and friends.

The fund-raising program should reflect what the institution needs most. As architects say, "Form should follow function." Thomas Broce explains:

> When a development program is being started, those persons responsible must determine the kinds of gifts needed to meet the institution's objectives and the kind of program that will best attract these kinds of gifts. . . . Institutions should not spend hard-earned dollars on nonproductive programs. Therefore, an institution with a small endowment but a great need for additional operating support should place its prime emphasis on aggressive annual gifts programs. It also should be active in corporate-support programs with a continuing interest in planned giving programs, but its primary staff and dollar concentration should be on securing operating funds. . . . The institution should also be attracting endowment funds, but that should remain a secondary activity. On the other hand, a research-oriented organization should focus on fund raising from foundations.[5]

Despite this logic, colleges and universities too often strive to replicate programs they observe and admire at very different types of institutions. Stretching their resources to try to do everything results in insufficient effort devoted to those elements of the program most likely to produce revenue or those most relevant to the institution's real needs. Trustees, presidents, and faculty are sometimes culprits in this phenomenon, encouraging development staff to implement programs that they have seen succeed elsewhere, without stopping to consider their appropriateness in a highly different situation.

Some institutions may undervalue annual gifts, which often comprise just a small percentage of the current operating budget. They may be tempted to confine their fund-raising efforts to obtaining the "big hit" that will capture headlines and transform the college or university quickly. But, pursuing that approach exclusively shortchanges the future by failing to build the tradition of giving and the broad base of donors from which tomorrow's major gifts may emerge. Other institutions may tend to overemphasize annual giving, with its immediate and tangible returns, at the expense of more long-term efforts to cultivate major gifts. Presidents and deans sometimes prefer outright gifts that can help them increase their spending now, while discounting the importance of planned gifts that will benefit their successors.

The practice of "benchmarking" has become widespread in higher education in recent years. Properly applied, it involves comparing an institution to that of similar or "peer" institutions to identify best practices that may be most usefully adopted. Misused, benchmarking can exacerbate the tendency to implement programs that are effective elsewhere but that may not fit a particular institution's unique situation. As Barbara Taylor and William Massey warn, "critical success factors will not be the same for all institutions but will vary depending on size, control, location, history, mission, goals, and other factors."[6]

The risk is especially great when the college's academic "aspirational peers" are used as the reference group for a comparison of fund-raising programs. Aspirational peers are institutions seen as "higher" in the academic pecking order, institutions that the college or university conducting the benchmarking study hopes to eventually match in academic quality and prestige. But, differences in current academic standing may reflect, among other variables, significant historical and cultural differences. Because history and culture are relevant to fund raising, the development programs of such institutions may or may not provide the best model for another college or university facing very different realities.

Again, no element of the development program should be ignored; the keys are timing and emphasis. Allocation of staff and budget among the various elements of the program should reflect a careful analysis of the institution's academic programs, needs, and history, as well as the capacities and inclinations of its constituency. The strategic allocation of effort and resources will become even more important in the years ahead, as budgetary pressures and demands for accountability continue to increase.

NOTES

1. David R. Dunlop, "Major Gift Programs," in *Educational Fund Raising: Principles and Practice*, ed. Michael J. Worth (Phoenix, AZ: Oryx Press/American Council on Education, 1993), 97–116.

2. Bruce R. McClintock, "Trends in Educational Fund Raising," in *Handbook*

of *Institutional Advancement*, 3rd edition, ed. Peter McE. Buchanan (Washington, DC: Council for Advancement and Support of Education, 2000), 369.

3. Ibid.

4. Robert L. Stuhr, ed., *On Development* (Chicago: GonserGerberTinker-Stuhr, 1977), 13.

5. Thomas E. Broce, *Fund Raising: The Guide to Raising Money from Private Sources* (Norman: University of Oklahoma Press, 1979), 20.

6. Barbara E. Taylor and William F. Massey, *Strategic Indicators for Higher Education* (Princeton, NJ: Peterson's, 1996), xii.

CHAPTER 3

The Historical Overview

Michael J. Worth

In 1641, William Hibbens, Hugh Peter, and Thomas Weld set sail from Boston to London on a mission to solicit gifts for a young American college. Their stated purpose was to raise money enabling the college to "educate the heathen Indian," a cause apparently viewed as worthy by wealthy British citizens of the time.

Weld remained in England, never to return to America. So too, in a manner of speaking, did Peter, who was hanged for crimes committed under British law. Only Hibbens returned to America, a year later, with £500 to support the struggling institution—Harvard College. As historian Scott Cutlip dryly observes, "Such were the rewards of early fund raisers."[1]

The adventures of Hibbens, Peter, and Weld often are reported as the first organized fund-raising activity undertaken for an American college. Throughout the eighteenth and nineteenth centuries, however, fund-raising methods were primitive by today's standards, mostly consisting of "passing the church plate, of staging church suppers or bazaars, and of writing 'begging letters.' "[2]

Early colleges were often connected with a sponsoring church, and their fund raising reflected a religious zeal, with gifts being solicited for the purpose of advancing Christianity in a young and "uncivilized" nation. The blending of religion and higher education was exemplified in the preaching tours of George Whitfield, who raised money for Harvard, Dartmouth, Princeton, and the University of Pennsylvania as well as for "the poor."[3] Even paid agents were often motivated primarily by their religious convictions, and many were principals in the college itself, sometimes playing roles in academic and business affairs in addition to their fund-raising activity.

THE BEGINNINGS OF MODERN TECHNIQUES

Despite their generally primitive methods, early fund-raising efforts do reveal the seeds of modern techniques. On their trip to England in 1641, Hibbens, Peter, and Weld needed "literature," and the first fund-raising brochure was produced. In 1829, a Philadelphia fund raiser named Mathew Carey introduced the ideas of rated prospect lists and advance promotion of the fund-raising appeal, concepts that Cutlip calls "in embryo, the elements of modern fund raising."[4] Benjamin Franklin's advice to Gilbert Thomas in raising funds for the Presbyterian Church in Philadelphia reflected a strategy that is still employed in today's campaigns:

> In the first place I advise you to apply to all those whom you know will give something; next to those whom you are uncertain whether they will give anything or not, and show them the list of those who have given; and lastly, do not neglect those whom you are sure will give nothing, for in some of them you may be mistaken.[5]

Despite these early beginnings of a systematic approach, fund raising before the twentieth century was generally amateur and personal, a transaction between two individuals, with no role for organization, strategy, or professional managers.

THE START OF THE MODERN ERA

The first organized fund-raising programs in higher education came in the area of alumni annual giving. Alumni interest and loyalty to the alma mater was evident as early as 1643, when Harvard alumni began returning to attend commencements and renew old acquaintances. The first formal alumni associations were created in the early 1800s; their primary purpose was to perpetuate memories and intellectual interests. Formal alumni funds also appeared in the 1800s, often promoting the concept of alumni as a "living endowment" for the school.[6] But the most significant revolution in fund raising was to come from outside higher education in the first decade of the twentieth century.

A YMCA executive, Lyman L. Pierce, had begun a campaign in 1902 to raise $300,000 toward construction of a new YMCA in Washington, D.C. With the help of a $50,000 gift from John D. Rockefeller and other gifts, his campaign had come within $80,000 of its goal when it stalled in 1905. Pierce then called on Charles Sumner Ward, a fellow YMCA executive from Chicago who had gained attention for his fund-raising skills. Ward came to Washington to help Pierce complete the floundering campaign. As Cutlip recounts,

> The collaboration of Ward and Pierce produced the first modern fund-raising campaign techniques: careful organization, picked leaders spurred on by team competition, prestige leaders, powerful publicity, a large gift to be matched . . . careful records, report meetings, and a definite time limit.[7]

Ward insisted on a carefully prepared list of prospects and showed prospective donors the names of those who already had given, adopting Benjamin Franklin's advice of more than a century earlier. Ward also introduced what is now known as the "campaign clock" or "thermometer," a graphic device to keep the pressure on to reach the goal by the deadline. Although Pierce and Ward collaborated on this historic campaign, Ward became "widely acknowledged as the prime originator" of what became known as the "Ward method" of fund raising.[8]

The first application of the new campaign techniques to higher education occurred when the University of Pittsburgh brought in Ward in 1914 to raise $3 million. Ward recruited others to work on the Pittsburgh campaign, including Carlton and George Ketchum, Arnaud Marts, and others destined to become prominent in educational fund raising.

Ward and his disciples subsequently established some of the best-known consulting firms in the field, some of which survive today. In their role as consultants, they introduced the new campaign methods to universities and other organizations across the country. With further refinements introduced by others over the years, Ward's campaign methods became standard practice in educational fund raising, still evident in today's development programs.

WARD'S CONTRIBUTION: THE BEGINNING OF A DEVELOPMENT PROFESSION

Ward's contribution went beyond the introduction of a new fund-raising method. First, his emphasis on "method" in itself represented a significant change from earlier fund raising, which rested primarily on the personal appeal of charismatic individual solicitors. Second, Ward himself represented a new breed of fund raiser, a fund-raising "professional" who developed strategy and managed the overall enterprise but who was not himself a solicitor of gifts—unlike the paid solicitors or agents who raised funds for the early colleges. The task of solicitation was carried out by volunteers and institutional leaders, with Ward providing the strategy, method, and overall direction of the campaign. Ward did not personally solicit gifts, yet he raised millions.

Indeed, Ward did not possess any of the personal characteristics associated with so many earlier fund raisers. One of his associates, Carlton Ketchum, described Ward as "an austere and reserved man, very far indeed from any of the campaign types which we all know." Ward's effectiveness, Ketchum said, "was that of the originator of a sane and practical method, and the firmness to insist on its thorough application . . . rather than any personal magnetism."[9]

By creating this new role of fund-raising strategist and manager, Ward paved the way for the growth of a development profession in the years that followed. In the first chapter of this book, a distinction was drawn between "development" as a process and "fund raising" as the narrower task of soliciting gifts. It was Ward who made this distinction a reality, with his emphasis on system and strategy, in contrast to the "beggar" fund raisers of earlier decades. In that sense, all who work as development officers today are truly Ward's descendants.

In the first half of the twentieth century, most college and university campaigns were directed by professionals from consulting firms like those founded by Ward and his contemporaries. Indeed, Kathleen Kelly identifies the period from 1919 to 1965 as the "era of consultants," in which these firms dominated the landscape of educational fund raising.[10] Typically, the consulting firm would send a "resident manager," who would work with the institution for a period of months to complete the campaign and then move on to the next assignment at another college or university—all the time remaining an employee of the consulting firm, not the institution. The actual fund raising was performed by the volunteers and institutional leaders, with the consultant providing the strategy and management.

As development programs became more sophisticated, more intense, and more continuous, institutions came to recognize the value of having such a fund-raising professional as a full-time member of the college or university staff and created the position of director of development. Kelly calls the period since 1965 the "era of staff fund raisers," but the transition was a gradual one.[11] A survey by the American College Public Relations Association in 1949 found only two members with the title director of development. In 1952, another survey discovered only thirteen.[12] By 1965, the number of staff development officers had become so significant that consulting firms began to change their emphasis from on-site resident management to part-time counseling.[13]

Today, nearly every college and university in the nation—four-year and two-year, private and public—has at least one and in many cases dozens, even hundreds, of development professionals on the institutional staff. Professional consultants have continued to be an important part of the field, and some smaller institutions still use resident managers from consulting firms to direct their major campaigns. As the size and capability of institutional development staffs have grown, however, the trend has continued to be toward using consultants for specialized services and periodic advice rather than full-time campaign management.

It is interesting to observe that the role of the college or university development officer originated in the for-profit consulting world. In the days before development professionals on the college staff became common, the fund-raising professional indeed came from "outside" the academic world and was clearly motivated more by the quest for profit than by loyalty to a particular institution. Alumni secretaries, by contrast, were more often institutional figures and served their colleges or universities for long periods of time. A perceived cultural difference between the disciplines of alumni relations and fund raising remains today.

Although development officers have become almost universally a part of college and university administrations, there continues to be a perceived cultural gap between them and members of the academic community, particularly faculty. Faculty are sometimes suspicious of development professionals, viewing them as apart from the academic world and lacking in institutional commitment. While this view is unjustified in many—perhaps most—cases, it is one probably encouraged by the degree to which development officers continue to follow the patterns of their consultant ancestors. Mobility from institution to institution is relatively high, and it is not uncommon for individuals to move from institutional development positions into consultancies and vice versa. This historical blurring of the for-profit and academic worlds may continue to have implications in the way development is understood and defined in colleges and universities, and the trend toward evaluating and compensating development officers using methods drawn from the business world could exacerbate the gap in the future.

EDUCATIONAL FUND RAISING SINCE WORLD WAR II

Three principal trends have marked the evolution of educational fund raising since World War II: first, the increasing professionalization of the field and the changing role of the development officer within the institution; second, the proliferation and growth of formal development programs, in the United States and abroad; and, third, a dramatic increase in campaign goals along with larger and larger gifts, leading to a "narrowing" of the fund-raising pyramid.

The Professionalization of Fund Raising

Whether or not fund raising is a bona fide profession in the nature of law or medicine is worthy of debate. But certainly, development has emerged within the past fifty years as an identifiable field within higher education administration, with its own specialized body of knowledge, standards, training programs, and career patterns. Concomitantly, the development officer or institutional advancement officer has risen to the most senior ranks of college and university administration, with a significant role in the overall management of the institution. In the past decade, development has become a common route to the college or university presidency.

A significant event in the history of the educational fund-raising profession occurred in 1958, when representatives of the American Alumni Council (AAC) and the American College Public Relations Association (ACPRA) met at the Greenbrier resort in West Virginia. Most members of AAC were development and alumni relations professionals, while ACPRA served campus public relations officers. Prior to the Greenbrier conference, these two organizations had been rivals, and on most campuses the management of their respective professional areas was fragmented.

The product of that conference, the "Greenbrier Report," gave birth to the contemporary definition and concept of institutional advancement. As Michael Richards and Gerald Sherratt describe it,

> The Greenbrier report was a comprehensive effort to define and improve the management of institutional advancement and its elements, as they were conceived in 1958. . . . The report advised institutions to select an organizing pattern for their programs that would encourage coordination of all advancement functions and that would lighten the responsibilities of the president. The report recommended the appointment of an "administrative coordinator" at each institution who would work in harmony with the president to oversee alumni relations, fund raising, and public relations.[14]

The Greenbrier recommendations gained ascendancy during the 1960s and 1970s, as advancement programs were increasingly placed under the direction of a single administrator, usually at the vice presidential level. With greater responsibilities and an enhanced function in the institution, vice presidents for institutional advancement, development, college relations—or however titled—became key players in the overall management of their colleges and universities as well as directing their own programs.

In the culmination of the movement initiated at Greenbrier, the AAC and ACPRA merged in 1974 to create the Council for Advancement and Support of Education (CASE), comprising professionals in all institutional advancement specialties. CASE has expanded its programs concurrently with the growth of the field and now offers a variety of conferences, institutes, publications, and online services.

In earlier decades, development officers could learn their trade only through experience or the tutelage of a senior practitioner. Francis Pray's experience, when appointed to his first development position in the 1940s, is typical: "When the president of the small college I worked for asked me to 'take over the alumni fund,' I accepted with alacrity, almost instantly afterward realizing that I knew nothing about it, either specifically or generically."[15] Today, programs offered by CASE, the Association of Fundraising Professionals (AFP), and other organizations provide much more systematic training and have greatly improved the professionalism and skill of educational fund raisers. The 1980s and 1990s saw the initiation of degree programs in institutional advancement at several universities and a flourishing of scholarly research on advancement and fund raising. In 1999, CASE initiated the CASE International Journal of Educational Advancement, the first scholarly journal dedicated to the field.

The 1980s and 1990s also saw a trend toward subspecialization in the development profession. For example, the Association of Professional Researchers for Advancement (APRA) was formed in 1987 as the professional association for individuals engaged in prospect research and advancement information systems. By 2001, APRA had more than 1,100 members.[16] The National Committee on Planned Giving (NCPG), founded in 1988, had grown to more than 11,000 members by 2001.[17] NCPG provides a variety of services and training programs for professionals engaged in planned giving, both in higher education and other types of organizations.

Despite its movement toward greater professional competence and standing, educational fund raising remains an evolving field. As noted in Chapter 2, confusion continues regarding definitions and roles. On many campuses, there is still a gap in understanding and mutual regard between development officers and their academic colleagues. Tension and rivalry still exist among the various specialties of institutional advancement, and some campuses have moved away from the advancement model of organization recommended by the Greenbrier conference, separating administrative control of development from that of communications and marketing programs.

There has been a noted decline in the involvement of volunteers in campaigns, attributable perhaps to the increase in two-career families and the pressures of an increasingly competitive economy. And, there has been a concomitant increase in the number of solicitations being undertaken by professional development staff. There is a growing emphasis on measuring the performance of individual staff members, and an increasing number of development officers are receiving a portion of their compensation in the form of incentives, such as bonuses. The number of independent "gift planners" is on the rise, creating a cadre of freelance fund raisers who may work either for institutions or directly for donors who are planning gifts. For-profit investment companies, such as Fidelity and Merrill Lynch, now employ "fund raisers" to solicit gifts to their commercial gift funds from among wealthy clients of the firm, most of whom also are prospects for individual colleges and universities.

These changes and the increasing pressure of high dollar goals have given rise to concern with fund-raising ethics and the proper relationship of fund-raising objectives to institutional priorities.

The Proliferation of Development Programs

As noted earlier, the first American colleges and universities were private institutions, and it was in the private sector that formal development programs originated. State universities were created much later, in the nineteenth and twentieth centuries, with financial support coming primarily from state government.

The history of private support for public institutions varies across the country. In the Midwest, state universities were often the first higher education institutions founded, and they enjoyed considerable prestige and support right from the start. For example, the Kansas University Endowment Association was established in 1891 to receive gifts from grateful alumni of the University of Kansas.[18] In the East, however, state colleges and universities were newcomers in an area dominated by the older private colleges. Their missions were initially limited to agriculture, mechanical arts, and teacher training, often due to political pressure from neighboring private colleges. Moreover, they developed in an era of relatively abundant state budgets and a national climate that placed a high priority on public funding for education. In sum, before the 1970s, most public colleges and universities had neither the ability nor the need to seek significant private support.

However, as the missions and roles of public colleges have expanded, so too have their financial needs. These needs have outstripped the ability of state and local governments to respond, forcing these institutions to seek new sources of support. And they have found such a source in private philanthropy. Private support for public universities totaled just $356 million in 1971–72, representing 21.6 percent of the total $1.6 billion given to all of higher education.[19] By 1998–99, private support to public institutions had grown to $7.4 billion—nearly 43 percent of all gifts to higher education that year.[20] Community colleges lagged behind four-year institutions in moving into the fund-raising arena, but they have moved aggressively in the past two decades, with impressive results. In 1988–89, about $44 million was contributed to public community colleges.[21] By 1998–99, that total had more than doubled to $99 million.[22]

In the 1990s, competition for the philanthropic dollar began to increase from the creation of fund-raising programs in organizations outside higher education, many of which have followed the example of public colleges and universities in establishing affiliated foundations. Many public school systems have created foundations to raise private support, and even government agencies, such as the Library of Congress, the National Park Service, and the National Institutes of Health, have initiated efforts to supplement government appropriations with gift dollars.

As development efforts have grown ever more ambitious at colleges and universities in the United States, educational fund raising has become an international enterprise. American colleges and universities now actively cultivate and solicit gifts from international donors. Higher education institutions in many nations, facing reduced government support, have implemented development programs based on the U.S. model. In 1994, CASE opened an office in London and by 2001 claimed membership in twenty-seven nations, including fifty-three European member institutions.[23] Although confronted by challenges related to their funding, history, culture, governance, and other factors, some European universities have begun to realize significant fund-raising results. By 2001, Oxford University was raising $15 million annually, and Cambridge University was reporting over $45 million in support.[24]

Ever-Higher Goals, Larger and Larger Gifts

Historian Scott Cutlip cites three campaigns run by Harvard University to illustrate the dramatic growth in fund-raising goals in the twentieth century. Harvard's campaign of 1904–5 sought $2.5 million for faculty salaries. A 1919–20 campaign raised more than $14 million for Harvard's endowment. Writing in 1965, Cutlip described Harvard's 1956–60 campaign as having raised "the staggering sum of $82,775,553."[25] In 1999, Harvard was the first to break the $2-billion barrier in higher education fund raising, completing a campaign that raised over $2.3 billion in just five years.[26] In 2000, UCLA completed a campaign for $1.2 billion, setting a new record for a public university, and Wellesley College set a new record for a liberal arts college with a successful $400-million campaign.[27] Even larger campaigns are undoubtedly in the planning stages at the time of this writing.

Along with higher goals, campaigns in the 1990s called forth unprecedented "mega gifts." In 1999, a single gift of $1 billion from the Bill and Melinda Gates Foundation to support scholarships for minority students set a record as the largest ever to higher education.[28] A $400-million gift from the Hewlett-Packard Foundation to Stanford University in 2001 set a new record for a gift to one institution.[29] It would not be surprising if both records were exceeded after the writing of this book.

The impact of large gifts has created a "narrowing" of the fund-raising pyramid, with a higher percentage of total support coming from fewer and fewer gifts at the very top. A 1999 survey by CASE revealed that 57 percent of total gifts to the campaigns it studied came from just 1 percent of the donors and that 80 percent of funds raised was attributable to the top 10 percent of donors.[30] Some observers have expressed concern that colleges and universities continue to focus on donors at all levels and not become totally dependent on a handful of large gifts.

The explosion of fund-raising goals in the 1990s reflected the strong U.S. economy, an historic bull stock market, and the increasing needs of colleges and universities being called upon to serve a lengthening national agenda. Colleges and universities are looked upon as vehicles for achieving social justice, enhancing national economic competitiveness, and advancing technological and medical knowledge, among other goals. The costs of needed facilities and equipment has continued to rise, as have faculty salaries, medical insurance costs, and all the other elements of the college or university budget. There appears to be no end to the forces driving educational fund raising to the center stage of American higher education and no limit to the goals that development professionals will be called upon to help meet.

Three hundred and fifty years after Hibbens, Peter, and Weld set sail for London, both the rewards and challenges of educational fund raising remain considerable. Contemporary development programs resemble the methods of these three early fund raisers about as much as today's jet planes resemble the sailing ships that took them to England. But private gifts are no less critical to our universities, colleges, and independent schools today than they were in America's earliest years.

NOTES

1. Scott M. Cutlip, *Fund Raising in the United States: Its Role in America's Philanthropy* (New Brunswick, NJ: Rutgers University Press, 1965), 4.

2. Ibid., 7.

3. Ibid., 6.

4. Ibid., 8.

5. Ibid., 6.

6. Gary A. Ransdell, "Understanding Professional Roles and Program Mission," in *Handbook of Institutional Advancement*, 2nd edition, ed. A. Westley Rowland (San Francisco: Jossey-Bass, 1986), 374.

7. Cutlip, *Fund Raising in the United States*, 44.

8. Ibid., 40.

9. Ibid., 86.

10. Kathleen S. Kelly, *Effective Fund-Raising Management* (Mahwah, NJ: Lawrence Erlbaum Associates, 1998), 139.

11. Ibid.

12. Francis C. Pray, ed., *Handbook for Educational Fund Raising* (San Francisco: Jossey-Bass, 1981), 2.

13. Kelly, *Effective Fund-Raising Management*, 151.

14. Michael D. Richards and Gerald R. Sherratt, *Institutional Advancement Strategies in Hard Times* (Washington, DC: American Association for Higher Education/ERIC Clearinghouse on Higher Education, 1981), 11.

15. Pray, *Handbook for Educational Fund Raising*, 2.

16. Association of Professional Researchers for Advancement Web site (http://www.aprahome.org), viewed February 26, 2001.

17. National Committee on Planned Giving Web site (http://www.ncpg.org/what.html), viewed February 26, 2001.

18. Michael J. Worth, ed., *Public College and University Development* (Washington, DC: Council for Advancement and Support of Education, 1985), 1.

19. Ibid.

20. *Voluntary Support of Education 1998–1999* (New York: Council for Aid to Education, 2000), 38–39.

21. Ibid., 5.

22. Ibid., 8.

23. Council for Advancement and Support of Education Website (http://www.case.org/about/belong.htm), viewed February 26, 2001.

24. Scott Hayter, "Stranger in a Strange Land: A North American Learns Advancement in the UK," *Currents*, 26 no. 8 (October 2000): 15.

25. Cutlip, *Fund Raising in the United States*, 480.

26. John L. Pulley, "How Harvard Raised $2.3-Billion While Trying Not to Look Greedy," *Chronicle of Higher Education*, November 5, 1999, A-45.

27. "UCLA Raises $1.2 Billion, a Record for a Public University; Wellesley's $400-million Is Biggest for a Liberal Arts College," *Chronicle of Higher Education*, April 28, 2000, A-40.

28. John L. Pulley, "A $1-Billion Experiment Seeks a New Way to Identify Talented Minority Students," *Chronicle of Higher Education*, June 23, 2000, A-41.

29. John L. Pulley, "$400-Million Is Pledged to Stanford," *Chronicle of Higher Education*, May 11, 2001, A-35.

30. John L. Pulley, "Campaigns Are Getting Longer and Relying on Fewer Donors," *Chronicle of Higher Education*, December 10, 1999, A-39.

PART II

Foundations of Educational Fund Raising

I n this section, authors establish a foundation for the chapters that
follow by describing the field's base of knowledge and emphasizing
two important prerequisites to successful fund raising: an institutional plan and a clear understanding of the roles to be played by development professionals, the president, and the volunteer leaders.

Fund raising practice is still a blend of science and art, informed by
the experience of practitioners and, increasingly, by findings of research.
In the past decade, scholars in various disciplines have shown an increasing interest in fund raising and philanthropy. There also has been
growth of university programs and centers dedicated to the study of
nonprofit organizations and philanthropy. In some instances, research
has helped to confirm long-held assumptions about donors and fund-
raising practices, and in other cases it has provided new insights that
contradict conventional wisdom. In Chapter 4, Kathleen Kelly, a professor whose work is focused on fund raising, summarizes the state of
theory and research in the field, and notes gaps that remain to be filled.

One accepted principle is that successful development programs are
built on academic priorities and institutional plans. In an environment
of increasing competition for the philanthropic dollar and sophisticated
donors who view gifts as a type of "investment" in the institution, establishing the link between planning and fund raising has never been
more important. And yet, sound planning is not the norm on all campuses, and others fail to establish the important link from academic
planning to fund-raising priorities. In Chapter 5, Jon Dellandrea and

Adel Sedra provide a case study, based on the successful University of Toronto experience, that provides a model for integrating development with the institution's planning process.

Another axiom of fund raising is that success requires a team effort, in which the institution's volunteer leaders, chief executive, and professional development staff all play key roles. As will be discussed later in this book, the roles of these critical players are evolving. There has been a noted decline in the participation of volunteers, presidents and other academic leaders are devoting an increasing portion of their time to fund raising, and development officers themselves solicit more and more major gifts. But, the most successful fund raising continues to require the full commitment and participation of all three. In Chapter 6, Sara Patton describes the important relationships that define the fund-raising team.

As the chapters in this section demonstrate, there is more to fund raising than just "asking for money." It is part of a complex process that brings together aspirations and leadership to accomplish important and tangible goals. In a sense, this section of the book introduces the three basic ingredients of educational fund raising: the goals and objectives of the institution, the knowledge and skills of the development profession, and the involvement of key individuals in appropriate roles. Securing these foundations is the right place to start.

CHAPTER 4

The State of Fund-Raising Theory and Research

Kathleen S. Kelly

A colleague on campus, who is a leading scholar in cognitive science, recently asked me for advice to prepare him for an upcoming meeting with officials of a large foundation. The foundation previously had given him a $1-million grant, and he now planned to request funding for a $5-million facility, which was needed to move his research to the next stage. His questions were many. My answers were swift and absolute. "No, do not ask for whatever they can give." "Do not bring up the possibility of spreading the cost with other funders." "Offer multiyear pledge payments if feasible." He was impressed with my authoritative counsel and thanked me profusely.

After I hung up the telephone, I felt like somewhat of an imposter. My fellow faculty member sought my advice because I study fund raising. He, like most faculty, respects knowledge generated by the scientific method and is uncomfortable with prescribed action based on other sources of knowledge, such as experience. He assumed that my answers to his questions would be grounded in theory and supported by research findings. This was not the case. Although my recommendations generally aligned with what we know scientifically about fund raising, by necessity, the bulk of my advice came from the wisdom of fund-raising professionals.

Fund raisers know a great deal about their function, as demonstrated throughout the pages of this book. But most of what we know comes from sources other than science. It has only been in the last 15 years that fund raising has moved beyond principles supported solely by anecdotal evidence to begin building a body of knowledge based on theory and research. The move toward a scientific basis is critical to the well-being of practitioners, the organizations they serve, the charitable sub-sector in which they play a unique role, and the democratic society that depends on voluntary action for the public good.

Educational fund raisers in particular have a vested interest and spe-cial responsibility in forging this new foundation. They operate in a corporate culture that reveres scientific explanation, without which re-spect and understanding are difficult to attain. They are greatest in num-ber and are the undeniable leaders of the overall fund-raising field. Educational practitioners also produce a substantial portion of the fund-raising literature. With this in mind, until research yields more scientific knowledge, there is no acceptable answer to the question I feared most from my colleague: "But how do you know?"

BUILDING KNOWLEDGE

The purpose of this chapter is to describe the current state of theory and research on fund raising and to provide an overview of areas in which there is knowledge derived from science. The numerous areas that are not covered represent significant gaps in our knowledge base. It should be noted that the chapter does not purport to review the fund-raising literature or to present a bibliographic essay. Rather, a few se-lective studies are discussed and cited to illustrate progress in building scientific knowledge. To set the stage for that discussion, the chapter begins with a brief outline of the principles of scientific study.

Scientific Method

Epistemology, or the study of how we come to know things, identifies various sources of knowledge, including intuition (truth is self-evident), authority (wisdom flows from experts), and tenacity (beliefs are passed from one generation to the next). Of all the ways of knowing, science is judged superior because it has built-in checks to detect errors. Indeed, the scientific method is a hallmark of modern industrialized societies and has been adopted by all occupations claiming to be professions.

The scientific method consists of five steps. First, the problem selected for study is defined with evidence supporting its background, importance, and timeliness. The second step is to review applicable scholarly liter-ature, particularly previous studies that addressed the same or a related problem. A comprehensive literature review places inquiries within the context of what has been discovered in the past. The larger perspective allows researchers to properly interpret their findings and add to a cumulative body of knowledge. This step identifies one or more theories to provide a framework for the study. It concludes by stating the hypotheses to be tested and/or the research questions to be answered.

In step three, the methodology deemed most appropriate to collect data is described. The population selected for study, sampling procedures, and measurement of variables are explained. The fourth step is to report the results of the study. Hypotheses are supported or rejected (never proved or disproved, because future developments are unknown), and research questions are answered. The final step involves interpreting the findings, particularly as they relate to previous studies, applying them to practice, pointing out weaknesses of the study, and suggesting directions for future research. In this methodical and meticulous manner, the scientific method allows replication through which errors can be detected, encourages new studies, and systematically builds knowledge.

Fund raising has a literature rich in practitioner wisdom and time-tested principles, which come from intuition, authority, and tenacity. Much of what we know represents research problems worthy of investigation and begging for study.

Fundamentals of Theory and Research

Theories are statements about the relationships between variables. They fulfill at least one of four general purposes: to describe, explain, predict, or control. Starting with the most basic, theories are developed to describe a phenomenon, to describe what takes place. Descriptive theories provide a vocabulary for studying and talking about the subject. Theories also explain a phenomenon, telling us not only what takes place, but why. Explanation promotes understanding and often is considered the most important of the four purposes.

To help solve real-world problems, theories should be able to predict and control. Although complementary, the two purposes are different. Prediction allows us to anticipate future events regardless of our own experiences. Control prescribes appropriate action for intervening and influencing predicted outcomes. Predictive theories answer the question, "What can we expect?" Control theories answer the question, "What should we do?" As scientists frequently state, there is nothing so practical as a good theory.

Theories and research are interdependent. Research is needed to test and revise theories, and theories are needed to identify what variables and relationships should be examined. Research lacking a theoretical framework produces findings that are difficult to interpret and contribute little to cumulative knowledge. In the behavioral sciences, in which fund raising belongs, theories are tested through empirical research, meaning observations are carefully defined so that they can be repeated.

Empirical research employs both qualitative and quantitative methodologies. While qualitative methods, such as in-depth interviews and focus groups, help us better understand a phenomenon, quantitative methods with large samples are needed for generalized description and explanation. Furthermore, only findings from quantitative studies, utilizing such methods as surveys, allow us to predict and control outcomes.

FUND-RAISING THEORY AND RESEARCH

Past assessments of theory and research on fund raising have been uniformly dismal. Even critics sympathetic to the field described fund-raising research as sporadic, fragmented, redundant, and disappointing. Reviewers primarily found one-shot, administrative studies that were limited to a single institution and concentrated on alumni giving. Theory building was largely nonexistent.

Most of the studies were conducted for doctoral dissertations by part-time students who were working full time as fund raisers and earning degrees in education, usually higher education administration. Little of the work was produced by full-time scholars. Research on fund raising did not hold much interest for the higher education professorate, and many of the students did not publish their studies once they had completed their degrees.

Significantly, the push for more and better research on fund raising has come from practitioners and their associations. In 1985, the Council for Advancement and Support of Education (CASE) sponsored the Colloquium on Professionalism in Institutional Advancement, also named Greenbrier II, after the 1958 conference that established the institutional advancement structure. The major topic of discussion was the need for a scientific knowledge base. Research was designated a top priority, and a call was issued for increased efforts to stimulate and disseminate research on advancement, including fund raising. The colloquium's report urged studies in three hierarchical categories: (1) theory-building studies, which produce general principles about the function; (2) introspective studies, which provide knowledge about the occupation and its practitioners; and (3) administrative studies, which help a specific organization solve a problem.

Progress Report

Recent progress is noteworthy, although much remains to be done. Focusing first on dissemination of research, in 1999, CASE launched a scholarly journal, the CASE *International Journal of Educational Advancement*. Another refereed journal, *Nonprofit Management & Leadership*, was started in 1990 by the Mandel Center for Nonprofit Organizations at Case Western Reserve University and the Centre for Voluntary Organisation at the London School of Economics and Political Science. They joined the much older *Nonprofit and Voluntary Sector Quarterly*, which is sponsored by the Association for Research on Nonprofit Organizations and Voluntary Action (ARNOVA). The fourth U.S. journal relevant to studies on fund raising is *Voluntas*, sponsored by the International Society for Third-Sector Research, which was founded in 1992. Discipline-specific journals, such as *The Review of Higher Education* and *Journal of Public Relations Research*, represent additional outlets for studies related to educational fund raising and advancement.

The "birth" of three new journals in the last decade provides strong evidence that research and theory building have increased substantially in the fields of philanthropy, nonprofit management, and fund raising. As a point of clarification, philanthropy (defined by Robert Payton as voluntary action for the public good, including voluntary giving, voluntary service, and voluntary association)[1] is the larger research domain. It encompasses nonprofit management, of which fund raising is a part. Although certainly related, the domains are not synonymous. For example, philanthropy concentrates on giving from the perspective of donors, while fund raising concentrates on managing donor relationships from the perspective of receiving organizations. Different perspectives result in different problems, and as philosophers of science explain, research domains are defined by the problems selected for study.

Regular reading of the journals just named reveals that, although overall productivity has increased, fund raising has not received its "fair share" of attention. Proportionately, articles dealing with fund-raising problems still are few. A 1993 study found that only 3% of the 472 articles published in *Nonprofit and Voluntary Sector Quarterly* during its first 20 years (1972–1992) dealt with "fund/resource raising."[2] Even this low proportion was inflated because philanthropy and fund raising were combined. It must be stressed that there is no scholarly journal exclusively devoted to fund raising. Monitoring of journals also indicates that more faculty in traditional disciplines and fields are conducting research on fund raising; however, their number still is minuscule. Established fields have demonstrated that the interests and attention of full-time faculty are essential to building a scientific body of knowledge.

There has been a surge in the establishment of academic centers for the study and teaching of philanthropy and nonprofit management. Some 36 such centers are now spread across the country. Almost all contain a component on fund raising, although a review of their courses and publications shows that fund raising is not a priority subject (an exception is the Center on Philanthropy at Indiana University in Indianapolis).

Similarly, there has been rapid growth of graduate education in nonprofit management, but fund raising has been given short shrift. In 1990, just 17 colleges and universities offered a graduate degree with a concentration in the management of nonprofit organizations; by 2000, the number had more than quintupled to 97. Yet fund raising has not been fully integrated into the programs because it is deficient in theoretical knowledge backed by research, which (reflecting a Catch-22 situation) makes it suspect to academics. As an illustration, many of the nonprofit management programs do not require fund-raising courses, offering them instead as electives. The vast majority of fund-raising courses today are taught by practitioner-adjuncts rather than by full-time educators.

In 1991, a milestone was reached in advancing knowledge on fund raising. Three books published that year converged to establish fund raising as a management function and a legitimate subject of theory and research.[3] They, and others that followed, such as Worth's 1993 book, assumed a critical voice essential to scientific study.[4]

Continued Weaknesses

Despite improvements, key elements of the research infrastructure have remained unchanged. In his 1987 introspective study, Carbone documented that the majority of fund raisers with doctoral degrees who belong to CASE majored in education.[5] In 2000, this author surveyed members of the Association of Fundraising Professionals (AFP, formerly the National Society of Fund Raising Executives) who hold a Ph.D. degree. In addition to other variables, the study examined their educational backgrounds. AFP was selected for study because it is the only one of the three major professional associations that represents practitioners who work for all types of charitable organizations, although the plurality of its members are educational fund raisers.

Results revealed that 40% of AFP members with Ph.D.'s majored in education, and almost all of them concentrated in higher education administration. Revealingly, 87% of the members who wrote a dissertation on fund raising earned their Ph.D. in education, which analysis showed is statistically significant. Nearly 40% of the dissertations on fund raising were produced by practitioners who work for educational institutions.

It is important to emphasize that less than one-fifth of all dissertations accounted for by AFP members dealt with fund raising. Yet 31% of the members who wrote a fund-raising dissertation did not publish any part of it, and another 31% published only some of the dissertation in a practitioner, as opposed to a scholarly, journal. In other words, findings suggest that about two-thirds of all dissertation studies on fund raising—which constitute the bulk of research on the subject—never enter the mainstream of scholarship.

Practitioners who earn doctoral degrees by conducting research on fund raising should try to publish their dissertations. Publication, particularly in refereed journals, is the formal system by which research is evaluated and findings become part of a permanent accessible record, which in turn forms the knowledge base for future endeavors. All studies have value, whether they offer promising paths to follow or point out dead ends that should be avoided. Without more publication, future studies will overlook previous work, research on fund raising will continue to be redundant and deficient, and efforts to build knowledge will be severely hampered.

AREAS INFORMED BY SCIENCE

Despite the paucity of scholarly inquiry, there is still a body of fund-raising research worth reviewing. The following section provides a brief overview of knowledge we do have based on research. It is divided into two parts: knowledge gained from research in related domains, such as philanthropy, nonprofit management, and the social sciences, and knowledge gained from fund-raising studies. The works discussed in both parts are selective, and this is not intended as a exhaustive review of the literature.

Knowledge from Related Domains

Fund raising is a new field of scientific inquiry, while studies on philanthropy date back to the late 1950s, and studies on nonprofit management started with the six volumes of research issued in 1977 by the Commission on Private Philanthropy and Public Needs. The time lag is due to the fact that philanthropy and nonprofit management began as subspecialities of academic disciplines (for example, sociology and public affairs), while fund raising developed outside the knowledge industry of universities. The field still lacks an academic home with an established core of scholars. Not surprisingly then, much of what we know about fund raising and its practice comes from work in the older domains.

Motives for Giving. Consensus exists that giving is best explained by mixed motives. As related to fund raising, donors have an interest in self and in a common good when making gifts to charitable organizations; that is, altruism and self-interest are not mutually exclusive. Based on social-exchange theory, the mixed-motive model of giving describes two levels of donor motivation: (1) raising the amount of a common good (for example, the number of minority students studying computer science), and (2) receiving some private good in return for the gift. Private goods are broken down into tangible, intangible, and internal benefits (for example, an expanded pool from which to recruit minority employees, greater prestige, and feeling good about the act of giving, respectively). The two levels are inextricably intertwined, whether the donor is an individual, corporation, or foundation.

Applying this well-researched theory to practice, donors do not give just for the sake of giving. They are more likely to contribute if they are offered opportunities for giving that are clearly consistent with their own interests and also have potential for successfully addressing societal problems they view as critical. This reinforces the often-cited fund-raising maxim that "the case must be larger than the institution."

Nonprofit Sector. Since the 1970s, numerous studies have described and defined the sector of our society that we alternatively refer to as nonprofit, voluntary, or independent. Also called the third sector, it consists of tax-exempt organizations that do not fit into the first two sectors of business and government. Based on this definition, both public and private educational institutions are considered charitable nonprofits.

Lohmann's theory of the commons explains why a sector separate from business and government exists in our society: to create a protected space for the collective expression of what people find most important in their lives.[6] The theory helps us understand why donors give to some organizations but not to others. Nonprofits (or commons) form to produce common goods, which are desirable outcomes within a particular commons, but not necessarily beyond. Benefits are restricted to those interested in the goods, although they are shared regardless of payment. In contrast, businesses produce private goods whose benefits are restricted to those who have paid for the goods (for example, a car), and government produces public goods that benefit all members of a society (for example, military defense).

Common goods, then, are not universally preferred. Indeed, outside a particular reference group, any common or a good it produces likely is a matter of indifference, or may even be considered a "bad." Stated another way, one's own good cause is not necessarily someone else's. Contributing to charitable organizations allows people to go beyond majority rule (government) and consumer demand (business) to join with others who believe as they do. Fund raisers, therefore, should concentrate on donors' interpretation of what is in the best interest of society.

Individual Donors. Schervish and Havens reached compatible conclusions in their well-established research program on motives of individual donors. In a 1997 study, for example, they found that of virtually all the factors suggested in the literature, one cluster of variables they defined as "community of participation" had the strongest and most consistent relationship to giving behavior, which prompted them to conclude, "Charitable giving is largely a consequence of forging a connection between the existing inclinations and involvements of individuals and the needs of recipients."[7] The two scholars' program of research has been particularly valuable in describing patterns of giving by high-income and wealthy families.

Corporate Donors. Galaskiewicz's work on corporate philanthropy represents another rich program of research.[8] His theory of contributions as social currency holds that U.S. companies make gifts because senior managers are expected by their peers to contribute corporate dollars. Studies have shown that giving is the norm in many business subcultures, and managers who want to remain in the inner circles have to conform by making appropriate contributions. In addition to social currency, corporations use contributions for purposes of marketing, public relations (including employee relations), social responsibility, and tax savings. Contrary to popular opinion, empirical evidence does not support the notion that marketing objectives dominate corporate contributions.

Tax Laws. In many ways, philanthropy and the nonprofit sector are defined by the tax laws that govern them. Extensive studies by economists have shown that tax laws explain a substantial portion of individuals' and corporations' giving behavior—as much as 50%. As tax rates go up, giving goes up, and vice versa. Foundation donors make grants partly because they are required by law to give away an amount equal to 5% of their financial assets each year. Studies of foundations, it should be noted, generally have been limited to historical and introspective investigations. Overall, the area of tax laws offers some of the most potent theories for predicting and controlling aspects of fund-raising practice.

Theories and research such as those just reviewed provide a core of scientific knowledge for fund raising. However, the majority of work emanating from studies in philanthropy and nonprofit management is of marginal value to fund-raising practitioners. For example, most philanthropy scholars study giving in isolation of donors' relationships to recipient organizations. Their concentration on one side of the philanthropic exchange assumes that fund raising has no effect on giving. Prominent benchmark surveys, such as those conducted by Independent Sector, deal with the "generic" act of giving, meaning donors are defined as anyone who has made one or more gifts of any amount to one or more charitable organizations, including churches. Variables related to such behavior (for example, religiousness) are not necessarily factors in giving to specific organizations (for example, a secular university), particularly when a major gift is involved.

Nonprofit management scholars tend to treat fund raising as something charitable organizations do, rather than a systematic function carried out by specialized practitioners. In comparison, few of them regard accounting as a collection of informal activities performed by whomever is willing to take responsibility. Scholars also equate fund raising to solicitation, only one part of the process by which gifts are raised. Clearly, fund raising cannot depend solely on related domains to build the scientific body of knowledge it needs.

Knowledge from Fund-Raising Studies

Most of the research on fund raising still is conducted by graduate students, and their studies continue to dwell on predictors of alumni giving to the exclusion of equally and more important problems. The John Grenzebach Research Awards in Philanthropy for Educational Advancement have been presented annually since 1989 by CASE and the American Association of Fund-Raising Counsel Trust for Philanthropy. During this time, the award for the outstanding master's thesis or doctoral dissertation usually has been won by studies dealing with some aspect of alumni giving (for example, factors related to institutional loyalty). The award for outstanding published scholarship, rather than student theses or dissertations, usually has been won by works that are not scholarly or are from related research domains (for example, Schervish and Haven's 1997 philanthropy study cited earlier).

Regardless, the Grenzebach Award winners, as well as publications selected for AFP's Staley/Robeson/Ryan/St. Lawrence Prize for Research on Fund Raising and Philanthropy, represent what we currently know about fund raising. They form a list of "must read" literature for practitioners interested in scientific knowledge. Studies reported in that literature and elsewhere have produced promising concepts in six areas: (1) alumni giving, (2) fund-raising productivity, (3) cost-benefit analysis, (4) the process of fund raising, (5) fund-raising models, and (6) roles of fund raisers.

Alumni Giving. Seeking simplistic answers to who will give and who will not denies the complexity of the problem and is unrealistic. Research in all the behavioral sciences is directed at the same fundamental question: Why do people behave as they do? One-sided concentration on donor attitudes and demographics yields little knowledge, producing instead mixed results, because both sets of variables are unreliable predictors of behavior. Findings of greater value come from studies grounded in social exchange theory that examine giving in the context of the organization-donor relationship. In other words, giving behavior is dependent on the recipient organization's behavior, which in turn is affected by the donor's behavior.

The strongest predictor of giving is previous giving to the institution, which verifies the well-known fund-raising principle that the best prospects are previous donors. Analyses of gift records show that alumni who have given before are significantly more likely to give in the future than nondonor alumni, and that past giving far outweighs other factors in explaining both annual and major gifts. One theoretical explanation is that giving engenders involvement, and a high level of involvement enhances long-term behavioral support. Moreover, recent "data mining" analyses reveal that almost 75% of multiyear donors, compared to less than 40% of first-year donors, renew their annual gifts to colleges and universities. These results indicate that how an institution treats donors after they have made a gift has an important effect on future giving. Stewardship, then, appears to be critical to successful fund raising.

Similarly, nurturing relationships through alumni associations returns valuable dividends. Alumni who pay dues to belong to their institution's association are more likely than nonmembers to make an annual gift—as much as three times more likely. Member donors also give more than nonmember donors. For example, Patouillet's 1993 study of 75 universities found that, on average, just one-fourth of all alumni join their alumni association; however, almost half of alumni association members (47%) make a gift to the annual fund, as compared to only 16% of nonmembers, and alumni association members donate 25% more money than nonmembers.[9] Recognizing interdependent behavior, astute fund raisers focus much of their programming on alumni association members and previous donors, paying special attention to major gift prospects and first-year donors. That approach maximizes dollar results and minimizes costs.

An institution's relationship with alumni extends beyond fund raising. Decisions and performance outside the control of practitioners can have positive or negative effects. Based on this premise, a recent stream of research has documented linkages between student experiences and alumni giving. Patouillet, for example, found from a 2000 study of one university's alumni association that donor members are significantly more satisfied than nondonor members with the quality of their educational experience, their overall university experience, and the quality of faculty.[10] Such findings suggest that current students should be treated as future donors and that doing so is a campus-wide responsibility. Characteristics of the early relationship predict fund-raising outcomes. For example, evidence shows that alumni who participated in intensive extracurricular activities, such as working on the student newspaper or playing in the orchestra, are more likely than other graduates to contribute annual and major gifts. Participation in intercollegiate athletics, however, decreasingly is a factor in alumni giving.

Fund-Raising Productivity. Results of numerous studies, which usually have been misdefined as dealing with effectiveness, support the axiom that "the rich get richer." The amount of money raised is positively and strongly related to indicators of organizational wealth, such as cost of tuition, number of students, amount of expenditures, and size of endowment. Other predictor variables include prestige of the institution and number of alumni in top corporate positions. Except for endowment, the variables are institutional characteristics over which fund raising has no control, making findings useful only for comparison purposes. In the case of endowment, although size is related to dollars raised, logic tells us that cause and effect flow in the opposite direction; that is, high productivity increases an institution's endowment, not the other way around, which makes findings helpful for demonstrating the importance of fund raising but of little use for improving the practice.

On the other hand, studies that have examined the relationship between fund-raising outcomes and characteristics of the fund-raising department—as opposed to its sponsoring institution—have revealed several ways to increase fund-raising productivity. Most notably, research consistently has shown that staff size and department budget are significant factors in the amount of dollars raised. Therefore, institutions that want to raise more money are well-advised to hire more fund raisers and allocate more dollars to their work. This scientifically based recommendation is validated by the common practice of increasing fund-raising staff and budget in preparation for capital campaigns.

Before leaving this area, it must be emphasized that studies repeatedly have shown that, contrary to conventional wisdom, win-loss records of such revenue-generating sports as football and men's basketball have no effect on giving to a college or university. The myth should be laid to rest.

Cost-Benefit Analysis. Research guided by enlightened thinking has challenged traditional ways of measuring fund-raising efficiency, which is often confused with effectiveness. Rooney, for example, conceptualized and tested a new method for analyzing costs and benefits of educational fund raising that accounts for time gaps in staff efforts and return on investments.[11] His findings corroborate practitioner principles that recognize significant delays from the time donors are cultivated and solicited to the time gifts are received. Likewise, practitioners know that some fund-raising activities are more expensive than others. To test the working hypothesis, Sargeant and Kähler surveyed the top 500 charitable organizations in the United Kingdom to present average returns for nine different fund-raising techniques and programs, such as direct mail and major gifts, respectively.[12] A parallel study currently is being conducted in the United States by Indiana University's Center on Philanthropy and the Urban Institute. Results from such research establish standards of efficient practice and contribute to developing a theory of fund-raising effectiveness that goes beyond the annual amount of dollars raised.

Process of Fund Raising. Recent studies have documented what practitioners have long known: Fund raising is much more than solicitation; it involves a multistep process that requires management. In a 1994 doctoral dissertation, Curtiss drew from a number of fund-raising studies to identify 57 elements of effectiveness (for example, a prospect tracking system and trustee involvement in cultivation), which he grouped into a five-step process consisting of identification, cultivation, solicitation, acknowledgment, and recognition.[13] He used the five-step, 57-element process, which he termed donor relations, to internally assess fund raising at one private liberal arts college. Durham and Smith replicated his study at a large public research university.[14] Findings from their in-depth interviews showed that all five steps are considered important to fund raising, with three to four elements per step viewed as most important.

In the 2000 survey of AFP members who hold a Ph.D. degree, this author tested the "ROPES" process of fund raising, which she had conceptualized in earlier work.[15] ROPES consists of five consecutive steps: research, objectives, programming, evaluation, and stewardship. Details of the process can be found in the cited publication. Whether raising annual, major, planned, or campaign gifts, the theory holds that fund raisers should spend 20% of their time on research, 15% on objectives, 30% on programming (equally divided between cultivation and solicitation), 15% on evaluation, and 20% on stewardship.

Results of the AFP survey showed that ROPES is a valid description of the process by which fund raisers generate gifts. The 101 participants reported that they or other fund raisers for their organization spend an average of 14% of their time on research, another 14% on setting objectives, 39% on planning and implementing programming, 11% on evaluation, and 21% on stewardship.[16] Educational fund raisers do not differ significantly from other types of practitioners in time allocated to the five steps. Cumulative findings of this study and two others show that fund raisers generally follow the ROPES process, although they devote less time to research and evaluation than advocated by the theory.

Fund-Raising Models. Through a program of research spanning almost 15 years, this author conceptualized and tested four models of fund raising, which describe the different ways fund raising was practiced in the past and still is practiced today.[17] First, theory from public relations was adopted to analyze the history of U.S. fund raising. This analysis concluded that fund raising has evolved through four historical stages, which represent the four models of practice: press agentry, public information, two-way asymmetrical, and two-way symmetrical. A critical analysis of practitioner literature provided evidence that all four models continue to be used.

A second phase of theory building tested the models in a national survey of 296 AFP members, segmented by the type of organization for which they worked. Findings showed that, as predicted by theory, charitable organizations represented in AFP practice all four models to some extent; however, all types—including those with educational missions—predominately practice press agentry fund raising. Ramifications of the findings and additional related research are explained in the book just cited.

Roles of Fund Raisers. Following a similar theory-building process, a study by this author conceptualized four organizational roles enacted by fund raisers: *liaison*, *expert prescriber*, *technician*, and problem-solving process *facilitator*.[18] The roles explain how individual practitioners behave in carrying out their job responsibilities and predict the outcomes of the action. As in other occupations, fund raisers adopt roles by taking on patterns of behaviors to deal with recurring types of situations and to accommodate others' expectations. Like the models, every practitioner plays all four roles to some extent, but enacts one predominantly.

Liaison is the role predominantly enacted by consultants, who do not solicit gifts but advise organizational managers and volunteers on doing so. They function as interpreters and mediators in bringing together organizational representatives with prospective donors. A weakness of this role is its reliance on other actors, which makes fund raising vulnerable to unmet goals and inefficiency. *Expert prescriber* is the exact opposite of liaison. Fund raisers in this role act and are viewed as the only ones in their organization with the skill and responsibility for raising gifts. Senior administrators, trustees, and faculty are content to leave fund raising in the hands of the "expert" and assume relatively passive participation. Among the role's many weaknesses, fund raising is isolated from the institution's operations, which hampers efforts to address institutional needs and establish meaningful relationships with donors. Commitment to fund raising and its success is limited to development officers, which often leads to unrealistic expectations and dissatisfaction with results.

Fund raisers usually begin their careers in the *technician* role, in which they primarily are concerned with producing and implementing the various techniques used in raising gifts (for example, phonathons). Technicians carry out decisions made by others. They are not part of the management team, and they generally are indifferent to the purpose of their work. Problems arise when fund-raising departments consist only of technicians. In such cases, the function contributes little to advancing the organization's mission or meeting its goals.

Professionals who are playing the *problem-solving process facilitator* role are part of the management team. They collaborate with others in the organization and manage key actors' participation in the fund-raising process. In turn, they participate in decision making on organization-wide problems. The role is superior to the other three because it integrates fund raising in the overall management of the institution.

CONCLUSION

Most of the areas just reviewed are in need of additional studies. Without findings for comparison, concepts cannot be advanced to general theories, and necessary modifications will not be made. New and better ideas also will be overlooked. Yet there are many more areas not covered here that require attention. For example, we have no studies on how negotiation is used in raising major gifts, or its effects. Cultivation, a critical prerequisite of solicitation, has been ignored. Similarly, although past donors are the best prospects, we know little about stewardship. Critics charge that fund raising should be "need driven" not "donor driven," yet philanthropy theory and practitioner wisdom dictate that donors' interests and needs must be satisfied to raise gifts. Theory building and research on the dual concepts of autonomy and accountability would help resolve the controversy, as would work in other areas. The field suffers from the absence of a general theory of fund-raising effectiveness. It is agreed that the function and its practitioners should not be evaluated solely by the amount of dollars raised. But, almost all definitions of effectiveness are based on dollar totals, even though fund raisers spend the majority of their time on nonsolicitation activities. Legal issues, such as determining Unrelated Business Income Tax (UBIT), and ethical issues, such as using solicitation firms, have not been addressed.

The research infrastructure now in place encourages increased efforts. However, a major weakness that must be corrected before significant progress can be made is the dearth of full-time faculty who are interested in studying fund raising. Practitioners who hold a Ph.D. degree are encouraged to pursue a second career as teacher-scholars. Professional experience would enrich theory building and research skills would improve inquiries. Although the pay likely is less, the opportunity to make a difference is great. It would be fitting if the field, which conceived and developed fund raising, provided the faculty needed to advance its own body of knowledge.

NOTES

1. Robert L. Payton, *Philanthropy: Voluntary Action for the Public Good* (New York: American Council on Education, Macmillan Publishing Company, 1988), 32.

2. Jeffery L. Brudney and Teresa Kluesner Durden, "Twenty Years of the *Journal of Voluntary Action Research/Nonprofit and Voluntary Sector Quarterly*: An Assessment of Past Trends and Future Directions," *Nonprofit and Voluntary Sector Quarterly* 22, no. 3 (1993): 207–218.

3. Dwight F. Burlingame and Lamont J. Hulse, eds., *Taking Fund Raising Seriously: Advancing the Profession and Practice of Raising Money* (San Francisco: Jossey-Bass, 1991). Kathleen S. Kelly, *Fund Raising and Public Relations: A Crit-*

ical Analysis (Hillsdale, NJ: Lawrence Erlbaum Associates, 1991). Henry A. Rosso and Associates, Achieving Excellence in Fund Raising: A Comprehensive Guide to Principles, Strategies, and Methods (San Francisco: Jossey-Bass, 1991).

4. Michael J. Worth, ed., Educational Fund Raising: Principles and Practice (Phoenix, AZ: American Council on Education/Oryx Press, 1993).

5. Robert F. Carbone, Fund Raisers of Academe, Monograph no. 2 (College Park: University of Maryland, Clearinghouse for Research on Fund Raising, 1987).

6. Roger A. Lohmann, The Commons: New Perspectives on Nonprofit Organizations and Voluntary Action (San Francisco: Jossey-Bass, 1992).

7. Paul G. Schervish and John J. Havens, "Social Participation and Charitable Giving: A Multivariate Analysis," Voluntas, 8, no. 3 (1997), 235–260.

8. Joseph Galaskiewicz, "An Urban Grants Economy Revisited: Corporate Charitable Contributions in the Twin Cities, 1979–81, 1987–89," Administrative Science Quarterly 42, no. 3, (1997): 445–472.

9. Cited in Leland D. Patouillet, "Alumni Association Members: Attitudes Toward University Life and Giving at a Public AAU Institution," The CASE International Journal of Educational Advancement 2, no. 1 (2001): 54–55.

10. Ibid., 53–66.

11. Patrick M. Rooney, "A Better Method for Analyzing the Costs and Benefits of Fundraising at Universities," Nonprofit Management & Leadership 10, no. 1 (1999): 39–56.

12. Adrian Sargeant and Jürgen Kähler, "Returns on Fundraising Expenditures in the Voluntary Sector," Nonprofit Management & Leadership 10, no. 1 (1999): 5–19.

13. Cited in Margaret L. Durham and Albert B. Smith, "Assessing the Fund-Raising Process at a Public Research II University and Refining the Process Framework," CASE International Journal of Educational Advancement 2, no. 1 (2001): 68–70.

14. Ibid., 67–78.

15. Kathleen S. Kelly, "ROPES: A Model of the Fund-Raising Process," in The Nonprofit Handbook: Fund Raising, 3rd edition, ed. James M. Greenfield (New York: John Wiley & Sons, 2001), 96–116.

16. Because the survey was administered by telephone, respondents were not asked to break down the programming steps by cultivation and solicitation. However, subsequent surveys, which were administered in person, showed that fund raisers spend equal proportions of time on the two types of programming.

17. Kathleen S. Kelly, Effective Fund-Raising Management (Mahwah, NJ: Lawrence Erlbaum Associates, 1998), 155–192.

18. Ibid., 192–200.

CHAPTER 5

Academic Planning As the Foundation for Advancement

Jon S. Dellandrea and Adel S. Sedra

A cademic planning is an essential foundation for successful fund raising, and advancement's participation in planning is vital to secure its rightful place in the priorities of the institution. The University of Toronto provides an example of how one institution was able to successfully shift its focus, and move advancement activities from the sidelines to the spotlight. Advancement moved from the periphery to the center of the University for one simple reason: The advancement program became highly relevant, if not crucial, to the quest to secure the University's position as one of the world's best public research universities. This experience and its lessons are, at one level, specific to the University of Toronto, but at another level are transportable and relevant to other institutions as well.

Founded in 1827, the University of Toronto is Canada's largest, and by most reasonable measures, leading university, with over 50,000 students and 10,000 faculty and staff. Along with McGill University, it is the only university outside of the United States to hold membership in the prestigious Association of American Universities. It houses the largest graduate program in Canada, with 10,000 students enrolled in master's and doctoral programs in 80 graduate departments.

Aspirations for the University are quite simple: it is and will continue to be a *public* research university with strengths across the full spectrum of disciplines, from the humanities to the social sciences to the physical and life sciences and the professions. Its mission is to rank with the best public research universities of the world and to offer students an educational experience commensurate with that rank.

The evolution of advancement activities at the University began in the early 1990's, a time when the Canadian and Ontario governments were engaged in a program of austerity, resulting in significant reductions in university funding. Rather than respond with across-the-board budget cuts, Toronto made cuts but at the same time identified areas to be strengthened through reinvestment. Budget reductions of 1.5 to 2 percent per year above what was required were used to create an Academic Priorities Fund (APF) to support strategic reinvestment. This reflected a decision to spend the decade making the University stronger rather than managing its decline.

THE WHITE PAPER

To accomplish this rather difficult task, an academic planning exercise was framed by a white paper entitled "Planning for 2000." The white paper focused on the objective to become one of the world's top research-intensive universities and provided a framework for developing multiyear academic and budget plans. What distinguished the process from other attempts at comprehensive academic planning was an inclusive top-down and bottom-up, open, interactive and iterative process. Released in 1994, the white paper defined a number of principles that would steer the decision-making process regarding the allocation and reallocation of resources. These tenets included selectivity, creativity, self-assessment, and accountability. "Planning for 2000" focused the planning exercise on various objectives and strategies, including linking teaching and research, improving the organization and format of academic programs, and recruiting and supporting outstanding faculty, academic administrators, and staff.

As part of this planning exercise, the Provost[1] asked the University's faculties, colleges, and schools ("the divisions") to identify their fundraising priorities. Those academic priorities that could not be funded completely through the University's reallocated resources became approved priorities for the University's campaign. A comprehensive list of divisional priorities later became the "Catalogue of Campaign Priorities."

By 1998, at the end of two cycles of APF allocations that formed the "white paper planning process," a total of $34 million* had been allo-

---

*All amounts given in this chapter are in Canadian dollars.

cated in base budget funding (about 10 percent of the total base budget for the academic divisions), $22 million of which was allocated for academic positions. In addition, $60 million was allocated in one-time-only funds for a range of purposes, including libraries, information technology, and equipment.

THE NEXT CYCLE: "RAISING OUR SIGHTS"

The second phase of planning began in 1999 with the release of "Raising Our Sights: The Next Cycle of White Paper Planning—Key Priorities for 2000–2004." This paper identified three key planning priorities for the period: Building the Faculty for the Twenty-first Century, Enhancing the Educational Experience, and Strengthening Our Academic Programs. The paper also set out a three-step planning process consisting of a self-study, an external review, and the plan development. As part of the exercise, academic divisions were asked to identify their fund-raising priorities, to carefully scrutinize their advancement activities, and to think very practically about what staffing they might need to meet their objectives. As a direct result, many divisions were allocated funding for additional advancement staffing as part of their APF allocation. A total of $27.4 million in base funding and $20.4 million in one-time-only funding had been allocated as of summer 2001, with a small fraction of the plans still to be reviewed. At the time of this writing, divisions were working to develop an updated list of campaign priorities, one which fully reflected the priorities incorporated in their plans.

Throughout the "Planning for 2000" and "Raising Our Sights" planning exercises, the process of formulating plans was highly iterative, involving extensive discussions within faculties, and between principals/deans and the Provost, before final plans were produced. The benefits of the planning process to the University were inestimable. In a period of fiscal uncertainty, planning provided stability, a rational framework for deployment of limited resources, and it helped both to focus and energize academic leaders. The allocations made through the planning process supported the development of emergent fields of disciplinary strength, enabling the University to establish itself as a world leader in certain cutting-edge areas, such as proteomics and bioinformatics. APF allocations also helped to consolidate graduate student funding in faculties where resources were badly needed.

Figure 5.1
From Academic Priorities to Campaign Objectives

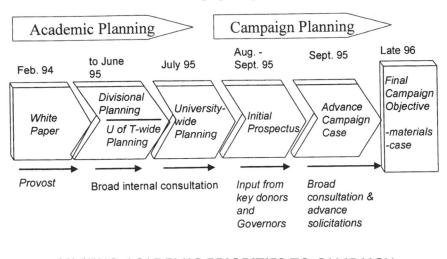

LINKING ACADEMIC PRIORITIES TO CAMPAIGN OBJECTIVES

The University of Toronto has established a process for academic planning that "works." Furthermore, academic planning that is very intimately linked to budget planning and fund-raising priorities has become an important element in the culture of the University of Toronto. Figure 5.1 provides a sense of the movement from academic priorities to campaign objectives and illustrates the link between academic priorities and advancement programs.

A dominant theme that emerged from the academic planning exercise was the need to invest in human capital, specifically, the creation of at least 145 new chairs endowed from private sources, in order to attract and retain excellent faculty and financial support for undergraduate and graduate students. From the academic planning exercise came the identification of key priorities totaling in excess of $800 million. This objective presented a real challenge, given that no institution in Canada had ever successfully executed a campaign with a goal greater than $200 million in private support. In fact, the University of Toronto itself had completed in 1991 a five-year campaign raising $126 million against a goal of $100 million, its largest campaign ever!

In September 1997, "The Campaign for the University of Toronto" was launched with a goal of "a minimum of $400 million." By May 1999, when the creation of the 100th endowed chair was announced, the goal was raised to $575 million. In October 2000, the goal was raised to $1 billion.

Transformation is never easy, and in this case transformation involved raising donor sights to a very high level. It involved the introduction of an equally high level of donor stewardship and accountability while at the same time rigorously protecting academic freedom. Key, too, was the involvement of the local community of faculty members, department chairs, and deans. The theory was simple: if the academic priorities are "owned" by the academic community, then the community has an important role to play in the process of generating the resources required to realize these aspirations.

The challenge then was to match donor interests with academic priorities. The process required a close partnership between the Provost (as the chief academic officer) and the Vice-President and Chief Advancement Officer. After approval by the relevant Dean, every funding proposal was approved by the Provost before being submitted to a prospective donor. This strong collaboration between the Provost and the advancement office ensured that the campaign remained responsive to the academic priorities.

By the summer of 2001, the campaign had raised $810 million and was on schedule to exceed the $1 billion goal. It had raised the standards for philanthropic support in Canada and had laid the groundwork for a sustainable post-campaign advancement program at the University. Resources had been raised for the specific academic priorities identified in the planning exercise. But, the University had set out to accomplish a number of objectives beyond the obvious one of meeting the campaign's goal. There was a commitment to have the advancement program be servant to the academic priorities, to transform the advancement culture of the University, and to "brand" the institution. The financial results of the campaign were less significant than the overall institutional impact.

LESSONS LEARNED

The campaign and the planning process leading to it provided seven important lessons.

1. *Faculty members play a key role in the process.* Achieving on-campus ownership of the advancement program is a challenge. When the objectives are critical to the future success and aspirations of a department or to the lives of individual faculty members, their interest and involvement can be intensified. But, the temptation to sit back and have the central development staff just deliver financial support is powerful, particularly when the funding objectives are abstract or removed from the specific interests of individual faculty or departments.

Some of the most significant gifts in the University of Toronto campaign resulted from the direct involvement of faculty members who provided the personalized bridge with the donors. Experience teaches that relationships between faculty members and former students are often deep and lasting and serve as a powerful motivation for graduates to give back to the institution. But, this faculty involvement requires that they accept the priorities of the campaign with enthusiasm.

2. *Anything is fundable.* If the institution's aspirations truly resonate with its communities, anything is fundable. Such resonance is evident when prospective donors ask to be informed of the priorities considered most difficult to fund. Early in the quiet period of the campaign it was suggested that the advancement staff "vet" academic priorities with potential donors in order to determine "fundability" and thus decide whether a given project would be included in the campaign. The suggestion was ignored, and the campaign went forward with all of the projects deemed by the academic leadership to be important to the University's future. In many cases, prospective donors were first presented with a menu of academic priorities from across the University to determine areas of potential interest for further discussions. This process resulted in a significant number of surprises for development staff and academic leaders—projects that were originally felt to be "unfundable" in fact attracted a surprising level of private support. At the same time, a number of "can't miss" academic priorities did not capture the interest of the donor community because they lacked strong academic champions or were not perceived as sufficiently unique or compelling by potential benefactors.

3. *A highly successful advancement program based on academic priorities creates a strong sense of institutional pride.* As mentioned earlier, the campaign coincided with a period of successive government cutbacks in university spending. In practical terms, these cuts meant that the University had to reduce its operating budget significantly and most academic divisions had to reduce their faculty complement. The University badly needed something to celebrate—and the campaign provided just that. Because the goals of the campaign were driven by academic priorities, it engaged academic leaders and their colleagues in ways that previous campaigns had not. At a time when many of the best scholars were retiring (and not being replaced), the endowed chairs program enabled the University to attract world-class scholars in its most prominent areas. The momentum and success of the campaign had a hugely transformational effect in helping achieve academic aspirations. In such a challenging fiscal climate, this was an enormous boon to institutional

pride and confidence. It enabled the University to move forward—to truly advance—at a time when it could easily have lost ground. And, success secured internal acceptance and support for the institutional advancement function.

4. *Linking the campaign to planning takes more time than "conventional fund raising."* One of the fundamental structural changes to occur in institutional advancement in the late twentieth century was the increased role of development staff in soliciting major gifts. While volunteers remain indispensable assets to institutions, the negotiation of major, transformational gifts requires the extended time and attention of the academic and advancement leadership of the institution. In the Toronto campaign, there were 169 gifts of $1 million or more. Each required an average length from first discussion to closure of something in excess of 14 months. This is not a task that volunteers can normally be expected to undertake.

5. *Staff retention is important.* An increased role for staff in advancement programs presents a critical challenge to institutions, namely, staff retention. The long process of donor cultivation and subsequent stewardship results in special relationships being developed between the advancement staff and the institution's donors. These relationships are precious and sometimes fragile. The departure of a senior advancement staff member can involve the fracturing of important institutional relationships. Institutions have a challenge to find ways to identify development staff who are committed to the cause of the particular institution and in turn, to develop employment terms designed to retain the very best staff.

6. *Transparency and accountability are required for advancement staff.* If we are to compensate advancement professionals at a level appropriate to their expanded role and sufficient to retain them, special care must be taken to ensure that their compensation does not attract resentment. The salaries of senior advancement professionals in many cases are similar to those of senior faculty members. The University of Toronto has undertaken two specific measures to build a climate that places a premium on transparency and accountability.

First, every week an e-mail is sent to principals and deans listing every contact made with a current or prospective donor, detailing the name, position, and division of the responsible staff member. This ensures that every academic leader knows not only what her development staff are doing, but equally important, what the development staff are doing in other divisions. Under these open conditions, any potential issues regarding lack of performance are quickly identified.

Second, the University has implemented a new human resources policy for senior advancement staff, in which a significant percentage of total compensation is "at risk" if specific performance measures are not met. In addition, all salary agreements in the advancement area are subject to a review process chaired by the Vice President and Chief Advancement Officer, with the advice of senior members of the academic community. This ensures that the academic leadership of the University is fully consulted regarding the return on investment from senior advancement staff.

7. *Anchoring a campaign in an academic plan results in balance across the institution.* There is a fear in the minds of some that the pursuit of private support will influence the institution's priorities toward areas of donor interest, that institutions will go in certain directions simply in response to the availability of money—in other words, that campaigns will be "donor-driven" rather than "need-driven." No better case can be made for the importance of strategic academic planning than this fear. In the absence of a real plan, such influence is inevitable.

Another concern about the pursuit of private support is the fear that the rich will get richer and the poor will get poorer; that is, that the humanities and social sciences will starve while disciplines such as business, medicine, and technology will prosper. The Toronto experience demonstrates the balancing effect of strategic academic planning on advancement results. Endowed chairs at the University are 26 percent in engineering and sciences, 23 percent in business and law, 23 percent in health sciences, and 28 percent in the social sciences, humanities, education, and social work.

CONCLUSION

The University of Toronto's experience illustrates the importance of institutional planning, both to the definition of academic objectives that can inspire the entire campus community and to the realization of these objectives through advancement. Toronto's experience indicates that the involvement of faculty and academic leadership through a top-down, bottom-up process is critical to the success of this process. Faculty, staff, students, and alumni know that private support is critical to the fulfillment of departmental objectives across the University. Their enthusiasm inspired more than 100,000 donors to support the University and created the base upon which was built the most successful advancement program in the history of Canadian education.

NOTE

1. The chief academic officer of the University is the Vice-President and Provost. The University's academic divisions are overseen by principals or deans, who are responsible for the administration of their unit, according to policies set by the Governing Council of the University, which includes representation from the faculty, students, staff, administration, alumni, and community.

CHAPTER 6

The Roles of Key Individuals

Sara L. Patton

F or an institution to realize its fund-raising potential, the key institutional players—the board of trustees, the president, and the
chief development officer—must clearly understand and effectively interpret their roles. While some areas of responsibility are and
should remain the exclusive domain of the board, the president, or the
development staff, many more call for understanding, cooperation, and
teamwork among these parties.

William A. Kinnison and Michael J. Ferin make this point in their
discussion of the "three-party relationship," in which they discuss how
"partnership roles" support and sustain the mission and priorities of the
institution. According to Kinnison and Ferin, an institution can effectively set and achieve development goals only if its staff and volunteers
know they must act together.[1]

At the same time, each of the three key players must exercise dynamic
leadership in his or her area. In his book *Successful Fund Raising for
Higher Education*, Frank H.T. Rhodes analyzes the relationships among
the CEO, trustee, and chief development officer (CDO) positions. He
writes:

> The president's role in fund raising is an integral part of his or her
> larger educational and support activities. The trustees . . . engaged in
> a campaign are performing a significant part of their fiduciary respon-
> sibilities. The Vice President for Institutional Advancement, devot-
> ing time to on-campus . . . activities and programs, guarantees the
> first-hand familiarity on which successful development rests.[2]

THE ROLE OF TRUSTEES

The environment in which schools, colleges, and universities seek to attract students, faculty members, and financial support becomes more intensely competitive every year. The most successful institutions are those with trustees who involve themselves fully in the planning, execution, and evaluation of development efforts and who can interpret the institution's goals with conviction and understanding within their individual spheres of influence.

In most cases, this involvement is inspired and sustained by the chair of the board. Jerold Panas states: "The Chair is your organization's chief executive volunteer, its driving force, the embodiment of all that is vital and effective about the organization."[3]

One feature unique to the governing board is that its members are responsible for every aspect of the enterprise. As J. W. Pocock writes, "the board is the ultimate seat of power and responsibility in the institution." Board members are policy makers, long-term planners, and asset managers; they "hold the assets of the institution in trust for the benefit of the institution, its supporters, and society."[4]

Board members set the standard for volunteer leadership and commitment. At the very top of the hierarchy of volunteers, they are expected to hold a broad view of the institution, to be able to consider it in the context of the larger society, and to be advocates for the particular mission and values of the institution they serve.

The board also is responsible for maintaining the creative energies and balance of the institution's leadership over time. Trustees should take an active role in identifying, cultivating, and recruiting new trustees, just as they help select and evaluate the institution's president.

Finally, the board bears ultimate responsibility for ensuring the institution's financial strength and vitality[5] (i.e., giving not only their time, but their resources, in generous measure). Board members' broad perspective and personal involvement can make them the most effective fund raisers—especially when they themselves are major donors. As Pocock says, "Fund raising is the one major activity in which trustees step beyond their policy and oversight roles and become active players."[6]

This is not to say that every single member of an effective board must be an active solicitor or make one-on-one presentations to major donors. Some trustees, even some who give generously themselves, simply may not be comfortable in this role. They may participate in other ways—perhaps by hosting an off-campus event for alumni and friends or by accompanying the president or development officer on a solicitation visit to a key corporation where the trustee is well known and respected. More important than actually "making the ask" is a trustee's ability to internalize the goals of the institution so that he or she perceives development activity—in a variety of forms—as a necessary and important component of the trustee's service. This perception is especially important when an institution is in a capital campaign; then, trustee involvement becomes not only desirable, but absolutely essential.[7]

Other trustees will relish the opportunity to seek support for a cause in which they are investing time and money themselves. Most boards have a "development committee" whose members are expected to promote development objectives, not only to the institution's various external constituencies, but also to other members of the board. In this sense, the board's development committee serves as a kind of in-house public relations agency for the advancement effort. Individuals with drive, enthusiasm, and the ability to relate to others with empathy— while practicing friendly persuasion—are well suited to this role.

Author and editor Bob Hartsook stresses that without the active participation of board members in identifying, cultivating, and soliciting peers who can advance the institution's mission, "a campaign is just potential energy."[8]

THE ROLE OF THE PRESIDENT

Whole books have been written about the college or university president's role in fund raising.[9] Within the three-way leadership partnership, the president's role is the most complex. The president must be at once the interpreter of the educational environment in general and the standard bearer for his or her institution's unique mission within that environment. The president must take the lead in "defining and articulating the [institution's] mission and priorities."[10]

Edward G. Coll asserts that "out of the many individual views of the future, the president must forge . . . an agenda for progress and change that is at once compelling, challenging, and achievable."[11] In a capital campaign, these skills help make presidential leadership vital. In the words of Edward Foote, former president of the University of Miami, "The campaign is the translation of a vision to the most demanding reality of all, money."[12]

The president must personify the institution's successes and aspirations while balancing various competing needs and special interests. He or she must be both an idealistic visionary and a steely-eyed realist— sometimes in the same half hour. Since presidents are people too, they will find some roles fit more naturally than others. As Madeleine Green points out, there is no set formula for successful presidential leadership. "The real issue is . . . a personally authentic approach . . . with a consistent philosophy and value system underpinning it all."[13] This "authenticity" is crucial in fund raising, where the president forges the vital link between trustees and professional development staff.

At most colleges and universities, the president is a member of the board of trustees. The president's involvement in fund raising sets the example for other trustees. If that involvement is positive, enthusiastic, and firmly tied to institutional priorities, trustees are likely to follow suit. If the president is indifferent to development concerns or distant from fund-raising activities, board members are likely to place a lower value on their own participation.

Similarly, the president's relationship with professional development staff, and particularly with the chief development officer, is pivotal. The best development work is never an end in itself, but has at its heart the academic mission of the institution. In this regard, the president must be a decisive leader who motivates and educates while giving fund raisers the support they need to attract resources to meet the real needs of the institution.

This support includes such elements as staff, budget, and access to the institution's decision-making structures. The president should also help create opportunities for development professionals to interact with trustees and other key volunteers.[14] Most important of all is the president's systematic dedication of time to assist both trustees and staff in cultivating and soliciting major donors.

THE ROLE OF THE CHIEF DEVELOPMENT OFFICER

The CDO, with other members of the professional development staff, must create specific strategies and action plans to meet fund-raising objectives. He or she must also create a climate of confidence for the staff's integrity and performance by making sure that all players understand and share the institution's short- and long-run goals. An effective development office works as a team to address the many practical tasks that must be undertaken to achieve these goals.

Frank Rhodes tellingly observes that

> Having three strong leaders in pivotal fund raising roles can create tensions, so the roles must complement one another. The Vice President (CDO) must be able to choreograph the dance in such a

way that the volunteer leadership occupies center stage but all necessary movements are completed in their proper order.[15]

The CDO must manage two complementary functions of development activity: creating materials and cultivating donors. The first is mainly internal and involves producing research, proposals, publications, case statements, operating plans, and the like. The second is an external function that requires the development team's being regularly involved outside the institution in identifying, screening, and cultivating prospective donors and volunteers. Like the trustees and the president, professional staff members must also be persuasive advocates and able to make the institution's case compelling to diverse audiences.

Above all, it is the CDO's responsibility to facilitate the trustees' and the president's participation in the fund-raising process. Because neither the trustees nor the president can devote full time to development, the time they do give must be used to its fullest advantage. When a capital campaign is in progress, the CDO must also provide effective training for volunteers at every level, including trustees.[16]

And, whether or not in the midst of a campaign, the professional staff should give top-level volunteers the best preparation possible for solicitations. That means giving them thorough briefings about a prospective donor's relationship to the institution as well as any written materials or illustrations that would strengthen the presentation. The volunteer who is successful is likely to welcome future assignments; it is in the CDO's best interest to lay the groundwork for continuing volunteer involvement.

CONCLUSION

Board members, with their broad perspectives and high levels of achievement in their fields, can attract strong support for the institutions they serve. As advocates who volunteer their time, interests, and resources, they are perhaps the best "authenticators" of an institution's claim of significance in the world beyond academia.

The president must lead the way in defining the institution's mission and making it comprehensible to a diverse constituency. He or she must also demonstrate by personal example, to both trustees and staff, the interactive nature of the fund-raising partnership.

Professional development staff use their practical skills and experience to support and enhance the fund-raising activity of trustees and the president in order to achieve institutional goals and meet educational needs.

The responsibility for an institution's fund-raising efforts is shared among these participants in this "three-party relationship." To be effective, the trustees, the president, and the CDO must all support one another's efforts, communicate within their roles, and involve themselves personally in the fund-raising process.[17]

NOTES

1. William A. Kinnison and Michael J. Ferin, "The Three-Party Relationship," in *Fund-raising Leadership: A Guide for Colleges and University Boards*, ed. J. W. Pocock (Washington, DC: Association of Governing Boards of Universities and Colleges, 1989), 57–61.

2. Frank H.T. Rhodes, *Successful Fund Raising for Higher Education: The Advancement of Learning*, ed. Frank H. T. Rhodes (Phoenix, AZ: American Council on Education/Oryx Press, October 1997), xxiii.

3. Jerold Panas, *Boardroom Verities* (Chicago: Precept Press, 1991), 22.

4. Pocock, *Fund-raising Leadership*, 3.

5. At public institutions, fund raising may be the job of institutionally related foundations—private organizations with their own directors or trustees. The members of the university's own governing board may be appointed without regard to their fund-raising abilities or inclinations. In this situation, the interaction between the university regents and foundation trustees is crucial to fund raising. Readers interested in the issue of private foundations and public universities may refer to Chapter 18 of this book, to Michael J. Worth's chapter entitled "The Institutionally Related Foundation in Public Colleges and Universities" in *Fund-raising Leadership*, Pocock, 63–74, and also to Eric Wentworth's "Primer on Institutionally Related Foundations" in *Handbook of Institutional Advancement*, ed. Peter McE. Buchanan (Washington, DC: Council for Advancement and Support of Education, 2000), 359–362.

6. Pocock, *Fund-raising Leadership*, 23.

7. Henry D. Sharpe, Jr., "The Role of the Board of Trustees," in *The Successful Campaign: From Planning to Victory Celebration*, ed. H. Gerald Quigg (Washington, DC: Council for Advancement and Support of Education, 1986), 63–72.

8. Bob Hartsook, ed., *Getting Your Ducks in a Row!* (Wichita, KS: ASR Philanthropic Publishing, 2001), 102.

9. One such source is *The President and Fund Raising* by James L. Fisher and Gary H. Quehl (New York: American Council on Education/Macmillan, 1989).

10. Kinnison and Ferin, "The Three-Party Relationship," 58.

11. Edward G. Coll, "The Role of the President in Fund Raising," in Buchanan, *Handbook of Institutional Advancement*, 515.

12. Edward T. Foote II, "The President's Role in a Capital Campaign," in Quigg, *The Successful Capital Campaign*, 73.

13. Madeleine F. Green, "Presidential Leadership: Changes in Style," *AGB Reports* (January/February 1986): 20.

14. Francis C. Pray, ed., *Handbook for Educational Fund Raising* (San Francisco: Jossey-Bass, 1981), 358.

15. Rhodes, *Successful Fund Raising for Higher Education*, 124.

16. Sara L. Patton, "Solicitation Methods and Training," in Quigg, *The Successful Capital Campaign*, 159–166.

17. Kinnison and Ferin, "The Three-Party Relationship," 58.

PART III

Raising Funds from Individuals

W hen the topic of higher education fund raising comes up among people who do not know much about it, they often seem to think first about corporations. Large corporations are perhaps the most visible "philanthropists," because their activities are reflected in their advertising and other communications efforts. Others may think of prominent foundations—household names like the Ford Foundation or the Gates Foundation—and assume that they must be among the most important sources of financial support for colleges and universities. People are often surprised to learn that the single largest source of philanthropy is *people*, that is, giving by private individuals.

The chapters in this section of the book explore four dimensions of raising funds from individual donors. The first three take us "up the pyramid" from annual giving to major gifts to principal gifts. (Chapter 2 describes the concept of the fund-raising pyramid and introduces these terms.) The section's final chapter provides an overview of planned giving (or "charitable gift planning"), including methods and vehicles that are increasingly applied in making major and principal gifts.

Annual giving remains the bedrock of the comprehensive development program, the "front door" through which many individuals will first enter into their philanthropic "careers." For most college and university alumni, the annual giving program is the most visible of the institution's efforts, arriving in their homes through their mailboxes, their telephones, or, increasingly, their computers. As Fritz Schroeder discusses in Chapter 7, the annual giving program serves many purposes, among them the opportunity to engage a broad base of individuals in advancing the institution, and perhaps beginning relationships that eventually will lead to higher levels of support.

The definition of a "major gift" is, of course, relative to the needs of the institution and the scope and scale of its development program. But, however defined, major gifts result from an individual's relationship with an institution that has grown to an intensity that calls forth a significant, even sacrificial, commitment. Chapter 8, on the subject of major gift programs, is written by David Dunlop, widely considered the "guru" of major gift fund raising. In his chapter, Dunlop reiterates some of the principles that he introduced in earlier writings, many of which have been incorporated into the common vocabulary and practice of educational fund raising. He also introduces new concepts, reflecting his continued thinking and analysis.

The term "principal gifts" has been introduced into the fund-raising lexicon within the past decade or so. The 1993 book *Educational Fund Raising: Principles and Practice* did not employ the term at all. In today's post-1990s environment, it would be a glaring omission not to include a discussion of such gifts, which in recent years have made headlines and transformed some institutions. In Chapter 9, Frank Schubert describes the impact of principal gifts and approaches to fund raising at the highest level of the pyramid.

As Chapter 2 emphasizes, planned giving is not itself reflected on the fund-raising pyramid, but is instead an important "tool" that is increasingly used in the construction of major and principal gifts. The growth in the importance of planned giving, and the role of planned giving officers and programs, has been explosive over the past decade. This reflected in part the booming stock market of the 1990s, which provided many people with substantial assets and the need to integrate giving with their overall financial planning. But, the growth in planned giving also reflects an aging population, to which many planned giving vehicles are most favorable, and the growing financial sophistication of the American public. Although the future of the economy and markets is always unpredictable, other trends seem to assure that knowledge of planned giving will become ever more essential for development professionals. Chapter 10, by Ronald Sapp and Peter Kimball, provides an overview of planned giving vehicles and the current state of the art in charitable gift planning. Readers with a particular interest in planned giving will need to remain constantly aware of changes in laws and regulations that might alter the landscape for this type of philanthropy.

CHAPTER 7

The Annual Giving Program

Fritz W. Schroeder

Annual giving is the foundation of every successful fund-raising program and an important source of revenue for many institutions. In recent years, many traditional annual giving techniques have remained effective, while myriad new strategies have been introduced. Phonathons and direct mail have been and will continue to be important tools in fund-raising efforts. People are still at the heart of every solicitation strategy. At the same time, it is possible to look into this new century knowing much more about the data behind fund-raising programs and how to analyze efforts. The maturity of the annual fund within the overall development effort is a significant factor in continued growth. The increased access to demographic information has pushed fund raisers to define the characteristics of certain cohorts of alumni and donors and appeal to the behavior of twenty-year-olds in a different tone than fifty-year-olds.

Newcomers and seasoned veterans alike will profit from a solid overview both of the tools and programs used in annual giving efforts and of several of the important themes and issues annual giving programs are facing in the new century. Naturally, the purposes and design of annual giving efforts are unique to each development program— they can vary dramatically from one institution to the next. While the principles are consistent everywhere, the issues and themes that affect a program can be quite different, depending on the size, history, and scope of the annual giving effort. The very general issues covered here will, of course, require different interpretations for different institutions.

ANNUAL GIVING

Beginning with a few straightforward concepts will serve to ground the discussion. Annual fund efforts represent the broad-based, regular solicitation of an institution's largest constituency, including alumni, friends, parents, grateful patients, and others. Annual fund revenue typically involves "current-use" funds—moneys that are raised today and spent tomorrow. The degree to which these funds are unrestricted depends on both the history of the organization and the needs of the institution.

The term "annual fund" is both an activity and a giving designation. We talk about our annual fund programs, implying phone, mail, parents, senior class giving, and so forth. In addition, we measure our success by how much was raised for the annual fund each year. Each institution may define the annual fund in a slightly different way, including:

- a single, unrestricted account
- a series of individual current-use accounts
- gifts within a certain dollar range, say $1–$10,000
- gifts raised as a result of phone, mail, and personal solicitation efforts (as tracked by appeal codes)

There is no ideal definition. The key is to define the annual fund in a manner that is consistent with the goals of the specific development program and is reasonably simple to analyze and track from one year to the next.

In addition to differences in the definition of the annual fund and which gifts are credited toward it, there are also various roles that an annual giving program can play within the overall development efforts of an institution. For example, some programs are steeped in tradition with very strong alumni participation (50 to 75 percent), outstanding reunion efforts, and a steady stream of current revenue that is an integral part of the institution's financial health. In such cases, the institution's financial officer views that annual fund as a significant revenue source with the expectation that the revenue is "protected" by the broad base of participation. The efforts in this program are focused on preserving and growing the base.

Conversely, major gift officers rely on the annual fund as a primary source of major gift prospects. Many institutions have determined that, among their alumni, the annual gift has been the single most important predictor for major gift potential, and therefore visit almost every donor who has consecutively made gifts of $100 or more. In this situation, while the revenue stream is important, the institution may primarily view the annual giving program as a feeder to the major gift effort. In this type of program, efforts are focused on carefully tracking the higher-end donors for consecutive giving and increased giving, and creating initiatives to increase this pool of major gift prospects. These are just two examples of the role of annual giving efforts. The critical issue is that each program clearly understands the role of the annual fund and takes determined action toward that goal.

Following, then, are possible goals and roles of an annual giving program.

Participation

All programs strive for broad-based participation, even though very few can actually claim participation percentages that cross the 50 percent mark. As in baseball, a batting average in the .300s is considered great. Those of us with participation rates in the 30 percent to 40 percent range should feel good (although we're not likely to get a three-year, $6-million contract or a place in the Hall of Fame). Overall participation, whether from alumni, parents, friends, or others, is a solid indicator of how our closest friends feel about supporting the institution. That endorsement carries weight with major donors, corporations and foundations, our own faculty and staff, and so forth. In addition, broad participation does provide a "cushion" of support. In the recent record economy, annual funds were in great shape because many donors gave at levels that exceeded expectations on an annual basis. However, in periods when the economy slows and some of these individual donors decrease the size of their gifts, it is the broad base of support that helps to sustain the revenue stream.

As a rule of thumb, pursuing broad participation is an expensive proposition (this is not meant to be a negative statement). Each institution has a "baseline" participation rate—the rate that can be achieved through the standard solicitation schedule. For example, if a program typically solicits every alumnus four times each year (two phone contacts and two mail contacts), and generally maintains a 28 percent participation rate, then that is its baseline rate. Each year alumni are added to the roster, and any subtle enhancements in the program may only allow for keeping pace with the growing alumni list. It will take a significant investment to move the participation rate in any substantial manner. It might be necessary to double the number of solicitations, increase alumni relations efforts, add staff, or take some other significant step to achieve a higher goal.

Major Gift Cultivation Program

Every annual giving program can serve as a cultivation and identification tool for major gift efforts. Many of the screening programs offered by national consulting firms point to consecutive annual gift patterns as the single greatest predictor of major gift success. Furthermore, many donors "self-identify" through their gifts to the annual fund. For example, a donor who increases her gift from $500 to $2,500 in one year is sending a signal about either her commitment to your organization or her personal financial situation. Finally, annual gifts are an important stewardship step for major donors. The relationship between annual gifts and major gifts will be explored later, but asking major donors to invest in the annual fund further strengthens their relationship to the institution.

Volunteer Identification and Development

Volunteers play a critical role in annual giving programs. The annual fund provides a wonderful opportunity to introduce volunteers to the philanthropic nature an organization. Annual giving volunteers are particularly important in overall volunteer efforts because their involvement can be short term and entry level. Most of the roles for annual fund volunteers span a fiscal year. While many of the volunteers renew year after year, this short term allows for careful evaluation of individual volunteers, moving those with a true commitment forward to longer-term endeavors.

Revenue

While it is almost too obvious to mention, one of the primary roles of annual giving programs is to generate annual, expendable, and primarily unrestricted revenue. One of the most effective ways to describe the importance of annual fund revenue is to talk about the cash flow it represents in terms of endowment. For example, an annual fund of $200,000 may not appear very significant for some organizations. How-

ever, that $200,000 revenue stream represents the equivalent of an en-
dowment of $4 million, assuming a 5 percent payout rate.

PLANNING IN THE ANNUAL FUND

In the simplest sense, annual fund raising is all about acquiring, retaining, and upgrading donors. The program operates on an annual cycle,
hence the term "annual fund." Each and every year, the annual fund
starts over at zero. The process involves efforts that convince last year's
donors to renew their support, while simultaneously developing a case
that encourages non-donors to join the ranks for the first time. The
effort to retain last year's donors not only relies heavily on the "habit
forming" aspect of making annual gifts but also demands that consistent
messages of stewardship and donor accountability be sent throughout
the year. Acquiring new donors is a more expensive effort that involves
regular, repeated solicitations with a clear, compelling case for support.

All of the fancy segments and high-profile volunteer programs that
are created, at their core, have three activities: acquiring, retaining and
upgrading. Therefore, planning efforts should also have these three actions at their core. The planning process involves a careful review of
past years with an eye toward growth in certain areas. The end product
of the planning process is a document that will serve as a work plan for
the year with details that should include:

- segmentation strategies
- mail and phone solicitation dates
- programmatic time lines (when to start planning for family weekend,
  when to schedule the first meeting of the gift society committee, and
  so forth)
- quantitative and qualitative targets for each program
- individual staff responsibilities and goals
- back-up plans (more about this later)

There are two types of planning fund raisers undertake in the annual
fund. Every year they go through the process of planning the next year.
For programs that run on a July 1 through June 30 fiscal year, this
planning process typically begins on January 1 and develops over the
next six months before the start of the new fiscal year. Here, this type
of planning is referred to as "regular planning." As this label implies,
regular planning occurs every year and incorporates analysis, goal-
setting, and timetables for regular annual fund solicitations and programs.

The second type of planning fund raisers undertake involves a much more detailed effort that includes researching peer programs, developing long term goals, securing new funding, adding staff, and so forth. Again, for the sake of this discussion, this type of planning is labeled "growth planning." Growth planning occurs when something or someone prompts the manager to do more. Backing up, most annual funds grow at a rate of 3 percent, 4 percent, or maybe even 10 percent in any given year, barring any outside interferences such as stock market slowdowns, institutional crises, and so forth. Proceeding from year to year and going through the process of "regular planning," fund raisers can rightly expect revenue increases in the range of 3 to 10 percent. Suppose, however, that the CEO announces he or she wants to see a 30 percent increase in revenue in the next three fiscal years. This demand necessitates fund raisers to enter the "growth planning" stage, because a program won't grow 30 percent with only a routine review of last year's program. The growth planning stage requires a strategic approach—developing new ideas, new solicitation techniques, new themes, and new resources to help achieve these heightened goals.

TOOLS AND PROGRAMS

Annual giving efforts combine two important components: (1) solicitation tools, such as phonathons, direct mail, web home pages, and personal visits, and (2) programs, such as young alumni funds, parent funds, class agents, reunion gift programs, leadership gift clubs, matching gift programs, and many others. The "art" of annual giving involves developing strong volunteer teams, creative programs for young alumni and parents, the aggressive marketing of leadership societies, and the exploration of new programs and opportunities. The "science" of annual giving implies using the solicitation techniques in the most effective, cost-efficient manner to bring in the largest possible number of donors and dollars. The basic solicitation tools have remained fairly consistent for many years; however, the application of the different techniques has changed rather dramatically.

Direct Mail

Although there are exceptions, direct mail is typically the least expensive program with the lowest response rate. While response rates, or "yield," can vary significantly, a 2 to 5 percent response rate on a large mailing is considered successful. In contrast, a smaller, targeted mailing to high-end or consistent donors may produce a 50 or even 75 percent response rate. There are several important reasons why direct mail is used:

- It creates a visual image of the annual fund and helps to make the program "tangible" to the donor.
- It has a long-term reminder effect—a donor can keep a direct mail response card in his or her "bill pile" for days, weeks, or even months, allowing the individual to make the gift according to his or her timetable.
- With the growth in answering machines, caller I.D., and other "screening" tactics for telemarketing, direct mail letters sometimes provide the only contact with a donor.
- Direct mail permits a level of creativity and innovation that is harder to accomplish with telemarketing scripts.

Phonathons

Phonathon programs, whether using volunteers or salaried callers, allow for high volume with a modest amount of personal interaction. In a three-to-five-minute telephone call, a caller can connect with a donor on several levels not possible in direct mail. Most importantly:

- Phonathons allow for two-way conversations, the exchange of information, and reminders of important dates and upcoming events. Most critically, phonathons allow a caller to more thoroughly build a case for support by responding to objections and offering clarification where needed.
- Phonathons allow the caller to negotiate the dollar amount of the pledge, the payment schedule, and other details that help to encourage a pledge.
- Phonathon solicitations can be tailored to individual donors and prospects—each script can incorporate certain messages, activities, and references to giving habits and affiliations in a way that targets the specific appeal to a level that is not possible with direct mail.

Personal Solicitations

Personal solicitations are the final component of a strong annual giving program. Personal solicitations allow an opportunity to meet with donors face-to-face, talk about the importance of their involvement in the organization, react to every clue (verbal and nonverbal), and make a very personal appeal for support. Fund raisers typically use personal solicitations in annual giving as a means to: (1) increase the gift of a current donor, (2) solicit a "VIP" donor for his or her annual gift, or (3) solicit the first gift from a non-donor with particularly exciting potential.

The principles that apply to major gift solicitation techniques are parallel to those for annual gift solicitations. The significant difference lies in the fact that the multiple steps found in major gift solicitation (identification, interest, cultivation, solicitation, and stewardship) are condensed into one, perhaps two steps for annual giving. In many cases, most of the work is accomplished in one visit, whereas the major gift process may take three, four, or more visits. Clearly, personal solicitations can be the most rewarding and exciting part of any annual giving program. It reminds us that the heart of any program lies with people, not numbers or percentages.

Programs to Address Special Constituencies

As mentioned earlier, the art of annual giving is found in the creation of effective programs to address the special needs of certain constituencies. These programs include parents funds, young alumni efforts, the senior class giving program, faculty-staff campaigns, class agents, reunions, and others. The applicability of these programs to a particular institution is determined by how well the program fits the culture and demographics of that institution. For example, a school of continuing studies with many part-time and returning adult students may not be the appropriate place to launch a parents program. However, this same continuing studies school may have an excellent opportunity for a successful faculty-staff campaign, given the large constituency of adjunct faculty members, who may derive substantial income from their other, full-time careers.

Regardless of which programs best fit each institution, the most important aspect of these "special" efforts is their ability to involve volunteers. Without question, a peer volunteer can be a stronger solicitor than a paid staff member. Involving volunteers as class agents, reunion gift chairs, parents fund chairs, gift society leaders, and other roles allows the staff to spread its reach. Volunteer involvement also represents a very strong endorsement of a program by your potential donors' peers. The four most important principles for enlisting annual giving volunteers (or any other volunteers, for that matter) are:

1. Providing potential volunteers with a clear understanding of their duties and responsibilities during the recruitment process, and reinforcing these throughout their involvement

2. Giving volunteers the tools and the opportunities to be successful. There is no greater mistake than placing volunteers in a position to fail

3. Training volunteers for their task. This includes teaching them about the organization, its case for support, and the "art" of fund raising

4. Recognizing that supporting volunteers is time-intensive, and they will require a significant commitment of staff effort

EVALUATION

The process of evaluating annual giving efforts is very closely linked to the process of planning. As stated earlier, planning involves setting accurate projections and goals that are quantifiable and qualifiable. The very simple approach to annual giving evaluation is to draw two columns on a piece of paper. In one column, list the goals (total dollars raised, number of donors, number of personal solicitations, number of volunteer solicitations, etc.). In the second column, list the corresponding results. The finished product should reveal successes as well as areas for improvement.

The more advanced approach to evaluation involves taking the two columns to the next step and identifying the underlying reasons why a goal was or was not met. If the goal for alumni participation wasn't met, the fund raiser needs to determine whether a certain decade, school, or demographic fell short of its potential. If only one-half of planned personal solicitations were made, the annual giving manager should try to account for the time in a way that will illustrate why. In addition, this is the stage at which it is relevant to examine external benchmarks from peers. While it may not be necessary to analyze peer data every year, it is important to periodically measure a program against similar institutions. These comparisons aren't made for the sake of competition, but to further explain success with certain goals, the reality of goals, and what peers' experiences have been.

Annual giving efforts are not insulated programs unaffected by the outside world. Programs can be helped or hindered by the economy, leadership changes at an institution, technology changes in the market (look at the challenge answering machines have presented), competition for the fund-raising dollar, and yes, even an NCAA tournament win (or loss!). A thorough evaluation of programs allows the annual giving manager to pinpoint which achievements or failures can be controlled, and which stem from other influences. The most important thing an evaluation provides is the answer to "What can/should be changed next year?"

ISSUES FOR A NEW CENTURY

With that primer on the basics of annual giving, it's important to examine the issues that face all annual giving programs in the context of today's educational fund-raising climate.

The Role of Annual Giving in the Development Program

The philanthropic support institutions receive continues to grow at a very rapid pace. "Mega gifts" of $100 million and more are seen with increasing frequency. Campaigns move from one to the next with shorter and shorter "down" periods between these mammoth fund-raising efforts. So where does that place the annual fund in the scheme of overall development efforts? In many ways, it simply increases the importance of the program to an even greater level. As the mega gifts and mega campaigns grow, the annual fund provides the average donor with the opportunity to express his or her philanthropic commitment to the institution. In many organizations, those unrestricted annual fund dollars provide the leadership with the day-to-day discretionary resources that sustain programs and activities. While mega gifts clearly have a transforming impact on an institution, annual gifts can allow for the continuation of those daily activities that make each school unique.

Combined Ask or Dual Ask

A significant challenge is how to maintain annual giving in the face of ambitious major gift campaigns. Many of the very best major gift donors have emerged as high-end donors to the annual fund, contributing, for example, $5,000 or $10,000 a year. A major gift strategy might be to solicit them for a $100,000 endowed scholarship with a four- or five-year payment schedule. If a component of that solicitation does not include the annual fund, a very vital stream of current-use income is lost while the donor is working to endow the scholarship. In many cases, it is not necessary to sacrifice one for the other: the major gift can be obtained while also continuing the donor's support of the annual fund.

The most straightforward way to accomplish this is to include the annual fund in the major gift solicitation, using a "combined ask." For example, a major gift proposal for $100,000 (payable over four years) might also include an annual fund request for $8,000. The donor's gift each year would be $27,000—$25,000 toward the major gift commitment and $2,000 for the annual fund. This strategy is most effective with donors who have strong, consistent participation in the annual fund.

Another variation is to invite the donor to earmark a portion of his or her major commitment for the annual fund. To continue the first example, the solicitation for the $100,000 commitment might include $96,000 for a capital project and $1,000 a year for the annual fund. This strategy is effective when the donor does not have a track record of gifts to the annual fund and may not have a clear understanding of the importance of both funds. Including this combined ask in the major gift solicitation allows the donor to grow in his or her understanding of the annual fund while fulfilling a major commitment. There is a negative side to this approach, however, in the perceived "discounting" of endowment and capital needs. If the organization requires $100,000 to name a scholarship, and it is offered to a donor for the $96,000 described above, the development officer will need to work carefully with his or her organization to determine a specific protocol for this process.

Another strategy is to use a "dual ask" approach. A fund raiser solicits a capital pledge; for example, $100,000 to establish a scholarship fund, and then he or she simply encourages the donor to also consider the annual fund when he or she receives regular annual fund solicitations each year during the pledge payment period. While this is not the strongest strategy, it is clearly better than sending no message at all about the importance of continuing annual support.

So, why is maintaining annual giving during the campaign such a big deal? Considered strictly from a financial perspective, it preserves and protects a vital stream of primarily unrestricted income for current use. In most situations, fund raisers approach major donors about large gifts to capital projects, endowments, and other permanent, long-term programs. If they neglect also to ask donors for an annual gift, that income stream is sacrificed while the donor completes his or her larger commitment. The distinction is a fine one, however. Clearly, a six- or seven-figure capital endowment gift will do more to protect the future of an institution than a $1,000 annual gift, but if a culture is created in which it isn't *necessary* to sacrifice one in favor of the other, the institution will be stronger now and in the future. In addition, it's possible to create a very compelling case for the annual fund by pointing to the most generous major donors and highlighting their continued commitment to the annual fund.

Finally, and perhaps most importantly, if fund raisers take a $1,000 donor to the annual fund and solicit him or her for a multi-year, six-figure capital commitment and nothing more, what happens at the end of the payment schedule? Has the hope or expectation been clearly conveyed that the donor resume annual giving once the capital commitment has been fulfilled? If not, then there is a strong chance that the individual may not return as an annual donor.

Designing a Program for Growth

Growth planning in the annual fund was discussed earlier in this chapter. It is the process by which programs are analyzed, perhaps compared with external benchmarks, and significant changes are made in order to achieve greater goals. While this process itself is very important for any program, the typical plan that emerges will seek growth through one of two strategies:

1. Adjusting the marketing of the annual fund
2. Adjusting the volume of solicitations

In today's climate, both of these strategies present many challenges. As a result of the explosion of nonprofit fund raising over the past twenty years, the pressure to distinguish one nonprofit from another is significant. In fact, many social service and health organizations can develop cases for support that are very tangible compared to the standard college or university annual fund case. For example, a local community kitchen can talk in great detail about the opportunities created by a $100 gift. Perhaps that gift buys enough food for twenty-five meals, enough groceries for a family of four for a week, enough fuel to heat a small house for two months, or automotive fuel to deliver 500 meals to homebound individuals. These are vivid images for donors and can be very effective in motivating their gifts. Compare this to the case that can be made for a college or university annual fund. While some institutions are fortunate to be able to identify very specific uses of annual dollars, in many cases, is only possible to be as specific as "scholarships, lab equipment, faculty development, and other initiatives."

The second strategy, increasing solicitation volume, has obvious challenges. As all fund-raising organizations use this strategy, the relative impact of each solicitation stays the same. The solution involves increasing volume strategically—choosing those segments and populations that will respond to more opportunities to give. For example, assume that an annual fund program solicits past donors from the previous five years at four different times of the year, two by telephone and two by direct mail. In the program's structure, if a donor responds with a gift, he or she is not included in the rest of the solicitation schedule. If the strategy for raising more from this group is to increase from four to six solicitations a year, the return on that investment may not be favorable because many members of the group have reached their peak giving rate. However, if segments within the overall group can be isolated, say, last year's donors of $40 or more, this smaller group may bring a positive return on the investment and help reach the overall goal of raising more money.

Staffing and Professional Growth

As the profession evolves, the expectations of staff in the annual giving office change as well. This shift requires annual giving managers to address staffing in several different ways.

Training. The annual fund of today requires a professional who is multi-skilled. The work involves elements of marketing, personnel management, fiscal planning, statistical analysis, personal communication, public speaking, and strategic planning. Increasingly, professionals in annual giving are seeking ways to grow all aspects of their skills through conferences, professional peer groups, mentoring relationships, and so forth. As new training opportunities develop, it is essential to keep these multiple facets of the job at the top of the priority list.

Professional Growth. Today's annual fund is more complicated and requires an increasing level of seniority to manage. In many institutions, the annual fund director is seen as a member of the senior management team of the division. While the issue of "job hopping" can apply to any part of development, the annual fund has more traditionally been seen as an entry level stepping stone to other development work. While this reputation has changed dramatically in the last decade, it is important to be aware of two issues. First, the relationships our annual fund officers develop with donors, volunteers, and members of the university community can be as important as many of the relationships our major gift officers build. The annual fund staff member's longevity in a position will allow those relationships to develop to their maximum benefit for the program, and longer commitments to these important positions should be encouraged. Second, it is crucial to provide opportunities for annual fund officers to develop the skills that will make them successful in other positions within development. These skills might include personal solicitation strategies, personnel management, and grant writing.

CONCLUSION

This is an exciting time for annual giving throughout the country and the world. American philanthropy is setting new records year after year, and yet the marketplace is growing and competition for the charitable gift is increasing. Additionally, with the climate of mega campaigns at many institutions, it is legitimate to wonder where the annual fund fits at all. But it very clearly fits. It remains the lifeblood of development programs because the great majority of major and leadership donors emerge after years of giving to the annual fund. The annual fund provides that precious unrestricted dollar to presidents and deans. It allows every constituent, regardless of the size of his or her gift, to participate in the future of the institution. It is the public face of fund raising to most of our constituents, and it describes the traditions of philanthropy that have sustained schools, colleges, and universities for generations. Finally, it educates the students, parents, and friends involved on campuses today about their role in assuring the continuation of such traditions.

CHAPTER 8

Major Gift Programs

David R. Dunlop

The patterns of philanthropy in American society have consistently demonstrated a small number of givers will provide a disproportionately large share of the total amount given to almost any fund-raising endeavor. It used to be said that 20 percent of the givers give 80 percent of the total given. There are now campaigns in which even fewer givers provide more of the total. Regardless of the exact percentage, the giving patterns reflected in the 20/80 rule highlight the importance of having a well-constructed major gift program in place. The existence of this type of fund-raising program will be a major factor contributing to the overall success of the institution's fund raising. If an institution does not have in place a fund-raising program that focuses on a few givers who will provide a large share of the total given, it may be time to reconsider how it conducts its major gift fund raising.

Many factors influence an institution's fund-raising success:

- wealth of its constituency
- state of the economy
- significance of the institution's mission
- quality of the strategic plans for accomplishing that mission
- constituents' confidence in the leadership implementing those plans
- dedication of those who represent the institution
- spirit and culture of the institution

Nevertheless, the quality of an institution's fund raising, and particularly of its major gift fund raising, is vitally important. It is a sine qua non without which the higher levels of charitable giving will not evolve. For an institution's major gift program to achieve the higher levels of success, it is essential that the concepts, principles, and requirements of major gift fund raising be understood by both the laypeople and professionals engaged in major gift fund-raising endeavors.

DEFINING CHARACTERISTICS

Typically, major gift programs are defined by the size of the largest gifts that the institution hopes to receive. However, because major gifts can have such a transformative effect on an institution, and because of the complex array of factors that influence major gift decisions, a more sophisticated definition is needed.

The audience addressed by the major gift program comprises those few individuals who will provide the largest share of the total given. It would be convenient to say that they are the 20 percent of the givers who provide 80 percent of the total given. In reality, however, it is essential to begin with a small enough number of individuals that each person can be given the quality, frequency, and continuity of attention that is needed in order to make an institution one of his or her highest priorities for charitable giving.

For any institution, and for any fund-raising endeavor, the small number of people who give the eighty, ninety, or ninety-five percent of the total given are not a homogeneous group. Their net worth may differ significantly. For some, the gifts they have made represent a significant part of their net worth. For others who give the same amount, the total may be a small percentage of their annual income. And for still others, payments must be extended over a number of years to enable them to give a gift of this size. This kind of disparity is understandable when some other factors are also taken into account. These other factors include:

- stage of life
- charitable nature
- history with the institution
- current involvement with the institution
- competing charitable interests
- outstanding charitable business and personal commitments

- liquidity
- relationships with trustees, administrators, faculty, staff, and alumni

A major gift program will differ from the institution's other fund-raising endeavors by the amount and character of the initiatives that it takes with the individuals it addresses. Much of what is currently written about major gift fund raising focuses on making "the ask." What is done before, during, and after soliciting a gift is an essential and important part of major gift fund raising. Almost every institution will take initiatives that will prepare an individual to be ready to consider a major gift before he or she is asked for it. At one level of major gift fund raising, initiatives are undertaken with a specific gift in mind. At a second level, initiatives are taken without a specific gift in mind, but rather to develop a working relationship with an individual that enables the institution and the individual to work out together what good they can mutually accomplish. The major gift program should function at both of these levels. If an institution's major gift program does not include this second level as a major component, it should consider adding it.

When contemplating adding this dimension to a major gift program, a complex array of factors comes into play. The language commonly used to describe these factors is sometimes inconsistent and imprecise. Therefore, it is important to have a clear understanding of the following elements:

- perspectives from which gifts are made
- types of gifts
- methods of fund raising
- basis for making fund-raising decisions

PERSPECTIVES FROM WHICH GIFTS ARE MADE

A person about to make a charitable gift is likely to consider that gift from one of three perspectives:

1. What should I give right now (today, this month, this year)?
2. What should I give while the institution needs it (typically over the pledge payment period of a campaign)?
3. What can I give and what can I do, both now and in the future, with whatever abilities and capacities I have (now and for the rest of my life)?

The second level of major gift fund raising is undertaken to foster giving from the perspective of what a person can do and give both now and in the future. This is a distinctly different kind of fund raising. It might be called "commitment raising," because the benefits that evolve from it are more than financial. These benefits may include gifts of time or expertise, as well as social, political, moral, intellectual, and spiritual support.

TYPES OF GIFTS

Regular Gifts

Regular gifts are made repeatedly and at regular intervals. Their timing is largely a function of the calendar. Because regular gifts are made over and over again, these gifts are usually the smallest gifts the individual will give. This does not mean that all regular gifts are small. Some individuals make six- or seven-figure gifts on a regular basis. To compare the size of regular gifts with other types of gifts, we can ascribe a unit value of one to the regular gift.

$$\text{Regular Gift} = 1X$$
(timed to the calendar)

Special Gifts

Special gifts are most often given to an institution to which the giver makes regular gifts. These gifts are not timed to the calendar; rather, they are influenced by an opportunity or a need of the institution that receives them. To help the institution meet a need or take advantage of an opportunity, the giver may extend payment over several years. Special gifts are typically five to twenty times larger than the regular gift the person makes to the same institution.

$$\text{Special Gift} = 5X \text{ to } 20X$$
(timed to the needs of the institution)

Ultimate Gifts

Ultimate gifts are an exercise of the giver's full giving capacity. They are the largest philanthropic commitment the giver is capable of making.

Consequently, many ultimate gifts are made by means of a trust or bequest. The timing of ultimate gifts is more influenced by the life circumstance of the giver than by the calendar or even the needs of the institution. A person's ultimate gift may be given to a single charitable institution or divided among several institutions and is often 500 to 1,000 times larger than the amount the same person has given on a regular basis.

$$\text{Ultimate Gift} = 500\text{X to } 1,000\text{X}$$
(timed to the life circumstance of the giver)

The objective of a major gift program is to encourage all three types of gifts from a select group of individuals. The experiences that these individuals have in making regular and special gifts to an institution will have a substantial impact on how they will feel about that institution when they consider their ultimate giving.

METHODS OF FUND RAISING

In some ways, fund raising is a lot like agriculture. The "Law of the Farm," about which Dr. Stephen R. Covey wrote in his book *Principle-Centered Leadership*,[1] applies to fund raising as well as it does to farming. The work in both must be done in season, or natural consequences will follow. This balance between growing the crop and bringing in the harvest distinguishes three methods of fund raising.

Speculative Fund Raising

Speculative fund raising focuses heavily on asking for, receiving, and acknowledging gifts. Much less is invested in preparing the individual to want to make a gift. Direct mail appeals, phonathons, telethons, and even personal solicitation to canvass the class, neighborhood, or congregation are examples of speculative fund raising. This kind of fund raising is most often used in the solicitation of regular gifts, but occasionally it is used for special gifts. It is based on the speculation that, if you ask enough people for gifts, the number of positive responses will be sufficient to make the whole effort worthwhile. The balance between what is invested in preparing the giver versus what is invested in asking for, receiving, and acknowledging gifts might look something like Figure 8.1.

Figure 8.1

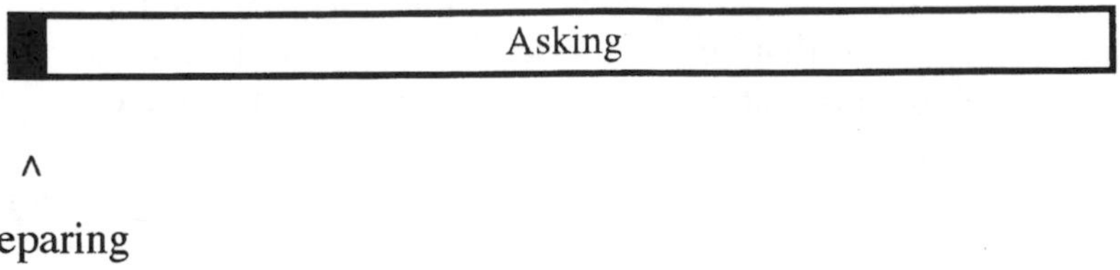

Asking

∧

Preparing

Campaign/Project Fund Raising

Campaign/project fund raising is primarily used in the solicitation of special gifts that are timed to the needs of the institution. A strong focus is placed on balancing the processes of asking for, receiving, and acknowledging gifts with more time and resources invested in preparing the prospective giver for the request. The additional work of preparing the giver is warranted because of the larger size of the special gift. The balance between preparing and asking in campaign/project fund raising might look something like Figure 8.2.

Nurturing Fund Raising

Nurturing fund raising for ultimate gifts focuses on creating a continuous stream of initiatives to develop an individual's commitment to an institution and its mission. Its objective is to develop sufficient awareness, understanding, and involvement so that the institution becomes a priority for all forms of the individual's giving, including an ultimate gift. Nurturing fund raising initiatives are undertaken without knowing what gifts will evolve from them, but rather from trusting that the interests and the values the individual and the institution share will provide a basis for working out whatever good they can accomplish together. The proportion of effort put into building the individual giver's sense of commitment before asking might look like Figure 8.3.

The individuals addressed by an institution's major gift program will be exposed to all three methods of fund raising. Experiences in the course of being solicited for gifts to the annual fund or a capital campaign will affect how an individual feels about making an ultimate gift to the institution. While the management responsibility for the annual fund and capital campaigns may fall to others, the major gift program must assure that the experience of being asked for and making any type of gift to an institution is a satisfying and rewarding one. To accomplish

Figure 8.2

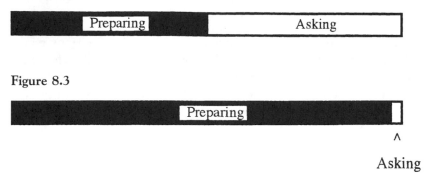

Figure 8.3

Asking

this, significant communication, coordination, and cooperation is required between the institution's various fund-raising programs.

BASES FOR MAKING FUND-RAISING DECISIONS

Fund raisers think a lot about the people who make gifts. They also think a lot about their own work and the thousands of transactions with which they are involved to accomplish that work. These transactions are as diverse as designing a direct mail piece, conducting a phonathon, recording a gift, doing a feasibility study interview, drafting a charitable trust agreement, or writing a thank you letter. The fund raiser's day is filled with decisions about what to do, why to do it, how to do it, when to do it, who should do it, where to do it, and even how well to do it. Making these decisions routinely takes into account both the transaction to be accomplished and the person or persons who will be affected. It is important for all fund raisers, and particularly for major gift fund raisers, to be aware of which of these two considerations comes first in any given situation. In speculative fund raising for regular gifts and campaign fund raising for special gifts, the transaction is the first consideration. In nurturing fund raising for ultimate gifts, the relationship with the individual should be considered first. This difference in the way decisions are made is the difference between the transaction-based aspects of fund raising and the relationship-based aspects of fund raising. Simply being aware of these differences can help fund raisers make better decisions and resolve differences of opinions about what to do, why to do it, how to do it, when to do it, who should do it, where to do it, and how well to do it.

SELECTION OF INDIVIDUALS FOR NURTURING FUND RAISING

Nurturing fund raising cannot be mass-produced. The decisions made, and the initiatives taken, are based on what is appropriate for each individual. Consequently, the number of individuals who can be addressed with this type of attention is very limited. Three criteria should be used in selecting the individuals for it.

Financial Capacity

The financial capacity to make major gifts is an obvious and unavoidable first criterion. Because the signs of wealth abound, they are not difficult to recognize. The homes people live in, the cars they drive, the trips they take, the gifts they make, the jobs they hold, the businesses they own, their lifestyle—all make this criterion relatively easy to apply.

Interest or Potential Interest

Like financial capacity, interest or potential interest is also not difficult to determine. For a school, college, or university, those who may have a potential interest in wanting to preserve the institution's well being include its alumni, its neighbors, those who hire its graduates, and those who share its values.

Charitable Nature

This attribute is often more difficult to confirm or deny. The presence of some fairly significant gifts does not necessarily confirm a charitable nature, and the absence of significant gifts does not deny it. Gifts are sometimes made for non-charitable motives. Nevertheless, the efficiency and effectiveness of nurturing fund raising depends on identifying not only persons who have means and interest, but those who are also charitable.

SOME THINGS TO WATCH OUT FOR

The enthusiastic pursuit of major gifts may lead a fund raiser to give priority to the first criterion of financial capacity over the second and third criteria of interest and a charitable nature. In the solicitation-focused aspects of the major gift program, this is usually all right. However, for the relationship-based aspect of the major gift program, balanced consideration must be given to all three criteria. The investment in creating the quality, frequency, and continuity of initiatives that nurturing fund raising requires is simply too costly if the individual's interest or charitable nature is in question.

When the first criterion of financial capacity is too heavily weighted during the selection process, there is another risk. Just as with a personal relationship, an institutional relationship that is founded solely on one aspect of a person's identity will not be complete or durable. A relationship that is developed with only one objective in mind, whether it is social, political, business, sexual, or financial, is not as fully functional or durable as one that acknowledges a wider range of the individual's abilities and capacities. When a relationship is pursued solely because of a person's wealth, without regard for other abilities and capacities, major gift initiatives may be considered akin to "loving them because they are rich." To develop functional, well-balanced, and durable relationships, the initiatives taken must address the whole person. An institution cannot ignore an individual's capacity to provide social, political, intellectual, moral, and spiritual support as well as financial gifts. This dimension distinguishes nurturing fund raising from other fund-raising endeavors. The time and effort this approach takes limits the number of individuals that an institution can address with nurturing fund raising.

While the individuals addressed with nurturing fund raising have some exceptional abilities and capacities, they are, of course, no more or less perfect than the rest of humanity. As a fund raiser works to develop the institution's relationship with these individuals, he or she will become aware of their virtues and, occasionally, traits that cannot be admired. At times, a person who makes thoughtful and generous gifts may do or say something that is unkind, rude, politically incorrect, or even bigoted. A fund raiser needs to develop a kind and forgiving nature and the ability to genuinely like and appreciate people who are not perfect. Fund raisers who are judgmental and fail to appreciate people who do not meet their expectations may find themselves in awkward situations and feel they are expected to express compliments they do not mean and feelings they do not feel. The ability to forgive others' shortcomings and avoid judgment is a valuable asset. To look past imperfections in a person's behavior, and to envision the better person an individual can become, opens the door to helping individuals become all that they can be for themselves and for the institution.

Figure 8.4

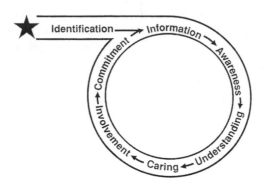

Building a Sense of Commitment

The individual experiences that lead a person to make the largest gift of a lifetime are, by necessity, unique to that person and to the institution. However, certain types of experiences are common to everyone who has ever made an ultimate gift. Such experiences are ones that develop the individual's *awareness, understanding, caring, involvement,* and *commitment* in respect to the institution and to the purposes served by the gift. If these types of experiences can be replicated for others, they too may feel the desire to make an ultimate gift to an institution and increase their regular and special gifts substantially. The process of building the sense of commitment may look something like figure 8.4.

Choosing the right initiatives of course requires an in-depth understanding of the individual's values, interests, capacities, and circumstances and a thorough understanding of the institution's mission, plans, priorities, and capabilities. The initiatives selected must go beyond communicating how great an institution is and the good that it accomplishes. They must enable the individual to connect with the leaders of the institution, the people who do its work, and to encounter the spirit with which that work is carried out. The initiatives taken must help to develop awareness, understanding, caring, involvement and commitment, in keeping with both the individual's own interests and the priorities of the institution. Additionally, these initiatives must allow the individual to express his/her growing sense of commitment not just financially, but with whatever unique capacities he/she has.

Foreground and Background Initiatives

Two types of initiatives are used to advance awareness, understanding, interest, involvement, and commitment. Foreground initiatives are conceived, planned, and executed with a specific individual in mind. Dinner with a faculty member, use of a home for a college reception, a student calling to express appreciation for his or her scholarship, and a note of congratulations on a promotion are typical examples of foreground initiatives.

Background initiatives are conceived, planned, and executed with a group of people in mind within which there may be one or more individuals that the institution is attending to with nurturing fund raising. Opportunities for background initiatives occur routinely in the normal functioning of an educational institution. Homecoming weekends, reunions, governing board meetings, alumni magazines, athletic and theatrical events, and alumni travel programs all may be used to develop awareness, understanding, caring, and involvement and to develop a sense of commitment. The challenge for the fund raiser is to be alert and responsive to possibilities for background initiatives that routinely occur. Occasionally a fund raiser has to be the one to create an event that serves as a background initiative. For example, an event to launch a fund-raising campaign can be a background initiative for the individuals addressed by the major gift program. The major gift program should be judicious about holding background initiative events because they can be costly in both time and resources.

Events Calendar Plus

Inertia is the enemy when it comes to capitalizing on institutional events. To overcome inertia, an institution needs to make it easy for staff and volunteers to take advantage of opportunities already in place for background initiatives. Most institutions publish an events calendar. For the major gift program, something more is needed. It might be called an "Events Calendar Plus." Ideally, the information it provides should be available online for the appropriate staff and volunteers to use. It should be "plus" in two dimensions. First, in addition to information about the institution's public functions, it should also have information about private functions to which a few additional participants could be added. For example, if the dean of a law school held a barbecue to welcome new students, a few "friends of the school" might be invited to participate in the welcoming. Second, an Events Calendar Plus should have additional information about the events listed. The additional information should indicate:

- staff and volunteers in charge (names, addresses, e-mail addresses, and phone and fax numbers)

- who is invited
- who has accepted, declined, or not yet responded
- what effect the event is intended to have on those who attend
- the limits on adding additional guests
- costs involved
- who to contact for additional information and to make arrangements

The late Harold J. "Si" Seymour used to remind his clients, "people like to be a worthwhile member of a worthwhile group."[2] This kind of Events Calendar Plus enables staff and volunteers to connect individuals with worthwhile groups. The creation of the calendar requires the campus-wide cooperation of all who manage events for the institution. Failure to employ this tool will result in wasting the wealth of background initiative opportunities that are available on and off campus.

Six-Step Discipline

The major gift officer must be prepared to execute at least one initiative per month—more if it can be managed—for each individual that he/she attends to with nurturing fund raising. Managing these initiatives requires the use of a six-step discipline:

1. Review what has transpired in the relationship
2. Plan what is appropriate to do next to advance the relationship
3. Coordinate with those you need to involve in the next initiative
4. Execute the initiative
5. Evaluate whether the objectives were accomplished and what to do next
6. Report and record the results of the initiative

Tracking System

The requirements for tracking systems used in nurturing fund raising go beyond the requirements for those systems used solely for campaign/project fund raising. An ideal system will meet the requirements of both. However, most of the tracking system software that can be purchased off the shelf is designed for campaign/project fund raising because there is a greater demand for it. Only now is a market for tracking systems that meet the distinctly different requirements of nurturing fund raising starting to develop. Do not use the wrong tracking system.

Tracking systems for nurturing fund raising must be able to record information about the overall strategy, recent history, and next initiatives planned for each person. This information should be expressed in plain language and without limit on the number of characters used. Systems that employ a series of codes to record information ignore the subtleties of relationship building.

Tracking systems for nurturing fund raising must clearly identify who has responsibility for initiatives with each individual. They also need to be able to hold in memory the record of successive strategies, recent histories, and next initiatives for later reference. Many include a tickler system that automatically reminds the user of when initiatives need to be taken. They should be able to print paper reports that can be distributed on a regular basis to all who have responsibility for the relationship so that those individuals remain up-to-date. And, those reports should not be loaded with distracting biographical or giving information. To meet all of these requirements, many institutions have found it necessary to either substantially customize off-the-shelf tracking systems or develop their own tracking systems.

While computer-generated tracking system reports are a primary tool for nurturing fund raising, they may not be appropriate for your volunteers. If they receive a tracking report, they will very likely wonder, "What do they have on me?" For volunteers, you must forgo the convenience of using the tracking report and, instead, consult with them by phone, letter, or in person.

NATURAL PARTNERS

In speculative and campaign fund raising, the determination of who should ask a specific individual for a gift is usually done with little effort or forethought. Either someone who knows the individual steps forward and volunteers, or the campaign chair or a staff person familiar with constituent relationships assigns an individual they believe will be the most effective solicitor. In person-centered nurturing fund raising, time and effort are needed to discover the individuals who are already part of the prospective giver's relationship with the institution and to enlist their help. Nurturing fund raising can be done best by those who have the type of relationship with the individual that will allow them to learn the individual's values, interests, concerns, achievements, aspirations, inclinations, and what they hope to accomplish with their assets and capacities. This kind of information is shared between close friends and not with recent acquaintances.

Twenty-five years ago, G. T. "Buck" Smith coined the term "prime" to describe the person in the best position to help guide and carry out the most appropriate foreground and background initiatives. Others who

are in a good position to help he called "secondaries." A prime or secondary might be a member of the faculty, a trustee, or some other volunteer. It is rare that development staff have the extensive history and
close bond with the individual to be able to function as a true prime or
secondary.

There are two kinds of primes and secondaries—the "Reals" and the
"Wannabees." Some people would like to be a constructive helper in
building the individual's relationship but may lack the length and depth
of familiarity and confidence required to carry out the role of a true
prime or secondary. Both "Reals" and "Wannabees" can play valuable
roles in nurturing fund raising, but it is important to recognize the difference.

A word of caution: as well-intentioned as a prime or secondary may
be in helping to facilitate the relationship between the friend and the
institution, days, weeks, and even months may pass before good intentions are carried out. A development staff person is needed to help
facilitate, communicate, coordinate, and stimulate the work of primes
and secondaries. This person, in consultation with primes and secondaries, will ensure that the six-step discipline is carried out at least every
month for each individual.

Development staff who perform this work function under many titles.
McLain Bybee at Brigham Young University has used the title "liaison"
for staff who serve in this capacity. This designation carries the helpful
connotation of being of service in connecting people with the institution.

ESSENTIALS FOR SUCCESS

Major gift programs are usually begun with a sole focus on campaign/
project fund raising without an organized effort to conduct nurturing
fund raising. The addition of an organized focus on nurturing fund raising is often delayed until the leadership becomes aware that ultimate
gifts from a few key people could transform the future of its institution.
Unfortunately, the existing organization, budgeting, staffing, procedures,
and tools in use for campaign/project fund raising are all too often simply
extended to serve the newly added nurturing fund raising aspects of the
major gift program. This approach occurs when the distinctly different
organization, concepts, principles, requirements, and potential of
relationship-based nurturing fund raising are not fully understood and
respected. To assure appropriate organization, budgeting, staffing, procedures, and tools, some educational institutions have established sep-

arate "principal gift programs" that are founded on the distinctly different concepts, principles, requirements, and potential of nurturing fund raising.

Regardless of whether campaign/project fund raising and nurturing fund raising are conducted by an institution's major gift program or by separate fund-raising programs, both of these methods require the help and involvement of staff, faculty, academic and administrative leaders, trustees, and other volunteers. Both must be integrated and coordinated with the rest of an institution's other fund-raising endeavors.

At times the initiatives taken by different fund-raising programs may appear to be in conflict with one another. When all the fund raisers involved understand the distinctly different requirements of relationship-based and transaction-based aspects of fund raising, the essential integration and coordination are more effectively accomplished.

For nurturing fund raising to be successful, some essential characteristics must be added to the work. These concern the *quality*, *frequency*, *continuity*, and *focus* of the foreground and background initiatives and the empowerment of natural partners who can help develop an individual's awareness, understanding, caring, involvement, and commitment.

Quality

The quality of an initiative can be determined by how well it fits the relationship with the individual for which it is intended and by how well it supports the mission and overall strategic plans of the institution. Quality initiatives are responsive to both.

Frequency and Continuity

Unless an institution enters the life of the person frequently and continuously, the decision about how his/her wealth will ultimately be used for charitable purposes will likely favor another interest with which he or she has been more regularly involved. One or two great moments with an institution rarely make up for deficiencies in the quality, frequency, and continuity of attention.

Focus

For most charitable institutions, there are a small number of individuals who share its values and have the capacity to make extraordinary gifts.

The transforming potential of those gifts makes relationship-based nurturing fund raising worth doing in its purest form.

In its pure form, nurturing fund raising is so time-consuming and costly that it must be limited to a relatively few individuals. Start with one or two individuals, then increase the number as you gain experience. In nurturing fund raising, in contrast to campaign/project fund raising for major gifts, the ratio can rarely exceed 50 individuals/families to one staff liaison.

Empowering Partners

Institutional friendships thrive when the number of people participating in them grows. The more an institution empowers the natural partners called primes and secondaries, the more likely they are to play a constructive role in developing the individual's awareness, understanding, caring, involvement, and commitment to an institution. Natural partners and others involved in a relationship are empowered by sharing information, providing opportunities for involvement, and sharing results.

CLOSING THOUGHTS

The major gift program attends to the individuals who are most able and likely to make major gifts. It has two objectives. One is to develop interest in specific gifts and solicit for them (gifts timed to the needs and priorities of the institution). The other is to develop each individual's awareness, understanding, caring, involvement, and sense of commitment so that when the time comes to decide how his/her wealth will ultimately be used, the institution will be selected to receive part or all of that person's ultimate gift (gifts timed to the life circumstance of the giver). The focus here has been on the concepts and requirements of the two distinctly different methods of fund raising needed to achieve both objectives and how they must be integrated and coordinated with each other and with the rest of an institution's fund-raising endeavors.

NOTES

Chapter is Copyright © David R. Dunlop.

1. Stephen R. Covey, *Principle-Centered Leadership* (New York: Summit Books, 1991), 161–162.

2. Harold J. Seymour, *Designs for Fund-Raising* (New York: McGraw-Hill Book Company, 1966), 6.

CHAPTER 9

Principal Gifts

Frank D. Schubert

A gift category that has begun to receive its own degree of special attention in recent years is that of principal gifts. Major gifts are of a large dollar amount, however that may be defined by any particular institution. Principal gifts are also usually defined in terms of their amount and are among the largest gifts an institution will receive. Some institutions may define principal gifts as gifts of $5 million, $10 million, or even more, depending on the scope of their fund-raising campaign or program. But principal gifts differ from major gifts not solely in terms of amount. They are important to consider in their own right for a more fundamental reason. These are the rare gifts in the life of an institution in which the institution's values become so exemplified in the benefactor's act of generosity that the gift itself serves to sharpen, refine, and, in a meaningful sense, rededicate the entirety of the institution to its deepest core values.

It is no surprise, then, that the principal gift benefactor can often become a celebrated figure, accorded a status alongside that of the institution's founders. What draws the focus of public attention is not necessarily the gift amount, however, but rather the way in which the act of publicly making the gift unites the deepest values of both benefactor and institution at a moment of great importance for both.

HEROES AND VALUES

This undeniable "heroic" quality accorded the principal gift benefactor has parallels in other domains beyond philanthropy. In statesmanship, for example, the deepest values embedded in, say, the U.S. Constitution might inspire in later eras an Abraham Lincoln or a Martin Luther King. In the area of sports achievement, the most compelling stories are those that recount sagas of humble beginnings and great odds overcome on the way to athletic success. Similarly, in the case of philanthropy, there will always be that rare individual who demonstrates through his or her selfless and visionary act of generosity a profound and inspired understanding of the deepest core values at work in the enterprise of education.

Probably the most famous example of a recent gift to higher education involved only a modest amount of money by today's million- and billion-dollar standards. But Oseola McCarty, a poor African American citizen of Mississippi, was so moved in her life by the ability of education to improve students' lives that in 1997 she gave away her entire life savings, earned from a career of taking in others' laundry, to establish a scholarship fund at the University of Mississippi.

In the end, what makes McCarty's story so compelling is its simplicity. Though she had no firsthand experience of higher education, Oseola McCarty seems to have understood its value more clearly than many of us who operate comfortably within its confines on a daily basis. It is her kind of understanding and commitment that inspires principal gifts and makes them so very transformational in the lives of colleges and universities.

THE DEFINITION OF A PRINCIPAL GIFT

While a principal gift is usually defined by its large amount, many principal gifts will also be "ultimate gifts" from the perspective of the donor. Such ultimate gifts represent *an act of giving over the largest share of one's life work to a given cause or purpose.* Several points follow from this understanding.

"An Act of Giving Over ..."

The idea of simply "writing a check" for a principal gift is a mistaken notion. Principal gifts are not so much paid out to an institution as they are entrusted to it. Much like a bank is entrusted not to lose, squander, or fail to account for one's life assets over many years, the educational institution is making a similar assurance to the principal gift benefactor that it is a wise place to entrust valuable assets. A degree of trust built up over a lifetime of positive experiences and interchanges between the institution and the potential principal gift benefactor is essential. A principal gift understood in these terms becomes a natural expression of one's deepest life values rendered into an act of philanthropy and not a singular response to a one-time solicitation for funds.

"... of the Largest Share of One's Life Work ..."

Since a principal gift usually involves the largest share of the assets that one's life work has produced, it is worth inquiring about the values that principal gift benefactors place upon their life's work experience. Did they work hard? Undoubtedly they did. But what inspired them to work as hard as they did? Was it for support of family, spouse, community? Have they spent segments of their lives in service to others as well as working toward enhancing their own personal living standards? Often, stories of a benefactor's values exemplified within his or her own work experience remain untold unless a deliberate inquiry is made about them. It is incumbent upon a representative of an educational institution calling upon a potential principal gift benefactor to initiate this conversation at a level of comfort and ease most suited to the prospective benefactor.

The most important trait an advancement officer of an educational institution can possess is the ability to make an honest inquiry and then to listen. The advancement officer should make an honest inquiry into a prospective benefactor's ultimate values and then listen patiently as the individual recounts them in the wider context of his or her life story. In such a conversation, a benefactor is giving the development officer a unique opportunity to present the case that the largest share of the product of his or her life's work might wisely and safely be entrusted to the "life work" of the institution.

"... to a Given Cause or Purpose"

No principal gift cultivation can take place unless the development officer can honestly articulate compelling answers to the following questions on behalf of his or her institution:

- What are the institution's deepest core values?
- How might they be stated and understood most succinctly?
- What are the standards of performance by which the institution measures itself in seeking their realization?

- How confident is the development officer in assuring the potential benefactor that the institution will be reliably faithful to the carefully expressed intentions of his or her gift long after that benefactor's lifetime?

Since educational institutions will survive their current staff, it is all the more important to articulate the answers to these questions with honesty and integrity. Just as a donor would not find any reason to mislead a listener in a discussion of his or her life's deepest core values and ultimate beliefs, so too must development officers offer a fair and honest assessment of their institutions' anticipated levels of trust and performance for the future, based on an honest assessment of past experience and a critical assessment of the present.

Of course, stories of gifts made in the institution's earliest years that continue to deliver value and performance in executing the intentions of early donors are valuable examples to cite in a discussion of values with a potential principal gift benefactor. These living stories, updated into the present, become the institution's citable "track record" of success.

A UNIVERSAL SET OF RESOURCE DEVELOPMENT CORE VALUES

Every institution has to develop a clear self-understanding of its mission and its fundamental core values. Not every institution will decide, as the University of Texas at Austin did in 1997, that its fundamental mission, at its core, is "to transform lives for the benefit of society." This mission statement goes on to cite six core values deemed essential to the performance of that mission: freedom, responsibility, discovery, learning, leadership, and individual opportunity.

If an institution needs assistance in articulating its deepest core values, it is worth spending a significant amount of internal time developing a succinct mission statement that encapsulates at once its identity and purpose. While core values and a mission statement will not be the same for every institution, it is possible to formulate an understanding of what a universal "resource development" mission statement might look like. That formulation is more or less as follows:

1. We are, fundamentally, *People*—a community.
2. We are a community of *People* committed to *Knowledge*.
3. We are a community of *People* committed to *Knowledge* and the *Communication* of that knowledge to others for their benefit.

4. If entrusted with your support, it is our responsibility to *Account* for your gift in a trustworthy manner.

5. If entrusted with your support, it is our responsibility to *Account* for your gift in a trustworthy manner and to be a wise *Steward* for your gift as we work toward a long-term future for our educational enterprise.

6. If entrusted with your support, it is our responsibility to *Account* for your gift, to be a wise *Steward* for your gift, and to *Link* you as closely as you desire with the people of our enterprise, especially those in our community who may be most directly touched by your act of generosity.

It will come as no surprise that the final goal of this exercise—the *Link* that is established over many years of fulfilling a mission with donors—becomes the single most important long-term factor in the cultivation for a principal gift. The goal of principal gift cultivation will always be a forging of a long series of ever-closer links between benefactor and institution over many years, steadily moving toward a convergence point where the values of benefactor and institution can be said to fully merge.

It is possible, of course, that this convergence of links between benefactor and institution can happen from a distance, and some principal gifts have come to institutions from "secret admirers." The very possibility of a potential principal gift benefactor evaluating an institution's performance anonymously from a certain distance, however, underscores even more the rationale for a strong and effective communication program (*people* committed to *knowledge* and the *communication* of that knowledge). Every outward communication of an institution—whether written, electronic or personal—should encourage anyone in the public domain to note what is underway in that institution as it carries out its mission and to consider a further link or two should they find it to be of possible further interest.

THE ROLE OF THE PRINCIPAL GIFT DEVELOPMENT OFFICER

Since it is true that any individual—dean, president, headmaster, faculty member, or development officer—may be the primary representative of the institution for a potential principal gift benefactor, is there a special role in the development office for a principal gift development officer?

The principal gift development officer should be a member of the senior management team of the development operation. In that capacity, he or she should assume a specific role as a primary resource person for individuals who have already made a gift of a very large segment of their "life's assets" to the institution or who have indicated that they might consider doing so. Primarily, the principal gift development officer monitors closely those who have expressed an interest in giving over the largest share of their life's assets to the institution. At the same time, he or she seeks to forge ever-closer links between the potential benefactor and the lives of those who will benefit from the donor's philanthropy.

Even with this special responsibility, however, the principal gift development officer must function responsibly as a member of a larger team that includes the institution's chief executive officer, chief advancement officer, and a host of other major gift and planned giving officers (the "gift planning" team). So what is a proper role for a principal gift development officer as a member of the development team?

An illustration might be illuminating in this instance. Consider the case of a large aircraft carrier setting out on an important military mission. The fleet commander (the chief executive officer) issues orders for getting the fleet underway. Working closely with the captain of the carrier (the chief advancement officer), the carrier is lined up in position and gets underway in formation.

Clearly the carrier is important to the fleet, but *not because the individuals on it are more important*. Rather it is because the carriers are entrusted with the *highest profile* and with the *most valuable assets of the fleet*, namely the planes that will take off on their respective missions and then return to safety.

The most sensible role in the operation for the principal gift development officer, then, is not that of chief executive officer (fleet commander) or chief advancement officer (carrier captain), since they have special responsibilities for setting forth the direction of the fleet and guaranteeing the well-being of the entire operation. In contrast, the role of the principal gift development officer is best understood as that of a "chief of the flight deck," responsible for the safe launching and return of the most highly visible and highly valued assets of the operation. Working closely with the entire flight deck team, this officer monitors the schedule of the entire aerial operation, notes prevailing atmospheric conditions, prepares for eventualities in mid-course, and ultimately ensures the final safety and risk of a given takeoff or landing. The job does not need to be highly visible, but it does need to be very unforgiving of mistakes, since so much value in lives and assets are at stake at the height of an important operation.

When success is achieved, the entire gift planning team, including the chief executive and the chief advancement officers, should be the "heroes" of the operation. The principal gift development officer, though, fulfills a critical role as guarantor of the highest level of performance of a "flight-deck" operation when success does emerge from a challenging situation.

NAMINGS, DEDICATIONS, PUBLIC ANNOUNCEMENTS, PRESS COVERAGE

It is natural that educational institutions will always return to their most essential concepts when speaking of principal gifts: the founders and the values that inspired them. If someone decides to "give over the largest share of their life's work to a given cause or purpose," they clearly believe in the values of that cause or purpose to the very depths of their being. But that belief is not a snapshot. It is a belief informed and inspired by a life of thoughtful evaluation of an institution over many years.

For those with this depth of gift commitment, there will always be great sensitivities at stake, extending to their immediate family and close associates, regarding issues of public naming and recognition, dedications, and press announcements. Why? This set of concerns is understandable if one stops to consider that there is probably just a single occasion in a person's lifetime that a principal gift might be made and publicly announced. Whether the gift is even made during a person's lifetime or through an estate, it is important that the principal gift development officer be someone who can appreciate the depths of these sensitivities and honor them to the degree possible, balancing at all times the interests of the institution with the desires of the benefactor.

As noted above, however, if the proper internal groundwork for a principal gift is in place, the "linking" of a benefactor's life values with the values of an institution over many years is not an uncomfortable experience at all. In fact, it is one of the most fulfilling experiences imaginable. Oseola McCarty knew the experience of this deep and fulfilling conviction firsthand. Your principal gift benefactor will too.

CHAPTER 10

Planned Giving

Ronald E. Sapp and Peter K. Kimball

In years past, charitable giving that made use of financial planning methods was called "trust and estate planning" or "deferred giving." Today, it is referred to as "planned giving," or more accurately, "charitable gift planning." These changes in terminology reflect the movement of gift planning programs away from a technical and *product* orientation to a more "donor friendly" *process* orientation—a shift that has helped to make gift planning a relevant program for any development effort.

Gift planning requires a blending of knowledge in charitable tax law and financial planning to enable a charitably motivated individual to make a significant gift at a minimum cost. A comprehensive gift plan can (indeed, some would argue, should) involve not only the donor but also the donor's legal and financial advisers.

In its most fundamental form, gift planning responds to three basic questions: (1) *What* gift asset should the donor use (cash, stock, mutual funds, bonds, real estate, family business, antiques, etc.)? (2) *How* should the gift be structured (outright, bequest, trust, deed, contract, bargain sale, donor advised fund, supporting organization, etc.)? and (3) *When* should the gift be made (during life or at death)? With the wide variety and flexibility that gift planning offers, individuals who have never thought of themselves as philanthropists are able to make significant contributions to the charities most important to them.

Gift planning, then, integrates "how" people give with "why" people give. The skilled fund raiser learns enough about each donor's assets in order to be able to suggest a gift planning arrangement appropriate to the individual's situation. At its best, a thoughtfully tailored gift plan can help to increase the value of a gift by reducing tax liabilities, enable the donor to dispose of cumbersome assets easily, or provide estate and financial planning benefits.

The discussion that follows will cover some basics of tax rules, assets, and instruments. It is essential to remember, however, that the mechanics of gift planning are always secondary. The basis of every major gift is charitable intent. Individuals give because they want to support a certain cause, mission, or purpose. How the gift is structured proceeds from that important starting point.

TAX RULES AFFECTING PLANNED GIFTS

Certain rules of the Internal Revenue Service (IRS) Code can make charitable giving an attractive option for a donor. Other rules can decrease the tax benefit and thus discourage gifts. To understand what sorts of planned gifts will be to the donor's advantage, the fund raiser needs to be familiar with basic charitable tax laws.

Tax Deduction Limits on Charitable Contributions

An individual (who itemizes deductions) is allowed to claim an income tax deduction for charitable contributions up to certain limits, based on that individual's contribution base. For the great majority of individuals, the contribution base is their Adjusted Gross Income (AGI). The most generous limitation, which is 50 percent of a taxpayer's contribution base, applies to public organizations such as colleges, universities, museums, private schools, religious organizations, and hospitals, as well as the foundations and endowments established by these organizations.

Gifts of cash, for example, to such "50 percent type organizations" are deductible in the year the gift is made, up to a limit of 50 percent of contribution base. Gifts of long-term held appreciated assets, such as securities, are subject to a limit of 30 percent of contribution base. Gifts valued in excess of these limits may be carried over for up to five additional years. Using a special election, a donor may choose to deduct a gift of long-term appreciated property under the 50 percent ceiling as long as the deduction is limited to the property's cost basis.

Private foundations are "30 percent type organizations," which means they have lower deduction limits—30 percent for gifts of cash and 20 percent for gifts of appreciated property.

Valuation of Non-cash Gifts

In order to claim a charitable tax deduction, a donor must follow certain rules and procedures. The recipient organization must also meet particular reporting requirements. These rules become especially important with gifts involving assets such as securities, real estate, and tangible personal property.

Donors of non-cash charitable gifts worth more than $500 must complete IRS Form 8283. Non-cash gifts worth more than $5,000 also require an appraisal. Securities are an exception. Non-publicly traded securities require an appraisal only if the value exceeds $10,000, and publicly traded securities do not require an appraisal at all. Gifts of significant art have additional substantiation requirements.

For non-cash gifts requiring appraisals, the recipient organization is required to sign IRS Form 8283. Then, if the organization sells, exchanges, or otherwise disposes of the property within two years of receipt, it must file IRS Form 8282 to report the amount received from the transaction.

To deduct any gift of $250 or more, a donor must have a written receipt from the charity detailing the type of gift, the amount of payment and a good faith estimate of any goods or services given to the donor in exchange for the gift. If no goods or services were received, the receipt should so state.

ASSETS

Cash is only one of the many assets donors can use to make gifts. Other assets—including securities, mutual funds, real estate, partnership interests, tangible property, and even life insurance policies—can form all or part of a gift. Most often, a donor can realize significant tax benefits by giving the asset itself, rather than converting an asset directly into cash. By reducing the amount of money lost to taxes, such a gift can, in effect, enable the donor to increase the value of the gift. Fund raisers who are familiar with these options, and who suggest them to donors who can benefit, will provide a valuable service to both the donor and the institution.

Gifts of Appreciated Securities

Donors who hold long-term appreciated securities—including publicly traded stocks, bonds, and private securities held for more than one year—can realize two important tax advantages from giving them to a charitable institution. First, the donor is entitled to a charitable income tax deduction based on the fair market value of the securities. In addition, the donor avoids paying tax on the capital gain that would be realized if the donor had sold the securities. For example, Mr. Smith transfers $5,000 in readily marketable securities, which he bought years ago for $1,000, to his favorite charity. He is entitled to a charitable deduction of $5,000 and avoids paying the potential tax on the $4,000 capital appreciation.

An individual can transfer securities directly to a charity or transfer them to a trust or a similar arrangement for the eventual benefit of charity. Fair market value of publicly traded securities is determined as the mean between the high and the low price on the date of delivery.

Generally, securities that have depreciated in value should not be donated directly to the institution. Rather, it is to the donor's advantage to sell the securities to establish a tax-deductible loss and then donate the cash proceeds.

With increasing frequency, mutual fund shares are being given to charity. Generally, a donor will send a signature guaranteed letter to the mutual fund company authorizing a transfer of mutual fund shares to an account at the company established by the charity. The transfer is effected by journal entry. Care needs to be given to determine any capital gain attributed to shares held for less than one year, especially short-term shares purchased through an automatic reinvestment program. The charitable deduction for short-term gain is limited to the original cost of those shares.

Gifts of private securities (closely held stock) can provide the same tax benefits as publicly traded securities, but this type of stock requires special handling. The significant difference is the lack of a ready market for the institution to sell the stock and convert it to cash. Various methods exist for converting closely held stock to cash, but all require caution. Institutions and donors should rely on the advice of qualified legal and tax advisers.

Gifts of Real Estate

Many donors have enjoyed significant tax benefits by making gifts of real estate. Gifts of real estate can consist of almost any type of property—a primary residence or a vacation home, a farm or ranch, a commercial building, subdivision lots, or an undeveloped parcel. The gift can be the entire property or a partial interest in the property. Real estate subject to debt presents special problems that need to be carefully considered when structuring a charitable gift. Legal and tax advisers can help in such cases.

The donor's financial needs, estate plans, and philanthropic objectives determine which of the various methods of donating real estate is most appropriate. Options include the following:

- *An outright gift.* The donor who wishes to provide an immediate benefit to charity can deed the property to the institution, which sells it unless there is a special investment reason for holding it.

- *A bargain sale.* The philanthropic donor who wants to receive some immediate financial benefit from a piece of real estate can sell the property to the institution for a price below its fair market value. The difference between the bargain sale price and the fair market price is a charitable gift. The institution can then sell the property at full value.

- *A life income gift.* The property may be transferred to a special trust (a charitable remainder unitrust discussed later in this chapter) and then sold. The proceeds are then invested to produce income for life to the donor and, if desired, to a second beneficiary. After the death of the last income beneficiary, the trust assets pass to the institution. Another method for receiving income is for the donor to deed the property to the institution in exchange for a gift annuity contract (discussed later in this chapter.)

- *A gift with lifetime use.* If the property is being used as a personal residence or farm, the donor may transfer ownership to the institution while retaining the right to use the property for life. At death, the life estate ends and the institution assumes full ownership of the property, which it can then sell or use for its own purpose. Under certain conditions in this gift plan, an income for life can be provided to the donor as well, using the remainder value (an actuarially calculated partial value) of the property as the funding basis for a gift annuity contract.

- *An undivided partial interest in real estate.* An undivided portion of real property can be conveyed outright. For example, the donor can make the institution a co-owner by giving a one-half undivided interest in a residence, vacation home, commercial property, farm, or ranch. When the property is sold, the donor and the institution share proportionately in the proceeds. Or, as with the preceding options, the donor can receive income by transferring an undivided fractional interest to a unitrust or exchanging it for a gift annuity contract.

- *A bequest.* The donor may leave real estate to the institution in his or her estate plans.

Gifts of Tangible Personal Property

The term "tangible personal property" refers to physical assets other than real property and financial instruments. Examples include art, antiques, collections, manuscripts, books, vehicles, and boats.

Donors can give tangible personal property for charitable purposes, but the tax value of the gift depends on the purposes of the charity. If the property can be used in a manner related to the charity's tax-exempt purpose, for example a gift of art to an art museum, then the donor may claim a tax deduction based on the fair market value of the donated asset as determined by an independent qualified appraisal. If the property is unrelated to the charity's exempt purpose, for example, a gift of a boat to a soup kitchen, the donor's charitable income tax deduction is limited to the lesser of the property's cost basis or fair market value.

The "related use" test does not apply in the case of tangible personal property gifts bequeathed in a will. All such property given by will is fully deductible for estate tax purposes.

Gifts of Life Insurance

Life insurance policies are a particularly useful means for making future gifts. There are several ways to use life insurance for charitable purposes:

- *Donate an existing policy.* A donor can designate the institution as the owner and irrevocable beneficiary of an existing policy that is not fully paid up. The donor is then entitled to a charitable deduction for the "present value" of the policy (approximately equal to the cash surrender value or the cost basis, whichever is less). The donor can then continue to pay the premiums to maintain the policy in force and be entitled to deduct the premium payments each year as a charitable contribution.

- *Establish a new policy.* A donor can establish a new policy, designating the charity as owner and beneficiary. The donor may then deduct the premiums as a charitable contribution.

- *Asset replacement.* Life insurance can be used as a "replacement" asset. For example, a donor gives appreciated property to the institution and replaces the dollar value of the asset with life insurance payable to family members. The income tax savings from the gift may be sufficient to pay for the "replacement" insurance. The insurance premiums are not a charitable contribution, however.

- *Establish a unitrust.* A donor can use life insurance to fund a charitable remainder unitrust for a spouse, for example. The unitrust provides income for the spouse after the death of the donor. At the spouse's death, the trust principal becomes the property of the institution.

- *Convert to cash.* A donor can liquidate a policy no longer needed for family protection and donate the cash value to the institution as a tax-deductible charitable gift.

GIFTS THAT PROVIDE INCOME

Some individuals would like to make significant gifts but cannot afford to give up the annual income they draw from the assets that would form the gift. Often, the loss of this income is a barrier to giving. Many potential donors, therefore, assume that the only alternative is to provide for a future gift through their estate plan. This need not be the case. Special provisions in the tax code allow donors to make charitable gifts while retaining the right to receive income during their lives.

These types of charitable gift arrangements—called "life income gifts"—have been in existence in one form or another for decades. The Tax Reform Act of 1969 introduced charitable remainder trusts (the unitrust and annuity trust) and pooled income funds. Another life income gift instrument, the charitable gift annuity, predates that law and is still in use.

The features and legal basis of these arrangements vary, but they can all provide similar benefits:

- Income for life or term of years to the donor(s) and/or another designated beneficiary(ies)
- An immediate federal income tax deduction for a portion of the value of the gift
- Elimination or reduction of capital gains taxes if the gift is in the form of an appreciated asset
- Transfer of the gift remainder to the institution upon the termination of the life income plan, usually at the death of the last designated beneficiary

While the various life income gift arrangements share these characteristics, they each have unique features that allow them to be used creatively to meet the requirements of the donor(s) and designated beneficiary(ies). Important factors to consider in setting up these arrangements include the approximate size of the gift being considered by the donor, type of asset to be donated, beneficiary selection, beneficiary income requirements, length of payment term, and income and investment risk tolerance.

Charitable Remainder Trusts

A charitable remainder trust is an irrevocable trust that creates two distinct interests. The first is the beneficiary's *income interest*, and the second is the charity's *remainder interest*. A donor transfers property to the trust and specifies the amount of payments to be distributed, to whom the income shall be paid, the duration of the payment (for life or a term of years), and the charity(ies) that will receive the remainder. There are two basic forms of the charitable remainder trust. One is the unitrust, which provides a variable income, and the second is the annuity trust, which provides a fixed payment. Given the legal and administrative costs of establishing and managing a remainder trust, most organizations that serve as trustee of the charitable remainder trust set minimum funding levels, usually in the range of $100,000. Additions to the unitrust form may be made any time at substantially lower levels.

Unitrust. The unitrust is an individually managed trust that allows a donor to contribute to one or more charities while retaining an income interest for life, a term of up to 20 years, or a combination of these. The income beneficiary's annual payment is determined by multiplying a fixed percentage, which must be at least 5 percent (but no higher than 50 percent), by the net fair market value of the trust assets, as determined each year.

For example, Mrs. Jones establishes a 5 percent charitable remainder unitrust with an initial cash contribution of $100,000. Her income that year will be $5,000 (5% × $100,000). If, in the following year, her unitrust is valued at $110,000, her income that year will be $5,500 (5% × $110,000). Thus, while the percentage remains the same, the payment increases or decreases each year as the value of the unitrust changes over time. For many donors, an attractive feature of the unitrust is the growth of income potential as a hedge against future inflation. Payment must be made at least annually but may be made in more frequent intervals, such as semi-annually or quarterly.

For each contribution to the unitrust, the donor is entitled to an income tax deduction for the present value of the charity's future remainder interest. This charitable remainder interest must be at least 10 percent of the net fair market value of the property as of the date the property is contributed to the trust. The remainder value is determined from government tables and takes into consideration the value of the gift, the trust percentage payout, the age and number of the beneficiaries or the trust term, the IRS monthly assumed discount rate, and the payout schedule. While the remainder value can be calculated manually, commercial computer software simplifies the process considerably.

The unitrust can be funded with a wide variety of assets, and additions to the trust are permitted. There are a variety of subcategories within the unitrust form that can be used to accommodate the objectives of the donor/beneficiary(ies) and the asset being used to fund the trust.

In order to meet the stated beneficiary payout requirement, a *standard unitrust* draws the payment first from the trust's ordinary income, then, if necessary, from capital gain income, third from tax-exempt income, and finally from tax-free return of principal. The most common assets to fund the standard unitrust are liquid assets such as cash and marketable securities.

An alternative to the standard unitrust is the *net income-only unitrust* (NI-CRUT), which limits payments to the stated percentage rate or to the actual income earned by the trust assets, whichever is less. This variation, which leaves principal and appreciation intact for the life of the unitrust, is especially useful when funding a unitrust with non-liquid assets that are earning little or no income. For example, if the donor funds the trust with real estate, the income-only provision allows time for the trustee to sell the real estate and reinvest the proceeds, free of any obligation to make payments before income is available.

A further variation of the net income-only unitrust allows the income beneficiary to recoup deficiencies in payments. This *net income-only with make-up unitrust* (NIM-CRUT) uses income earned in excess of the stipulated annual payment to make up for shortfalls earlier in the life of the unitrust. This variation of the unitrust is useful in retirement planning when the objective is to use low-income, growth-producing investments to minimize payments in early years and shift to high-yield investments to produce increased payments in later years.

A hybrid version of these forms of the charitable remainder unitrust is the *flip unitrust*. The flip unitrust starts out as a NI-CRUT or NIM-CRUT but then switches to the standard version upon the occurrence of a permissible triggering event specified in the trust document. This event might be the sale of the illiquid asset (e.g., real estate, or closely held stock) used to fund the trust, a specific date in the future (e.g., anticipated date of retirement, child's 40th birthday), or a specific event (e.g., birth, marriage, divorce, or death).

For example, Dr. Smith transfers the deed to a parcel of highly appreciated undeveloped real estate to a 5 percent flip unitrust. Because her real estate generates no income, she receives no income as long as the property is held in her trust. In the unitrust document, Dr. Smith has specified that on the first business day of the year following the sale of the property, the trust will "flip" from a NI-CRUT to a standard unitrust. This provision then will allow the trustee to invest the real estate sale proceeds in the trust for a total return, thereby providing Dr. Smith with the full income she seeks. Had this trust not flipped, her income would have been limited only to the dividends produced by the trust assets, which may be less than her 5 percent payout expectation.

Annuity Trust. A charitable remainder annuity trust is a life income plan that pays a fixed dollar amount (annuity) to one or more named beneficiaries. The payments may continue for life, for a term of up to 20 years, or some combination of these options. When the beneficiary dies or the term is up, what is left in the trust—the "remainder"—goes to the charitable institution.

The annuity payment is a fixed dollar amount (equal to at least 5 percent but not more than 50 percent) of the initial fair market value of the trust's assets. The annuity, once set, cannot change, and no additional contributions can be made to the annuity trust after the initial transfer of assets. If the invested assets produce more income than needed to pay the annuity, the excess is added to the trust principal, thereby increasing the amount ultimately payable to the institution. If the annuity trust's income is less than required to meet the annuity payment, the difference is taken from the trust principal, thereby reducing the amount that will ultimately go to the institution.

The charitable remainder interest must be at least 10 percent of the initial net fair market value of the property placed in the trust. Moreover, when the annuity trust is established, the IRS requires an actuarial test, called the "5 percent probability test," to evaluate the possibility that the trust will be depleted before the end of its natural term. If the test determines there is a greater than 5 percent probability that the trust will exhaust its assets before the remainder passes to charity, the donor may not take a charitable deduction.

The charitable deduction (remainder interest) is calculated based on the annuity rate, the initial value of the assets transferred to the trust, the date of transfer, the age and number of beneficiaries and/or the term of years, the initial payment date and frequency thereafter, and the IRS monthly discount rate. This calculation, as well as the 5 percent probability test, can be done manually or with computer software.

As with the unitrust, a significant factor affecting the charitable deduction is the annuity rate. A higher rate—which means more money paid out to the beneficiary(ies) over the trust's life—produces a smaller deduction (remainder) than does a lower rate. Age of the income beneficiary(ies) is also significant. Younger beneficiaries, who stand to receive more payments over time because of their longer life expectancy, produce a lower charitable deduction than do older beneficiaries whose life expectancy is shorter.

Taxes on the annuity income paid to the beneficiaries depend on the type of income earned and accumulated by the trust. Space does not permit a full discussion of this point, but details are available in IRS publications and other planned giving guides.

Pooled Income Funds

Charitable remainder unitrusts and annuity trusts are self-contained fiscal entities that, by their nature, require a minimum size that may preclude some donors from making this type of gift. Fortunately, there are two alternatives suitable for donors of smaller gifts: pooled income funds and charitable gift annuities.

A pooled income fund is a type of charitable remainder trust that operates like a mutual fund. A donor's gift to a pooled income fund is commingled with gifts from other donors and invested by the institution, acting as trustee (or by a bank or trust company designated as trustee by the institution). In return, the donor or a designated beneficiary receives an income for life, typically in quarterly payments. Payments vary depending on the beneficiary's share of the income earned by the fund. When the beneficiary dies, the corresponding share of the fund's principal is released from the fund to be used by the institution as directed by the donor at the time of the original arrangement.

An important feature of a pooled income fund is the combination of many donors' gifts in a single trust, which spreads administrative costs as well as investment risk. As a result, each gift can be considerably smaller than would be necessary for a stand-alone unitrust or annuity trust. Institutions that establish pooled income funds usually set the initial gift minimum at $10,000, with additional gifts set at a lower level. Pooled income funds generally accept gifts of cash and publicly traded securities that are not tax exempt. While real estate is not prohibited, most funds prefer not to accept an asset that is not readily convertible to an income-producing investment.

Pooled income funds can be a particularly useful fund-raising tool because institutions can structure the fund in different ways to appeal to different types of prospective donors. A pooled fund might seek to achieve a high rate of income (a high-yield fund) and therefore would be invested in a bond portfolio. Alternatively, it might be designed to achieve a balance of income as well as growth in value over time (a balanced fund). This kind of pooled fund would invest in a blend of stocks and bonds. A pooled income fund might be invested primarily in stocks to achieve growth and, to a lesser extent, income (a growth fund).

A pooled income fund donor is entitled to a charitable deduction for a portion of the remainder interest in the gift transferred to the trust. The deduction amount is based on IRS mortality tables, the number of beneficiaries, and the rate of investment return. The beneficiary must report all of the income received as ordinary income for federal tax purposes.

Charitable Gift Annuity

The charitable gift annuity differs from the charitable remainder trusts and pooled income funds in that the actual agreement is a contract, not a trust, between the charitable institution and the donor. A charitable gift annuity is part gift and part annuity. A donor makes a gift to the institution and, in doing so, purchases a fixed and guaranteed income for one or two beneficiaries for life. With the *immediate payment annuity*, the lifetime income commences within the year the contract is established. The *deferred payment annuity*, which can be an attractive retirement planning device, specifies income to commence at a date a year or more in the future. A donor, for example, can fund an annuity today and receive an immediate income tax deduction but specify income payments to begin on a future date, typically coinciding with retirement.

Like a charitable remainder annuity trust, a gift annuity contract requires payment of a fixed income. However, the payment obligation differs. An annuity trust can pay the annuity income only to the extent of the trust assets. If the trust assets run out, the annuity ends. A gift annuity is a binding contract, obligating the institution to pay the annuity from its general assets. The relative high degree of safety associated with this contractual guarantee is one reason for the popularity of charitable gift annuities.

The amount of the annuity payment is usually based on the age of the beneficiary(ies). The American Council on Gift Annuities publishes recommended annuity rates that charities are not required to use, but which are broadly accepted. These uniform rates serve to discourage the use of unrealistic annuity rates and also to provide a degree of self-regulation among charities.

A gift annuity donor is entitled to a charitable income tax deduction for a portion of the value transferred. The deduction calculation is based on the age of the beneficiary(ies), payment frequency, annuity rate, IRS mortality tables, and the IRS monthly discount rate. It is worth noting that a charitable gift annuity and an annuity trust using identical actuarial factors of age, annuity rate, frequency, and IRS tables result in an identical charitable deduction. However, taxation of the annuity income payments differs.

Payments from a gift annuity funded with cash are taxed in part as ordinary income and in part as a tax-free return of the donor's original investment. For many donors, this tax-free return of principal is another attractive feature of the gift annuity. If the annuity is funded with appreciated securities, part of the long-term capital gain is spread over the annuity payments and taxed as capital gain income, thereby reducing the tax-free portion. In both cases, the tax-free portion continues for the actuarial life expectancy of the donor. Should the donor outlive expectations, all of the income becomes fully taxable as ordinary income.

In addition to cash and securities, real estate and tangible personal property are generally suitable assets to exchange for a gift annuity. However, insurance regulations in some states not only restrict such transactions but also regulate investment policies and reserve requirements for organizations offering gift annuities.

Part of the popularity of gift annuities with institutions is the ease with which they can be established. Unlike the other life income arrangements described above, gift annuities do not require a trustee. However, the institution must carefully consider the legal as well as administrative responsibilities of this type of contractual obligation.

Like pooled income funds, gift annuities offer an economy of scale that permits gifts as low as $10,000. Small size is not a requirement, though. Gift annuities and pooled income funds also work well with large gifts of trust size. In fact, many planned giving programs direct large gifts to their pooled income funds or gift annuity program, recommending annuity trusts and unitrusts only when the donor's unique requirements call for a custom-designed life income plan.

OTHER PLANNED GIVING INSTRUMENTS

In addition to the methods that provide a life income, other planned giving arrangements exist. These arrangements provide more gift planning options, allowing fund raisers to further address donors' individual needs.

Charitable Lead Trusts

The charitable lead trust works like a life income gift in reverse. Income from a lead trust goes to the charitable institution. When the trust terminates, the remainder transfers to the donor or other beneficiary(ies). Generally, a lead trust provides one of two benefits to the donor. If the trust is a "grantor lead trust," the donor can take an income tax deduction for the present value of the payments the charity is to receive from the trust over a specified period of time. At the conclusion of the trust period, the principal reverts to the donor. If the trust is a "non-grantor lead trust," the donor's tax benefit is a reduction of gift and estate taxes that would otherwise apply when property is passed to heirs such as children and grandchildren. The unitrust form of the charitable lead trust provides a variable income to charity, and the annuity form provides a fixed income.

The use of lead trusts has diminished steadily through the 1980s due to changes in tax rules. Given the current limitations, charitable lead trusts are far less popular than life income gifts. Their best place is in planning a sizable estate, with help from legal and tax advisers experienced in using lead trusts in estate planning.

Charitable Bequests

A charitable bequest is a legal provision made by will or revocable trust, naming a charitable organization as the recipient of all or part of the donor's estate. The bequest may be in the form of cash, real estate, securities, or other property as specified in the estate plan. Estate tax laws are particularly generous in allowing the donor to pass assets to charity free of estate taxes and of many of the limitations that normally apply to gifts given during life.

The most common method of testamentary giving is an outright transfer at the time of death. The property transferred can include tangible property, capital gain property, ordinary income property, and more, without regard to the charity's exempt purpose and without percentage limitations.

As with outright gifts, the tax deductibility of a gift by will reduces its cost to the donor. The cost of gifts made through an estate provision varies with the size of the taxable estate and the applicable tax bracket. For example, if a donor whose estate is taxed in the 45 percent bracket makes a bequest of $100,000, the real cost of the gift to his estate is only $55,000—because the other $45,000 would have been lost in estate taxes had the gift not been made.

Bequests can take various forms depending on the donors' wishes for heirs and for other charitable organizations.

- *Specific bequest.* The institution receives a specific dollar amount or specific assets such as securities, real estate, or personal property.

- *Residuary bequest.* The institution receives all or a percentage of the estate remaining after the payment of expenses and any specific amounts designated to other beneficiaries.

- *Contingent bequest.* The institution receives a bequest only in the event that a named beneficiary predeceases the donor.

A will and other estate planning documents are important legal instruments that should be prepared by the donor's attorney. In some cases, the institution has the opportunity to provide sample language for a new will or a codicil for an existing will.

In addition to outright transfer, bequests can also be used to create life income gifts. Testamentary gifts to establish life income plans are subject to requirements similar to the income tax rules. The gift must be in the form of a charitable remainder trust, pooled income fund, or charitable gift annuity. The estate tax charitable deduction is determined using the same tables and factors as the living forms of these gifts.

Gifts of Qualified Retirement Plans

For many people, retirement plans, including IRAs, 401(k)s, 403(b)s, Keoghs and non-qualified deferred compensation plans, represent a substantial portion of the estate. These retirement plans, if left in the estate, are subject to both income taxes and estate taxes. These two taxes, when combined, can consume as much as 70 percent of the assets in those plans. For high net worth individuals, this tax liability makes retirement plans one of the worst assets to leave to children, but one of the best to leave to charity. The value of the interest from a retirement plan passing on to charity is fully deductible for estate tax and income tax purposes.

Donors can transfer retirement plan assets to charity at the end of their life with favorable tax consequences. Some of the options include designating charity as a direct beneficiary of the retirement account or transferring the plan assets to a testamentary charitable remainder trust. Another option includes transferring the plan assets to a non-charitable trust, known as a qualified terminable interest property trust (QTIP trust). This trust provides income, as well as access to principal as needed, to a surviving spouse for life, after which the remaining principal passes to charity.

THE TIME FOR PLANNED GIVING

Gift planning has come of age, due in large part to the innovative tools and creative strategies that fund raisers and others have developed in recent years. The mutually beneficial result has been to provide valuable financial and estate planning benefits to donors while at the same time achieving generous support for charitable organizations.

To advance this effort, today's fund raiser needs to know the basics of gift planning strategies and should keep abreast of the ever-changing charitable and estate tax laws. But to truly succeed, it is essential to be able to communicate the benefits of planned giving to donors in ways they can understand. Achieving that objective will result in major gifts from which everyone will benefit, both now and in the future.

PART IV

The Campaign

"The campaign" stands alone as the subject of a section of this volume because of its visibility and central importance as a fund-raising strategy of colleges and universities. As discussed in Chapter 3, the principles of the modern campaign were developed by YMCA fund raisers in the early years of the twentieth century and introduced to higher education by consultants. The definition of the campaign has evolved over the decades, from the simple "capital campaign" to today's "comprehensive campaigns," encompassing objectives for annual support, endowment, and facilities under one umbrella and typically crediting outright gifts, planned gifts, and other commitments toward the goal of the campaign.

The dramatic increase in the number, frequency, and magnitude of campaigns has been a hallmark of higher education fund raising in recent decades. These trends also have given rise to considerable discussion regarding campaign practices and even the continuing relevance of the campaign as a fund-raising strategy. Many of the criticisms of the campaign that are voiced today were raised in an insightful essay written more than twenty years ago, in 1981, by Joel P. Smith, former vice president of Stanford University. Smith's essay was first published as a chapter in Francis Pray's *Handbook for Educational Fund Raising* and was reprinted in 1993 as a chapter of *Educational Fund Raising: Principles and Practice*.

In the context of a thoughtful broader commentary on the fund-raising profession, Smith raises challenges to the conventional wisdom regarding the benefits of campaigns. Among other points, he levels three criticisms. First, he questions whether the episodic nature of campaigns and their emphasis on short-term goals are consistent with professionalism and the reality that successful fund raising is "patient, subtle, and sustained."[1] Smith says that the sustained approach (akin to David Dunlop's concept of "nurturing fund raising," discussed in Chapter 8) may be especially important when campaign goals emphasize endowment over facilities projects. Many endowment gifts will involve some form of gift planning, with the timing influenced more by the donor's life cycle than by the institution's timetable.

Although campaign objectives are presumably based on an institutional agenda resulting from a planning process, Smith argues that this approach is often more appearance than reality. Campaigns inevitably focus attention on the bottom line. He says this may lead fund raisers to ignore the differing "utility" of gifts, that is, the fact that support toward core institutional needs is more "valuable" than gifts for more marginal purposes, although both count equally toward the campaign's dollar goal.[2] In other words, as Rick Nahm and Robert Zemsky wrote in 1993, "When you go hunting where the ducks are, you tend to get the ducks available, no matter how odd they might be."[3]

Writing in 1981, Smith notes rising campaign goals and speculates that "some major university will soon boldly announce the first billion dollar campaign."[4] (Ironically, it was Stanford that first broke the billion-dollar barrier in 1987, subsequent to Smith's tenure as vice president.) Smith voices concern that such goals may be perceived as "reaching way beyond whatever even the most faithful [will consider] a legitimate realm of need—in short, as grasping for all that [the institution] can get."[5]

In the 1990s, more than a decade after Smith's essay, college and university campaigns erupted as a subject of considerable controversy within the educational fund raising profession. One line of criticism was aimed at inconsistent accounting standards that were making it difficult to compare campaigns across institutions and, some believed, undermining the credibility of goals. Responding to this concern, the Council for Advancement and Support of Education (CASE) formed a Campaign Reporting Advisory Group, chaired by Vance T. Peterson, then vice president for institutional advancement at Occidental College. After considerable debate and discussion, the CASE Campaign Standards were published in 1994, recommending practices for campaign management and uniform standards for reporting campaign results. But, this did not end the controversy over campaign accounting. Some continued to argue that the definition of a campaign should reflect the specific objectives and circumstances of each institution rather than a uniform standard. For example, while the CASE standards do not include counting any public funds toward the campaign goal, some state universities hold the view that state matching grants, made in response to private gifts, should be counted toward the goal because they directly reflect campaign efforts. There are also varied opinions on the appropriateness of including testamentary commitments (that is, bequest intentions) as campaign support. At the time of this writing, CASE was considering revision of the standards.

The campaign debate of the 1990s reflected more than concerns about accounting. Some challenged the very model of the comprehensive campaign, echoing many of Joel Smith's arguments from a decade earlier. In 1993, Nahm and Zemsky saw higher education fund raising "at a crossroads" and shared Smith's concern about the utility of gifts. They pointed to the criticism that big campaign goals were focusing attention on the overall bottom line, causing campaigns to become "donor-driven," rather than reflecting the core needs of institutions. They called for a closer link between campaign objectives and institutional planning.[6] Writing in 1990, Charles Lawson, then chair of the consulting firm Brakeley, John Price Jones, Inc., reflected Smith's worry about the image of institutional greed. "Unless our not-for-profits act more responsibly in this area," he wrote, "I believe we will experience a very real donor backlash."[7] And, in 1992, then president of CASE Peter Buchanan called the episodic, start-and-stop model of the campaign "the dumbest thing I think I have ever seen," and recommended continuous fund raising as a "cheaper" and "better" alternative.[8] However, these criticisms were not sufficient to reduce the popularity of the campaign model in the booming economy and stock market of the decade. Campaigns flourished as the principal strategy for higher education fund raising throughout the 1990s, increasing in their boldness, visibility, and success.

In these early years of the twenty-first century, the campaign remains a subject of discussion, but new themes and directions have emerged. More speakers and writers are acknowledging both the advantages of the continuous fund-raising program and the continuing benefits of the campaign model. The scope of comprehensive campaigns has broadened to encompass virtually all fund-raising efforts of the institution, and the interval between campaigns has shortened to the point that the end of one campaign and the beginning of another are virtually indistinguishable in the intensity of fund-raising activity. In this environment, the difference between a "continuous program" and a series of "campaigns"

has become less pronounced. Indeed, in the second edition of his book
Conducting a Successful Capital Campaign, published in 2000, Kent Dove
includes the "continuous major gifts program" as one of four "forms" of
the campaign. He calls the continuous program, when linked to institutional strategic planning, the equivalent of "perpetual campaigning."[9]
At a CASE district conference in 2001, Robert Lindgren described the
Johns Hopkins decision to begin the quiet period of a new campaign
immediately following the victory celebration marking the end of a successful $1.5-billion campaign.[10] The concept of the "continuous fund-
raising program" may be evolving into an era of the "continuous" or
"perpetual" campaign.

Despite criticisms, the campaign has continued to be a key strategy
of colleges and universities and has evolved to meet the changing circumstances of higher education fund raising over the decades—expanding from the traditional capital campaign to the comprehensive
campaign, and perhaps now moving into a new era of continuous campaigns. In some form, the campaign is likely to remain as a central
element of educational fund raising for two reasons. First, it is a good
fit with several fundamental characteristics of human nature. People are
motivated by specific goals and deadlines. People like to participate with
others in an organized activity and will follow the example of those they
see as leaders. Giving is emotional, and people respond to inspirational
themes and grand visions. While fund raising may in fact become continuous, the campaign remains the single best strategy for mobilizing the
focused attention and effort of the institution, its volunteer and academic leaders, and its fund-raising staff. Second, campaigns have become
more than just fund-raising strategies. They also offer an unequaled opportunity to communicate the institution's academic vision and plans
in a way that, because they are attached to the excitement and sus-
pense—indeed the drama—of ambitious goals and deadlines, attracts
broad attention and understanding.

In Chapter 11, William McGoldrick and Paul Robell, both veteran
campaigners, provide a detailed view of the modern campaign from start
to finish and summarize in specific terms the tasks that must be completed in each phase.

NOTES

1. Joel P. Smith, "Rethinking the Traditional Capital Campaign," in *Handbook for Educational Fund Raising*, ed. Francis C. Pray (San Francisco: Jossey-
Bass, 1981), 65.

2. Ibid., 66.

3. Rick Nahm and Robert M. Zemsky, "The Role of Institutional Planning in Fund Raising," in *Educational Fund Raising: Principles and Practice*, ed. Michael J. Worth (Phoenix: Oryx Press/American Council on Education, 1993), 57.

4. Smith, "Rethinking the Traditional Capital Campaign," 67.

5. Ibid.

6. Nahm and Zemsky, "The Role of Institutional Planning in Fund Raising," 56–66.

7. Charles E. Lawson, "The Nineties: Worrisome Trends in Fund Raising," *The Journal* (National Society of Fund Raising Executives, Washington, DC) (Winter 1990): 11–12.

8. Kathleen S. Kelly, *Effective Fund-Raising Management* (Mahwah, NJ: Lawrence Erlbaum Associates, 1998), 547–548.

9. Kent E. Dove, *Conducting a Successful Capital Campaign*," 2nd edition (San Francisco: Jossey-Bass, 2000), 18–19.

10. Robert R. Lindgren, "The Campaign: Same Purpose, New Approaches," Presentation, CASE District II Conference, Pittsburgh, February 5, 2001.

CHAPTER 11

Campaigning in the New Century

William P. McGoldrick and Paul A. Robell

I s there a college, university, or independent school anywhere in the world that is not at this moment considering a major campaign, involved in a campaign, or completing a campaign? Probably not. On nearly every campus—be it an elite and wealthy Ivy League university, a small and struggling church-related independent school, a publicly supported land-grant university, or an urban community college—the idea of fund raising and the words "capital campaign" are ubiquitous.

Trustees hire presidents they think can lead campaigns. Fund-raising prowess or potential is one of the major prerequisites for an individual vying for a presidential appointment in American, and increasingly in international educational institutions. Presidents hire vice presidents with "campaign experience." Vice presidents call colleagues everywhere looking for a major gifts officer who can persuade wealthy donors to support Old Siwash. The campaign has become one of the most important programs on American and Canadian campuses as well as on campuses abroad, both in England and increasingly in many other European countries.

In the 1950s, universities debated whether to begin campaigns. In the 1970s, they debated how often to begin campaigns. In the 1990s, they debated how large the campaign goal could be. Today, they worry about how often they can successfully utilize the tried-and-true campaign strategy to raise their fund raising to new heights.

Since the 1950s, the campaign itself has undergone changes. The "capital" campaign of the twentieth century has been generally transformed into a "comprehensive" development campaign. The comprehensive campaign counts in its totals all gifts to the university. Although not consistent with campaign accounting guidelines promulgated by the Council for Advancement and Support of Education, some campaigns include bequest expectancies, government support, and other revenues from non-gift sources. Campaigns once were relatively short; today, they are planned to extend over five or more years. Once, campaign gifts were solicited by volunteers who were encouraged by a small staff on campus; today, large professional staffs are the primary major gift solicitors in many campaigns.

This chapter will help institutions understand the choices they must make before recommending plans for a major campaign to their board of trustees. It outlines the phases through which every campaign passes, the roles of the people who can make it happen, and some specific issues that will need to be addressed along the way.

WHAT IS A CAMPAIGN?

A campaign is an organized and intense effort to secure extraordinary gift commitments during a defined period of time to meet specific needs crucial to the mission and goals of an institution.

As discussed in Chapter 3, fund-raising efforts for American education started not long after the founding of Harvard in 1636. But the "campaign" as we know it today was born in the early 1900s when the YMCA movement introduced the concept of specific goals and fixed time limits for fund raising. The American Red Cross followed with campaign efforts during World War I that included the solicitation of corporate support.

Until after World War I, the solicitation of support for American higher education most often fell to the president alone. And while a few colleges and universities began organized efforts in the first half of this century, it was not until the 1950s that broad and massive efforts to support education emerged.

During the 1960s, Harvard completed an $82 million campaign, and several other universities demonstrated that $100 million efforts could succeed. As the 1970s came to a close, Stanford University raised the stakes of campaigning with a successful $300 million program. In the 1990s, 27 American universities completed or had underway campaigns with goals of $1 billion or greater. These mega-campaign goals have had the effect of causing many other institutions to expand their visions of goal possibilities. As a result, campaigns at even the smallest colleges and universities seek millions and tens of millions of dollars, while large institutions chase goals of hundreds of millions, even billions of dollars. The skyrocketing economies of the United States and other countries during the 1990s, and the increase in educational institutions' assets as a result of the booming equities markets, have propelled many institutions' endowments into the billions. Partially as a result of this economic growth, since 1998 there have been at least 23 individual financial commitments to American universities of $100 million or greater.

BEGINNING A CAMPAIGN

The financial threats to the American system of higher education—aging facilities, spiraling tuition, the need to increase faculty and staff salaries to remain competitive for qualified personnel, the increasing demand for financial aid—have increased the pressure to secure philanthropic support. But pressure is what campaigns are about. They are not easy to plan. They are not easy to carry out. They are highly visible. And their progress is judged differently by various constituencies.

Like military campaigns, fund-raising campaigns involve leadership, planning, logistics, volunteers, execution, and persistence. The planning often takes months, even years, to complete. There are considerable risks associated with campaigning, and an institution must make the decision to move forward very carefully.

Six key tests will help determine if a campus is ready to campaign. They are all vital to an informed decision, and it may be helpful to involve outside counsel in answering these questions.

1. *Does the institution have a clearly understood and easily recognized mission?* Is the mission written and widely shared and accepted enthusiastically by volunteers and donors? Donors want to be certain that they understand the role of a college or university in society, how it differentiates its role from that of other institutions, and what impact the institution has upon its constituents. This mission is the foundation for all the plans and goals that will be developed.

2. *Is there a written long-range plan?* The entire campus community must understand and endorse the strategic plan. The plan should contain measurable milestones and present a clear vision of what the institution will look like when the plan is executed successfully. It must state the academic, financial, administrative, and admissions goals for the campus over at least a five-year period. It must demonstrate great aspirations centered on the mission. From this document will come the clear, concise, and compelling document called a case statement.

3. *Is campus and volunteer leadership strong and capable?* The role of the president and the trustees in campaign success cannot be overstated. Campaign activities may require as much as 50 percent of the president's time. Is the president prepared to devote the necessary amount of time and effort to cultivate and solicit key donors? Does the president plan to remain in office through the completion of the campaign?

Are the trustees eager to begin a campaign? Do they understand the need for a campaign, and are they willing to commit their time to development activities? Are the trustees committed to their personal leadership roles and prepared to make generous financial contributions to the campaign?

Are there volunteer leaders who are ready to assume key campaign roles, including campaign chair and chairs of volunteer committees?

Without strong and dedicated leadership, a campaign cannot succeed. If the preceding questions cannot honestly be answered in the affirmative, the institution is not ready to launch a campaign.

4. *Is there compelling urgency to campaign now?* As the internal planning and discussion of a campaign proceeds over several months, the campus begins to believe in the need and the urgency for greater resources. Too often, trustees and key volunteers are brought into this process far too late. The campus is off and running (or wants to be) and cannot understand why trustees, key volunteers, and top donors have not "bought in" to a major campaign.

The skill with which the president and the chief advancement officer inform and involve the volunteer leadership in the planning process will prepare them for the timely decision of campaign readiness.

5. *Are there potential donors?* More campaigns fail for lack of donors than for any other reason. That is not profound, but it is true.

Has the market been tested? A market survey, or feasibility study, is crucial to understanding the ability and willingness of donors to support a university. This study will help set an aggressive but realistic campaign goal and will also help make clear which campus needs are perceived as attractive gift opportunities by donors. The feasibility study should be done by an outside agency, such as a fund-raising consulting firm.

6. *Are the elements of a campaign plan present?* With a strategic plan, an eager president, a committed board, an experienced staff, an aggressive campaign chair, a flashy case statement, and a ready list of potential donors, it's time to go. Right? Wrong!

The chief advancement officer is responsible for the written campaign plan. This business plan sets timetables, outlines philosophical approaches, states campaign accounting rules, discusses the roles of each major campus and volunteer player, outlines the roles of public relations and alumni relations in the campaign, and covers the myriad details that enter into such a major effort. The outline for such a plan should be in place so that details can be incorporated during campaign planning discussions.

With these six questions answered, development officers and campus leadership can decide if they are prepared to campaign. Since all aspects of the institution—its strengths, weaknesses, people, and programs—are exposed to public scrutiny during a campaign, the risks are great. But the rewards can ensure the health of the institution for many years to come.

THE SIX PHASES OF A CAMPAIGN

While it is easy to oversimplify complex topics such as campaigning, it is also easy to overcomplicate them. Every campaign passes through six successive phases. While following the steps outlined here does not guarantee success, understanding the importance of each phase is essential to reaching the goal.

Phase 1: Pre-campaign Planning

Pre-campaign planning is that period during which the institution's officers develop a strategic plan, define needs and priorities, and test the feasibility of a campaign among important constituents. This period might last from six to eighteen months. In this time, the president and vice president must determine whether to recommend to the board that a campaign should commence.

During this phase, you and your team must:

- engage campaign counsel
- complete the institutional strategic plan
- define the institution's needs and priorities
- begin-donor research and evaluation
- define the campaign program and priorities
- write a campaign rationale
- enlist eight to ten key volunteers
- determine the role of alumni relations staff in the campaign
- involve public relations staff in writing a communications plan
- develop gift tables

- determine a rough budget and possible funding sources
- determine the current base of gift support
- determine a possible campaign starting date
- begin intensive staff and volunteer training

All the elements of this phase must be completed before Phase 2 begins.

A few of the Phase 1 tasks deserve further discussion here. When determining the current base of support for the university, neither last year's total giving nor the highest total the university has achieved should be used as the sole standard. To determine the true base of support, take the average total giving to the institution over the last three to five years after any extraordinary major gifts are eliminated. Also, the changing demographics of the constituency and region must be kept in mind. The old methods of screening and rating prospects will probably have to be modified to account for the rise and fall of certain industries as well as the sources of wealth that enable the institution's constituencies to make major gifts.

Preparing the campaign rationale involves writing down succinctly why this campaign is needed for the university and why it is needed now. If a compelling case for urgent support cannot be created, it is not time to begin major gift discussions with donors.

During this period, the institution must address campaign staffing and budget very directly. Can it execute the campaign with current staff, or will it need additional staff? How will it pay for the campaign? Out of the university's operating budget? From unrestricted gifts? From a tax on all gifts? To avoid great unhappiness later, these problems need to be solved early. It is generally not advisable to plan to pay for the extra costs of staffing or conducting a campaign from the anticipated proceeds of the campaign fund-raising dollars.

Phase 2: Campaign Planning

Phase 2 is a short and relatively intense period of three to six months. During this time, support with important opinion leaders on and off campus must be built. During this phase, you and your team must:

- complete a market survey (feasibility study)
- refine the analysis of needs and priorities
- write the formal case statement
- intensify research of the top 100 to 500 potential donors
- write a detailed campaign plan

- determine the goal of the nucleus fund
- prepare a smooth budget and determine the funding sources
- continue intensive staff and volunteer training

By this time, there is a real possibility that someone will want to jump the gun and "just start the campaign." That temptation must be resisted. Each planning step must be well executed, and the president and volunteer leadership must possess confidence in the plan. Their enthusiasm will depend upon the confidence of success that a well-formulated plan provides.

Even as the plan is prepared, another document essential to establishing the credibility of the campaign will be underway. This involves translating the institution's needs and aspirations into a clear, concise statement of objectives, relating those objectives directly to the campaign's monetary goals, and supporting the credibility of those goals with a realistic plan to succeed. The document that does this is the case statement.

Harold J. Seymour called the case statement "the one definitive piece of the whole campaign. It tells all that needs to be told, answers all the important questions, reviews the arguments for support, explains the proposed plan for raising the money, and shows how gifts may be made and who the people are who vouch for the project and will give it leadership and direction."[1]

Phase 3: The Nucleus Fund

Few campaigns are announced publicly before enlisting the commitment of several key donors who, by their statement of generous support, bring credibility to the campaign, its goals, and its leadership.

Nucleus donors are often well-recognized board members, alumni, and key major donors of long standing. Since these donors are usually the most knowledgeable and most involved in the life of the college or university, their willingness to back the campaign is invaluable evidence of their belief in its cause, plans, and leadership. Such commitments, far more than verbal endorsements, demonstrate the generous financial commitment of the institution's leadership.

This stage of "quiet" or "private" campaigning may take one to two years. Generally, when a campaign is publicly launched, the nucleus total is announced along with the names of the key donors and the purposes that their gifts will serve.

During this phase, you and your team must:

- enlist a cadre of volunteers
- continue intensive staff and volunteer training
- solicit the first gifts to the campaign
- build campaign enthusiasm among volunteer leadership
- begin to cultivate the next group of major donors
- analyze success and recommend a campaign goal
- complete all targeted nucleus fund solicitations

One purpose of the nucleus phase is to convince those most important major donors to make large commitments that will set the sights of other donors at a high level. With this start, fund raisers can then seek support from the next group of leadership donors. Years ago, George Brakeley, Jr., former chair of the campaign consulting firm Brakeley, John Price Jones, referred to this process as "sequential fund raising." He meant that one should approach those capable of making the largest gifts early in the campaign and then move through the list of potential donors to smaller gifts. This approach makes sense because major donors often need the time to organize their affairs to make a large commitment as well as the flexibility to pay their commitment over time. Also, generous gifts tend to encourage others to give generously.

Because major donors, properly approached during this phase, may surprise by making gifts 10 times, 100 times, or even 1,000 times greater than their previous largest gifts, it is worth being patient before announcing a public goal. Until now, the campaign will have proceeded with a "working goal." Understanding the base of support the university has had historically, adding to that the gifts from successful nucleus fund solicitations, and analyzing the ability of the remaining donor pool, it is now possible to intelligently recommend a public campaign goal. (How to set that goal is a subject that will be discussed later in this chapter.)

Phase 4: The Kickoff

Balloons, parties, and gala celebrations often accompany the announcement of a major campaign. It is important that all potential donors be aware that the campaign is under way and that they will be approached. The kickoff may be as short as a day or as long as a year, depending on whether the plan calls for one celebration on campus or a series of celebrations all across the country.

During this phase, you and your team must:

- announce the campaign goal and nucleus fund success
- introduce the campaign volunteer leadership
- present the case statement
- demonstrate the president's clear leadership of the campaign
- expand the volunteer base
- continue intensive staff and volunteer training
- continue to solicit the "critical few" donors who are able to make major gifts
- begin cultivation activities for the several hundred to several thousand donors who are able to support the campaign at levels below your "principal" gift or major gift level

Prolonging the enthusiasm of the kickoff with alumni events and publications is crucial to the ongoing credibility and success of the campaign. Success, in turn, will maintain enthusiasm. Staff and volunteers should thus be prepared and trained to solicit and close gifts early.

In this phase, the team should still be focusing most of its energy and resources on the "critical few" prospects who are able to make major gifts. Once there was a rule that said 80 percent of the giving to a campaign came from 20 percent of the donors. Later the rule was amended to say that 90 percent of the giving came from 10 percent of the donors. Today, many universities find that 95 percent of the giving comes from 5 percent or fewer of the donors.

This is not surprising considering the immense goals of campaigns and the distribution of wealth in America. Very, very few people can give $1 million to support a university; fewer still can give $5 million or more. Yet more and more goals require gifts of $5 million, $10 million, $25 million, or more to succeed.

The "critical few" capable of such gifts must receive the appropriate attention from the president and the campaign leadership early in the campaign. They need information germane to their interests and to the goals of the campaign, as well as the opportunity to learn how their support will make an important difference to the future of the institution.

Phase 5: The Plateau of Fatigue

Not everyone agrees with the name of this phase of the campaign. Some feel it is too negative, and that the label becomes a self-fulfilling prophecy. But the experience of many veteran campaigners indicates that every campaign that stretches its goals and pushes its programs beyond "business as usual" eventually runs into problems.

At this stage, the enthusiasm of the kickoff has worn down. Donors are not responding enthusiastically to each solicitation. Volunteers are not completing their assignments as quickly as suggested. And staff are more than a little frustrated by their inability to move their programs forward according to the wonderful plan the vice president wrote quite some time earlier.

Careful planning can help to minimize the negative effects of this phase of the campaign. This is the one- to three-year period of hard work that will ultimately determine whether the campaign succeeds in reaching all its goals and whether it heightens or lowers the morale of volunteers.

During this phase, you and your team must:

- continue intensive staff and volunteer training
- continue the programs of cultivation and stewardship
- continue the solicitation of leadership donors
- begin the active solicitation of donors who were newly identified during the early phases of the campaign
- assess the results of each program
- adjust plans as donor response to requests and new campus needs become apparent
- overcome volunteer and staff burnout
- analyze cash flow

Regional programs, discussed later in this chapter, are most apt to suffer the effects of fatigue because they are frequently used to target first-time major gift candidates—a difficult prospect group—and because they often employ volunteers who have little or no experience with major gift solicitations.

Development professionals must take positive steps to maintain the campaign's momentum. The mental toughness of the vice president, director of development, and staff will often determine the attitude of the president, volunteer leadership, and volunteers. Activities to rebuild enthusiasm should be planned.

Phase 6: The Home Stretch

During the last 12 to 18 months of the campaign, the successes achieved to date in the campaign can be demonstrated. Opportunities will be available to highlight goals that have not yet been achieved and to focus on their completion.

People give to winners. As the campaign begins to accomplish major objectives and achievements are celebrated, people who have considered giving but have not yet made their commitment will step forward to be part of the success. Recognizing this phenomenon and planning to capitalize on it can help a campaign reach or exceed its goal.

During this phase, you and your team must:

- continue intensive staff and volunteer training
- celebrate goal achievements
- recognize the generosity of many donors
- thank and honor volunteers
- if appropriate, resolicit donors who are now ready to give again
- communicate actively with all donors to thank them
- begin the strategic planning for post-campaign activities

Recognition events for major donors are also cultivation events for donors who have not yet made commitments. Be certain that close attention is paid to a potential donor's reaction to the thanks publicly offered to committed donors.

Resolicitation of donors is a very tricky process. It is crucial to carefully examine the donor's past giving, potential for support, and present attitude toward the campaign, the campaign leadership, and the unmet goals. Rarely do donors with outstanding payments due on pledges increase their commitment before completing their initial pledges. Donors who have completed their commitments should be examined carefully.

By this time, the president and vice president should already be discussing the plan for post-campaign development activities. When will the university be ready for its next campaign? When will the president be ready? The volunteers? The staff? The donors?

A new written plan should be in the works to avoid the post-campaign blues. Without careful planning, volunteers will move on to other causes, staff will move on to other jobs, and the program built so carefully will become shaky.

THE PEOPLE WHO MAKE IT HAPPEN

Although raising money is the object of every campaign, it is crucial never to lose sight of the fact that it is people who will achieve the goal. Campaign leaders must be thoroughly convinced of the importance of the campaign and be able to inspire others to adopt the cause. Staff and volunteers must know their contributions are important and feel their work is valued and appreciated. It takes many people, each fulfilling a specific role, to make a campaign successful.

The President

People give to people. And people make extraordinary gifts to leaders who convey great vision, aspirations, conviction, and the ability to succeed. The role of the institution's president is central to the success of any campaign. No one will carry a greater burden of public responsibility.

Since the campaign is the outgrowth of strategic planning, the immense responsibility of the president makes sense. According to Edward T. Foote II, former president of the University of Miami, "The campaign is the translation of a vision to the most demanding reality of all, money. The president is both the principal author of the vision and, as the university's chief advocate, the ultimate asker for big money."[2]

Today, presidents are selected not only for scholarship, vision, and leadership, but also for their perceived ability to raise great sums of money. Fund-raising willingness, experience, and prowess are basic tenets of any presidential search in colleges and universities in the United States and internationally.

The Vice President

The vice president is responsible for preparing the campaign strategy, executing campaign plans, organizing the time and activities the president and trustees devote to the campaign, and recruiting the necessary staff.

The timely execution of the campaign plan is crucial to its success. This time-limited activity exemplifies the simple concept, "When you're ahead, you're ahead; when you're behind, you're behind." Once a campaign begins to lose momentum, it is very difficult to get it back on schedule.

The vice president is the conductor who sees that every player knows and carries out his or her part. The vice president directs the activities of the staff, the deans, the faculty, and the volunteers. In large campaigns, there are obviously many staff members, each performing specific assignments. But it is the vice president who is ultimately responsible to the president and to the board for all campaign logistics.

The Campaign Chair

The campaign chair is the role model for all other volunteers. This person will commit untold hours to working with the president, the vice president, and key volunteers. He or she will play a major role in articulating the importance of the campaign, in setting an example for personal giving, and for actively soliciting major donors.

Because people give to people who also give, the campaign chair and trustees will be called upon for leadership giving early in the campaign. Without their generous financial commitments, the campaign will falter quickly. Since people volunteer when they are asked by other volunteers, the campaign chair and key lieutenants will set the pace for volunteerism in the campaign. Their belief in campaign goals will inspire others. Their commitment of time to visit potential donors will encourage others to join them in this activity. Their oversight of campaign progress will require staff to remain aggressive in their daily activities.

Alumni and Public Relations

Those planning and executing major campaigns often fail to employ the advice and participation of alumni relations and public relations professionals. Their experience working with volunteers, publications, and the media can help development staff understand and communicate effectively with their constituents.

Alumni relations and public relations leadership should be involved from the beginning and delegated the roles they must assume to make the campaign effective. Alumni officials can ensure appropriate alumni programming during the campaign and help gain the personal support of alumni leaders for the campaign. The public relations staff can provide needed publications and media relations support.

IMPORTANT STEPS

Some of the tasks mentioned above deserve additional discussion here. The way these steps are implemented will affect the nature of the entire campaign.

Setting the Campaign Goal

The campaign goal is often a matter of considerable debate on campus and among volunteers. Some people advocate goals based upon need alone. Others believe that whatever goal the president desires is right. Some feel a modest goal will ensure success. Others point out that low expectations will never produce great accomplishments. And some may believe that campaign goals are determined by local psychics or on a Ouija board. But only accurate information and sound advice will help determine a campaign goal.

In setting the goal, institutional decision makers should consider the priority needs of the college or university, the identified potential of prospective donors, the institution's past experience in development, and the effectiveness of the campaign plan. As mentioned earlier, a feasibility study will provide additional information about the reaction of important donors to proposed campaign objectives.

While it is dangerous to use mathematical formulas to set campaign goals, it is highly unlikely that a college raising $1 million per year will be successful in a $50 million campaign. A random look at several recent comprehensive campaigns indicates that goals of eight to ten times the most recent year's total are common. As goals get larger, the length of campaigns typically extends to five years or more, and accounting periods for receiving payments often extend beyond ten years.

In 1994, the Council for the Advancement and Support of Education (CASE) published recommendations for campaign standards that deal with the length of the campaign as well as counting methodologies. Any educational institution contemplating a campaign should examine the CASE standards and reach a considered decision as to the methodology that will be employed.

By postponing announcement of the official goal until well into the nucleus phase of the campaign, it is possible to make a more informed decision based on the total raised during the nucleus phase, the number of identified donors "used" to reach that total, and the number and potential of donors remaining in the major gift pool. If more than half of the known potential major gift donors have made commitments and the total of their gifts reaches only 30 percent of the hoped-for goal of the campaign, that goal is probably unrealistic. Conversely, if only 10 percent of the known potential major givers are committed and their gifts total 75 percent of the planned goal, the goal is too conservative.

From 40 to 50 percent of the goal should be accumulated during the campaign's nucleus phase. The thinking is that a majority of the most important donors will make commitments during this period, and their gifts will often be among the largest. If the nucleus total is considerably less than 40 percent, the goal needs to be examined carefully before proceeding.

Keep in mind that these rules are poetry, not science. Nevertheless, they are based on experience and should help calibrate the campaign goal.

Setting the Campaign Budget

Like every other budget, the campaign budget is a political as well as a practical issue. Certainly the budget determines how much is available to be spent for each particular campaign purpose. It also is a statement of the confidence of the institution in the campaign director's personal leadership and professional credibility.

There is no recipe for what a campaign should cost. It will greatly depend on circumstances. Is this the institution's first campaign? Will there be a substantial volunteer effort? If the ongoing development program already possesses a reasonable budget, the incremental amount needed for a campaign may be a very small percentage of the campaign goal.

In a 1990 study of 65 universities, total development costs averaged 16 cents per dollar raised. The report cautioned, however, that such a figure, taken alone, may badly mislead, and that costs reflect the unique characteristics of each institution.[3]

A budget needs to be developed in considerable detail. Assumptions and budget needs should be documented thoroughly and shared widely with other institutional officers who can provide suggestions and questions. Regular accounting of spending is crucial. The campaign staff creates the budget, and is responsible for its use.

Conducting Regional Campaigns

Most comprehensive campaigns are a combination of many smaller campaigns. Sometimes these campaigns are organized around specific purposes. Sometimes they are organized by alumni classes and incorporate reunion giving. Often they are organized geographically, as a practical means of reaching hundreds or thousands of potential donors.

The regional campaign is a brief, intense microcosm of the overall campaign executed on a local basis, with local leadership, local volunteers, and a local goal. Events to kick off and to support regional campaigns provide momentum and importance. Solicitation of attendees should begin rapidly following such events to capitalize on their effect.

Such campaigns succeed best when they are completed within three to six months. If a region is large enough to necessitate a longer campaign, it may be wise to divide the region into smaller areas that can be managed more quickly.

The relatively swift nature of these efforts enables volunteers to accomplish their tasks efficiently, permits many rapid successes for the campaign, and maintains a sense of momentum for the greater campaign effort. When regional campaigns founder, however, morale deteriorates, momentum is lost, and the fatigue of campaigning overwhelms volunteers and professionals alike.

CONCLUSION

The concept of capital campaigns will be as important, if not even more so, during the early part of the new century as it was during the 1980s and 1990s. There will be many new techniques employed by the successful institutions, however, such as electronic prospect screening. Goals will continue to increase, and major and principal gifts will play an even more crucial role in the success of campaigns. The basic concepts of fund raising have not and will not change. Philanthropists are more generous than ever before, and there are more and more individuals practicing philanthropy. Principal gifts in the $50 million, $100 million, and greater range are more prevalent than ever before. The differences in campaigns will be in scale and scope rather than in the basic principles of fund raising. Some critics say that mega-campaigns have focused efforts on how many dollars are sought rather than the purposes for which funds are sought, that billion-dollar goals cause even million-dollar donors to question the impact of their support, and that annual fund donors feel lost among the hoopla created for major donors. Some say that the mega-campaign goals reflect institutional greed.

The imagination and skill of fund-raising professionals will be tested during this century, which has begun with a far less optimistic economic environment than prevailed the last two decades of the twentieth century. Professional development officers have the responsibility to provide optimism and confidence, reality and pragmatism. They are often the source of donors' imagination and vision and volunteers' energy and enthusiasm. They will be the architects of a new era of campaigning.

Education's need for philanthropic support will not diminish. The challenge will be to understand and react to the changes required and to lead institutions to success.

NOTES

1. Harold J. Seymour, *Designs for Fund-raising* (New York: McGraw-Hill, 1966), 42–43. Other excellent discussions of the case statement can be found

in Richard D. Chamberlain's chapter in *The Successful Capital Campaign: From Planning to Victory Celebration*, ed. H. Gerald Quigg (Washington, DC: Council for Advancement and Support of Education, 1986), 87–94, and in Kent Dove's *Conducting a Successful Capital Campaign*, 2nd edition (San Francisco: Jossey-Bass, 2000), 59–67.

2. Edward T. Foote II, "The President's Role in a Capital Campaign," in *The Successful Capital Campaign*, 73.

3. Council for Advancement and Support of Education and National Association of College and University Business Officers, *Expenditures in Fund Raising, Alumni Relations, and other Constituent (Public) Relations* (Washington, DC: Council for Advancement and Support of Education, 1990).

PART V

Corporate and Foundation Support

orporations and foundations—important sources of support for higher education—differ from individual donors in important ways. This means that development professionals who work with these organizations must have specialized knowledge and skills.

Whereas individual donors may be motivated by altruism and perhaps make giving decisions based on emotion as well as reason, corporate and foundation giving is generally based almost entirely on reasoned strategies. Corporations increasingly determine their philanthropy in relationship to their overall business plans and goals. They may prefer to establish partnerships or outright commercial relationships with colleges and universities, instead of, or even in connection with, more traditional forms of support. Corporate giving officers must demonstrate that the company's relationships with colleges and universities have a positive impact on its business success.

There are several categories of foundations, and their approaches to giving (or "grant making") differ significantly. For example, family foundations reflect the priorities of family members, and relationships with them will follow the principles of individual fund raising. But, many foundations have become highly professionalized and make their decisions based on well-defined missions and guidelines. The purpose of such foundations is to advance the mission of the foundation rather than the growth of any specific institution, and they will select their grant recipients based on their "capability" rather than their "need."

To say that the support of corporations and foundations reflects their own interests and purposes is not to disparage. Indeed, the boards and executives of these organizations have both legal responsibilities and moral obligations to their stockholders or founding donors that require that approach. While positive human relationships are helpful in any endeavor, developing support from corporate and foundation sources must recognize their goals and responsibilities. It requires the corporate or foundation development officer to seek a match between the goals of his or her institution and the goals of the funder, to develop a "partnership" that serves mutual interests.

Increasingly, campus professionals who work with corporations and foundations need to have more than fund-raising skills. They also need to have a deep understanding of academic programs and research, and possess an understanding of complex business relationships. Some campuses are altering the organization of corporate and foundation relations to include new reporting relationships and structures to provide this perspective across the institution.

In Chapter 12, Chris Withers describes the current landscape in corporate support of higher education, elaborating on some of the trends mentioned in this introduction. In Chapter 13, Marianne Jordan provides a similar overview of the evolving relationship between higher education and foundations.

CHAPTER 12

New Patterns of Corporate Support

D. Chris Withers

W hy do corporations make contributions to colleges, universities, and other organizations? After all, they exist to make money, and when they give it away it eats into their profits. Traditionally, there have been at least three justifications: (1) altruism (to improve society), (2) perceived political interest (funding organizations that support specific political positions that benefit the corporation), and (3) to increase a company's reputation and image. These reasons still exist, but today, more and more corporate giving is focused on the single goal of improving the corporate bottom line.

"True corporate giving is dead." "The days of 100 percent corporate philanthropic giving are gone." "Most corporate giving is really just marketing money now." These are just some of the very direct and pointed statements heard in 2001 when this author informally polled a variety of nationally known and respected fund-raising consultants and corporate-giving officers from Fortune 500 companies. Their bluntness aside, it is clear that those in higher education cannot seek support within the corporate community in the traditional manner.

Support can no longer be assumed because a large number of alumni are employed by the corporation, nor because the company recruits on a particular campus, or because faculty consult with the company, or because the company is a vendor, or because there is a trustee sitting on its corporate board. Long the basis for receiving support from a company, none of these relationships any longer assures a major gift. These time-tested traditions have been replaced by words like "marketing," "branding," "cause-related marketing," "partnerships," "marketing contracts," and "in-kind giving."

Carolyn Cavicchio, in her analysis "Corporate Philanthropy in the New Millennium," indicates that "Corporate community involvement [has] become more attuned to trends in business, rather than the philanthropic sector: cause-related marketing, with its emphasis on consumers; employee volunteerism, as a tool in workforce recruitment and retention; and venture philanthropy, as an adaptation of the business model [are] fueling the growth of the new economy." She also notes that there are fewer corporate donors as mergers and acquisitions continue to play a major role. "In a *Business Week* survey of 46 companies that have been involved in a merger in 2000, only one company reported that its giving would increase. . . . As the new entities [AOL and Time Warner, Philip Morris and Nabisco, J. P. Morgan and Chase Manhattan] integrate their giving programs and seek to blend their often different philosophies and approaches, the experience of recent years suggests that fewer dollars and tighter giving guidelines will prevail. . . ."[1]

Corporate giving is different than individual giving. In the past, many large corporations were owned or controlled by single families, such as the Rockefellers or Fords. Thus, the company's philanthropy was motivated by the personal interests of the family. Later, as corporate management was transferred from founders to professional executives, corporate giving still often followed the personal interests and loyalties of top executives. But, corporate giving has changed. Now managers have to justify corporate philanthropy to stockholders based on how it serves the interest of the corporation. Today, giving is largely justified as marketing and public relations, as a tax strategy, or as a strategy for increasing the satisfaction of employees by enabling them to more fully participate in the life of a community.

This chapter will expand on the changing landscape in hopes of providing readers with a better understanding of how to navigate through the maze and continue to obtain corporate dollars for their institutions.

DEFINING THE SHIFT

Corporate giving made up 5.3 percent of all giving in 2000, totaling about $11 billion. This was an increase of just over 8 percent from the previous year. Corporations contributed about 1.2 percent of pre-tax profits, the same proportion as the previous year, but down from the highs in the mid-1980s, when they gave 2.6 percent. Giving to education

Figure 12.1
Giving by Corporations, 1970–2000

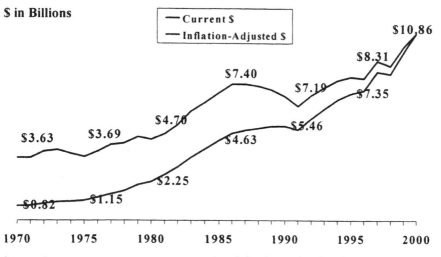

$ in Billions

Legend:
— Current $
— Inflation-Adjusted $

$10,86
$8.31
$7.40
$7.19
$7.35
$4.70
$5.46
$3.63 $3.69
$4.63
$2.25
$0.82 $1.15

1970   1975   1980   1985   1990   1995   2000

Source: *Giving USA 2001*, AAFRC Trust for Philanthropy (used with permission).

was the slowest growing category, down .7 percent from the previous year.

Compounding the overall reduction in corporate giving, the focus of corporate giving has shifted to institutions and causes outside of higher education. For example, K–12 education is a major emphasis of corporations now, as are other social causes.

More and more consumers expect companies to take action in support of social causes. They are acting on their feelings where it matters—at the cash register. Increasingly, a corporation's identity and reputation are tied to the causes it supports. Target Corporation is a good example because it donates 1 percent of individual purchases to the purchaser's favorite charity. The traditional notion of corporate philanthropy has been replaced by a much broader concept that is more akin to corporate activism. The Home Depot, Ben & Jerry's Homemade Holdings, Inc., and Starbucks Corporation are three retailers that have raised the bar with a wide range of initiatives benefiting employees, the environment, and the communities they serve. The Home Depot is one of the few retailers to issue an annual social responsibility report. The company's community service emphasis is on affordable housing, at-risk youth, and environmental and disaster relief. Ben & Jerry's gives back a whopping 7.5 percent of its pre-tax earnings to the community through corporate

Figure 12.2
Corporate Giving As a Percentage of Pretax Income, 1970–2000

% of Pretax Income

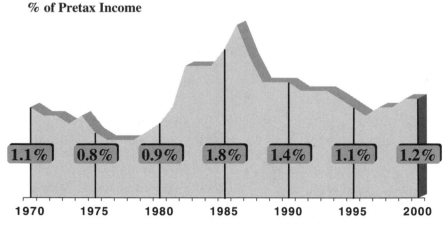

Source: *Giving USA 2001*, AAFRC Trust for Philanthropy (used with permission).

philanthropy that is primarily employee led (remember the national average is slightly over 1 percent).

Businesses today have become very creative in establishing links with
their communities. These links reflect a philosophy of "hands-on philanthropy." For example, in Richmond, Virginia, Ukrop's Super Markets,
a local grocer, has a "Golden Receipts" program whereby they contribute
up to 2 percent of the total cash receipts to the charity of the purchaser's
choice. The Home Depot builds houses for Habitat for Humanity, and
LensCrafters distributes glasses to the needy.

Canon USA, Inc., established a program they called "Ambassadors,"
enabling employees to apply for Canon grants to use toward the charity
they actively support. It helped provide grants of up to $500 for indi-
vidual employee projects and up to $1,500 for projects involving two or
more Canon employees as a team.[2]

Agvortal.com, Inc., a company that provides comprehensive internet
solutions for small- and medium-sized businesses involved in small-town,
rural economies, has created a community partners program whereby
they donate 50 percent of sales to institutions that have a focus on
revitalizing small-town America. Basically, they are funding a community development bank for venture capital and social venture capital
investments in small towns. The objective is to invest in higher-risk,
yet high-impact potential economic opportunities in those small towns
that have never received their share of American risk capital.[3]

In order for colleges and universities to capture the interest of companies operating in this arena, it will be necessary to go beyond describing their own educational programs to demonstrating how they also are working as partners in serving local community needs. But, this is not always easy to accomplish and does not address the needs of higher education institutions for support of their own core mission of education and research.

Another changing pattern of corporate giving that affects colleges and universities is the reduction in matching gift programs. Some companies once matched on a 4-to-1, a 3-to-1, or a 2-to-1 basis. Now 84 percent of the companies offer only a 1-to-1 match. IBM, which once had one of the most generous matching gift programs, is cutting back its program and is giving more computers and other gifts in-kind.

Higher education benefited from higher matching ratios, since these corporate dollars multiplied the impact of alumni giving. In today's new environment, this "automatic" corporate support is reduced, and colleges and universities must compete with other kinds of organizations for corporate giving.

Finally, it is not just changes in corporate financial support that have affected colleges and universities. Some also note a decrease in the voluntary participation of corporate officers, who once were the backbone of volunteer leadership for many institutions. J. David Ross, President of Ross, Johnston & Kersting, Inc., observes, "It is . . . more difficult than ever to get the very senior corporate executives to play key volunteer roles in upcoming campaigns. Many of them are on planes most of the time, which leaves little time for local commitments. They only make four or five calls in two or three years which is significantly less than in previous campaigns." He concludes, "For higher education, it's not good news."[4]

CAUSE-RELATED MARKETING

Corporate contributions regularly come through the "marketing" department now, and a tangible return to the company is expected. Cause-related marketing is straddling the line between philanthropy and advertising, yet it's becoming increasingly common because it promotes the company's product by making a gift to a nonprofit organization.

Sandy Stoddart, Executive Director at Circuit City Foundation, emphasizes the growing relationship between corporate giving and its marketing strategies. Circuit City, for example, is now developing marketing and is branding community partnerships by working with their human relations department. The goal is to position the corporation so that it is known as the "employer of choice" and to build their brand around it. Stoddart calls it "very measurable, targeted giving." They are no longer "just handing out checks." In this strategic change, Circuit City has decided to focus its annual giving on a single national organization rather than making small contributions to a number of groups. They recently announced a partnership with the national Boys and Girls Clubs of America, committing $3 million to be distributed over three years to assist Boys and Girls Clubs with creating a photography program and sponsoring a national photography contest. Those funds will help Boys and Girls Clubs buy cameras and other photographic equipment, build darkrooms, and train students. Circuit City also has conducted a fund-raising event at a store opening in Louisville, Kentucky, where the University of Louisville basketball coach signed basketballs that were sold for $50 each, and the funds were donated to the Boys and Girls Clubs. The company's partnership with the Boys and Girls Clubs allows for significant mentoring and training, so thousands of volunteers will see the Circuit City name every single day, strengthening the brand and its image.[5] It is this type of visibility and impact that corporate philanthropy today is intended to achieve.

MARKETING CONTRACTS

Some corporate gifts are tied directly to the sale of corporate products. Often these arrangements involve vending contracts with the institution. For example, a number of institutions have signed contracts with major beverage companies agreeing to dispense only their products both on and off campus, including at alumni events. Universities also have outsourced certain services to corporate providers, for example, bookstores that are outsourced to Barnes & Noble, coffee shops run by Starbucks, and facilities maintenance contracted to ServiceMaster or one of the other firms in the industry. In many cases, contracts for such services also include a commitment by the company to make some gifts to the college or university.

These gifts are often made without much fanfare, and some people question whether they are truly "gifts" in the traditional sense of the word. But, it is clear that many companies do tie their support of colleges and universities to such business relationships, and it is becoming more difficult than ever to obtain support from the competitors of companies with which the institution does business.

SPONSORSHIPS

Corporate sponsorships, rather than typical corporate grants, are becoming increasingly common in higher education and throughout the nonprofit sector. For example, colleges and universities across the country are granting significant naming opportunities in return for corporate sponsorship of their arenas, theaters, or playing fields. Other examples might include having the corporate logo on a brochure being distributed at an event, such as homecoming weekend, or the company's visible sponsorship of a gala opening or tour of an art exhibit.

According to Patricia Martin, a marketing consultant with The Martin Resource Group, Inc., "Sponsorship has grown into a $6 billion business world-wide."[6] The goals of sponsorship are far different from those of grant making, and the funds generally come from a completely separate part of the corporation. Sponsorship funding requires a major shift in concept. Sponsors measure the effectiveness of their investment by how well their affiliation with a cause or event helps shape consumer attitude, raise brand awareness, and generate sales.

Development officers are used to "making the case for support" to the corporate contributions staff based on the merits of an institution. With sponsorships, the case must be made to the marketing and public relations department based on the business benefits to the company. Development officers once would start with the corporate CEO, perhaps working through a member of the college or university board who knows the CEO. But, promoting a sponsorship relationship usually starts with staff in the sales or marketing department rather than any personal relationships with senior corporate leaders.

IN-KIND GIVING

More corporations are making in-kind contributions rather than monetary gifts or grants. For example, technology companies are giving computers, printers, and software, but consumer product manufacturers are using gifts-in-kind as well. For example, Avon, which contributed over $57 million to charity in 2000, says that 30 percent of it represented company products, including skin care and personal care products, fragrances, clothing, jewelry, and other types of goods. These contributions were made to an organization called Gifts-in-Kind International. This organization serves as a "middleman" for in-kind gifts of company products, receiving them from the companies and then redistributing them to United Way affiliated organizations and others across the country.[7]

Some other points help to show the increase of in-kind giving:

- The Conference Board, a business membership and research network based in New York City, calculates that 28 percent of all corporate charitable contributions in 1999 were in the form of gifts in-kind. Office Depot and Gifts-in-Kind International have created a unique program that provides high quality office merchandise to charities that impact health, welfare, and educational institutions. Their product gifts range from computers and printers to Post-its and paper.[8]

- The July 26, 2001, issue of *The Chronicle of Philanthropy* reported that the Microsoft Corporation gave 85.2 percent of its philanthropy as gifts-in-kind. Kroger, Minnesota Mining & Manufacturing Company (3-M), Hewlett-Packard, IBM, Sears Roebuck, Johnson & Johnson, Bristol-Myers Squibb, Merck, and Pfizer all did more than 50 percent of their giving in products.[9]

- The same issue of *The Chronicle of Philanthropy* also detailed how Pacific Gas, J. C. Penny, Aetna, and Kimberly Clark are changing the way they give. J. C. Penny, for example, will have all its support go as in-kind gifts to after-school programs. All four companies are more carefully aligning their philanthropic programs with corporate business goals.[10]

PARTNERSHIPS AND JOINT VENTURES

Some of the most interesting relationships between corporations and higher education institutions today involve partnerships, often based on common interests in research, and even joint business ventures in which both the corporation and the university hold a financial stake. Many of these relationships are complex, and negotiating them requires the expertise of the institution's business officer as well as the chief development officer. While more common at research universities than at smaller institutions, and especially prevalent at universities with strength in fields such as engineering, medicine, and science, such partnerships continue to grow as an aspect of relationships between higher education and the corporate world.

CONCLUSION

This author's chapter on corporate support in *Educational Fund Raising: Principles and Practice*, published in 1993, said, "Times have changed because of the recession. . . . This is not a good time to seek major corporate support." After the long economic boom of the 1990s, it is ironic that this chapter is being written in 2001, when those 1993 words seem relevant again. Hopefully, by the time the reader is studying this chapter, the environment will have changed for the better yet again. Even so, corporate relationships with higher education are forever changed.

Corporations are no longer persuaded by emotional appeals or such perks as special seating at events or parking privileges. There must be far more accountability in building a justifiable relationship. The corporate emphasis on developing long-term partnerships with specific institutions is one that those in higher education development will need to understand and work within. Colleges and universities must begin to build multifaceted relationships, which may include research partnerships, opportunities for on-campus recruitment, executive exchange, professional training, and a variety of other contacts.

Although the state of the economy will most likely eventually strengthen substantially, it seems unlikely that corporate giving will ever return to the high levels of the 1980s, and it seems equally unlikely that the patterns of corporate support of higher education will ever return to the traditional model.

NOTES

1. Carolyn Cavicchio, "Corporate Philanthropy in the New Millennium," onPhilanthropy.com (http://www.Changingourworld.com), viewed June 21, 2001.

2. "Canon U.S.A. Creates Ambassadors Program to Support Local Volunteer Efforts," *Fund Raising Management* (June 1999): 7.

3. "Agvortal.com Announces Paradigm Shift in Venture Philanthropy," *Dow Jones Interactive Newstand* (May 1, 2001): 1.

4. David Ross, telephone conversation with author, June 28, 2001.

5. Sandy Stoddard, telephone conversation with author, April 19, 2001.

6. "It's Not Just About Applying for Grants Anymore," *Corporate Giving Watch* 20, no. 2, (April 2000): 1–2.

7. Elizabeth A. Amery, "In Kind Giving: It's a Beautiful Thing," onPhilanthropy.com (http://www.Changingourworld.com), viewed June 21, 2001.

8. Elizabeth A. Amery, "Expanding the Strategic Role of In-Kind Giving," onPhilanthropy.com (http://www.Changingourworld.com), viewed June 21, 2001.

9. Debra E. Blum and Martha Voelz, "Corporate Donations Cool Off," *The Chronicle of Philanthropy* 23, no. 19 (July 26, 2001): 14–15.

10. Ibid., 13.

CHAPTER 13

New Patterns of Foundation Support

Marianne Jordan

T he roaring stock market in the middle to late 1990s boosted all private giving, including that of foundations. The Dow Jones Industrial Average quadrupled from 1993 to 2000, growth that created this country's most prosperous peacetime economy. Foundation assets parallel stock and bond market performance and soared during the 1990s. In 2000, foundation grant dollars increased by an estimated $4.3 billion, surpassing an increase of $3.9 billion in 1999, reaching a total of $27.6 billion. Overall, foundation giving doubled from 1996 to 2000, outpacing all other private giving.[1] It accounted for 12% of all private philanthropy in 2000, compared to 7.3% in 1990.[2]

Federal law requires foundations to pay out at least 5 percent of their assets each year. During the flush times of the late 1990s, some suggested that the federal government increase foundations' required payout rate. Some experts in philanthropy have also suggested that foundations spend from their endowments and not try to preserve their assets in perpetuity; in other words, that they set a finite time frame for spending all of the foundation's assets in order to make a bigger social impact. Some foundations are doing so, for example, the Whitaker Foundation in Arlington, Virginia. Others would not be permitted to spend their assets in order to be in keeping with the original intent of the donor.

While some foundations are being liquidated, new ones have been created. Investors made a tremendous amount of money in the stock market in the 1990s, and some used their disposable income and assets to create foundations. In 1999, more than 3,300 foundations were created (with assets of $1 million or more), and existing family foundations' assets grew as well. The Bill and Melinda Gates Foundation led this growth curve; by 2001, its assets stood at $21.8 billion, and the foundation was distributing $1 billion annually in grants to local nonprofits and to large international organizations.

TYPES OF FOUNDATIONS

Most of the growth in foundation giving has been from the independent and family foundations, including the new health foundations, formed from nonprofit healthcare conversions.[3] The Council on Foundations (www.cof.org/glossary/index.htm) defines various kinds of foundations as follows.

Independent Foundations (Also Called *Private Foundations*)

Independent foundations usually are created by one individual, often by bequest. They are also called *non-operating foundations* because they do not run their own programs. Sometimes groups of people, usually family members, form a foundation while the donors are still alive. Such foundations are known as *family foundations* since the assets come from one family and family members are often involved in managing them. Many larger foundations were once run by family, but are now run by professional staff members. Independent foundations are the primary type with which higher education works.

Family foundations are one of the fastest growing categories. The highly touted intergenerational transfer of wealth from the WWII generation to the baby boomers has begun and is having an impact. In addition, many of the entertainers and entrepreneurs who have made their wealth in the last 20 years are establishing foundations that are closely aligned with their personal interests, including Doris Duke, Barbra Streisand, Steven Spielberg, Michael Milken, David Geffen, and Ted Turner. Among grant makers in the late 1990s, the Foundation Center identified 20,500 family foundations.[4] Between 1980 and 1989, more than 3,000 foundations with assets of $1 million or more were created. More than 3,300 foundations were established in 1999 alone. For comparison, only 600 foundations were created before 1940. The Council on Foundations notes that most family funds donate locally. Today it is estimated that family members advise two-thirds of private foundations.[5]

Most new foundations have not targeted higher education as a priority, or if they have, their giving to higher education is local, or to the donor or his or her family members' alma mater(s). The donor or his or her designated executive runs many of these foundations, and the foundation's programmatic interests are tightly connected to their personal interests or the impact they can have globally.

Some colleges *are* developing relationships with these smaller foundations, but again there has to be a tight fit between the donor's interests and the college's existing programs or strengths. A question for development officers to contemplate in the next decade is how to identify and cultivate more of these family foundations.

Community Foundations

Community foundations are autonomous, tax-exempt, nonprofit, publicly supported philanthropic institutions composed of permanent funds established by many donors for the long-term benefit of a defined geographic area.

Operating Foundations

Operating foundations support their own programs and rarely make outside grants. Examples include the Carnegie Endowment for International Peace and the Getty Trust.

Corporate Foundations

Corporate foundations are formed through donations of the parent corporation to its own specific foundation, such as the AT&T Foundation. Such foundations are sometimes the exclusive giving arm of the company; in other cases the corporate foundation exists alongside direct giving programs administered within the company itself.

FOUNDATION TRENDS AFFECTING HIGHER EDUCATION

Witnessing the robust economy of the 1990s and the corresponding increase in foundation giving, some people may have thought that grant money was there for the taking. But, this is not true for higher education, especially not for undergraduate institutions.

Higher Education's Share Is Declining

Education as a whole received 24% of all foundation dollars in 2000, totaling $2.8 billion. This included support for colleges, universities, and nonprofit foundations for elementary and secondary schools, libraries, tutoring and literacy agencies, as well as vocational and technical schools. As indicated in the following tabulation, higher education accounts for the largest share of these education dollars. But, foundations' level of commitment to higher education has changed. Undergraduate education accounted for 12.1% of all grant dollars in 2000, up from 11.3% in 1999.[6] However, that percentage had been 14% in 1994, reflecting an overall downward trend.

Education Dollars from Foundations

Higher Education	46%
Precollegiate Education	25%
Graduate and Professional Schools	15%
Libraries and Educational Services	10%
To Foundations	4%

Source: Steven Lawrence, *Foundation Giving Trends*
(New York: Foundation Center, 2001), 11.

The established, older foundations (for example, Ford, Carnegie, Rockefeller, and Pew) are no longer significant players in the field of higher education. They have turned their attention to the support of more socially oriented nonprofits. Part of the reason for this change is that beginning with the Reagan Administration (and especially after the 1994 midterm congressional elections and the "Contract with America"), public funding for nonprofits decreased. Federal programs turned funding over to state and local municipalities and to foundations, none of which has the resources to fund the seemingly infinite social needs at the same level as the federal government. During the 1990s, foundations continued to support all kinds of organizations providing for the common good—healthcare organizations, human service groups, public/societal benefit agencies, arts and cultural institutions, as well as K–12 private and public educational institutions. The 1990s foundation agenda also included social causes, such as civil rights, women's rights, and science and technological development. This new role for foundations as public welfare provider, however, has cast their giving to higher education in a new mold.

As noted above, several national foundations that were key supporters of higher education in the 1980s and early 1990s withdrew altogether from higher education funding. Of the top 25 foundations defined by total giving in 1999, only a handful funded undergraduate programs on a regular and national basis. Prominent supporters continued to be the Andrew W. Mellon, Arthur Vining Davis, Henry R. Luce and Starr Foundations. Some national foundations funded college and university consortia, but within these arrangements colleges simply cannot play up their individual or unique strengths, which was the basis for a strong case in a grant proposal. This loss is profound for the colleges that had come to rely on the participation of the old stalwarts of higher education funding, such as the Pew Charitable Trusts, to bring about change and innovation on their campuses.

Foundations made this change because their trustees felt as if they could no longer make grants that would have lasting impact upon an individual campus. Colleges' needs have become more complex with the advent of technology and are too expensive compared with the limited resources of foundations.

In addition, some family foundations believe that grants for social needs have greater impact than those made to the "sacred cows" (including higher education), where $50,000 is just "a drop in the bucket."[7] It is hard, if not impossible, to argue that problems such as HIV, malaria and other diseases of the underdeveloped world, air and water pollution, the depletion of biodiversity, and world peace are unimportant issues. They *are* important, to colleges and universities as well, but support for organizations serving these causes directly clearly has reduced the foundation resources available to higher education.

Increased Emphasis on Relevance and Accountability

One reason for higher education's diminishing share of grants is an increased focus on "goods delivered" and some question as to whether higher education institutions can deliver the most "bang" for the foundation's "buck." For example, the Pew Charitable Trusts is currently gathering data on whether higher education is serving its constituents well. Some also question how much "need" many colleges possess. As of 2000, there were 47 private and public colleges and universities with endowments of $1 billion or more. It may be that recent flush economic times, which increased colleges' capacities to self-fund, made colleges appear less needy and thus less deserving of foundation support. The self-funding that colleges were able to do in the middle to late 1990s in turn may have led to a complacency among college faculty members, who could ask their institutions to fund their research and teaching needs rather than having to rely on a riskier competitive external grant process.

During the 1990s, foundations began holding their higher education grantees more accountable. During the 1980s and early 1990s, evaluation plans in a proposal could be minimal; today they are essential for success. Foundations are requiring serious evaluation plans so that the donor will have a record of how their dollars were put to use. Program officers emphasize the importance of evaluation plans so that they can justify their work to their boards.

An opposing tension is that many educational institutions did not previously have a sophisticated knowledge of program evaluation. Although books on the subject abound, such evaluation is very often alien to a college campus culture, where faculty efforts are directed at the more abstract notions of good teaching and learning. Following on the stringent, congressionally mandated requirements of federal agencies to require of their grant recipients a clear evaluation plan, foundations will no longer accept a proposal that does not show evidence of an outcome assessment plan. This positive trend could result in continuous improvement on the part of the colleges and could provide foundations with the measure they need to assure themselves and their boards that their grants are being put to good use.

Undergraduate Education Is Less Favored

Undergraduate colleges were once an institution type that foundations favored because many of their family members and trustees attended them, and foundations regarded them as synonymous with quality—for example, Harvard, Princeton, Yale, Rice, Amherst, Swarthmore, and Williams. This too has changed.

Today, when foundations do support higher education, less than one-quarter of grants are for broad educational programs. When broken down as to type of award within the category of education grants, 34% of dollars benefited specific disciplines, most found at research universities but not undergraduate colleges. A subject breakdown by the Foundation Center shows that of the foundation dollars granted to educational institutions, the largest areas of benefit were health (32%), followed by science (18%), arts and culture (12%), social science (10%), public/

society benefit (9%), human service (7%), environment and animals (5%), and international affairs and religion, 3% each.[8] Grants being made are mostly programmatic, and they are restricted to narrow program areas.

Running somewhat against this trend are the Lilly Endowment and the Freeman Foundation. Lilly's assets grew to $15 billion in 2000, and Freeman's to $1.6 billion. In 2000, for the first time, Lilly invited undergraduate institutions from outside of Indiana and the Midwest to submit proposals. The Lilly Request for Proposal (RFP) targeted the development of religious vocations, broadly defined. Non-Indiana undergraduate colleges were happy to be on Lilly's radar screen and scrambled to make strong proposals. The endowment made sizable grants to undergraduate colleges. Some colleges approached Lilly to ask to be included on their invitation list, also a growing practice among grants officers. Freeman also issued a broad-based RFP, and granted close to $100 million to 87 institutions for undergraduate Asian Studies programs. Most grant recipients were first-time Freeman awardees.

Pew is a good example of changing foundation priorities because it was once at the core of undergraduate educational funding. The trusts are now funding high-level policy issues; where they once funded constituents' needs, they are now looking to be honest brokers on social issues and to address problems that affect the whole constituency. Foundations want impact and are trying to be focused and strategic. The trusts' work focuses on presidential campaign finance reform, public school reform, performance assessment of higher educational institutions, and the environment. On the latter, the trusts have taken an assertive stance and are confronting the government and private corporations on vast issues such as protection of old-growth forests and wilderness areas, climate change, energy conservation and renewable resources, and ocean protection. Unless a college or university has a special niche in one of these areas, or has built a special mousetrap, they will not receive Pew grant funding in the near future.

Bricks and Mortar Foundations Have Become Few and Far Between

In the mid-1990s, the F. W. Olin Foundation became a beacon, lighting the way toward the rejuvenation and replacement of aging facilities. In 1995, the foundation doubled its funding to $40 million a year, leading many colleges to hope for their turn with Olin. Because they paid for the entire cost of a building, Olin's grants were especially appealing (and difficult to obtain). In 1997, the foundation awarded a $300 million grant to establish and endow the F. W. Olin School of Engineering adjacent to the campus of Babson College. Since then, the foundation has continued to fund only this new university and one or two other institutions.

Another primary funder of undergraduate colleges' capital needs in the 1990s was the W. M. Keck Foundation. As of the late 1990s, this foundation too had moved away from capital to programmatic grants, hoping to have more of an impact by funding national program models rather than a small handful of facilities on individual campuses. The only national bricks and mortar foundation remaining for higher educational institutions is the Kresge Foundation.

The Shift to Request for Proposals

A Foundation Center report (customized report) comparing higher education grant patterns in 1992 and 2000 illustrates the changing nature of foundation giving to higher education. In 1992, 12.6% of foundation support went toward capital projects, including building/renovation, endowments, equipment, and computer systems. In 2000, this percentage was 9.4. On the other hand, program support increased from 32.3% to 35.4% over this same period. There is a sense among foundation boards and program officers that they have supported higher education's capital and endowment needs in the past, and the current role of foundations in our society is to promote new activities and programs.

The point of leverage with foundations has changed. Whereas college leaders and grants officers once visited foundation program officers to review the college's list of funding priorities, now they can hope only to influence the nature of future RFPs, or discuss "the fit" within existing RFPs. It is harder for a college president to initiate or get a hearing on the college's needs and dreams. Foundations see their jobs as trying to get out ahead of social problems and to stay focused on a few themes or programs.[9]

Grants from national foundations once provided the quintessential "edge" for undergraduate colleges, enabling them to add that little bit of extra value to make students' experiences that much better. Because of the downturn in the economy in 2000 and 2001 when the Standard & Poor's Index dropped 25% and many colleges' endowments dropped, the lack of federal or state funding increases, and the increased cost of doing business, colleges need those enrichment dollars now more than ever. However, foundations are not funding colleges' and universities' core needs.

Since the early 1990s, foundations have been looking for impact through the seeding of programs. They have asked grant recipients to use their grants to leverage other philanthropic dollars, thus allowing foundations to catalyze change and innovation. Foundations place the burden for sustaining innovation on the college or university campus squarely on the institution. In reaction, colleges have become very cautious about new programs, projects, or faculty positions. And so, program funding cuts both ways.

Foundations are defining their own programmatic areas of interest, sometimes in consultation with colleges and universities, and sometimes not. The Andrew W. Mellon Foundation conducted consultative practices during the 1990s. Mellon executives and program officers invited groups of college representatives to their offices to discuss critical issues in higher education. Then they issued RFPs based on these conversations. The Henry R. Luce Foundation also consulted broadly before making recommendations for new programs to their board. Many of Mellon's and Luce's programs are targeted to undergraduate colleges and universities, and both foundations' assets are among the top 50.

Some foundations that traditionally supported higher education made their decisions about RFPs and changes to programs based on expert and board opinion, not consultation with colleges.

ADDITIONAL TRENDS IN FOUNDATION SUPPORT

Science Funding Is Down

Many experts in philanthropy predicted that the 1990s would begin an era when science funding would continue to grow. In the early 21st century, this trend has begun to taper off, with grants to science being slightly down in number. Foundation funding for science increased in the number of dollars awarded for science from 1998 to 1999. However, there was a minus 1% change in the number of grants awarded in the sciences. Between 1999 and 2000, the share of foundation grants to science did not grow at all. This trend is significant for undergraduate colleges, many of whom ratcheted up their science programs to meet workplace demands for scientifically literate employees and citizens. Now, many of these colleges must fund their own science teaching and research needs and can do so in collaboration with the federal government, especially the National Science Foundation. Several foundations still favor the sciences over the other academic areas, including the Beckman Foundation and the Keck Foundation in California. However, these grants grow increasingly competitive as the number of colleges paying attention to the quality of their science programs has increased.

Geographical Shift

During the 1960s and 1970s, the majority of new foundations created were to be found in the Northeast. As the population began to shift west and south, so did foundation wealth. In 1998, for example, the South experienced the fastest growth in the number of new foundations, followed by the West. Much of the foundation growth in the West is a result of bequests received in the late 1970s or early 1980s, such as the J. Paul Getty Trust in California.[10] And now, of course, there is the Gates Foundation. The Northeast still reports the largest gain in actual number of foundations, but the rate of growth favors the South and West. In fact, a recent study states that California foundations' giving and assets grew at a greater rate than the total giving and assets of all grant makers in the United States. California foundations were second only to New York.[11]

Changed Patterns in Corporate Foundations

Corporate foundation giving accounted for one-quarter of corporate giving in 1999, and foundation corporate giving grew slightly faster than overall corporate contributions. In 1999, corporate foundations targeted close to a quarter of their grant dollars for program support. In addition, they allocated 10% for capital expenses and only 1.3% for research. Operating support accounted for 10% of their contributions, a decline from previous years.[12] While this differs from the trend in foundation giving in the type of dollars awarded, the amount of corporate foundation dollars is relatively small.

More charitable dollars come from the corporations themselves rather than through their corporate foundations, and (as discussed in Chapter 12) many corporations make contributions in forms other than gifts or grants—through their marketing, public affairs, and research and development departments. These contributions might be cash or equipment or personnel donations, and they involve mutually beneficial partnerships.

Web Connections

No foundation had a Web site until the early to middle 1990s. More than 1,500 (of the 55,000) foundations currently maintain Web sites, making them more accessible to their public. Still, only the larger foundations have Web sites. Many of the smaller family foundations do not wish to be this accessible to the public, or they do not have the staff to create and maintain such communications.

Foundations offer Web-based information about grants made, deadlines, contact information, and program descriptions. Web connections at colleges and universities are nearly ubiquitous, and so this trend has enhanced communication between grant maker and grant seeker. Grant seekers can easily and seamlessly ask questions of program officers via electronic mail as they read through the foundation's Web pages. This kind of electronic process provides the grant seeker with the power of current information and frees up the program officer to concentrate on more substantive issues.

Program-Related Investments

Program-Related Investments (PRIs) are low-cost loans for projects at organizations, which match the foundation's stated interests. They represented a new trend in foundation giving in the 1990s, whose origin and growth coincided with the stock market rise. Since 1997, PRI distributions have climbed by more than four-fifths.[13] PRIs have primarily been made to help community development projects, which eventually become self-funding. While PRIs total only 1% of the grants total, this strategy is growing in significance for the community development sector. However, PRIs are not relevant for most colleges, who can already borrow at favorable rates.

CONCLUSION: BASIS FOR A NEW PARTNERSHIP?

As this chapter has noted, the historic relationship between foundations and higher education institutions has, with the exception of some family foundations, changed significantly in the past decade to the disadvantage of colleges and universities seeking foundation support. Some wonder if there is any basis for renewing the interest of national foundations in the programs of higher education institutions. One college president I interviewed said that he hoped the tragic events of September 11, 2001, might prompt foundations such as Ford to do something "counter-cyclical," and return to supporting undergraduate education, perhaps starting with international studies programs and other international aspects of the curriculum. Colleges have been including courses on globalism in their curricula, and many students travel overseas on Junior Year Abroad programs. However, the connection between these courses and experiences and the world's business is now much clearer. Higher education with an international dimension is clearly more relevant than ever before.

Foundations and corporations contributed $1 billion in response to the events of September 11. But these are short-term and perhaps once-in-a-lifetime grants. Some college presidents and foundation heads are asking about the longer term and are reflecting on their values, reexamining their larger purposes. How can colleges help solve the terrible worldwide problem of terrorism? Foundations are also talking about funding programs that address the causes of global unrest. To make this sort of change would indeed be counter-cyclical; and, it could enable foundations and educational institutions to join together in a meaningful partnership to ameliorate a serious societal problem.

NOTES

1. Loren Renz and Steven Lawrence, *Foundation Growth and Giving Estimates, 2000 Preview* (New York: Foundation Center, 2001), 3.

2. Melissa S. Brown, ed., *Giving USA 2001*, The Annual Report on Philanthropy for the Year 2000 (Indianapolis: AAFRC Trust for Philanthropy, 46th Annual Issue), 30.

3. Renz and Lawrence, *Foundation Growth and Giving Estimates*, 3.

4. Council on Foundations, Website, glossary (http://www.cof.org/glossary/index.htm).

5. Ibid.

6. Steven Lawrence, *Foundation Giving Trends* (New York: Foundation Center, 2000), 6.

7. Charles Weiss, "Family Foundations," in *Approaching Foundations: Suggestions and Insights for Fundraisers*," ed. Sandra A. Glass (New Directions for Philanthropic Fundraising, No. 28, Summer 2000).

8. Steven Lawrence, ed., *Foundation Giving Trends*, 33.

9. Council on Foundations (http://www.cof.org/future/index.htm).

10. Steven Lawrence, ed., *Foundation Center Yearbook* (New York: Foundation Center, 2001), 34.

11. "Giving and Assets of California Foundations Grow Faster than Those

of Other U.S. Grant Makers," *The Chronicle of Philanthropy* (December 13, 2001), 16.

12. Steven Lawrence and Loren Renz, *Foundation Giving Trends* (New York: Foundation Center, 2001), 62.

13. Brown, ed., *Giving USA 2001*, 71.

PART VI

Traditions of Giving

One advertising slogan that found its way into popular language said, "It's not your father's Oldsmobile." Indeed, the United States and the world today are not the ones our parents or grandparents would have recognized. The implications for educational fund raising in particular are considerable.

The subjects of demographics and cultures were not emphasized in the 1993 *Educational Fund Raising: Principles and Practice*. Although the trends were clear, many higher education development officers continued to think primarily in terms of the types of students and alumni who had traditionally attended colleges and universities and to think mostly about raising funds within the United States. In many instances, fundraising professionals in the nonprofit sector outside of higher education were quicker to recognize the ongoing changes in society and to reflect them in their strategies and methods. That is understandable, since their constituencies are more diverse and reflective of the broad society than are college and university alumni. Today, no institution can ignore the realities of a changing American population and a shrinking planet.

In Chapter 14, Judith Nichols discusses how individuals' generational cohorts influence their approach to giving. In Chapter 15, Andrea Kaminski outlines the philanthropic perspectives of women, who will comprise half or more of college and university alumni in the future and who are increasingly leaders in philanthropic activity. In Chapter 16, Joanne Scanlan and John Abrahams discuss the giving traditions of minority communities that comprise an increasing proportion of the American population and that will be increasingly represented in higher education in the decades ahead. Finally, in Chapter 17 Scott Nichols provides a review of international fund raising. Although not related to the changing American population in the way that the other chapters in this section are, Nichols's chapter illustrates that we live in a world in which the practice of educational fund raising crosses boundaries of all kinds—generational, cultural, and geographic.

CHAPTER 14

The Impact of Demographics

Judith E. Nichols

A quote often attributed to Albert Einstein goes as follows: "Insanity is when you do the same thing over and over and expect a different result." This sums up the dilemma many fund raisers find themselves in today as they attempt to make the tried-and-true fund-raising methodologies of the twentieth century work for the twenty-first. Too many fund raisers are still working under the old rules: assuming an unlimited pool of donors to be acquired, treating everyone as if they share common "generational anchors," and clinging to methodologies that today's savvy consumers are rejecting.

The reason the old techniques will not and cannot work is simply that the demographics and psychographics of the American people are changing. Demographics are sets of characteristics about people, for example, age, sex, marital status, education, and income. Psychographics are the measure of attitudes, values, or lifestyles, which may make one group behave differently from another. To effectively raise money, it is crucial to understand this new world and how it affects the reactions of prospective donors to fund-raising requests. This world is being shaped by the following trends:

- The populations of the developed world are aging. Proportionally, fewer new adults are entering the population than in past decades.
- Americans are living longer and are concerned about outliving their assets.

- Most Americans are idealistic middle-aged baby boomers with very different psychographics from the older audiences upon which institutions have depended for support.

- Women are making up a larger portion of our older population and thus gaining increasing responsibility for determining the disposition of large amounts of wealth.

- The United States is becoming more diverse ethnically and racially. Members of the white, non-Hispanic audiences have traditionally felt welcome as donors and volunteers in traditional organizations such as college and universities, but members of most minority groups have not.

- There are five key generations that will dominate the next 25 years, each with differing psychographics and financial lifestyles. Development professionals need to develop a different communication style for each.

- Lifestyle, not life state, determines a person's attitude toward philanthropy and the ability to act philanthropically.

- Baby boomer audiences are now middle-aged and pressed for time. Growth in involvement in formal activities may not keep pace with growth in population. Attendance at many types of special events will peak, slowing down and even dropping.

- Technology has moved rapidly, and younger audiences have different communication preferences. Whereas direct mail works best with those born before World War II, midlife audiences respond better to phone requests coupled with an advance letter or video, and young adults expect to be contacted via the computer.

THREE PARADIGM SHIFTS

Three major paradigm shifts—a fear of economic instability, a lessening of the bonds of community, and an increasing cynicism—can be traced to two key overall population changes encompassed in the above trends: increasing longevity and increasing diversity. Greater longevity is producing an increased reluctance to make significant charitable gifts from assets during one's life. The increasing diversity of the population, increasing mobility, and the growth of "virtual" communities are leading individuals to exhibit less donor loyalty than pre–World War II generations. And, the idealistic baby boomers and reactive generation Xers are demanding more results from their giving than did their parents and grandparents, who trusted colleges, universities, and other nonprofit organizations, viewing them as knowledgeable authorities.

Increased Longevity and the Fear of Economic Instability

The world is turning gray. Increasing longevity and declining birth rates are leading to a dramatic increase in the number of older persons throughout the world. At the start of the twentieth century, life expectancy was just 49 years. Today, at birth, Americans can expect to live past 76 years and, if they reach 75 years of age, may well live past 90.[1]

As a result of these trends—increasing longevity and falling birth rates—the number of persons age 45 or older grew almost 30 percent more than the rest of the population over the past two decades. In the forseeable future, America will not be a society of youth. A similar situation will be found in Canada as well as every developed nation. Older Americans increasingly will be the focus of society. When the twentieth century closed, there were 31 million people over 65, comprising just 12 percent of the population. The senior population will explode between now and 2030, when 70 million elderly will account for 20 percent of the U.S. population, up from just 34.5 million (13 percent) in 2000.

There have been lifestyle changes as well. Rather than viewing retirement as an end to active life, many older Americans now see it as a transition to new activities and for setting new goals. But, with retirements lasting 20 or 30 years or longer, the risk of outliving assets has become a major concern for many. It takes about 15 years for our perceptions to catch up with reality. Americans are just beginning to accept the fact that so many are living well into their eighties and nineties, rather than the "three score and ten" that previous generations assumed to be their lot in life. Donors, fearing the costs of aging, are concluding that giving away major assets during life rather than at death is foolish.

Increasing Diversity

Today's fund raisers face increasing diversity in the American population, defined by ethnicity, race, gender, and generation. While all forms of diversity are relevant to fund raising, this chapter focuses on diversity among various generations. Other chapters in this section discuss the changing philanthropic roles of women and members of minority communities.

The American population today can be divided into five generational groupings or cohorts. The terms "cohort" and "generation," though often used interchangeably, are not exactly the same. A generation is usually defined by its years of birth. Cohorts are better defined by events that occur at various critical points in the group's lifetime and that influence its views and attitudes. These five cohorts include today's and tomorrow's alumni, and the differences among them will require that colleges and universities involve them and communicate with them in varied ways.

Depression Babies. Currently aged 65 and older, persons born prior to 1935 have "civic" personalities. They believe it is the role of the citizen to fit into society and make it better. These "civics" came of age during the Depression, and many of them fought in World War II. Their shared experiences gave them two key characteristics: frugality and patriotism.

Shaped by memories of the stock market crash and the Great Depression, they have cautious spending habits. They tend to be cash payers and distrust the technology of the "cashless" society.

They are the twentieth century's confident, rational problem solvers, the ones who have always known how to get big things done. Civics have boundless optimism and a sense of public entitlement. They respect authority, leadership, and discipline. They are loyal to traditional institutions such as colleges and universities. Their preferred message style is rational and constructive, with an undertone of optimism.

Eisenhower Babies. Born between 1935 and 1945, this smaller group of "young elders" was taught to be "silent," believing in the will of the group rather than individuality. The ending of World War II, with the dropping of the atomic bomb on Hiroshima, and the Cold War, symbolized by the Berlin Wall, are their key life events.

Consensus builders rather than leaders, they are inclined to see both sides of every issue and are more concerned with fair process than with final results. They are value-oriented and loyal to traditional institutions. Their financial style is "save a little, spend a little." Their parents drilled the lessons of the Depression into them, but Eisenhower babies reached adulthood in golden economic days. Now in early retirement, many are willing to spend on themselves and giving. Their preferred message style is sensitive and personal, with an appeal to technical detail.

Baby Boomers. Our society's adult "idealists," born between 1946 and 1964, have been hard for the world to swallow. Boomers were told they could do anything and that life is a voyage of self-discovery. They display a bent toward inner absorption, perfectionism, and individual self-esteem. Taught from birth that they were special, boomers believe in changing the world, not changing to fit it. Key events in their lives include the assassinations of John and Robert Kennedy, Martin Luther

King, worldwide rock music, the campus-based activism of the 60s, and Watergate.

Having always lived in a world of inflation and having no memories of the Depression, they have a different understanding of money. They tend to buy first, pay later and like monthly payment plans and using credit cards. However, now in midlife, many are refocusing on non-materialistic values and are demanding a new assertion of community over individual wants. Their preferred message style is meditative and principled, with an undertone of pessimism.

Baby Busters (Generation X). The young adults born between 1965 and 1977 are the first generation that does not believe life will be better for them than for their parents. Twenty- and thirty-somethings—the "young alumni" of colleges and universities today—have a different view of the good life. They are less concerned with financial success and are more concerned with the acquisition of intangibles: a rich family and spiritual life, a rewarding job, the chance to help others, and the opportunity for leisure and travel or for intellectual and creative enrichment. Highly computer literate, they prefer the "cashless society."

Members of generation X also hold a skeptical view and will need convincing that your institution is worthy of their support. They prefer volunteer service before giving, and many will select only one or two organizations on which to focus their support. Their preferred message style is blunt and kinetic, with an appeal to brash survivalism.

Baby Boomlet. Individuals born from 1978 through 1992 hold many of the values of an earlier generation. Many are "civics" like the Depression generation. Technology and globalism will play important roles in shaping their lives. Often nicknamed "generation net," they are growing up in a world without boundaries and are likely to extend their philanthropy well past their own countries. Most of them have yet to hit our campuses, but many of them will be joining the ranks of alumni within the next decade.

A Growing Cynicism

Attitudes toward educational institutions and charitable organizations have become more critical. Although philanthropic organizations still enjoy more confidence than business corporations or government, Americans also know that some organizations are not ethical in their practices or in their use of gift funds. Some may be concerned that their money will not be used well.

In charitable giving, as in other areas of consumer decision making, the twenty-first century may well be the decade of the "smart shopper." In charitable giving this means choosing a few priorities and funding them more intensely.

CHANGING PHILANTHROPIC PRIORITIES

The top charitable recipients in the United States remain religious, educational, and health-related organizations, and the fine and performing arts. But, as a result of the trends discussed above, many individuals' priorities for giving are also changing. And, these changes do not necessarily favor traditional recipients such as colleges and universities.

With the advent of the global economy, Americans have begun to shift some support toward organizations serving national and international concerns. The availability of the Internet has created among younger donors a new way of researching charitable interests. With a click of the mouse, it is possible to browse through a worldwide list of potential charitable partners and contact them pro-actively rather than waiting passively for a letter or phone call.

As the older civics move off scene and younger idealists take center stage, society is moving from one that views philanthropy as a duty to one that sees it a "reward." Perhaps as a result of their more inner-directed attitudes, many middle-aged and younger Americans want to feel good about their giving and are less motivated by a sense of obligation. Less institutional, often smaller charities may find themselves in a better position than higher education institutions to connect to those with these desires.

The majority of higher education's private contributions come from older individuals. As the mature civics born at the first half of the twentieth century reach the end of their lives, many are making one-time major and planned gifts, which has obscured the fact that younger prospects do not necessarily see their colleges and universities as their giving priorities.

The majority of college and university alumni are, in fact, individuals born after World War II. It will take effort to communicate the rationale for giving to mid-life boomers and, increasingly, to generation Xers and netters. Higher education institutions face a particular challenge; the loyalty of these alumni is not automatic. With the expansion of college enrollments, younger generations' college experiences were not necessarily the positive, bonding ones their parents and grandparents experienced. Many post–World War II Americans have stopped seeing the college experience as unique.

CHANGING PATTERNS OF GIVING

The donor pyramid long has been a fundamental assumption of fundraising practitioners. But, it depicts a linear form of donor growth. The thinking goes like this: a prospect makes his or her first gift to your organization and, hopefully, moves on to become a regular annual donor. If the institution cultivates the relationship and the donor responds, the gifts become larger, and ultimately, the organization will receive a bequest or life income arrangement.

This linear approach made perfect sense when people led predictable lives and did not live as long as they do today. But, with today's life span of eighty or ninety years or more, lifestyle is as important as life stage in influencing giving. This may require a more cyclical approach to major gift fund raising, tied to the donor's changing priorities and interests. Development officers will need to be more attuned to finding the moments when individuals are ready to give, which means keeping more in touch with donors and prospects.

Thinking about broad-based fund raising for the annual gift must change as well. The proportion of the population that will consist of new adults entering the workplace will diminish. This will make it more and more difficult to acquire a broad base of donors at a cost-effective price. Therefore, it makes more sense than ever to work hard to keep and upgrade existing donors.

NEW FUND-RAISING STRATEGIES

Successful fund raising in this new environment and among the rising generations of alumni will require programs that reflect three important qualities:

1. Selectivity—the ability to reach an individual based on knowledge of his or her background, interests, and habits

2. Accountability—the ability to trace the individual's response to a particular communication/appeal

3. Interactivity—the ability to cultivate a continuing dialogue and build rapport with each individual in order to retain his or her interest and loyalty

The world is rapidly changing. Continued success for educational fund raising will require that colleges and universities adapt their methods to the demographic realities of their primary donor prospects. Perhaps demographic pressures will be the impetus leading educational fund raisers to develop more effective and productive ways of fund raising.

NOTE

1. Except when noted otherwise, all statistics are taken from the U.S. Bureau of the Census. The overall material comes from Dr. Nichols's book, *Pinpointing Affluence in the 21st Century* (Chicago: Precept Press, 2001), and her articles in *Contributions* magazine.

CHAPTER 15

Women As Philanthropists

Andrea Kaminski

W omen have a long tradition of voluntary giving to support education in the United States. More than a century ago, Emma Willard and Mary Lyon applied their fortunes and talents to pioneer education for girls and women equal to that offered by the Ivy League schools to boys and men. After her husband's death in 1891, Phoebe Apperson Hearst pledged an annual gift of $1,500 to the University of California–Berkeley to be used for five $300 scholarships for "worthy young women." This was the beginning of "an exceptional personal history of support for the University that continues to benefit Cal faculty, students, and alumni to the present day."[1] In 1904, Mary McLeod Bethune opened the Daytona Literary and Industrial Institute for Negro Girls, which later merged with another Black school to become Bethune-Cookman College.[2]

Committed women who could not give large amounts of money to support education were adept at raising funds from others. For example, Spelman College was founded by Sophia B. Packard and Harriet Giles, two friends who were commissioned in 1879 by the Women's American Baptist Home Mission Society of New England to study the living conditions "among the freedmen of the South." Appalled by the lack of educational opportunity for Black women, the missionaries returned to Boston determined to effect change. On April 11, 1881, they opened a school in the basement of Atlanta's New England Friendship Baptist Church. The first eleven pupils were mostly ex-slaves. They went on to raise several thousand dollars from the Black community, as well as from major philanthropists on the East Coast.

WHY FOCUS ON WOMEN PHILANTHROPISTS?

Today, more women have more control over much more money than ever before, and more women view strategic philanthropic giving as an opportunity to help shape the future of society.

Consider the facts:

- There were almost 1.6 million female top wealth holders in 1995 with a combined net worth of more than $2.2 trillion. The average net worth for the group was $1.38 million, slightly higher than for male wealth holders, and the females carried less debt.[3]

- In 1999, there were 9.1 million women-owned firms, employing almost 28 million people and generating over $3.6 trillion in sales.[4]

- There are more than ninety women's funds across the United States, up from the "original eleven" created in the 1970s.[5]

- An estimated $41 trillion to $136 trillion will be passing from one generation to the next by 2044.[6] Women outlive men by an average of seven years. An estimated 85 to 90 percent of women are left in charge of family financial affairs,[7] so women will be determining what becomes of much of this transferred wealth—how much is spent, how it is invested, how much will go to heirs, and how some will be returned to society through taxes or philanthropy.

WHAT DO WE KNOW ABOUT WOMEN AS PHILANTHROPISTS?

It is clear that women have money and that they give. But what do we know about *how* women give? What are women's motivations, fears, expectations, and rewards for giving? A number of qualitative studies have examined women's giving patterns through focus groups and personal interviews with hundreds of women nationally.[8] Some studies have produced a more quantitative measure of women's giving, as well as comparing women's giving patterns with those of men.[9]

These studies indicate that women have the same core motivations for giving as do men—altruism, gratitude, and the desire to make a better world. However, women take a different approach to philanthropic giving, just as they have different styles of communication and management.[10] This is a result of women's socialization in a society that has long had a double standard in economic, social, and power structures.

THE SIX Cs OF WOMEN'S GIVING

The culture of women's giving is described in the book *Reinventing Fundraising: Realizing the Potential of Women's Philanthropy*, by Sondra C. Shaw and Martha A. Taylor, co-founders of the Women's Philanthropy Institute.[11] These authors summarized the recurring themes in their discussions with women philanthropists in six words beginning with the letter C:

1. *Create.* Women often give to create a new institution, as did Sophia Smith and Mary Lyon. In other cases, women create new programs in existing institutions, as did Lucille Puette Giles, who left $2 million in her estate to Randolph-Macon Women's College in Virginia to create a Global Studies Initiative in her name.

2. *Change.* Women give to bring about social change. Mary Elizabeth Garrett did this in 1881, when she gave $350,000 to The Johns Hopkins University to establish a medical school on the condition that the medical school open its doors to women.[12] At the University of Virginia Law School, a group of alumnae had noted the absence of women in the photographs and plaques on the walls of the school. In the mid-1990s this group of women lawyers, with the assistance of Director of Development Laurel Alexander, raised $1 million to fund a new lobby in the law school's renovated and expanded facility. Highly visible on the wall of the lobby are the names of the women lawyers who contributed to the project.

3. *Connect.* Women often seek a sense of personal connection with the program or project they fund. Fund raisers report that they can often meet this need for connection by providing continuing information after the gift has been made. Women donors want to know how their money will be used, how the project is progressing, and how it is helping people.

This is consistent with the findings of a study by Deloitte & Touche, Inc., which found that women seek to build a close, working relationship with their financial advisors.[13] The women in this study expressed a desire for ongoing guidance and information from their financial advisors. Women seek the same sense of partnership with people connected to the projects they fund.

Faculty members can also play an important role in motivating women donors and creating a sense of connection. At the University of Wisconsin–Madison, Martha Taylor coaches faculty members in how to speak to female donors and prospects and often invites the professors to talk about their research to a select group of women donors the evening before a women's philanthropy event on campus. When the professors share their passion for their work, the women are often fascinated by and enthusiastic about the research being conducted at the university. This experience creates a sense of personal connection for donors who support research. At the same time, Taylor believes this is a valuable skill for helping female professors to advance in their departments and fields.

4. *Collaborate.* Women like to collaborate, or work together as a group—in part this is why they often don't respond to competitive fund-raising appeals. For example, a group of eight anonymous alumnae made a pooled $2.2 million gift to Mary Baldwin College, in honor of President Cynthia Haldenby Tyson, to establish a new endowment fund to support leadership development programs.[14]

Women's funds, women's giving circles, and women's philanthropy councils in higher education are examples of collaborative philanthropy. Members of these programs usually engage in donor education and active involvement in the programs they support.

The high value women place on collaboration and connection is consistent with what has been learned about women's management styles in business settings.[15] Women managers in general foster cooperation, consensus, and networking. That's how women do business.

5. *Commit.* Women are committed to the causes they support—they want to give not only their money but also their time. According to Independent Sector, volunteering is still more significant among women than men. In their national survey on giving and volunteering, 62 percent of women reported volunteering, compared to 49 percent of men. And people who volunteer give more. Over the six biennial national surveys Independent Sector has conducted on giving and volunteering, contributing households with a volunteer gave more than twice the percentage of household income as contributing households in which the respondent did not volunteer. Even in periods of uncertain economic conditions such as 1991 and 1993, this relationship held.[16]

6. *Celebrate.* Finally, women like to celebrate their accomplishments and have fun with philanthropy. This preference is also grounded in women's tradition of raising money through events. Events are still an important way to recognize the contributions of major donors and volunteers—and to have fun.

BARRIERS TO WOMEN'S GIVING

Of course, every donor is an individual who has been shaped by unique socioeconomic and family influences. In addition to gender, there are differences based on generation, region, religion, ethnicity, and race.[17] Individuals with inherited wealth are likely to view giving differently from those who have earned it in their adult lives. Understanding these differences can be helpful when working with donors.

It is also important to understand that these differences can be additive. For example, the issue of gender may compound generational difference. While both men and women who came of age during the Great Depression are likely to want to hold onto their savings for a rainy day, for women this tendency is heightened by the fact that they may never have brought home a paycheck. In addition, women are more likely to outlive their husbands.

Recent pacesetting research by Cindy Sterling, Director of Gift Planning at Vassar College, indicates that in planned giving women are more likely to give through bequests, while men are more likely to make life-income gifts. This was backed up by a recent survey by the National Committee on Planned Giving, which found that more than half of charitable bequest donors are female (53 percent compared to 47 percent men). On the other hand, 56 percent of charitable remainder trust donors are men, compared to 44 percent women.[18] Sterling speculates that a bequest may feel "safer" to women, who may fear outliving their resources, than would an irrevocable, income-producing gift.[19] Based on a survey of women donors, Cheryl Altinkemer, Director of Development for the Purdue University School of Consumer and Family Sciences, has developed planned giving materials designed to reach and motivate women.

Women of this older generation may feel that "my husband earned that money." As widows, they may believe their responsibility is to safeguard the family money, spend as little of it as possible, and then pass it on to their children. Or, they may believe the money should be given, out of a sense of loyalty, to the causes and institutions that their husbands supported. Mature women often defer to male financial advisors or family members in their financial and philanthropic decisions.

Many women in this generation have devoted a life of unpaid service to family and community, and they rightfully may not believe that society values these contributions. They may be suspicious of administrative costs, and they may restrict their gifts to programs or scholarships, rather than supporting operating funds.

Women born between 1931 and 1945 represent a "sandwich generation." They share many of the characteristics of the mature generation, but may have been influenced by the feminist writings of Betty Friedan[20] and others. Many women in this cohort entered college and the workforce before the days of affirmative action or at midlife. Either way, they were pioneers. Women in this generation tend to be wary of issues related to money and power, and they prefer to give to programs that serve the traditional interests of women—child welfare, education, and health care.[21]

Baby boomer women, born between 1946 and 1964, are more likely to earn their own money and make their own money decisions. While boomers have tended to be spenders rather than savers, men and women in this generation have begun to take more interest in planning for retirement.

Of course, it is critical to begin planning now for how to reach the next generation, often called the baby busters, especially in light of the great wealth that has been generated by the high-tech industry. Like the mature women, the busters have been shaped by economic uncertainty in their childhood. They were born into a period of economic recession, corporate downsizing, and high divorce rates. Women in this generation know that they cannot count on anyone—a husband or an employer—to support them.

If there is anything uniform about the buster generation, it is a resistance to being typecast as uniform in any way. The Women's Philanthropy Institute has found that women in this generation resist a separate focus on women. At one seminar, a young woman said that women and men are now equal in the workforce and in society, therefore separate programs will only "ghettoize" women. Unfortunately, salary studies do not support her claim.[22]

For many women, these barriers to giving are internal fears that they themselves have to overcome. Donor education will help. However, the most pernicious barrier—one that came up again and again in the focus groups—is that *women don't believe they are being asked to give at the same level as men.* This was even found in 1999 in a study of high achieving businesswomen by the National Foundation for Women Business Owners. More than half the women in the study donate $25,000 or more annually, yet one out of four said they do not think they are taken seriously by the fund-raising community.[23]

MOTIVATING WOMEN AS MAJOR DONORS AND VOLUNTEER LEADERS

In the focus groups and interviews conducted by the Women's Philanthropy Institute, women philanthropists have illuminated ways that development officers and nonprofits can partner with them to shape a better world for future generations. They have described what motivates them as philanthropists, as well as what turns them off. Following are suggestions for transforming everyday development procedures to help reach, involve, and motivate more women as major donors and volunteer leaders.

1. *Concentrate fund-raising efforts on relationship building.* Potential women donors may first identify themselves through volunteer work.

2. *Examine what women see when they look at your organization.* Review your boards, committees, administration, as well as your publications. Are women represented? Are they represented in leading roles or supporting roles? Women want to see that your institution affirms and values their contributions of expertise and talent.

3. *Review your standard development procedures.* Are the six C's represented in your work? Do women know about opportunities to be involved in *creating* new programs at the institution? Do they know how the programs will bring about *change?* Are there opportunities for meaningful volunteer involvement? Is ongoing information provided so they feel *connected?*

4. *Analyze current giving statistics, broken down by gender.* Choose a time period, say the past three years, and answer the following questions:

- What percentage of donors were women?
- What percentage of total gift dollars came from women?
- What percentage of members of major gift clubs or higher giving categories were women?
- What percentage of your planned gifts, and of the total dollars given in planned gifts, came from women?
- What percentage of those on prospect tracking are women? (How many women are you actively talking to about major gifts?)

Note: The results of this inquiry will depend, in part, on how you credit contributions, in particular those from married couples. When looking at the data, it may be impossible to know which spouse had more influence on the philanthropic decision. Start by examining how your institution credits joint gifts, and you may want to recommend a change in policy for the future. A recent study of women's philanthropy programming at research universities found that all of the development offices surveyed used systems, including Advance, Ascend, or Millennium, that are capable of crediting spouses separately when a gift is received from a married couple.[24]

5. *If you do nothing else, make at least 50 percent of your fund-raising*

calls on women. And, ask for enough. As mentioned, women in focus groups have said they do not believe they are being asked at the same level as their male peers. Imagine the good work institutions can accomplish if women are helped to realize their philanthropic potential!

6. *Partner with both partners.* If your development office is working with a committed couple, learn about both spouses, or partners, and try to include both in solicitation calls and recognition. Schedule the call at a time and place that is convenient for both partners.

7. *Pay attention to stewardship.* How you accept the gift, acknowledge the donor, and maintain the relationship is crucial. In the research, women have expressed an overwhelming preference for personal, as opposed to public, recognition.

CONCLUSION

Women have emerged as leaders with a new approach in business, government, and the professions. Now they are poised to make a major impact with their philanthropy. They are passionate in their belief that education is key to providing opportunities for individuals and to advancing and improving society. They are seeking connection and guidance to help them make active choices about what becomes of their wealth—how much they spend, how they invest, how much goes back to society in the form of taxes, and what they accomplish through strategic philanthropic giving.

Development professionals, administrators, and faculty can help women become stewards of their wealth by identifying them as potential major donors and learning about their motivations, preferences, expectations, and fears with regard to giving. It is critical to ask women to give and to inspire women to fulfill their philanthropic potential. This must be followed by appropriate acknowledgment and careful stewardship.

Women are seeking a sense of connection with the institutions they fund, as well as a sense of partnership with the professionals they work with. Educational fund raisers can encourage women as philanthropists by providing guidance through donor education and programs, as well as in every contact with women donors and their families. This is what women expect from institutions and the professionals who represent them. This is how women will make philanthropy more rewarding for the donor, the people who work for the institution, and the students, researchers, and public who benefit from the institution's good work.

NOTES

1. "Women of Generosity and Vision," *Cal Futures* 14, no. 1 (Spring 2001). University of California, Berkeley, Office of Planned Giving, 1.

2. Amy Alexander, *Fifty Black Women Who Changed America* (Secaucus, NJ: Carol Publishing, 1999), 47.

3. Internal Revenue Service, *Statistics of Income Bulletin* (Winter 1999–2000).

4. National Foundation for Women Business Owners, press release, 1999.

5. Brochure, Women's Funding Network, 1999.

6. John J. Havens and Paul G. Schervish, "Millionaires and the Millennium: New Estimates of the Forthcoming Wealth Transfer and the Prospects for a Golden Age of Philanthropy" (Boston: Boston College Social Welfare Research Institute, Press Release, 1999).

7. Brochure, Kelly Bolton, Merrill Lynch, 1999.

8. S. C. Shaw and M. A. Taylor, *Reinventing Fundraising: Realizing the Potential of Women's Philanthropy* (San Francisco: Jossey-Bass, 1995); *The UCLA Women and Philanthropy Focus Groups* (Los Angeles: The UCLA Foundation, 1992); *Perspectives on Women's Giving: Findings from the 1999 Focus Groups* (Los Angeles: The UCLA Foundation, 1999); Martha A. Taylor, *Study on Women's Philanthropy for Health Care: St. Luke's Medical Center, Milwaukee* (Women's Philanthropy Institute, 1995); *Philanthropy Among Business Women of Achievement* (Washington, DC: National Foundation for Women Business Owners, November 1999); *Rutgers University: Women in Philanthropy: Analysis of Focus Groups* (Women's Philanthropy Institute, 2001).

9. Peter D. Hart Research Associates, "Toward 2000 and Beyond: Charitable and Social Change Giving in the New Millennium, Part 2. A Craver, Mathews, Smith & Company Donor Study," *Fund Raising Management* (June 1999):24–28; *Leaders in Business and Community: The Philanthropic Contributions of Women and Men Business Owners* (Washington, DC: National Foundation for Women Business Owners, November 2000), 36.

10. Carol Gilligan, *In a Different Voice: Psychological Theory and Women's Development* (Cambridge, MA: Harvard University Press, 1993), 29–31, 61; National Foundation for Women Business Owners Web site, "New Study Quantifies Thinking and Management Style Difference Between Women and Men Business Owners" (http://www.nfwbo.org/Research/7-19-1999/7-19-1999.htm, viewed April 10, 2002).

11. Shaw and Taylor, *Reinventing Fundraising*, 83–100.

12. Joan M. Fisher, "Celebrating the Heroines of Philanthropy," in *Women and Philanthropy: A National Agenda*, ed. A. I. Thompson and A. R. Kaminski (University of Wisconsin–Madison, 1993), 18.

13. "She Said: A Study of Affluent Women and Personal Finances," Deloitte & Touche, 1998.

14. *Women's Philanthropy Institute News* (May 2000): 8.

15. *Styles of Success: The Thinking and Management Styles of Women and Men Business Owners* (Washington, DC: National Foundation for Women Business Owners, 1994).

16. *Giving and Volunteering in the United States: Findings from a National Survey* (Washington, DC: Independent Sector, 1999), http://www.independent sector.org/Gand V/s-rela.htm. Last viewed April 11, 2002.

17. M. A. Abbe, "Inspiring Philanthropy by Women of Color," *Women's Philanthropy Institute News* (Madison: Women's Philanthropy Institute, May 2000), 1.

18. *Planned Giving in the United States: 2000: A Survey of Donors* (Indianapolis: National Committee on Planned Giving, 2001), 29.

19. Cindy Sterling, "Gender Differences in Planned Giving: The Way Women Give," *Planned Giving Today* (December 2000): 2.

20. Betty Friedan, *The Feminine Mystique* (New York: Dell Publishing, 1984).

21. Shaw and Taylor, *Reinventing Fundraising*, 98–100.

22. *Frozen in the Headlights: The Dynamics of Women and Money* (Englewood: National Endowment for Financial Education, February 2000), 4.

23. *Philanthropy Among Business Women of Achievement: A Summary of Key Findings* (Washington, DC: National Foundation for Women Business Owners, November 1999), press release.

24. M. Marcello, G. Van Dien, and K. Vehrs, *Women's Philanthropy at Research Universities: 1998–1999 Study* (Madison: University of Wisconsin Survey Research Center, February 2000), 18.

CHAPTER 16

Giving Traditions of Minority Communities

Joanne B. Scanlan and John Abrahams

According to the Census 2000 results, the United States is more diverse than ever before. Approximately 274.6 million people currently live here, and about 35.3 million of them, or 12.5 percent, are Hispanics, who may be of any race.[1] The Hispanic population has grown so fast over the last decade that it is about equal to that of African Americans. The number of Blacks ranged from 34.6 million to 36.4 million in the 2000 Census. Those who classify themselves as Hispanic grew by nearly 60 percent in the 2000 Census, and people of Mexican descent accounted for 58 percent of that growth.[2] If current trends continue, almost half of the population of the United States will be non-white by 2050.[3]

UNDERGRADUATE MINORITY ENROLLMENT IN HIGHER EDUCATION

Minorities are overall still less likely to attend college. But, the increasing diversity of the nation will be reflected on its college and university campuses in the years ahead. Minority[4] enrollments at the undergraduate level have increased at all types of institutions in the past 20 years. Minority enrollments increased from 17 percent of all undergraduate students in fall 1976 to 26 percent in fall 1995.[5] This rise was primarily due to the increased enrollment of Asian/Pacific Islander and Hispanic students. Black enrollment kept relatively steady as a percentage of total enrollments.[6] Minority women recorded higher enrollment gains in higher education in recent years than minority men. Between 1991 and 1996, minority women experienced a 25 percent gain in enrollment. These enrollment trends imply that the base of alumni and other individuals on whom colleges and universities rely for support also will be more diverse in the decades ahead.

THE STORIES BEHIND THE NUMBERS

As one sees the growing number of African Americans, Hispanics, and Asians who are in professional positions earning income that places them in the middle classes, obtaining undergraduate and graduate degrees, purchasing homes, and showing other signs of financial success, it would be easy—but inaccurate—to think that America's "melting pot" is finally succeeding as it did with European immigrants in the early years of the twentieth century.[7] This might lead us to expect that members of these groups will eventually develop similar relationships with their colleges and universities. But, it is important to remember that the experiences of these groups are different in important ways. Other groups did not experience the kind of legal, economic, and cultural exclusion over centuries (for African Americans) and decades that minority populations experienced. These and other historic facts, together with the prejudice and racism that were used to justify restrictive laws and customs, began to be addressed by the Civil Rights Act of 1965 and by affirmative action policies adopted by employers and educational institutions in the early 1970s. These policies have been criticized, dismantled, and resurrected on various campuses, adding to the layers of uncertainty that make it difficult to build open communication and collaboration across color lines and across ethnicities.

But minority families are sending their children to college in increasing numbers, and development staff will need to find ways to work successfully with groups that have had such different histories and experiences. It is important to become familiar with the history and culture of minority groups and to understand how they think about charitable giving. They do have strong traditions of philanthropy, although these may differ from those of groups with which educational fund raisers have traditionally worked.

LEGACIES OF PHILANTHROPY

Minority groups have faced legal and economic barriers that other immigrants did not experience. But each group also had great cultural and spiritual resources, and while they were excluded from the rest of society, they built and supported vibrant institutions of their own. The giving and volunteering that sustain these institutions reflect how minority donors think about and act on their charitable interests.

In interviews with over eighty wealthy people of color, researchers for *Cultures of Caring* found that very wealthy individuals have some traits in common with each other and with wealthy white donors. They prefer to support organizations that they feel are serving communities or interests that are important to them. They want to see that the leadership of the organization (staff and volunteers) includes some people like them. And, they like to be involved in an organization. Not all want to be on the institution's board, but they do appreciate and expect some contact with senior officers of the organization.[8] However, these individuals are not representative of most minority donors, as will be discussed below.

In her research for the Council on Foundations report *Cultures of Caring*, Jessica Chao developed a useful model that describes "stages of giving."[9] It is important to note that her research was based on Asians and may not apply to all groups. Among minority groups, Asians are most like European immigrants in their experiences in America, although they have faced more racial prejudice than European immigrants.

In the first stage, called "survival," the group is struggling to become accustomed to American ways, still prefers its native language, and its members are often employed in less-skilled positions with low-to-moderate incomes. In this stage, the group's giving supports organizations that provide immediate assistance, such as churches or helping organizations that provide direct support to their community. They may prefer to contribute as volunteers rather than give money. Some of these organizations may be arms of well-known agencies and service groups from their country of origin.

In the second stage, the group "thrives." Its members have a good command of English, which now may be preferred over the native language. Many have become small business owners or have entered white-collar and professional jobs. At this stage, their giving still includes indigenous organizations that benefit their community, but it may expand to include colleges and universities that have enabled them to get ahead, medical and cultural institutions, and organizations committed to social justice. They still volunteer and are able to also make larger cash gifts.

In the third stage, the donors in the group "invest." They may still support organizations and causes that help those from their countries or immigrants of similar background, but they have become sophisticated philanthropists who support many interests, serve on boards, and are generally quite similar to wealthy people of other backgrounds. They are culturally fluent in both their own traditions and American culture. They seek to make change as well as to support ongoing services.[10]

Chao's research shows that for Asian donors educational institutions are frequently the first recipients of gifts given beyond their own communities. This pattern also applies when other minority giving is analyzed.[11] It is important to remember that today most people in minority communities are still in the "survive" or "thrive" categories. It is essential to understand the importance of community institutions and how much their traditions and styles of giving have been built around those institutions. Being aware of how fund raising works in these institutions will help the college fund raiser understand how his or her outreach efforts are being interpreted as well as the competing demands on the donor's time, interest, and money.

African-American Giving Traditions

The African-American community has had the longest history of exclusion and also has the greatest number of indigenous charitable entities. Religious congregations—the "Black Church"—are consistently rated as the primary recipients and vehicles for charitable activity within the African-American community. Social clubs, sororities, and fraternal orders attract a small part of the more affluent African-American communities. National scholarship programs such as the United Negro College Fund (UNCF) obtain strong support, as do major civil rights organizations. Helping others, building and strengthening their community, and giving back for help received are common explanations of what motivates African Americans to give to charities.[12]

Hispanic Giving Traditions

Family support is a primary focus of charity. Although not tax-deductible, gifts are frequently made to help with medical care, schooling, emergency travel, or other needs. Within this community, the Catholic Church has been the major community institution and is a major recipient of gifts. Mutual aid societies that were founded in the country of origin also receive support. Supporting the schools that are often part of a Catholic parish combines family and religious obligations.[13] Among more urban Hispanic populations, there is also interest in support of civil rights and social justice causes,[14] programs that support youth, and emergency relief appeals, particularly when the areas affected are in Central or South America.[15]

Helping others, caring for children, and religious teachings about giving to the poor are concepts that help explain Hispanic motivations to give.

East Asian Giving Traditions

Members of the Asian groups that the authors have researched, Chinese, Koreans and Japanese, have emigrated to far reaches of the world in search of land and jobs. They have been supported for centuries by mutual aid associations organized by province or village, or by surname or dialect. These organizations, temples, and monasteries have provided aid to newcomers and means of communicating and transmitting funds to homelands. Well-organized community groups, including local relief programs, scholarships, and cultural events, also sponsor charitable programs. Individuals and families also frequently support religious institutions, clinics and hospitals, and public-works projects in their native provinces and villages.[16]

Christian, Confucian, Taoist, and Buddhist teachings of charity to others, family honor and obligation, honoring other important people (through memorial gifts, etc.), and upholding professional and peer relationships are concepts that motivate Asian donors in their charitable acts.[17]

Native American Giving Traditions

There are over 800 tribes that are recognized as separate legal entities by various states and the U.S. federal government. Since the 1980s, more tribes have been able to assert their rights as sovereign nations and have sued to gain control over their financial and natural resources.[18] The mid-1990s saw an increase in the well-being of some Native American tribes, particularly those who successfully took over management of their reservations' natural resources and those who developed successful gambling enterprises. A few tribes have begun to establish their own giving programs and foundations. The Pequot Tribe in Connecticut is probably the most well-known tribe to participate in philanthropy.

However, only about 22 percent of all Native Americans live on reservations. Depending on an individual's sense of connection to his or her heritage, tribal customs and beliefs will play a larger or lesser role in their giving. Among those who identify themselves as Native Americans, the extended family and tribe are the primary focus of charity, followed by tribal membership organizations and nonprofit organizations led by and serving Native Americans. Many of these donors describe giving as a part of a circle of relationships (the circle is an important symbol in most Native spiritual teachings).[19]

PYRAMIDS VERSUS CIRCLES

Development staff are familiar with the classic giving pyramid. But, numerous researchers who have studied the topic say that the pyramid doesn't work for minority donors.[20] What doesn't work are the traditional methods used to advance people to higher levels of the pyramid. Rather than defining donors as people who have to be "moved up" the pyramid, a more successful approach may be to use the "circle of giving" concept. Janice Gow Pettey describes individuals who cite strongly held beliefs in the mutual benefit and humanizing elements of gift giving.[21] They say such things as:

- Giving strengthens the whole community that I live in.
- Giving is something that is an honor to be able to do and it's a way of showing my respect for my community.
- Giving is part of how we connect with each other as fellow beings.
- I want to be able to pass on the help that I was given.

Five different themes can be heard in these statements:

1. There isn't a distance between the population that gives and the population that receives.
2. The act of giving benefits the giver. It provides a way of showing respect, fulfilling an obligation, demonstrating worthiness of respect from others, etc.
3. The act of receiving enables the recipient to demonstrate a bond with the giver, provides an opportunity to show appreciation and respect, and of course helps the recipient financially.
4. Gifts are part of an ongoing social exchange and communication within the community.
5. Giving is a continuous cycle, extending over time and through numerous iterations in which the giver will become a recipient and again a donor.

STRATEGIES FOR WORKING WITH MINORITY DONORS

Understanding diverse traditions and perceptions of giving will be essential if educational fund raisers are to increase minority people's support of higher education. Development professionals will need new ways of extending their communications to new groups of donors. Here are some strategies to help:

- Find people who can meet with potential donors and who will know how to behave in diverse settings. According to a 1990 Council for Advancement and Support of Education (CASE)-Ketchum Survey of Institutional Advancement, African Americans and other minorities constituted only about 4.5 percent of CASE member representatives. Recent estimates place this figure between 7 and 9 percent.

- Demonstrate that your campus is committed to serving the donor's community. Partnering with local schools, churches, or social clubs in the communities to provide coaching, mentoring, and tours can start opening up communication.

- Build reciprocal relationships with donors and potential donors. If you have a few potential donors identified, do some research and find out what organizations they support. Offer some of your resources—a meeting room, access to a staff training day, a special day at the campus swimming center—to their favored community organizations.

- Learn more about minority giving. Stay current with the latest research.

- Value, acknowledge, and reward all kinds of giving—volunteer service well as money—in order to make diverse donors feel appreciated.

- Make personal contact with minority donors at early stages in their giving to encourage the relationship. Most of the donors in these groups need more personal contact than do other donors at their giving level. Yours may be the first organization that has tried to involve them in alumni activities. Make special efforts to help them feel more comfortable.

- Acknowledge the first gift so that others will follow. A personal note from a high-ranking volunteer or official, a phone call, or other personalized way of saying thanks should be part of the process.

- Include minority donors in significant events to build trust and mutual respect. Asking for advice, sharing challenges, and discussing how the institution is trying to resolve various situations are important ways to involve donors.

- Let donors support each other to build peer networks that benefit them and the institution. Consider "giving circle" options as ways to involve donors. Inviting several donors with similar backgrounds (not just the same year of graduation) to pool gifts for a commonly recognized need is being done successfully elsewhere. Host a gathering of the circle and let the group self-determine its goals and giving plans. You may encourage a more comfortable and culturally appropriate outreach program that ultimately involves more donors.

In the next 25 years, 25 percent of college enrollment will be from communities of color. These future alumni may become substantial supporters of the institution. More knowledgeable and thoughtful efforts to reach out to them, to learn from them, and to position the institution as a vital support to the donor's community are important steps for development staff to take now in order to succeed in the future.

NOTES

1. M. Elizabeth Crieco and C. Rachel Cassidy, *Overview of Race and Hispanic Origin: Census 2000 Brief* (Washington, DC: U.S. Bureau of the Census, 2000), 3.

2. D'Vera Cohn and Darryl Fears, "Hispanics Draw Even With Blacks in New Census," *Washington Post*, March 7, 2001, A-1.

3. Hispanics are projected to overtake Blacks early in the twenty-first century. The non-Hispanic white population is projected to fall gradually from 72 percent in 2000 to 64 percent in 2020 and 53 percent in 2050.

4. In all subsequent discussions, "minority" is used to describe people who are of the following minority races: American Indian or Alaska Native, Asian, Black, Hispanic or Latino, Native Hawaiian or other Pacific Islander, and other racial groups excluding Whites. For a complete overview see U.S. Office of Management and Budget, "Standards for Maintaining, Collecting and Presenting Federal Data on Race and Ethnicity," Statistical Directive 15, 1997.

5. This figure excludes non-resident aliens as cited in the U.S. Department of Education, National Center for Education Statistics, *The Condition of Education 2000*, NCES 200 0-062 (Washington, DC: U.S., Government Printing Office 2000), 28.

6. Ibid. The enrollment for both Asian/Pacific Islanders and Hispanic groups increased by 4 percentage points between fall 1976 and fall 1995. In fall 1976, Blacks accounted for 10 percent of undergraduate enrollments; Hispanics, 5 percent; Asians/Pacific Islanders, 2 percent; and American Indians/Alaska Natives, 1 percent. In fall 1995, black undergraduates accounted for 11 percent of the total enrollment at colleges and universities. Hispanics represented 8 percent of enrolled undergraduate students; Asians/Pacific Islanders, 6 percent; and American Indians/Alaska Natives, 1 percent.

7. For a full development of this theme, see Michael Barone, *The New Americans: How the Melting Pot Can Work Again* (N.p.: Regnery Press, 2001).

8. Joanne Scanlan, ed., *Cultures of Caring: Philanthropy in Diverse American*

Communities. (Washington, DC: Council on Foundations, 1999), 11–12. Also, interviews and conversations with wealthy donors attending various Council on Foundations events, 1990–present. Also, see Francie Ostrower, *Why the Wealthy Give: The Culture of Elite Philanthropy* (Princeton, NJ: Princeton University Press, 1995).

9. Jessica Chao, "Asian-American Philanthropy: Expanding Circles of Participation," in Scanlan, *Cultures of Caring*, 11–12. Also, Jessica's model is fully developed in Mindy L. Berry and Jessica Chao, *Engaging Diverse Communities for and through Philanthropy* (Washington, DC: Forum of Regional Associations of Grantmakers, 2001), 189–254.

10. Paul G. Schervish, "Major Donors, Motives: The People and Purposes Behind Major Gifts," *Major Gift* (Indianapolis, IN: Center for Philanthropy) 16 (Summer 1997): 6.

11. Berry and Chao, *Engaging Diverse Communities*, 12.

12. Alice Green Burnette, "Giving Strength: Understanding Philanthropy in the Black Community," *Philanthropy Matters* (Indianapolis, IN: Center for Philanthropy) 11, no. 1 (Spring 2001) Also, see Mary Frances Winters, "Reflections on Endowment Building in the African American Community," in Scanlan, *Cultures of Caring*, 107–146.

13. See, for example, Eugene D. Miller, *Latinos and the Development of Community Philanthropy, Associations, and Advocacy*, Multicultural Philanthropy Curriculum Guide no. 7, Series ed. Barbara Luira Leopold (New York: Center for the Study of Philanthropy of the Graduate School and University Center of the City University of New York, 1999).

14. Henry A.J. Ramos, "Latino Philanthropy: Expanding U.S. Models of Giving and Civic Participation," in Scanlan, *Cultures of Caring*, 147–188.

15. Ibid.

16. Jessica Chao, *A New Heritage of Giving: Philanthropy in Asian America* (New York: Asian American Federation, 2001).

17. Chao, "Asian-American Philanthropy," 209.

18. Lawsuits filed by several Indian nations charge that the Bureau of Indian Affairs and Land Management has lost or stolen over $10 billion of income from land leases that the bureau managed for the tribes in previous decades. See "Interior Tries to Fix Indian Trust Accounting System," *Washington Post*, August 26, 2001, A-5.

19. Mindy Berry, "Native American Philanthropy: Expanding Social Participation and Self-Determination," in Scanlan, *Cultures of Caring*, 29–106.

20. For a full discussion, see Diana Newman, *Opening Doors: Pathways to New Donors* (San Francisco: Jossey-Bass, 2002).

21. Janice Gow Pettey, *Cultivating Diversity in Fundraising* (New York: Wiley and Sons, forthcoming 2002).

CHAPTER 17

International Fund Raising

Scott G. Nichols

A ldous Huxley was right. It is indeed a brave new world. And for the fund raiser, this is especially true. Consider the following.[1]

- In November of 2000, the first ever Asia-Pacific Symposium for Institutional Advancement was held in Hong Kong. Some 270 individuals attended from 89 educational institutions representing 13 countries.
- A month earlier, a similar gathering was held in Brazil. Attendance was 500.
- Over the past 20 years, the per-student expenditure in the United Kingdom by the government has dropped almost 50%.[2]
- In the past five years, 15 new private colleges have been successfully established in Turkey.[3]
- Over a 20-year period, the Massachusetts Institute of Technology sought and received 32 endowed professorships from separate Japanese sources.[4]
- In 2001, the Council for the Advancement and Support of Education (CASE), the premier educational association for fund raisers, listed members in 44 countries.[5]
- Each year, approximately 500,000 students and scholars from abroad study in the United States.[6]
- The University of Toronto has had a functioning, full-time, successful alumni and development operation located in Hong Kong for over a decade.

• Recently, two educational institutions in the United States have received gifts of $100 million from donors outside the country.[7]

These facts, and many others, are clear and dramatic signs for the advancement officer of today and tomorrow. Although there are precious little data to analyze and no experts to consult, the anecdotal evidence is overwhelming. Maximizing support for educational institutions—missions past, present, and future—requires most in the field to think in global terms. Mirroring the larger world, internationalization is a pervasive force that impels new thinking and effort on the part of advancement officers everywhere.

THE NEW REALITIES

Whether imposed by others or self-designed, the world requires that development officers reorient themselves and their programs to meet the new realities. For years, many professional have conducted their work under the mythology that educational fund raising is uniquely American. As one esteemed colleague used to say, "I've never seen a trip abroad that beat going to New York City one more time." The self-fulfilling prophecy kept this author domestic for too long. Yet the simple truth is that advancement officers who are now venturing offshore are experiencing noteworthy success. The steady flow of seven-, eight-, and even nine-figure gifts from offshore is certainly an attention getter. If educational philanthropy is a uniquely American tradition, institutions from Princeton to Berkeley are shattering the shibboleth.

It is especially important to understand the larger and shifting context of the fund-raising environment that is now producing so many successes. Several trends are obvious and dominant, mandating somewhat dramatic changes in where and in which way we seek support. It is important to examine some of the more dominant environmental factors.

All societies are charitable. Although this chapter does not permit serious analysis of this sweeping variable, it is necessary to recognize that from the moment a surplus economy evolved, humans have always been inclined to help the needy and less fortunate. From Hammurabi's code requiring the care of "widows and orphans" to the teachings of Buddha to the Judeo-Christian precepts from which American philanthropy evolved, charitable principles and practices are ubiquitous. Priorities certainly vary between and among societies geographically and throughout history. Translating them into support for education may be a challenge in countries where government has traditionally been the sole provider. Nevertheless, the underlying charitable impulse is everywhere.

Government support for education is shrinking worldwide. The most dramatic shift in the international landscape has been a remarkable, pervasive diminution of government support to educational institutions. Sometimes the process has been a slow but steady reduction, as in England. Other withdrawals of government funding have been more catastrophic. At the largest university in the world, the Autonomous University of Mexico, the introduction of tuition as a second source of funding not only closed the institution for a year but also led to violent, tragic demonstrations. In Korea, concern over the inability of government to finance education adequately prompted one *chebu* (corporate conglomerate) to open its own medical and law schools. And the United States is not immune. In the post–Howard Jarvis Proposition 13 era, state governments routinely have reduced or not kept up with financing of educational institutions. Whether in the United States or elsewhere, private philanthropy is receiving increased attention as the most relevant, viable alternative to government and tuition financing.

There has been an explosion in international wealth. The tremendous growth in wealth transcends all borders. In the United States, there are some methods of measurements. One is the intergenerational transfer of wealth data that has received so much attention. The data appears to show that wealth in the United States quadrupled in the 1990s. While reliable data on wealth internationally is elusive, a review of the Forbes 500 reveals an increasing number of the world's wealthiest coming from outside the United States. And the wealthiest of the planet seldom live in only one country. Many top prospects are now residents of several countries, forcing development officers to think about them and treat them as citizens of the world.

Institutions require development officers to be more international. For most U.S. advancement officers, there is no choice. Students are increasingly non-American. Faculty is broader in outlook, background, and geography. Satellite campuses, distance learning, and regional studies pressure development officers to take a worldview. Curricula are more global. At the Harvard Law School, almost one-fifth of the courses is focused on international or comparative studies. The graduates are more mobile and diverse geographically. Alumni activity abroad is now common. The real world of most alumni means more travel, business, and vacation abroad. It is certainly possible to serendipitously run into the important prospect on the street in Paris or the airport in Seoul.

There is a lot of competition already. Did you know that there are fully staffed development offices in New York for the London School of Economics, Oxford and Cambridge Universities, the American University in Beirut, and others? They have been there quite a while. As the opening facts conveyed, advancement professionals are more prevalent than most think, and they are active. The fund-raising profession is especially vigorous in Europe, complete with lots of consultants. CASE Europe has hundreds of members.[8] Capital campaigns, annual giving, phonathons, direct mail appeals, and many traditional fund-raising tools are being employed with rapidly increasing success. Far from being deleterious, the competitive activity is reinforcing. The introduction of the importance of alumni support helps break the existing belief that government takes care of all educational needs. Any training and enculturation of supporters in the life of the educational institution, including what competitors do, should be applauded. Good philanthropy begets better philanthropy. There is a warning associated with the proliferation of advancement activity. Like domestic prospects everywhere, prospects in the United States are not immune from being identified, cultivated, and solicited by others. If a development officer is not working your prospects abroad, it is likely someone else is.

Development officers are all fingerpainters in the art and science of fund raising abroad. An expert in raising money internationally is a development officer with two or more stamps in his or her passport. At best, American fund raisers are neophytes in pursuit of the Euro, yen, or dirham. Without data, with limited experience, and with the bewildering array of cultural, political, economic, and historical factors, development officers are making this up as they go. Happily, many professionals have not let the fear of the unknown stop them from trying. Fund raising's history has been one of ready, fire, aim. Although not everyone has succeeded, the majority has found it well justified.

International fund raising is not for the faint of purse or those in a hurry. Two commonalties of successful international development operations are resources and patience. Building relations far away takes additional budget and time. Despite the miracle of affordable travel, the budget required for international activities is significantly above domestic efforts. The University of Toronto estimates that its Hong Kong office did not recover its investment *until it had been in existence for a decade.* Several colleagues have observed that every day of international roadwork generally equates to *six* days of work in the office. There is ample evidence to indicate that building relations abroad, given cultural differences in particular, requires more time than is common domestically.

STRATEGIES FOR SUCCESS

Despite the lack of data and experience, some recognized strategies for success in international fund raising are emerging. Over the past few years, various conferences, articles, and informal sessions have attempted to determine how to obtain the faraway support that all seek.

Develop a Strong Case for Support

Whether dealing with the local community or one across the globe, the starting point for successful fund raising remains having the strongest possible case for support. For the international fund raiser, the starting question may be, "Are we seeking support for our international priorities or are we seeking support from sources abroad for all of our priorities?" Most international fund raisers have probably concluded that sources abroad are much more interested in regional or national interests than they are in general internationalization or basic priorities on the home campus. It is difficult convincing Japanese prospects that they should support unrestricted operating budgets. Similarly, it is a very tough sell to ask Saudi Arabian prospects to support Asian scholarships. What will support do to enhance Japanese focused interests? Or what is the common ground for support that might appeal to someone in the Middle East? I received a wonderful lesson in translating a case for support in Asia once. A loyal alumnus, after hearing what I thought was a solid, compelling case for building a better world for the next generation, gently told me that I must recalibrate. He said "We are more interested in building a better world for our parents rather than our children."

Those who target the nationalist/regional perspective appear to be succeeding. Before stepping on a plane, it is imperative to know what the *targeted* case for support is. Financial aid, teaching positions, program support, research projects, and other targets for gifts are far more likely to succeed when they address the immediate world around the prospect. There is no place called "international land." Requests are directed to residents and citizens of other countries. Solicitations should reflect common interests with the locals.

So, what is the best thing to pack? A well-crafted, targeted case for support written in the local language.

Commit to a Three- to Five-Year Time Frame

Quick success is rare. The business of building strong relationships requires a multi-year time frame. It is common to hear those on the international track sigh about the slowness of the process. There appear to be few shortcuts. Most of us are used to making a series of cultivation "moves" on prospects prior to attempting serious solicitation, but the process abroad is elongated. Most faraway prospects probably begin with an assumption that U.S. development officers may be carpetbaggers, interested solely in getting fast commitments and then disappearing. Hence, the process requires more care and effort than ever. If one were to measure the cultivation moves on prospects, one would most likely find that those from other countries require more, not less. Development officers therefore are well advised, like the University of Toronto in Hong Kong, to not expect results until solid relationships have been built over a several-year period. It is wise to have a formal plan that includes multiple annual trips, systematic cultivation programs, regular events, formal organized volunteer groups, and specific three- to five-year dollar goals.

Sell Internally First

The extra expense and elongated time frame for successful international fund raising must be supported inside the institution. Most academic communities have a predisposition to supporting internationalization. Most communities also recoil at the thought of a healthy additional budget that does not promise relatively short-term results. International fund-raising results are directly tied to the long-term commitment of the institutional leadership, not the development office. It has been sad to see successful but fledgling efforts scuttled when campus leaders have changed or shifted priorities. The successful development office must involve and educate institutional leaders in the effort. To attempt otherwise has a high risk of failure.

Tactically, getting support internally seems to benefit mightily from the involvement of faculty, particularly in regional studies, as well as parent and alumni leaders abroad. Many have also had success seeking targeted gifts just to finance international advancement efforts. This external support usually has an internal salutary effect on the skittish budget types.

Target Specific Countries and Cities

A clear lesson from successful programs is targeting. The harsh reality of limited budget, time, and staff makes it imperative to target a very few places that have promise. For Brown University, this meant starting

with Greece, where there were sufficient suspects and prospects to indicate possible success. Interestingly, the best and most numerous prospects were parents of students or graduates. Based on success in Greece,
Brown then prioritized Japan where they have had excellent success
obtaining support. The exercise of narrowing options begins in the office
and is determined by conversations on campus. The Willie Sutton syn-
drome—"Why do I rob banks? Because that's where the money is"—
serves as a guide. It is not continental, it is not regional, and in many
cases, it may not even be national. It is city focused. Pick two or three
cities that, after good research, have the best prospects. One should
follow a most-favored nation or city policy.

A word of warning: There is inherent risk in targeting. For several
decades, Bucknell University forged strong, deep ties within Burma. As
geopolitics lowered the Bamboo Curtain on Burma, the productive relations were severed, never to be reestablished. Despite the goodwill
created, politics can shift matters radically. Far from being an excuse
not to try, the example serves as a testimonial perhaps to the importance
of having cross-border relations that will help prevent an institution
from suffering such a setback in the future.

Research and Network Internally

Before stepping on a plane, it is imperative to know who the potential
prospects *and links to those prospects* are. The best sources for institutional
linkages are often on the home campus. In essence, it is wise to conduct
feasibility interviews to determine if there are sufficient prospects and
linkages before attempting travel. Faculty, particularly those in regional
studies, have proven to be a consistent wealth of information about who
potential supporters might be. They can be interviewed in the same way
consultants interview for campaign feasibility studies: Who might be
supporters? Who are key influencers that might approach them? Who
do you know? What historical or institutional linkages do we have? Why
is it important for those from a particular region/country/city to support
our efforts? It is often necessary to have the partnership with faculty and
researchers not only to build a strong case but also to have a defined
set of suspects and prospects. Many faculty scholars have developed relationships abroad that can be built upon successfully.

Many institutions, particularly at the independent school and college
level, have experienced the majority of their international successes
based upon building relationships with students' parents and grandparents. Family ties are a fabulous basis for building relationships and ob-

taining support. Education is highly prized universally, but there seems to be accentuated value abroad for schools that play a multi-generational family role. Princeton's $100,000,000 pledge from Gordon Wu was certainly influenced by the fact that two generations of the family had attended. There are numerous examples of small independent schools receiving seven-figure gifts from families very far away and commonly those having sent more than one child to the school. Homework on looking at the families of foreign students and alumni is well justified. The development office is well advised to spend significant time researching who the parents of students are and their potential ability to be major donors. Be especially attentive to families that have sent more than one member to the institution.

Major Gifts

The expense of international cultivation and solicitation requires thinking big. Development officers are ultimately responsible for ensuring that efforts are cost efficient. Without big gifts, six- and seven-figure ones, in the equation, fund raisers run the risk of appearing as junketeers. Furthermore, they must communicate the forthrightness of the message that they are seeking *and must obtain* big commitments if the campus is to justify far-flung efforts. What does it take to warrant visits that may be costing $100 a minute? Results!

Very often, getting started is the most difficult exercise. For the majority who find that budget is just not available, there is an alternative that has been employed quite successfully. Within any constituency there are usually those prospects who are quite keen on internationalization. It is a good idea to ask for their financial patronage in sponsoring forays abroad. A particularly good approach is to ask for "international venture capital" to enable starting from an experimental point of view, one not reliant on the usual difficult tradeoffs within operating budgets. A seed gift of $5,000 to $10,000 can remove many of the budgetary, political, and energy-consuming impediments to getting on the road. It is not uncommon to find enthusiasts in the prospect or alumni ranks, particularly those who work in the global marketplace, who are eager to provide seed funds to launch efforts abroad. In the long run, however, it is advisable to have the steadiness of institutional financial support.

Show Up

Woody Allen's precept that 90 percent of life is showing up applies heavily to international fund raising. Development officers are never well enough prepared, face innumerable unknowns, and always have competing demands for the lengthy blocks of time required for travel. Yet the biggest obstacle may be desk paralysis. I remember one frightening experience of traveling to the Middle East with our professor of Islamic Legal Studies who assured me that the lack of appointments prior to our arrival was not a problem. After two days of sitting in our hotel with no one returning our calls, I was convinced that I would be fired immediately upon my return to campus. Happily, the professor knew that it was obligatory to show up before attempting scheduling any visits and to be somewhat patient. Within the following week, we saw 72 various prospects and ultimately received several major commitments. How many development officers would travel without firm appointments?

A strategy that has great merit involves the "state visit." Too often, the thinking is to put the leader of an institution on a plane to have a few events and visits. In theory, prospects are thus identified and cultivated, yet this is a limited, almost haphazard approach. Instead, the advance trip should be considered in all circumstances. The advance team, ideally a regional specialist, like a professor, and a development officer visit in advance to ask advice and counsel about a potential visit by the president, dean, headmistress, and so forth. Utilizing any existing network and contacts, several questions should be posed: Is it advisable to have the leader visit? Who should be seen? Can you help get access to those who should be seen? What are common goals that could be established for the visit? What is the possibility of obtaining some significant support in advance of a visit so that announcements could be made? In essence, the state visit becomes partially stewardship if some support can be announced. I confess to brinkmanship in one country where I indicated to our friends and alumni that we would "lose face" and be unable to bring the leader if there were not some news (as in support) to announce. The scheduled trip for the leader was postponed indefinitely, much to the personal dismay of the leader. Within several months a major commitment was obtained and the state visit proceeded as an altogether very happy sojourn.

Think Mission over Culture

One of the more controversial issues debated by fund raisers concerns cultural sensitivity. The profession may well have erred on the side of letting social and cultural issues get in the way of the mission, that is, getting "asking" done. Development officers must stay focused on the fact that international journeys pivot on their ability to make a good case and solicit support. There are many reasons to be deflected—tax concerns, cultural differentiation, customs, mores, protocols. The impulse to be fully aware and sensitized to the local environment is strong. More often than not, we have let our nervousness about making missteps be an excuse not to solicit. Fund raising by indirection does not work anywhere. Perhaps it takes longer, perhaps the cultivation process differs, perhaps the solicitor(s) vary, but development officers should not escape their responsibility to have someone ask directly for support. It is clear that the creation of goodwill is a far cry from directly seeking support. The development office and leadership should not confuse the two. It may be necessary to solicit lightly, but it is vital to solicit somehow.

The desire to be fully informed can also deflect fund raisers from the mission. In preparation for a first trip to Asia with a new dean, we prepared a six-inch-thick briefing book. It was a superb tome encompassing historical, economic, social, and political facts of every place we were to visit. The dean digested it carefully over many hours. After the trip, he concluded that he would never read a briefing book again. He decided that his preparation time was better spent studying the individuals he would come into contact with and understanding local headlines—contemporary issues that popped up in conversations. He decided that knowledge overload and oversensitivity to culture differences inhibited him from his appointed mission.

Prepare for Quid Pro Quo

One of the significant differences in raising money abroad is the much greater prevalence of quid pro quo issues. Much of it is very understandable—how will my country, my city, benefit from this relationship? But there is also a clear perspective about direct benefits. How will the individuals, their businesses, their families, their friends benefit from the relationship? There are examples, mostly disastrous, of expected honorary degrees. One international philanthropist was renowned for offering gifts of $1 million—highly restricted—with the understanding that an honorary degree would be awarded. For others, there is a strong implication that family and friends will be admitted. And for others, access to professors, research, and the leadership of the institution is seen as part of the package. There are examples where supporters presume that the institution will offer some endorsement to favored politicians.

Some years ago, a phone call from a major insurance company overseas interested in making a contribution was routed to me. After some pleasant talk, the voice at the other end of the phone said, "So, we will be pleased to send a significant gift. But we have one question. Since I am the one the board of the company has chosen to attend your institution next year, should we send the check with my application form or send them separately?" Neither the student nor the check ever ended up at the institution.

Most institutions face quid pro quo issues regularly. Still, fund raising internationally requires much more attention to these matters. The best defense is preparation. What can and can't be done in terms of special attention and access? It is good to know in advance.

Recruit Local Surrogates

Even the best of operations are only able to spend a limited numbers of days a year in faraway locations. Short of opening a regional office, as more and more institutions are doing, the need for ongoing "eyes and ears" is large. They can provide critical information and extend the institution's presence on a regular basis. The governmental tactic of appointing honorary general consuls is very likely an option that would work in education. Alumni networks are, of course, invaluable tools. Yet the quest for major support sometimes transcends the level at which loyalists work. Frank, candid discussion about the needs and mission of the international efforts should be followed by recruiting adjunct pro bono staff, formally or informally. They can and should be ongoing researchers and major gift and stewardship officers.

INTERNATIONAL *TOPAS*

On a trip to Mexico, I learned the hard way that *topas* was Spanish for "speed bump." A few quick words about avoiding axle-bending mistakes many have made at the tactical level.

Bring Presents for Everyone

Manners and protocol are accentuated abroad. Gifts, sometimes expected, are important parts of the equation. Traveling development officers should bring something for everyone, including drivers and almost anyone they may come into contact with. Expense is not as important as the gesture. They should check with local guides about appropriate gift selections.

Know Something about the Tax Situation

Be sure to get some local tax knowledge or a link to a local tax expert before arriving at your destination.

Stay at Full-Service Hotels

Scrimping on hotels is a very bad idea. It is essential to have access to good phone lines, fax machines, transportation, travel agents, and other services, all of which are usually available at hotel chains that cater to the business traveler.

Translate Business Cards

Volumes are spoken when you present yourself in local terms. The low cost and easy availability of getting your business card printed in the language of your destinations is professional, polite, and effective in communicating the seriousness of your mission.

Document en Route

The physical fatigue of international travel works against good paperwork. Many have to use a "daily diary" approach to get the notes that refresh the memory of contacts. By the time one returns to the office, much can be lost to the brain-drain of travel. Notes along the way are the antidote.

CONCLUSION

There are bright days ahead for international fund raising. The amount and quality of educational fund raising is rising very fast. Many institutions, of every type, are trying and succeeding. The prospects are numerous, the potential is enormous, and the competition is probably already at work. With a thought-through case and a laser-like focus on solicitation, a bias for action is essential. Despite trepidations about the foreign environment and limited knowledge, development officers must forge ahead, always remembering the clear mission of identifying prospects, building strong relationships, making a compelling case, and actually asking for support. The fundamental lesson for international fund raising is simple: Try it, you'll like it. The only losing move is not to play.

NOTES

1. CASE Conference on International Fundraising, Edinburgh, Scotland, March 2001. Many of the practices of educational institutions cited in this chapter are from presentations at the conference. Consult the CASE Web site (http//:www.case.org).

2. *Annual Report*, University of Edinburgh, 1999–2000, 3.

3. David Cohen, "The Worldwide Rise of Private Colleges," *The Chronicle of Higher Education*, March 9, 2001, A-47.

4. "Your Passport to . . . Advancement's Global Marketplace," *Currents* (October 1999): 31.

5. CASE International Plenary, Trustees meeting, University of Edinburgh, March 2001. For further information, consult the CASE Web site (http//: www.case.org).

6. Nicole Lewis, "Have Expertise, Will Travel," *The Chronicle of Philanthropy* (July 13, 2000): 39.

7. Laura Smith and William Boardman, (Harvard University Development Office, 2000), Cambridge, MA: *Survey of Principal Gifts* 1–41.

8. For further information, consult the CASE Web site, International (www.case.org).

PART VII

Special Institutional Settings

The American educational "system" is the most diverse in the world in the variety of its institutions—some private, some public, some small, some large—and, increasingly, all supported by a combination of public and private funds.

Although the basic principles of fund raising apply in all situations, differences among institutional settings influence how they may be applied, the organizational and management strategies that are needed, and the problems and issues that must be addressed. The authors in this section explore such special considerations in four different settings.

In Chapter 18, Curtis Simic provides an overview of institutionally related foundations affiliated with public institutions. Although the chapter is focused on large universities, many community colleges also have foundations, and the same principles apply to them.

While most of this book emphasizes higher education—colleges and universities—independent primary and secondary schools also are an important component of the American educational system and have a long tradition of fund raising and philanthropy. In Chapter 19, James Theisen and Patricia King Jackson consider the unique aspects of fund raising for these institutions. In recent decades, community colleges have seen enormous growth in the number of institutions and enrollment. As discussed in Chapter 3, despite their relatively late entry into the arena of private support, many have developed highly successful fund-raising programs. Special considerations in community college fund raising are explored by Susan Kubik in Chapter 20. In the final chapter in the section, Linda Steckley discusses the complexity of raising funds for a professional school situated within a large university.

Again, the principles of fund raising—like those of medicine—are the same in every case. But each college, university, or school—like each patient—is unique and may call for a slightly different prescription. Educational fund raisers need to adapt their tools and skills to specific institutional settings, and their ability to understand the characteristics of each is essential to their success.

CHAPTER 18

Institutionally Related Foundations in Public Colleges and Universities

Curtis R. Simic

Private contributions are now as important to public institutions as they have always been to private ones. Although total dollars appropriated by state legislators have gone up over the years to cover the rising costs of a public education, the percentage of the operating budget that they cover is going down; at the same time, federal grants to both public and private institutions are declining. Auxiliary enterprises at colleges and universities, such as dormitories, are not intended to generate profits. Tuition and fees can be increased only so much if higher education, especially public higher education, is to fulfill its mandate to be accessible to as many qualified students as possible.

As a result, fund raising among America's public institutions of higher education—from state universities to community colleges—has increased dramatically over the past quarter century. Revenue from fund raising has been growing at rates much higher than increases in public funding.

So what is the best way for a public institution to pursue private contributions? In higher education, there are as many models for development operations as there are types of public institutions. But the one model that has seen the greatest growth in recent years is the separate, institutionally related foundation.

INSTITUTIONALLY RELATED FOUNDATIONS

Most public colleges and universities have found that a separate foundation maximizes the effectiveness of their fund-raising efforts. An external fund-raising operation offers advantages that have major, long-term benefits for an institution.

Key Advantages

Institutionally related foundations have unique features that make it easier for a public institution to raise and distribute private funds. By virtue of their separate existence from the public institutions they serve, foundations offer these key advantages:

- greater flexibility in the expenditure of funds
- increased investment opportunities
- protected donor confidentiality
- responsive accountability systems
- extensive opportunities for making "insiders out of outsiders"
- essential support from a larger, more diverse board of directors

Flexibility in Expenditures. By allowing the institution to keep private funds separate from state funds, a separate foundation gives the institution far greater flexibility in the expenditure of funds. For very good reasons, state dollars can be spent only in tightly prescribed ways.

State funds carry stringent requirements on bid procedures, limitations on expenditures, and specific time frames to meet various obligations. As a result, public institutions, including publicly assisted educational ones, are considerably limited in the way that they can disburse funds. They are asked to budget two or four years in advance, and, once the appropriation is made, they have limited flexibility in determining how the money is spent. A certain amount is designated for salaries and wages, capital projects or improvements, maintenance of the physical plant, and so on.

Also, certain kinds of expenditures simply cannot be funded with public money, although these vary from state to state. For example, money for faculty or staff relocation expenses are often not covered by state funds, but such funds can help attract the best candidates to the institution.

Utilizing the foundation enables an institution to seize opportunities with a minimum of red tape but with adherence to good business practices. Often, valuable educational opportunities are at stake. For example, a special library collection might hit the market between legislative sessions or out of sync with the budget year. A bid procedure would not be practical, and the money, not having been budgeted, might not be available. Gift funds donated and held for just such opportunities could be used immediately. Considered but quick action might determine whether the institution receives the collection.

Investment Opportunities. Another benefit that comes from the separation of state and private gift funds is the investment opportunities it opens up. Because of the restrictions imposed by some states' statutes, publicly assisted agencies are often limited in the way that they can invest. With millions of dollars in an endowment at stake, the difference between even a few percentage points on returns can make a significant impact on the long-term health and growth of an institution.

Nonprofit corporations, such as foundations, are subject to different laws and regulations, which sometimes allow them to invest more productively. While taking only a reasonable degree of risk, nonprofits can often realize better annualized returns. Since the foundation is holding funds in trust for departments, schools, programs, and campuses, maximizing the value of gifts through prudent and productive investment strategies is a fiduciary responsibility.

Donor Confidentiality. A third advantage of keeping private funds separate is the additional confidentiality foundations can offer donors. Though some state laws provide for a degree of confidentiality, rarely is it enough to protect most donors' concerns.

More than half of the funds given to any institution come from relatively few major donors. These are the donors who will almost certainly want their privacy protected because they are most likely to have disclosed privileged and personal information about their families and finances in the course of making their gifts. Many donors will have made planned gift arrangements with the institution, and no one wants their estate plans splashed all over the front page of the newspaper. By giving through a foundation, wills, trust agreements, and highly personal correspondence can be protected from public scrutiny.

Accountability Systems. A separate foundation can be organized to be fiscally accountable to its most important external constituency—donors. Accounting systems used by the states are not designed for use by fund raisers. On the other hand, an accounting system can be devised by a fund-raising organization that goes beyond the minimum accounting standards to answer donors' and account managers' questions, report on investments, and return information to the staff about productivity, among other uses. Such a system meets the special needs of the fund-raising office while complying with all accounting and auditing standards for private-sector corporations.

Making Insiders Out of Outsiders. It is important for foundations to involve people from outside the institution to increase the number of individuals who understand and support the institution's and the foundation's mission. According to the model of "philanthropic identification" developed by Boston College researcher Paul Schervish, "serious philanthropy results from a process through which a donor identifies with an organization and its cause. Individuals identify with the cause by becoming involved in an organization whose benefits can be learned and internalized and where they can interact with others who share similar values."[1]

Opportunities for involving outsiders include steering committees, special academic or athletic events, and advisory groups. Foundation volunteers, especially students, often become lifelong advocates for the institution. Even those individuals who help only with special events see the importance and long-term impact of the work being done.

It is essential to engage donors and alumni by inviting them to be on the foundation board of directors. Through foundation board membership and its responsibilities, individuals become involved in an organization that is vital to the well being and progress of the institution. As a result of their commitment, and in partnership with the institution's governing board, members of the foundation board become allies, advocates, and major donors to the institution.

The foundation's board of directors is frequently larger, sometimes much larger, than the institution's governing board. In addition to the core group of directors, foundations often have "consulting members" on foundation board committees. By including more members, the board can better represent the true gender, geographical, racial, and ethnic diversity of an institution's different constituencies. The job of the directors is not only to offer their expertise and make wise decisions, but also to engage in public relations activities and relate to the institution's key constituencies. They will represent an institution best if they reflect its diversity as truly as possible.

In choosing foundation directors, the criteria of "work, wealth, and wisdom" should apply. The more people who can contribute all three, the more successful the institution will be in fulfilling its mission. Effective foundation board members must possess a blend of integrity, expertise, and an ability to communicate and advocate effectively with community and national leaders. In addition, foundation board members must be able to provide financial support within their means and to influence others in their peer groups to do likewise.

The connections a foundation's board of directors brings to the institution are essential to the success of the fund-raising effort, and one of the primary functions of the foundation board is fund raising. While an institution's governing board is busy with the entire institution, the foundation board can focus on fund raising and all the associated functions that support it and make it a success. Since a foundation board exists in perpetuity, its history and relationships build continuously for the good of an institution.

In addition to fund raising, the foundation board is responsible for setting policies that refine the mission of the foundation in the areas of funds administration, asset management, and creating and developing relationships. These policies then become the goals of the foundation staff who take responsibility for their implementation and management.

MODELS OF FOUNDATION ORGANIZATION

In developing an institutionally related foundation model, institutions will want to consider whether to set up (1) a single foundation or multiple foundations, (2) centralized or decentralized operations, and (3) comprehensive or partial service offices.

Single Foundation or Multiple Foundations

Basically, the character of the institution determines the character of the foundation/s associated with it. A multi-campus university with a strong and effective central administration can successfully create a single foundation to serve its purposes. If the individual campuses of a multi-campus university have a tradition of substantial autonomy, little chance exists that a single foundation can be effective. Instead, individual fund-raising operations can focus on the unique character and needs of each campus.

The University of California system, which has several foundations, is an example of a multi-campus institution in which each campus has considerable autonomy. The system's governing board has created operational guidelines for the entire system, and these allow each foundation to discharge its responsibilities within system-wide policies and procedures. Indiana University, with an eight-campus system and a traditionally strong central administration, is an example of the multi-campus, single-foundation model.

It is possible, although more difficult, for a single campus to successfully operate multiple foundations. In this situation, each foundation board is charged with setting its own priorities, and each functions as an independent element, not necessarily in concert with the other foun-

dations or institutional priorities. Effective management of prospects—
"who will ask whom for what when"—is considerably more complex if
a single organization is not coordinating solicitation and stewardship
efforts. Finally, it is nearly impossible for a governing board to interact
effectively with the boards of multiple foundations.

Centralized or Decentralized

An institutionally related foundation can exist as a centralized operation
where all services—fund raising, investments, planned giving, and so
forth—are provided by a single, central foundation operation. This
model allows a foundation to have more control over the execution and
coordination of fund-raising activities. By assembling and centrally managing a core of specialists, the foundation can offer the institution highly
specialized legal, marketing, investment, publications, and prospect management services.

In a decentralized operation, fund-raising functions are spread out
over the institution to serve the different needs of various departments
and schools. Although this model allows individual development staff
to focus on their units' specific needs, it is much harder to coordinate
donor contacts and realize the economies of scale offered by a centralized
operation.

A very workable solution for an institution may be to establish a
foundation that is both centralized and decentralized at the same time.
All key services—legal, publications, prospect management, investments, and so on—could be centralized, while major gift fund raising is
decentralized.

Comprehensive or Partial Service

Comprehensive foundations obtain private support and manage gift assets as well as provide all the associated services and infrastructure required for raising, investing, and administering funds in compliance with
donor intent. Partial service foundations only manage assets raised by
their institutions' development staffs, or they focus on fund raising exclusively.

By taking advantage of economies of scale, comprehensive foundations can offer highly specialized services and save each fund-raising unit
within the institution the cost of duplicating those services. Direct mail,
publications, marketing, telemarketing, and database management services are all highly consistent and coordinated in a full service system.

As a result, comprehensive foundations have in place all the elements necessary to react quickly to the institution's needs, whether it be for a campaign or a new volunteer-focused program.

Considered the preferred model, a comprehensive foundation may not be feasible for a smaller institution or program. In such cases, partial service foundations allow institutions to keep costs to a minimum while simplifying different aspects of the fund-raising process.

ROLES AND SERVICES

As an old saying goes, only 10 percent of getting a gift is asking for it; 90 percent is preparation. In other words, depositing the check is just one act in the lengthy fund-raising process. Besides gift administration, there are donor acquisition mailings and publications, prospect research, events, telemarketing programs, in-person solicitations, donor recognition, and volunteer coordination. And these are just the basic services a foundation provides in its roles as a fund raiser. A comprehensive, institutionally related foundation fulfills several roles. Although fund raising comes first, a foundation also manages investments, provides central services and support, and maintains internal foundation operations.

Fund Raising

In the broadest sense, fund raising involves finding donors, developing and deepening their relationships with the institution, matching donors' interests and the institution's needs, and recognizing donors for their support. Services that sustain the basic fund-raising process include research and feasibility studies, publications and mailings, telemarketing, individual donor solicitations, major gift management, and campaign coordination.

Good fund raising also involves detailed follow-up and stewardship efforts. Donors want and should expect the reporting, stewardship, and accountability that a donor-responsive organization can give them. This level of attentiveness requires careful data entry and reporting, prospect management, and timely publications or correspondence.

On the other side of the equation, fund raising requires working with all constituent groups. Relationships should be cultivated with board members, volunteers, the institutional administration, faculty, staff, students, institutional governing boards, and the general public. These relationships can be built through communications that include in-person visits, publications, special awards or recognition ceremonies, and detailed and accurate gift reporting.

Investments

The investment management area of the foundation serves the donors and the institutional representatives as it strives to maximize the return on the endowment and preserve the purchasing power of the principal. Investments should be diversified to achieve a reasonable rate of return with a reasonable degree of risk. Services to support this mission include strategic planning, research, in-house portfolio management, donor reporting, and annual endowment statements.

Investments often involve planned giving services. Planned gifts have become a way for more donors to effectively and economically make major gift commitments to fulfill their philanthropic goals for an institution. In order to grow a successful planned giving program, a foundation needs dedicated legal services, specialty publications and reporting, and in some cases, real estate management.

Managing investments and planned giving in-house also allows a foundation to build strong donor relations. By keeping donors informed on the performance of their endowment funds, in addition to the results of the overall endowment, a foundation builds personal relationships with major donors that often result in additional gifts.

Central Services and Support

A foundation has two supporting roles to play. There's the fund-raising support a foundation provides individual units, and the flexibility it provides an institution to react to unique opportunities. On the one hand, a foundation provides all the central services that support fund-raising operations—database access and management, planned giving, legal, investment, publications, and events. On the other hand, a foundation can offer an institution as a whole innovative and flexible solutions.

Through its central services, foundations free up individual development officers and their departments to pursue major gifts and donors. A separate core of foundation services—like a single donor database—keeps different units from duplicating services and potentially generating inconsistent records.

In its role as the catalyst, a foundation assists an institution in ways that do not directly involve just fund raising. Real estate purchases are a good example. Often such opportunities arise on short notice, and the institution has to go through a lengthy approval process to purchase real estate. Alternatively, the foundation can purchase the real estate and lease the property to the institution, which purchases the property when it can. Another example would be providing an institution with start-up funds for a campaign.

Internal Foundation Operations

In order to sustain an institution, the foundation itself must run smoothly. Such internal operations—facilities management, accounting, information systems, and human resources—are the "invisible" functions that are critical to the success of the foundation and its institution.

Without a solid internal structure, a foundation quickly becomes caught up in its own housekeeping issues instead of providing for the institution. However, with strong core operations, a foundation not only offers consistent, high-level service to the institution it serves but also better represents itself and the institution to the general public.

LINKAGES: THE FOUNDATION AND THE INSTITUTION

A foundation is one of the best partners an institution of higher education can have. Public institutional governing boards and their foundations need each other in order to be successful. In creating effective links between the two organizations, foundations and institutions should begin by building strong, interactive communications, setting well-defined priorities, and finding funding solutions.

Opening Communications

Formal communication structures are a good place to start in creating stronger links between foundations and their institutions. For example, governing board members can also be members of the foundation board. The Indiana University Foundation's charter includes a provision that three of the more than 40 foundation board members must be trustees of the institution. Governing board members can serve on foundation board committees as consultants even if they are not members of the foundation board. It is also important that the foundation chief executive be a member of the institution's top management team. Likewise, foundation board members can serve on ad hoc committees of the governing board. Such formalized connections clearly establish the foundation's role as a separate organization that serves the institution as a key partner.

The faculty must be also be a full partner in the university fund-raising operation if the program is to succeed. This is true in any development operation, but tensions can be greater when an independent foundation is involved. An inherent faculty distrust of administrators is often over-laid by the recognition that the faculty has no control over a legally separate foundation. However, the foundation staff needs to remember that although they supply the technical expertise, the faculty provides the "inspiration" for potential donors. Regular meetings between the foundation head and a faculty committee are a good way to address important faculty concerns.

Foundation partnerships with other groups that deal with external constituencies of the university can also promote unity. These groups include the alumni association, university or community relations offices, intercollegiate athletics programs, and government relations and public relations offices. Together, members of these groups can develop a unified approach to a specific opportunity or to an anticipated problem.

Finally, the foundation board should consider inviting guests to its board meetings and including consulting members on foundation board committees. These involvements help make "insiders out of outsiders" from within the university family and result in more thorough discussions and constructive relationships. Perhaps most important of all, the governing board and the foundation must communicate like good partners. Good communications create synergies that make both organizations more effective.

Setting Priorities

When independent organizations work together, areas of responsibility must be clearly defined, and all parties must keep in mind their specific missions and capabilities. Setting fund-raising priorities is an area in which ambiguity over "who's in charge" may arise. The issue affects the foundation's relationship with all parts of the university, from the governing board to individual faculty members. Ideally, the process of setting fund-raising priorities should be carefully constructed and completely open to examination by any and all constituents.

However, the foundation is not in the business of setting priorities for the university. That is the responsibility of the governing board, the administration, and the faculty. The foundation *is* in the business of determining which of the priorities might be achieved through private funding and should provide the expertise on how to go about raising those funds.

Once the governing board, administration, and faculty have decided on overall institutional goals, a committee of the president, other administrators, faculty, and perhaps students, reviews requests, needs, plans, and proposals to determine specific priorities.

After this review is completed, the projects assigned to "private gifts-annual" and "private gifts-capital" are forwarded to a development group, chaired by the president of the university, that includes other administrators (such as the chief financial officer), faculty, students, and the chief executive of the foundation. At this point, the foundation assumes its responsibility for determining the feasibility of raising private funds for the proposed projects.

This process is made easier by foundation and governing boards that are willing to sit down together to determine policies and procedures based on what is best for the institution and what will make best use of the unique capabilities the foundation has to offer.

Finding Funding

The facts of life have been stated many times in many ways for years: "You can't raise money without spending money; within reasonable limits, the return is likely to be commensurate with the investment."[2] Returns on investment in fund raising are phenomenal. "[P]ast experience has proved that one of the best investments universities have made in the past twenty to thirty years has been providing seed money from university funds to launch a foundation."[3] Often 8-to-1 or 10-to-1, the return on investment in fund raising is strong. Once everyone is convinced fund raising is a good investment, the next hard task is to figure out where to find those funds.

Ultimately, there are only two sources of funding for a foundation: the institution and the gifts themselves. Whatever creative variations and combinations foundations or their institutions use to generate funding, they come down to these. The process of making the decision about how to fund a foundation, or to change the way an existing foundation is funded, will call into play all of the intangibles associated with resources and how they are expended, with all of the perceptions and priorities of the individuals involved. When making this decision, foundations and institutions should begin by considering the five most common sources of funding.

Flat Fee. The most direct form of funding is a fee from the institution for development and related services. This can come in a lump sum from the president's office or in pieces from various schools or campuses. The difficulty in breaking the fee out into pieces, of course, is the inevitable conflict over who pays how much, and how a fair share is determined. The final decision on whether or how to break out the fee is one that must be made by the institution for the foundation.

Fee-for-Service. It is possible to assess fees for individual foundation services. For example, an institutional account manager could decide to pay the cost of a telemarketing call from the gift funds accumulated because the calling program was optional and by contract. This is a change from historical institutional practice, where each department or administrative office provided its services for free to all other departments and offices in the spirit of institutional cooperation. Without losing the spirit, an increasing number of institutions are, however, turning to some form of responsibility-centered management or financial accountability by unit. This may make the concept of fee-for-service more palatable as it relates to the separate, institutionally related foundation.

Gift Fund Fees. Fees can be directly assessed against, or paid from, gifts once they are received. The foundation might decide to base a fee on the total dollar amount in a particular institutional unit's gift accounts. These fees are similar to the ones charged for services, but in this case either the foundation or the institution has decided that the fees will be paid from gift funds. Alternatively, some foundations keep the earnings on a gift for the first year only. A final option is for a foundation to keep a set percentage of every gift it receives—an approach few donors consider appropriate.

Asset Management Fee. Another source of funding is assessing a management or administrative fee on the market value of the endowment accounts. These fees range at various institutions from half to twice as much as is commonly charged by outside investment management firms. Currently, the prevailing fee charged is 1 percent above the cost paid to outside portfolio managers. Along with the fee-for-service from the institution, the investment management and administrative fee provides the most stable and consistent source of funding for a foundation.

Unrestricted Gifts. Funding for the foundation could also come from unrestricted gifts—those gifts that come to the institution without any restrictions on how they must be used. Unrestricted gifts are valuable to the institution in many ways. Not only do they give the institution the critical advantage of flexible funds that can be drawn on to further priorities and fend off the unexpected, but they are also a possible source of operating funds for the institution's foundation. So desirable are these gifts, in fact, that it is important that the institution and the foundation decide early on with how they will be handled.

Given the various options, most foundations and institutions opt to use multiple sources of funding. Royster C. Hedgepeth found in his 2000 survey of 47 colleges, universities, and institutionally related foundations that "Only 7 percent of the surveyed respondents' fund-raising programs rely on a single source of funding for the fund-raising budget, and 70 percent of the respondents' programs rely on three or more sources."[4] Whatever the mix, the funding plan should be straightforward and easily implemented.

Once the final funding solution is established, it is vital that the foundation and the institution have a written, contractual agreement that states the fee, the time period that it covers, and the services that will be provided by the foundation. It is becoming increasingly important that foundations formalize their separateness from their institutions for reasons ranging from privacy of donor records to flexibility in investment of gift funds. The written agreement also helps the foundation focus on its mission and not, in its zeal to be a partner in furthering the university's goals, step beyond its intended role.

WITH RIGHTS, RESPONSIBILITIES

The relative freedom that enables separate, nonprofit foundations to better serve their institutions is a right that cannot be abused. There has been, and should be, an increasing awareness and concern on the part of the public, legislators, and colleges and universities about accountability, openness, and the responsible use of funds. Separate foundations associated with colleges and universities have an obligation and a duty to inform those they serve. In fact, foundations could routinely make accessible to their constituencies and the general public the following items:

- financial audit, conducted by an outside auditor
- annual report, including an honor roll of donors
- operating budget, including funding sources
- policies on disbursement of gift funds
- investment policies, expenditure guidelines, and performance
- report on the cost of fund raising
- contract for service between the foundation and the institution it serves

- policies regarding the establishment of fund-raising priorities
- Form 990, the annual tax return for nonprofit corporations

The best foundations are the ones that strike a balance between their responsibility to be open and accountable against their responsibilities to those they serve. It is important to remember, after all, that "philanthropy and scholarship are each, separately, among the most powerful influences to shape the future of our society. In combination, they may be unsurpassed in their power to improve the human condition."[5] Colleges and universities are, as they have always been, a means for people to have access to a wider world and broader opportunities. The hope offered by education is inextricably linked with the success of our society.

NOTES

1. Aaron Conley, "Breaking Away in the Race for Donors," in *Philanthropy Matters* (Indianapolis: Center on Philanthropy, Indiana University), 10, No. 2, Fall, 2000, 10.

2. Harold J. Seymour, miscellaneous memoranda, American Association of Fund-Raising Counsel, New York, 1960.

3. Darrell D. Wyrick, "Financing and Budgeting a Foundation," in *Raising Money Through an Institutionally Related Foundation*, ed. Timothy A. Reilly (Washington, DC: Council for Advancement and Support of Education, 1985), 58.

4. Royster C. Hedgepeth, *How Public College & University Foundations Pay for Fund-Raising* (Washington, DC: Association of Governing Boards of Universities and Colleges and the Council for Advancement and Support of Education, 2000), 9.

5. W. B. Boyd, address made to donors and faculty at a recognition dinner hosted by the Indiana University Foundation, Bloomington, Indiana, November 1989.

CHAPTER 19

Raising Funds for Independent Schools

James M. Theisen and Patricia King Jackson

Independent school fund-raising programs have evolved along the same path as the rest of educational fund raising. However, independent school programs started one to two decades behind most of their higher education counterparts. This lag allows a look to higher education fund-raising models for trends and perspectives that might guide the growth of school programs.

Forty years ago, independent school fund raising was the province of a network of volunteers, mainly parents, who gave their time each week to help organize auctions, plan dinners, and author the school newsletter. The professional staff person often came from either a volunteer position in the school or was co-opted from another administrative or teaching post. Usually part-time, these early development directors spent their time—as did early college and university fund raisers—engaged in activities concerned with receipting gifts rather than raising them.

When inflation skyrocketed to double digits in the 1970s, and salaries rose more slowly than the cost-of-living index, trustees and school heads realized that resources and personnel needed more specific focus. By the 1980s, institutional planning and program development—combined with capital campaigns to shore up endowment and building assets—appeared to be a solution to school financial needs. This solution, however, required a programmatic, controllable, and goal-oriented fund-raising program. The pressure for increased, predictable results placed on independent school fund-raising programs forced greater specialization and larger staffs.

With large staffs of highly focused specialists, the larger independent school fund-raising programs today are indeed beginning to resemble those of colleges and universities. Yet, such specialization—simply because it requires the luxury of size—is beyond the capacity of most independent schools. The typical school development officer, unlike his or her colleagues at colleges and universities, embraces almost every aspect of institutional advancement—development, alumni and parent relations, and communications—and everything from working with the trustees to running the auction to writing the parent newsletter.

WHAT MAKES SCHOOLS DIFFERENT

The director of development at an independent school leads a highly centralized, manageable program that can respond quickly and directly to both opportunities and challenges. Schools are relatively free of the complexities and competitiveness of large universities. In most schools, all fund-raising activities originate with the development office. While development deals with sports associations and parents issues, few schools deal with "friends" groups that offer separate and competitive fund-raising appeals. Development works closely with faculty, and rarely does the staff have to coordinate individual faculty requests concerning particular projects. Although there are the usual complaints about bureaucracy, there is frequent and seamless interaction with the school head, the business manager, admissions officers, trustees, and faculty.

The successful independent school development program contains all of the elements of its higher education counterpart, but on a more controllable scale. Each staff member may fulfill several traditional development functions; for example, the annual fund director may also run the auction; the alumni director may also edit the magazine; the director may raise major gifts as well as foundation, corporation, and government grants. These multiple roles lead to greater flexibility. This flexibility, combined with a relatively small staff of individuals well known to the director, encourages innovation and offers an ability to quickly see the results of new efforts in order to realign resources and personnel when necessary.

The development officer is a member of the institution's management team, aware of broad concerns and the school's pressing needs. Development officers strive to meet common goals of faculty, the administration, and the school's board of trustees. The focus is on the whole, not on individual areas or departments, and it is on the long-range vision of the school.

Because independent schools are relatively small, uncomplicated organizations, most school development officers get to know their faculty and students personally. Many development officers today, as in the past, have some responsibilities beyond their office duties. They serve as coaches, student advisers, chaperons, club sponsors, or members of a faculty committee. This is a perfect way for a development officer to be well acquainted with the institution and its future constituency of alumni. The presence of the development officer also gives students an appreciation for how alumni and parents contribute to the financial strength of the school and how their help has enriched and broadened the educational programs.

SUPPORT FOR DAY AND BOARDING SCHOOLS

The fund-raising programs of day and boarding schools differ principally in the proportion of support they receive from their parent and alumni constituencies, respectively. The influence of these constituencies has molded both the shape of the institutions' development programs and various institutional policies, such as the proportion of either alumni or parents on the governing board and the preferences given to the various constituencies in the admissions process.

Boarding schools receive up to 80 percent of their support from alumni, paralleling support for residential colleges. For many alumni, the boarding school was their first experience away from home. The school acts "in loco parentis," and thus the student develops strong bonds with the faculty and staff. Since many boarding schools have a long history, alumni associations are often well developed and serve to link the school with graduates. Boarding school boards of trustees tend to be heavily weighted with alumni. Parents are relatively less involved and visit the campus less frequently.

At day schools, as much as 80 percent of all capital and annual gifts come from parents. Parents of day school students have chosen a private school education because they want to give their children the best. They see and measure their children's progress daily, and they develop first-hand knowledge of the strengths and weaknesses of the school, and also of the school's needs. In addition, day schools get to know the parents very well, including their financial capacity. Parents make up a majority of the school's trustees, and this closeness provides them an opportunity to respond to the school's programs with both their time and financial resources.

Over time, the lines between day and boarding schools are beginning to blur as more and more boarding schools develop strong parent programs and day schools develop strong alumni relations programs. The question remains whether the discrepancy between alumni and parent support at boarding and day schools is an immutable characteristic—or whether it simply results from each type of institution responding to the easiest and most accessible fund-raising constituency first, and then tailoring its programs accordingly. If the latter is the case, the future may bring a degree of leveling off in the proportions of alumni and parent support for boarding and day schools.

KEY PLAYERS

All successful organizations are managed from the top. The success of the school development effort depends on the vision and leadership of trustees, working in concert with the school head and supported closely by the development officer. This triumvirate is often also referred to as the "three-legged stool of fund raising."

Trustees are the stewards of the school's resources—people, plant, and financial assets—and, as such, they have a central role in school fund-raising efforts. Years ago, board members were selected because of their prominence in the community or through an "old boy" network. Today, independent schools emulate their colleagues in higher education and select trustees to represent the diversity of the school and the specific needs of the institution. All trustees should share a strong sense of loyalty and relationship to the institution, a desire to see the institution succeed, a willingness to make the institution their own philanthropic priority during their time as trustee, and, hopefully, a collective ability to make a quantitative difference in the fund-raising program. All trustees must support the annual fund to a level commensurate with their capacity. During a major campaign, each trustee should make a commitment that credibly demonstrates the priority that they, as a board, wish the community to give to the fund-raising effort.

A well-managed institution has a good working partnership between the board and the head. The head is the educational leader, and all academic, student, faculty, staff, and legal issues are ultimately channeled through this office. In a fund-raising context, the head is the chief fundraiser. Donors considering a major investment in the school want to talk to the head, and he or she will necessarily be involved in most all of the top solicitations. It is estimated that a school head needs to spend at least 20 percent of his or her time on fund raising during non-campaign periods, and as much as 50 to 60 percent during the early stages of a campaign.

The travel that may be involved in fund raising complicates the job for a school head. The boarding school head leaves the campus for days or weeks to visit and solicit a national constituency. Some heads of day schools are able to concentrate their fund-raising efforts on parents who live near the school, although this may be changing as day schools reach out to their alumni.

The development director is the third key member of the fund-raising team. He or she usually leads an office of increasingly professional individuals who support the governing board and head of school and implement an array of ongoing fund-raising programs. At independent schools, the institutional investment in fund-raising programs amounts to an average of 5 percent of the institution's budget, falling in line with the profile at most private colleges.

THE ANNUAL FUND IS THE FOUNDATION OF THE DEVELOPMENT PROGRAM

Every good development effort starts with a well-planned and carefully managed annual fund. Major gifts and planned gifts rest on this all-important fund-raising platform. The level of sophistication varies with different schools, but the principles remain the same. While yielding dependable yearly support, the annual fund provides a ready means of identifying and cultivating donors and a way for staff to learn how to work with volunteers on a specific task in a defined period of time. Lessons learned in the annual fund and knowledge gained about various donors should contribute directly to the major and planned giving program, as well as to campaigns.

Annual fund programs include alumni, parents, past parents, grandparents, and friends, but the degree of support from each has tended to depend on the type of school—day or boarding. While this distinction directs resource allocation, staff time, and volunteer efforts, it should be noted that successful annual fund programs at all schools will address each of these constituencies.

The parents fund is paramount in day schools where parents are close at hand. Parents know each other and are known to the school. They usually contribute the majority of volunteer support and provide most of the yearly revenues. Often organized by school division—or class—the successful parents fund usually relies on peer solicitation of leadership donors, backed by direct mail and telephone efforts conducted by volunteer parents.

In recent years, grandparents are playing an increasing role in their grandchildren's educational experience, and in the philanthropic program of their grandchildren's schools. Grandparents funds are usually nominally headed by volunteers, although most of the solicitations are done by mail or by school staff. Today, "grandparent days" are built into the school academic calendar.

Parents of former students—called "past parents" or "parents of alumni"—also play an important role in the school annual fund. As children progress from one educational level to the next, parental support and attention necessarily shift to the next school. However, the appreciation of the education and community represented by the independent school often remains. A grateful parent may not be ready to support the school immediately after a child's graduation but may express appreciation years after that child has completed college or graduate school. Those names shouldn't be removed from the lists too soon!

The alumni fund plays the paramount role in annual fund raising for boarding schools, and many day schools now look to the boarding schools to structure their own alumni funds. Most are based on a class system—relying on layers of volunteers, with classmates soliciting classmates. The five-year reunion cycle presents opportunities to raise larger-than-usual gifts, both for the annual fund and special projects. Reunions are the rallying point. They serve to reintroduce alumni to their alma mater and to articulate the school's most pressing needs. In the largest alumni funds, schools are emulating colleges by structuring their class and reunion campaigns using capital campaign techniques of advance planning (in some cases two years in advance), feasibility studies, and prospect screening.

In all annual funds, various approaches are used to solicit gifts: letters, telephones (phonathons), and—the most effective method—personal visits. Knowing that face-to-face solicitation is not possible in all cases, schools are turning to techniques of market segmentation, dividing the constituency into similar groups and targeting each with a specific appeal and combination of approaches. As schools shift to larger and more specialized staffs, market segmentation and other sophisticated fund-raising methods will become more common.

MAJOR AND PLANNED GIFTS

Independent schools today rely increasingly on major and planned gifts as an intrinsic part of their ongoing fund-raising program, rather than turning to major gifts only in times of capital campaigns.

In order to maintain a program of ongoing major gift fund raising, an institution must have a strong and well-articulated case for why major gift support is needed, a sense of priority projects, and a knowledge of the institution's constituency of potential major gift donors. In non-campaign fund-raising periods, solicitations tend to be more driven by prospect readiness than by project need. Good prospect research and a well-organized prospect-tracking system are indispensable tools for major gift fund raising in non-campaign periods, as they are during campaigns. Volunteer involvement in major gift solicitations, a popular character-istic of independent school fund raising, does begin to decline as staff are able to engage in more direct solicitation themselves.

As more individuals consider larger gifts, planned giving must be part of the development effort. Planned giving programs generally begin with bequest awareness and do not have to be highly sophisticated or expen-sive efforts. You can include bequest reminders in alumni and parent newsletters and suggest to board members and key volunteers to remem-ber the school in their estate planning. As the program begins to include more sophisticated planned giving vehicles, an outside consultant can be retained to help with specific questions, so the school need not invest in a full-time, trained planned giving director until the size of the pro-gram merits one. The marketing of planned gifts is facilitated for inde-pendent schools because so many donors are already familiar with these methods through long exposure at the university level and by other nonprofits that promote planned giving as a charitable option. Inde-pendent schools need to capitalize on this environment and develop a compelling case for this form of long-term support.

The planned giving program's cost-effectiveness cannot and should not be measured in immediate terms. The school should evaluate the program each year, but measure the investment versus financial payback on at least a five-year basis. Many schools invest time and energy in donor cultivation only to reap the benefits ten, twenty, or thirty years later. The real question is, how long can a school afford to wait before starting a planned giving program, even on a modest scale?

FOUNDATION AND CORPORATION PROGRAMS

Anyone who has worked in an independent school will have heard a well-meaning parent or graduate say, "I think you are missing the boat. There are real opportunities to raise dollars for this program from foundations and corporations. My college just received a grant for the same kind of program. Not only would it answer our needs, but it would also take the burden off the parents who are already paying a sizable tuition."

The truth is that independent schools—whether day or boarding— receive relatively little support from foundations and corporations. Most foundation support at the school level comes when a parent or graduate has a special relationship with the foundation. Some foundations independently support elementary and secondary education for specific programs, but they are few in number. Foundation grants will rarely, if ever, be the financial backbone of a school's fund-raising program.

Corporations support independent schools primarily through matching gifts to the annual fund program. Today, nearly 500 corporations match gifts to independent schools. Outright corporate gifts to schools usually occur when there is a community partnership or a direct benefit to the corporation. For example, a local computer software company might make a gift-in-kind of software to a school because many of the employees' children attend. Often, corporations that support colleges and universities hope to attract future employees or benefit from research in which an institution is engaged; schools can offer no such direct benefits.

Corporate and foundation grants have a place within the independent school development effort, but they are not the panacea some might imagine them to be, and a hard-worked school development director should be wary of putting too many resources into trying to raise funds from either corporate or foundation sources. Development staff must consider the time invested against the return and spend time cultivating alumni or parents who will do more over time than an occasional foundation gift.

SPECIAL EVENTS

Auctions, dinners, and carnivals are popular fund-raising events. For some schools, special events yield hundreds of thousands of dollars each year.

These events take an inordinate amount of staff and volunteer time. However, they serve the important function of bringing people together for a common purpose. The functions allow trustees, administrators, and volunteer leaders to meet their constituents and to further the school's cause.

An event is worth repeating only if it proves to be a money raiser and a popular rallying event in the school's academic year. It is important for staff to determine the time and effort needed to run it and the dollars it will raise, then compare that to the results expected from channeling the same resources into personal solicitations of the top 100 donors.

CAMPAIGNS

Thirty years ago, educational institutions viewed campaigns as one-time isolated events during which they suspended their annual funds in order to put all resources behind the capital effort. Eventually, institutions realized they had closed the door to an important volunteer network and donor base. Since not every person would contribute to the capital campaign, donors fell out of the habit of supporting the institution and shifted their loyalties elsewhere. Rebuilding annual support took precious time and cost significant revenues.

Today, most schools, like colleges and universities, view campaigns as strategic events designed both to raise significant amounts of capital and to bolster the entire development program. Most either integrate the annual fund with the campaign or continue to run the annual fund drive separately.

A campaign cannot be successful if run by the staff alone; the board, administration, and volunteers must be committed and work as a team. The school must have a clear image of itself, and the campaign must be based on legitimate institutional planning, long-term goals, and an adequate budget and staff.

The board's role is crucial. It is sometimes held that the board should contribute about 25 percent of the announced campaign goal. While that specific percentage is debatable, it is true that the board's leadership will set the tone for the rest of the campaign. Trustees must step forward before the campaign is publicly announced and pledge their support at a level that they believe to be a credible demonstration of their commitment to the institution. Momentum comes from the announcement that "100 percent of the board gave!"

Even when the development staff at an independent school has campaign experience, consideration should be given to bringing in an outside consultant to help with the preparation and implementation of a campaign. Outside counsel provides experience and serves as an objective barometer for the campaign's progress. The search for a consultant should begin as soon as a campaign is seriously considered. Choose a consultant who has a proven track record at similar institutions, good working chemistry with the development director, and credibility with the board of trustees.

THE FUTURE OF SCHOOL FUND RAISING

What challenges do schools face in the coming decade? Endowments in the near term are unlikely to grow at double-digit rates characteristic of the 1990s. Tuition will likely follow the path of prices in higher education, with declining increases or even a leveling off in the next decade. Fund raising, as a means of bridging the gap between income and expenses and of meeting urgent capital needs, will become even more vital to the financial integrity of schools.

With limited budgets, the development officer must review how resources will be allocated and weigh programs on a cost-revenue basis. Questions like, "Can we afford to continue this event or program?" and "Are we receiving a maximum return on the dollars spent?" will merit careful consideration. "Nice-to-have" programs will be eliminated.

Schools must also do a better job of stewardship—of maintaining a close, ongoing relationship with donors. Individuals who have given in the past will be even more important in future funding. Individual cultivation will consume more time. Recognizing, thanking, and showing donors consistent appreciation will be imperative.

More donors will consider planned gifts to meet, first, their own financial needs and, second, the institution's needs. While many of these gifts will not mature for ten years or more, schools cannot sit idle and let other nonprofits reap the benefits. Planned giving programs must be on every development officer's menu.

Reports of mega-campaigns at colleges and universities fill fund-raising journals. Donors' sights are being raised, and the effects will certainly filter down to independent schools. Schools must not be afraid to take advantage of the current fund-raising climate and ask for larger gifts.

Development staff must vigilantly monitor new trends and tools to assess how they will affect their institutions. State-of-the-art technology provides opportunities for institutions to have better and more communications with constituents. However, the people side of the equation remains crucial. People give to people, and the successful development campaign will always hinge on the dynamic interaction of a solicitor talking to a donor. School development officers must be familiar with the latest techniques while retaining the broad overview to communicate effectively and motivate donors persuasively. The world has changed, but the human need for personal interactions and involvement remains the same. People give to institutions when they feel that their support makes a difference.

CHAPTER 20

Raising Funds for Community Colleges

Susan K. Kubik

Community colleges marked their centennial anniversary in 2001. Having begun with the founding of Joliet Junior College in Illinois, community colleges now educate more than 10.4 million students annually. Spurred by a 1948 report from the Truman Commission, which called for the creation of a network of community-based colleges, the growth of this form of higher education has been dramatic. Today there are more than 1,100 community colleges in the United States alone, with many other countries adapting the model to their unique situations.

Coupled with the increase in the number of community colleges came a concurrent growth in enrollment. Forty-six percent of all first-time U.S. college freshmen now begin their studies at a community college. Community college enrollment represents 44 percent of all U.S. undergraduates. The student profile breaks out as follows:

- 58 percent female; 42 percent male
- 64 percent part-time; 36 percent full time
- Average student age is 29 years
- 46 percent of all African-American students enrolled in higher education; 55 percent of all Hispanic students enrolled in higher education; 46 percent of all Asian/Pacific Islands students enrolled in higher education; 55 percent of all Native American students enrolled in higher education

• More than 50 percent are first generation college students[1]

Learning the unique characteristics of community colleges is important to developing an understanding of institutional advancement
within this setting. In addition to the colleges' student profile, these
characteristics include low cost, open access, and the ability for quick
response to community and workforce needs. Community colleges reflect
the communities in which they are based. Since no two communities
are identical and since much community college development, at least
in its earliest stages, has tended to be community based, it follows that
successful advancement programs at community colleges do not tend to
follow a cookie-cutter mold. What works in one setting may not be
easily replicated in another.

Unfortunately, there is a scarcity of in-depth research on community
college development.[2] The benchmark most often used for comparative
purposes in higher education fund raising is the annual *Voluntary Support
of Education* report, published by the Council for Aid to Education
(CAE). This report includes data from less than 10 percent of all community colleges. There is some speculation that those community colleges that annually report their figures to CAE are among the most
successful in raising funds, but that has not been confirmed.

What is known is that for those who do report the success of their
efforts, philanthropic support per student at two-year colleges overall is
minimal, particularly when compared to other categories of institutions
within the higher education community. But, it is growing. "Voluntary
support per student is estimated to have been $41 (constant dollars) in
1981. It gradually moved upward to a high of $84 in 1990. It hovered
near that point, varying between $74 and $89 until it began growing
annually in 1996. By 2000, it stood at $128 per student."[3]

And, as it grows, what is emerging is a pattern of support that is
somewhat different from that of most other forms of higher education.
From the years 1995 through 2000, for example, alumni giving occupied
the number-one position in sources of support for institutions of all types
in the CAE report. Alumni contributed between 28.5 and 30.5 percent
of all gifts received. Sector breakdowns show alumni occupying either
the first or second spot for those five years, with a few exceptions, for
research/doctoral private and public institutions, master's private, and
liberal arts private institutions. Alumni giving accounted for anywhere
from 23.6 to 47.1 percent of gifts raised by those institutions. Even in
master's degree granting public institutions, where alumni gifts were only

the third largest source of support, giving hovered around 16 to 20 percent of total gifts received. Throughout that same time frame, however, alumni giving to public two-year colleges never exceeded 3.3 percent of total gifts received nor occupied a position higher than fifth.

Other individuals connected with the college were the primary source of support for community colleges for all five years, with ranges reaching from 37.7 percent in 1995 to 61.6 percent in 1996, and back down to 40.5 percent in 2000. They were followed closely by corporations, which occupied the number-two spot, accounting for anywhere from 20.8 to 32.2 percent of gifts received. Foundations occupied the third spot, with ranges of 9.8 to 19.8 percent, while other organizations were fourth.[4]

A fall 2000 survey of the 700 CEOs whose institutions are members of the League for Innovation in the Community College's Alliance helps to add broader validation to the CAE data by citing private donor and corporate solicitation as the most effective fund-raising methods employed by community colleges. "Regarding the types of donors that contribute to community college foundations, individuals not associated with community colleges were cited as contributing the most, followed by foundation board members and trustees, and community college employees."[5] Ninety-six percent of the colleges surveyed raised private funds through a foundation. Special events fund raising, a category not tracked by CAE, was mentioned as the third most effective method in the league's survey. That finding reinforces the results of a 1999 survey conducted by the Council for Resource Development, an American Association of Community Colleges affiliate council with 1,200 members. That survey found that foundation staff spent more time on special events than other activities.[6]

Special events are used by community colleges as both friend raisers and fund raisers. Many of the events usually associated with traditional four-year institutions are foreign to community colleges. Few have homecomings, major athletic competitions, or reunions that serve to connect prospects to the institution. Instead, events are created to bring the community to the college and to raise funds in the process. Events range in scope from golf tournaments to community dinners, to galas to theater performances, to live and silent auctions. And, while the event itself may not raise funds commensurate with the staff time devoted to it, it does serve to introduce the college to future prospects. In the case of Northampton Community College in Pennsylvania, one of its events reintroduced a lost donor who later made a six-figure gift to its endowment.

Before leaving the CAE data, it is perhaps also instructive to note that, while the sample is small, the variation in the amounts of money raised is not. Of the 98 community colleges reporting in 1996, for example, dollars raised ranged from $30,000 at the low end to more than $28,000,000 at the high end. That range was the most extreme in the five-year period, although it was followed in 1997 by a range of $37,000 to $18,000,000. In each of the five years cited, more than 20 colleges were raising more than $1,000,000 each.

PROGRAMS TEND TO BE SMALLER AND LESS DEVELOPED

In *Educational Fund Raising: Principles and Practice*, published in 1993, Nanette Smith noted that "because private fund raising is a relatively recent development on two-year campuses, programs are generally newer, smaller, and sometimes less sophisticated than at the more experienced senior institutions."[7] Although much has changed in the years since, including that fact that, "over the last decade, almost every one of the 1,100 community colleges in America has become a fundraiser,"[8] it is probably safe to say that Smith's words still hold true today. The League for Innovation survey cited earlier found that 53 percent of those surveyed raised under $500,000 in 1999. Seventeen percent raised between $500,000 and $999,000, sixteen percent between $1,000,000 and $2,499,000, and only five percent over $2,500,000.[9]

What appears to be changing, however, is the sense of urgency with which community colleges are now cultivating private support and the levels of success some are experiencing. "A report by the National Commission on Responsibilities for Financing Postsecondary Education (1993) revealed that federal dollars for postsecondary education decreased by 64 percent from 1970 to 1990."[10] "Since 1980, state support has dropped from one-half to one-third of community college budgets."[11] In an article on community college finance, Miller and Seagren contend that "for at least the foreseeable future, as through the 1990s, most evidence points to a continuation of financial constraints for most institutions of higher education."[12]

"Declines in federal and state support, along with the realization that increases in tuition and student fees can only be raised so far, has emphasized the importance of fund raising."[13] Development seems to be coming of age in the community college out of necessity.

In 2001 this author conducted a random sample survey of 90 community college members who belong to the Council for the Advancement and Support of Education (CASE). The response rate was 33 percent with respondents representing 15 different states. Although the sample size was small, the hope was simply to catch a glimpse into or get a feeling for the current state of community college advancement. Result showed that, like the league's survey, which revealed that 96 percent of the respondents had a foundation and 85 percent operated with a staff of five or less, all of the respondents had a foundation and all but two had staffs of four or less devoted to development.

SOURCES OF MAJOR GIFTS VARY

As in the CAE data cited earlier, friends of the college, corporations, and private foundations occupied the top three rankings in the sources of funds raised. But, individual differences could be seen emerging in some of the colleges, particularly as they related to the source of major gifts. Fourteen of the respondent colleges, for example, had received gifts of $1,000,000 or more at some time in their history. Nineteen had not. Of the 14 that did, nine colleges received large gifts from individuals. But Delta College in Michigan received a $3 million gift from a foundation; Community College of Allegheny County in Pennsylvania received two million-dollar gifts from two different foundations; Community College of Philadelphia received a million-dollar gift from a foundation; St. Louis Community College in Missouri received a $6.3 million in-kind gift of CAD/CAM (Computer Aided Design/Computer Aided Manufacturing) software from a corporation; and Monroe Community College in New York received four gifts in excess of $1 million, two from the same corporation, one from a foundation, and one from an alumnus. Ray Clements, president of the Salt-Lake-City-based Clements Group, a consulting group that is widely experienced in the community college market, is quoted as saying that his research shows that million-dollar gifts are "usually replicated within three or four years."[14] Of the group I surveyed, nine of the 14 had that experience.

Of the 19 colleges that had not yet received a million-dollar gift, most were getting close. One had received a $900,000 in-kind corporate gift and another a gift of land valued at $850,000. Three had received $500,000 gifts, and four had received a $250,000 gifts.

A 1999 article in The Chronicle of Higher Education, "For Community Colleges, Fund Raising Has Become Serious and Successful," highlighted a number of other community college success stories. Among them:

- A $43.2-million campaign conducted by the Kentucky Community and Technical College System

- A $10-million gift in cash and equipment donated by local corporations to the Maricopa Community College District, in Phoenix, Arizona
- Three community colleges in Washington—Olympic, Seattle Community, and Bellevue Community—among the first nine institutions to receive gifts from the Gates Foundation
- A $19-million art collection donated by Allen and Isabelle Leepa to St. Petersburg Junior College in Florida
- A $63.5-million gift to Young Harris College from a Coca-Cola Company fortune heiress[15]

The article goes on to point out that "in most places, they [community colleges] are stressing the same points: their ties to business, approaching sources other than the traditional alumni base, and the bargain of giving to a community college."[16] Giving to a community college can indeed be a bargain. The donor's dollar goes farther than it might in a different type of institution. Since tuitions tend to be lower at community colleges, named scholarships, for example, can be endowed for $5,000 in some cases, with $10,000 a more common starting point. Community colleges are also much less likely to stick with the notion that a donor should come up with 50 to 100 percent of construction costs to name a building. Lead donors to a project are often given the opportunity to name the facility, even though their gifts may not approach 50 percent. In the survey that this author conducted, $1,000,000 was the most commonly mentioned figure. Some community colleges have also become entrepreneurial and will name existing facilities after donors who contribute to endowment or for other purposes.

In a twist on the traditional endowed chair approach, Florida community colleges, with assistance from the state in the form of four-for-six matching grants, started a program that has become a model for other states when they endowed chairs for $100,000. Rather than support salaries, these endowed chairs pay for faculty development and program enrichment. The endowed chair matching gift effort was one of several initiatives in which the state of Florida used public money to challenge community colleges to raise private support, including programs to expand scholarships, address health-care training needs, and upgrade facilities and equipment. Tying public support to the generation of private support is not unique to Florida. For the past two years, Pennsylvania, for example, has had a Workforce Development Challenge Grant program that links state dollars to the generation of matching private support to be used to expand workforce training and development.

PHILANTHROPY OR RESOURCE DEVELOPMENT

The action by state governments of tying additional public funds to
private dollars raised has caused some community colleges to view philanthropy as one component of resource development, which many view
as a larger, more encompassing umbrella. When CASE was inviting
comments on its Campaign Standards draft in the early 1990's, one of
the criticisms voiced by community college practitioners was that not
counting matching dollars contributed either by the federal or state government to stimulate private giving would give an incomplete picture
of the total scope of many community college fund-raising efforts. This
"incomplete picture" notion is also advanced by some of the community
colleges that do not routinely report giving data to CAE.

"Stressing ties to business" is one way of saying that community colleges are beginning to implement a development approach that capital-
izes on their unique connections to their communities. "No other
segment of higher education is more responsive to its community and
workforce needs than the community college."[17] It's not surprising,
therefore, that "other individuals" and corporations are the dominant
sources of support for many community colleges. Pride and support of
one's local community are powerful motivators. "Proximity to a donor
base that is mostly local also gives community colleges an edge in fund
raising. Local pride and identity can be great assets to the institution as
area residents come to view it as 'our college.' "[18]

Corporations have also begun to recognize the value of supporting
"their college." One of the tenets of community colleges is to aid in the
economic development of communities by training and retraining the
community's workforce. This training not only occurs as company employees take courses on the college campuses, but often also in a contractual relationship between the company and the college. It is not
uncommon for community colleges to develop such relationships and
for these relationships to span years. These training relationships lead
to other partnerships. Company employees may serve in advisory capacities for academic programs, chief executive officers may be invited to
serve as "executives in residence" or on the college foundation's board.
This aspect of the colleges' mission serves as a catalyst in attracting
corporate gifts.

A Higher Education Issues Survey, commissioned by the National
Education Association and issued as a report in 2001, explored state
legislators' views toward higher education and captures some of the pre-

vailing thought about the role of community colleges in workforce development. "When asked to identify their state's most important strategic needs, almost without exception, state legislators framed their responses in terms of the state's economic development interests and emphasized that higher education must contribute directly to these efforts. . . . Higher education plays a critical role in furthering states' efforts to 'grow the workforce from within' as a way to attract new businesses to the state and to provide employment opportunities for state residents."[19]

Of the four types of higher educational institutions state legislators were asked about in terms of their responsiveness, legislators "consider the public two-year sector to be the most responsive overall to state, as well as to local, education and training needs. . . . Several legislators cite the public two-year sector's willingness to develop new programs or make curricular changes that are 'in tune' with the needs of business and industry."[20]

DEVELOPMENT BASED ON CORPORATE RELATIONSHIPS

Community college development officers are beginning to capitalize on the special relationships many of their institutions have established with local companies. Veteran development officers recognize that training may be the way in to the company, but that good stewardship on the development officer's part can turn what began as a training relationship into a college/company partnership that benefits both. Delaware County Community College in Pennsylvania, for example, received an in-kind gift of software valued at $900,000 from a company with whom they enjoy a long-standing training relationship. Company employees are involved in an advisory role with the institution, and one is an active member of the college's foundation board. Monroe Community College in New York was able to secure two seven-figure gifts from a company that understood that the college's success and the community's success were inextricably tied. More than 10 percent of the company's workforce had attended the college, employees of the company were currently doing so, the company had contracted with the college for training, and company employees were members of college advisory boards. More important, according to the president of Monroe's foundation, the senior leadership of the company understood the college, had a role in its founding, and held leadership positions on the college's foundation board and in its capital campaign.

STRONG BOARDS ARE CRITICAL TO SUCCESS

The vast majority of community colleges are now using the structure of a foundation to help in the development effort. Foundations are separately incorporated, 501(c)3 organizations with their own boards of directors. Strong foundation boards appear to be one factor that is helping to catapult many community colleges into raising more support than they previously thought possible. Several of the six-and seven-figure gifts previously mentioned came from members of the colleges' foundation boards. Butler Community College in Pennsylvania, for example, recently received a gift of land valued at $850,000 from one of its foundation board members. Several years earlier, four different members of the board were personally responsible for the nucleus fund of the college's first capital campaign, which raised $4.4 million.

While many community colleges have arrangements that call for certain numbers of members of the trustee boards to occupy seats on the foundation board, foundation boards serve a purpose that is distinctly different from that served by most public two-year college trustee boards. The focus of foundation boards is to create an awareness within the private sector of the college's needs not met through public support, and to implement a plan or strategy by which those financial needs can be met by private gift support. In the process, they involve community leaders who more closely tie the institution to its philanthropic supporters. These leaders likely do not get involved in the governance structure of the institution because of its political nature. They are, however, actively concerned and interested in their communities and their community's college and see the two as closely related.

Components of the job description given to prospective Northampton Community College foundation board members are universal. Board members are asked:

- to be aware of those individuals and businesses who need the institution as a resource and to invite those individuals into a relationship with the college
- to serve as a bridge to the industrial, business, and professional communities
- to help interpret the college to the community and, in the process, gain the interest and support of the community
- to procure and allocate financial resources
- to be donors to the annual giving, planned giving, and capital gifts programs

- to ensure that the advancement program is designed to affect all of the college's stakeholders in a positive way

In the introduction to the book *Successful Fund Raising for Higher Education*, editor Frank H.T. Rhodes writes that "the development of a fund-raising program involves the continuing interaction and cooperation of four major participants—the president; such campus leaders as the provost, deans, and faculty; the chief professional development officer (typically a vice president); and a committed group of volunteers— alumni, parents, faculty, students, friends, and, especially, trustees."[21]

Community colleges successful in development appear to have made some substitutions in the formula. The committed group of volunteers is most likely to be composed of community leaders who see the college as important to the health and welfare of the community and who are willing to work in leadership capacities, most often as members of a foundation board, to ensure its ongoing success.

NOTES

1. American Association of Community Colleges Web site (http://www.aacc.nche.edu/allaboutcc/snapshot.htm), viewed August 21, 2001.

2. Karen Luke Jackson and J. Conrad Glass, Jr., "Emerging Trends and Critical Issues Affecting Private Fundraising Among Community Colleges," *Community College Journal of Research and Practice* 24 (October/November, 2000): 729.

3. *Voluntary Support of Education 2000* (New York: Council for Aid to Education), VSE-006, 007.

4. *Voluntary Support of Education*, Table 6, 1995, 1996, 1997, 1998, 1999, 2000.

5. League for Innovation in the Community College Web site (http://www.league.org/league/projects/fundnet/files/foundations.doc), viewed August 21, 2001.

6. League Web site (http://www.league.org/league/projects/fundnet/events.htm), viewed August 21, 2001.

7. Nanette J. Smith, "Raising Funds for Community Colleges," in *Educational Fund Raising: Principles and Practice*, ed. Michael J. Worth (Phoenix, AZ: American Council on Education/Oryx Press, 1993), 347–358.

8. Martin van der Werf, "For Community Colleges, Fund Raising Has Become Serious and Successful," *The Chronicle of Higher Education*, April 9, 1999, A-42–43.

9. League Web site, viewed August 21, 2001.

10. Larry W. Jenkins and J. Conrad Glass, Jr., "Inception, Growth, and De-

velopment of a Community College Foundation," *Community College Journal of Research and Practice* 23 (September, 1999): 594.

11. van der Werf, "For Community Colleges," A-42–43.

12. Michael T. Miller and Alan Seagren, "Community College Finance: Department Chair Perceptions of Selected Financial Issues and Responsibilities," *Community College Journal of Research and Practice* 21 (January/February, 1997): 44.

13. Jenkins and Glass, Jr., "Inception, Growth, and Development," 595.

14. van der Werf, "For Community Colleges," A-42–43.

15. Ibid.

16. Ibid.

17. American Association of Community Colleges Web site (http://www.aacc.nche.edu/research/researchnew/past_present.htm), viewed August 21, 2001.

18. Smith, "Raising Funds for Community Colleges," 351.

19. Sandra S. Ruppert, "Where We Go From Here: State Legislative Views on Higher Education in the New Millennium," National Association of the United States Web site (http://www.nea.org/he/leg-news/gofrom.pdf), viewed August 28, 2001.

20. Ibid., 12.

21. Frank H.T. Rhodes, "Successful Fund Raising for Higher Education," *The Advancement of Learning*, ed. Frank H.T. Rhodes (Phoenix, AZ: Oryx Press, 1997), xix.

CHAPTER 21

Raising Funds for a Professional School within a University

Linda G. Steckley

*P*rofessional school—the term itself suggests constraints and expectations, binding standards that extend beyond the traditional academic environment. The professional school trains its students to take their place in a career with a tradition, a specific role in society, and ties to professional associations. Some professional associations share responsibility with the educational community for the depth and breadth of the academic curriculum, even overseeing accreditation, ensuring a strong professional influence in the evaluation of academic quality.

This chapter will look at the relationship of the professional school with its host university, the critical role of the dean in professional school fund raising, and the challenges that especially influence fundraising efforts at professional schools. Throughout the chapter there are references to technology changing the way business is done. New systems enable communication within and outside the university to occur almost spontaneously. Technology has created avenues for communicating with graduates at a speed and ease unimagined just a few years ago. However, it is vital to keep in mind that in this discussion technology is referred to as a tool to improve the quality of the relationship between the professional school and its constituents, not a replacement for personal contact.

RELATIONSHIP WITH THE HOST UNIVERSITY

Typically, a professional school owes its existence to a host university. Its academic standing and reputation are often tied to the strength of the host university. Yet faculty and administration at the professional school usually enjoy a high level of autonomy in governance and program development. Tensions develop between professional schools and the "central" university for resources and personnel. Those tensions are often most acute in the fund-raising realm.

Professional schools run the gamut from architecture to veterinary medicine. The organizational models are equally diverse. Harvard University is the model for autonomous units. It is decentralized, with most of the schools having their own development, alumni relations, communications, gift management, recognition, and stewardship functions. Indeed, Harvard Law School has published its own alumni directory since 1888. The first directory offered chronological and alphabetical listings of all those who had attended the law school since its establishment in 1817.[1]

Some private universities include development and alumni relations for their professional schools within a highly centralized university structure, while others have a combination of centralized and decentralized operations. At many state universities, development is based in a separately incorporated foundation. The foundation serves as a centralized organization serving the various schools.

Although the strengths and weaknesses of each model are frequently debated, no one design stands out as the best approach to raising money. The important factors for fund-raising success are university-wide systems providing needed information to the broadest number of people and a culture to encourage cooperation and discourage concealing information or stealing prospects. The vice president for university advancement must establish the culture of shared information and prospect management. He or she sets the tone and puts the procedures in place to foster cooperation and must make clear to all units that participation in the process is mandatory.

Technology can make the process manageable. The campus e-mail network facilitates sharing information about contacts with prospective donors. Most universities have sophisticated database systems that make biographical information and other donor research, giving records, and reports of contacts available to a select few or a large number of fund raisers simultaneously. When the prospect clearance system provides an equitable process for assigning management of prospects, and professional school requests are given equal weight to other parts of the university, there is no reason for complaints of "prospect stealing." Information regarding primary and secondary relationships with prospects should be readily available on the shared database. It is easy enough to pick up the phone or send an e-mail to work out potential conflicts. Management protocols can smooth the path to success with prospective donors who value access to many aspects of the institution—intellectual, athletic, social. The wise fund raiser is the development officer who graciously opens the door to many institutional assets for the benefit of a prospective donor.

DEANS AND DEVELOPMENT

The legacy of any dean's tenure is measured by the quality of faculty retained and recruited and successful fund-raising efforts to underwrite the school's growth. The dean is often under pressure to fulfill major fund-raising expectations, yet many deans are attracted to academia because of a love of teaching, research, and writing. The prospect of numerous social occasions required to build positive relations, and the thought of actually asking for money from a donor, can be daunting. Many step into the position of dean with dread at the external demands of the position.

The development officer plays a key role in assisting the dean to make the transition from scholar to professional school CEO by reassuring him or her that in a short time he or she will find that development and alumni relations can be the most enjoyable part of the job. Just as the academic year has its cycle, so does the development year. The development officer should urge a new dean to take a year to experience and learn the external aspects of the job. Remind him or her to take time to develop and articulate a personal vision for the school by modifying the strategic plan or beginning the process to develop a new one. The dean should get to know the leadership of the various boards, and ask questions of faculty, students, and alumni and get current on challenges facing the profession. The development officer can help the dean to develop a core of respected outside advisors, people in the profession who, whether graduates of the school or not, can offer valuable advice about the skills and knowledge needed in the field. During this time, the dean and the development officer can form a trusting, confidential relationship, and within a short time she or he will be deeply involved in the fund-raising process and appreciate the amount of effort that goes into a well-run development operation.

The dean will quickly realize that his or her leadership will influence loyalty and financial investment from alumni. The vision articulated by the dean can determine when a gift comes to the school. As momentum builds, other donors are attracted, and their giving is motivated by the excitement of the vision communicated by the dean.

To best serve the school and assist the dean to be as effective as possible, the development officer must become knowledgeable about the profession and active in the life of the school. It is not enough to be simply a competent development professional. Whether the fund raiser has a degree in the professional area is less important than a willingness to acquire an understanding of the profession and the professional school experience. Talking and listening to the students about why they chose this profession and this school can be informative. Engaging the faculty about their areas of work and research is beneficial. Talking with graduates in the profession and those who have traveled down alternative paths serves as prospect cultivation at the same time as it instructs. Listening to visiting speakers and attending academic conferences whenever there is an opportunity is crucial. Becoming comfortable with the language and understanding the thinking of members of the profession are key skills. The most successful development officers have a chameleon quality enabling them to connect quickly and with authenticity to the world of the prospective donor.

CHALLENGES TO RAISING MONEY

During the last century, fund raising from private sources evolved as the third prong, along with tuition and government support, funding American higher education. Alumni emerged as the primary source of private funds, and professional fund raisers were hired to facilitate relationships between alumni and their schools. And the twenty-first century presents new challenges for development officers in meeting their institutions' needs for philanthropic support.

Diversity: The Changing Face of the Graduate Student

Stunning changes in the composition of graduate student bodies in the last decades of the twentieth century will produce a base of prospective donors in the twenty-first century very different from the well-to-do white male alumni who built today's classrooms and endowed the professors who teach in them. As Part VI of this book discusses, fund raising in the years ahead will be about quality relationships with men, women, people of color, and successful graduates from around the world.

In the 1970's, growing numbers of women applied, and were admitted, to law schools, business schools, and medical schools. By the end of the decade, nearly all professional schools, including engineering, architecture, dentistry, veterinary medicine, and schools of the environment, were admitting a critical mass of female students. The 1980's and 1990's saw a steady increase in the percentage of African Americans, Hispanic Americans, and Asian Americans entering the professions. In the spring of 2001, *The New York Times* announced that enrollment of women in American law schools was expected to surpass fifty percent with the next entering class.[2]

In higher education, and particularly in professional schools, the vast majority of gifts continue to be given by white males who completed their schooling in the 1950's and 1960's. However, the composition of the donor population will change dramatically over the next ten years as the women and minorities who began their careers in the late 1970's and early 1980's reach their peak earning years and patterns of wealth increasingly reflect enrollment shifts.

Professional schools will be tested to determine whether they have met the expectations of women and minorities in the long-term cultivation process. Have the schools remained sufficiently relevant to prompt regular giving when the prospective donor is ready? Studies show that professional women and minorities expect results from their giving, to see that gift money is being used wisely. Young alumni will be less likely to make a gift to an unrestricted annual fund without explanation as to what the money will accomplish. The size of the gift and the frequency of giving will be determined by the ability of the professional school to remain relevant in the lives of its graduates. The development officer working with these donors will need to provide a case for giving that is straightforward, thorough, and compelling. They must eschew the old platitudes about the value of higher education and contributions to society. Whether the professional school's message is delivered in a colorful brochure or through a detailed proposal, the donor will expect a clear explanation of the rationale for making a gift and the ways the gift will make a difference.

The expectations of the new donor will not stop at the time of giving. The donor will expect continued accountability—regular reports on outcomes—whether it is the quality of the students, the results of faculty recruiting, or the conference produced by a newly funded program. Professional school graduates expect the same level of professionalism in the relationship with their school that they receive from other professional organizations.

Internationalization

The increasing numbers of students coming to the United States for graduate study and the increasing numbers of Americans living and working abroad create a complex challenge for development officers to maintain contact with alumni and engage them in a meaningful way with the intellectual life of their professional school. A foreign student may study at an American professional school for only a brief period and arrive with a professional degree in medicine, engineering, or law completed in their home country. They attend the U.S. school for a post-graduate degree or additional concentrated study in a particular area. With the rapid development of distance learning programs, men and women around the globe are combining online work in their home country with periodic classroom contact at a U.S. university or at one of a growing number of international sites. The opportunity to build allegiance is limited, but schools are discovering the great advantage of classes composed of students from around the world. There is a valuable exchange of customs and experience among students from various countries.

The American academic experience can be enormously important in the foreign professional's career advancement. It not only enables networking with other professionals around the world, it also creates the opportunity to develop a lifelong, personal relationship with an academic institution, a type of relationship unknown outside the United States. Many foreign students are surprised to see graduates involved in the intellectual life the school—supporting the basketball team or the women's soccer team or the jazz ensemble or other programs of a university having no connection to the professional school. This is a new, and often very appealing, feature of American academic life.

The international graduate has become a potential source of financial support for the American professional school. In recent years, there have been several multimillion-dollar gifts to U.S. schools from foreign alumni. There have been even more gifts in excess of $100,000, and growing numbers of international alumni are joining efforts to raise annual scholarship funds and support for program development.

International donors are especially important to professional schools for two reasons. First, the number of professional school students from abroad is already large, and it continues to grow. Second, the common experiences within professions are not defined by geographic boundaries. The barriers to successful fund raising from international alumni and friends are the expense involved in cultivation of prospects, the challenge to maintain regular meaningful contact, and the difficulty in obtaining accurate information about a person's wealth. In Chapter 17, Scott Nichols discusses the challenges of international fund raising in greater detail.

Economic Volatility

Changes in the economy can affect professional school fund raising almost immediately. Economic volatility exerts a particularly strong influence on professional school prospects and their ability and willingness to make a gift to their school. One way to counter or try to even out the effects of market volatility on fund raising is to identify segments within the ranks of professional school alumni. Engineering school graduates take jobs that match their areas of specialization—structural, electrical, mechanical, civil. A graduate school of journalism has alumni in advertising, broadcasting, public relations, and in print and online media. Business schools and medical schools can identify almost unlimited areas of specialization. Sorting alumni according to their career specialization enables a development office to customize its communication according to economic times.

As a professional school develops programs to involve alumni in the continuing life of the school, it is important to be sensitive to the ups and downs of the marketplace. When some segments are experiencing a business setback, provide programs but avoid asking for a major gift. Look to the particularly successful segments at the time for a solicitation. It is appropriate and intelligent to gear programs, as well as alumni publication articles, e-mail information, and contact with alumni in general, to the needs of the profession. With the abundance of information available on the Internet and in the media, there is no excuse for professional school fund raisers to be unaware of the issues confronting the graduates of the school. With the ability to gather information from alumni and to segment communication, fund raisers should be able to provide information specific to alumni that will help them to do their business more effectively. When a faculty member publishes an article that might be particularly useful to certain professionals, it is important to get the word out to that segment. Development officers can include a program during alumni weekend that is pertinent, and if a geographic region of the country is particularly affected by economic changes, take a faculty speaker to the region to share relevant information. The important message is that the school is aware of market conditions and wants to serve the alumni population.

Fund raising in a graduate professional school is a multifaceted approach to building and maintaining a life-long relationship with the alumni and friends of the school. When the school is relevant to the professional life of the graduate during tough economic times, the case for financial support in good times is legitimized. Admittedly, alumni and friends will drift in and out of active involvement with the school because there will be times when the programs, services, and contacts will be more important than others. The school, with its wealth of programs, bears responsibility to remind graduates of its value. As individuals take advantage of the professional school connections, they will become donors in a natural way. Those who have the capacity to make a major contribution can be identified, developed as leaders, and cultivated for an important gift that is meaningful to the interests of the donor.

Competition for Alumni Loyalty

The professional school graduate faces constant and competing demands on his or her time and money. The value of the professional school during tough economic times has been discussed, thus providing a very business-oriented rationale for financial support.

The relationship with the undergraduate institution poses a very different problem. While alumni recognize that their success is largely due to the quality of their professional education, they often feel a much stronger emotional tie to their undergraduate school. Even when an alumnus may have an undergraduate degree from the same university, there is going to be competition for the person's allegiance and financial contributions. This competition creates a special challenge for professional school fund raisers because gift-giving tends to follow emotional ties.

Undergraduate school is usually experienced during an important transition between youth and adulthood, is often residential, and is a place where having fun can be a primary focus. Undergraduate friendships tend to be important for life. It is no surprise when professional school alumni remind development officers that their first loyalty is to their undergraduate college or university.

There is equal truth in the development officer's response that they could not afford to support their undergraduate school, or much else, without the professional degree and the enhanced income that it has brought them. The credibility of this argument is supported by a review of the boards of undergraduate colleges and universities, filled with men and women who have gone on to earn professional degrees.

Along with the professional school curriculum goes a good dose of leadership development. Men and women who are members of the professions are also the leaders in their communities. They sit on corporate and nonprofit boards. They are officers of the PTA, the United Way, and the homeowners' association. They are selected to lead their churches, their hospitals, and their schools. There is an empowerment that comes with a professional degree that is recognized in communities throughout the world.

What persuasive argument does the professional school development officer have when the graduate is busy raising funds for a new hospital in her home community hundreds of miles away from the campus? What benefit does the businessman receive from his name on a campus building in Philadelphia when he is trying to build his business in Denver?

Every conversation with a prospective donor should remind the person of the importance the school's quality and current reputation gives to his or her degree. If the quality of the professional school drops, so may the value of the graduate's degree. The perception of diminished quality can affect the decision of a patient, a client, an investor, or a partner. The reverse is also true. When the quality and reputation of a professional school is enhanced over time, the perceived value of the professional graduates' skill is also enhanced. Much criticism has been levied at the rankings published annually by a number of national publications, but they attract attention, and they appear to provide a measure of relative quality of professional schools. There is a strong argument for alumni support when a school's resources can dramatically affect the media's evaluation of the school.

It is foolish for the professional school development officer to attempt to compete with the organizations and institutions that vie for the graduate's loyalty and financial support. Rather, the graduate should be commended for being philanthropic. Remind the graduate of the value of competent, well-trained new professionals coming out of school and available for recruiting. Emphasize the importance of maintaining quality in the professional degree for the benefit of the graduate and possibly for sons and daughters. A gift at a later time can be considered; the professional school is not likely to become less important in the professional life of its graduates. There will continue to be critical funding needs at the school. The challenge to the development office is to file the information and design a strategy that will lead to a major gift. With regular contact, annual gifts tend to increase in size and a leadership gift is just down the road. A bequest or a gift of a trust or gift annuity may be the perfect acknowledgment of the value and importance of the professional education to the life of the graduate. A close working relationship with the university office of planned giving can result in numerous gifts to the school. Bequests are frequently unrestricted and enable the dean to fund the school's most critical projects. If the long-term relationship has been consistent and meaningful, the graduate will want to do something for the school that enabled him or her to have a life of accomplishment.

Professional Standards and Values

Most professions have well-publicized standards that guide members in their professional lives. The development profession also has strict guidelines. But the fund raiser in a professional school must bring a level of integrity to the job that can stand up to the kind of scrutiny that permeates the profession. Members of a profession will expect those who represent their school to demonstrate strength of character and professional ethics consistent with their own.

A career as a professional school fund raiser can be most rewarding. It is a way to be a part of a research university's development effort while retaining the closeness and personal relationships of a small school. While having the benefits of the systems, training, and collegiality of a large university development office, there is a degree of independence in the professional school that gives the development officer the chance to be creative and try new ideas. There is an engagement with the life of the school that gives variety to each day while enhancing the ability of the development officer to build long-term relationships with prospective donors.

NOTES

1. *Harvard Law School Alumni Directory 1993* (Cambridge, MA: The Harvard Law School, 1993), 5.

2. Jonathan D. Glater, "Women Are Close to Being Majority of Law Students," *New York Times*, March 26, 2001, A1.

PART VIII

Managing and Supporting Development Programs

The scale of fund-raising programs has increased substantially in the past decade. Even small colleges may have several professional staff members working in development and related advancement disciplines. Some universities have staffs numbering in the hundreds. At the same time, there are demands for accountability and measurable performance. Goals and budgets are high—and thus so are the stakes. In response, fund-raising managers have adopted many practices from the business world.

In the following four chapters, authors address the management of today's sophisticated development programs. In Chapter 22, Robert Lindgren provides an overview of structuring and managing the development program. In the following chapter on prospect research and management, Eric Siegel explores an area of activity that is not new, but that has taken on increased importance as institutions work to focus resources on the best prospects and assure that fund-raising resources, both human and budgetary, are efficiently deployed. Prospect research and management are also activities that have been dramatically changed by advances in information and communications technology.

There was a time when development "office systems" consisted of 3 × 5 cards and typewriters. Today, sophisticated and complex electronic information systems are the nerve center of most fund-raising programs. The resources invested in such systems are substantial, and it is essential that they be carefully selected and well used. In Chapter 24 Gail Ferris provides a look at this important aspect of fund-raising management.

James Langley's Chapter 25 concludes this section of the book, exploring the subjects of benchmarking, accountability, and measuring performance. In today's environment, development officers must justify their use of resources and demonstrate the results produced. Increasingly, their own performance and compensation are based on such measures. The simplest variables to monitor are, of course, dollars spent and dollars raised. But, as Langley shows, the subject is more complicated. It is not always an easy matter to determine which variables are relevant and appropriate in a specific institutional setting. And, it is essential to select and apply measurements that are consistent with fairness and with ethical values.

CHAPTER 22

Structuring and Managing the Development Office

Robert R. Lindgren

evelopment operations, like the institutions they serve, have grown in size and complexity over the years. The first college development efforts in this country—if not performed by the president—were often in the hands of paid agents, who earned a percentage of what was raised. This personal solicitation of gifts by a single representative was the accepted technique for college fund raising in the United States until the close of World War II. Higher education gradually adopted the fund-raising campaign techniques commonly practiced in the YMCA movement, and the concept of development offices and officers located within the organizational structure of the institution was born. Initially, one or two professionals were responsible for all of the fund raising: annual appeals, campaign solicitations, and the corporate and foundation relationships. As institutions placed more emphasis (and budget support) into the development process, the staffs grew and became more specialized.[1]

STRUCTURING THE DEVELOPMENT ORGANIZATION

College and university fund-raising organizations were initially organized by the *sources and types* of gifts. A development staff was often structured around traditional functional areas: *annual gifts*, which were solicited by mail, volunteers, and eventually by telephone appeals; *individual gifts*, which were garnered by staff who made personal calls on prospects or motivated volunteers to do the same; *corporate and foundation gifts*, which were sought by staff who focused on the myriad companies and foundations that might have an interest in their institution and its programs. Later, the field of *planned giving* created still another functional area for staff knowledgeable about charitable trusts, annuities, and bequests—and even more complicated gift mechanisms. A small development operation might have had specialists in one or more of these areas, concentrating on their particular "markets" and assisting each other when necessary.

Along with the functions of fund raising, successful development programs have a series of *infrastructure* components, which serve the institution as well. *Prospect research*, as described in Chapter 23, is an essential resource to successful development officers. The role of *stewardship*, what happens to a donor and to a donor's gift once it is made, is taking on increasing importance in all institutions—such that many have established separate positions and offices to deal with this important activity. Gift processing and donor and alumni biographical information database maintenance are extremely important "back office" functions and are crucial to the overall effectiveness of a development operation, as outlined in Chapter 24. Indeed, development operations are intensely *information dependent*, and information systems, and the professionals who support them, have become increasingly important members of the development team. It is not unusual for institutions to spend up to 12 percent of their annual development and alumni relations budgets on information systems and personnel. The era of shoe boxes and index cards has given way to complicated information management systems that not only track the donor records of alumni and friends, but hundreds of individual data elements about each donor and potential donor.

ORGANIZATION BY AFFINITY

Institutions have realized that alumni often develop stronger loyalties to their own academic disciplines, and most sophisticated development structures now reflect a strategy of appealing to the alumnus's personal affinity. Professional schools, such as law, medicine, and business administration, were among the first to organize development activities specifically for their own alumni. Today, it is not uncommon for each of the academic schools or colleges within a university to have its own development program and staff. "Constituent-based" fund-raising organizations in complex institutions often extend to the campus library, the athletic program, museums, theaters and musical groups, television and radio stations, and even individual academic departments, particularly in schools of medicine. Moreover, specific constituencies such as parents, young alumni, and "grateful patients" are treated as unique markets by separate staffs with specialized strategies. As described in Chapter 21, professional schools within universities often develop complete programs including individual, planned, and annual giving; corporate and foundation relations; and even specific infrastructure elements such as gift processing and prospect research.

Smaller and less complex universities and colleges tend to organize their development programs by function and are thus much more highly centralized in their approach. In these types of programs there is control over the entire fund-raising organization by the vice president or director of development. All fund-raising staff have a direct responsibility to this individual, what is often called "solid-line" reporting relationship. Such a structure often allows for greater efficiency among the development functions, that is, there is less duplication, particularly in support services. Fund-raising budgets, strategies, and key personnel decisions tend to be made centrally in this model. Finally, and perhaps most importantly, centralized programs tend to allow for a greater sense of focus on institutional fund-raising priorities.

Programs that are organized by both function and constituent affinity, in other words, where the schools have their own development offices, are often more decentralized. There are three primary ways of organizing in this case. The first model involves development staff hired and evaluated by the *central development structure*, with assignments to cover constituent areas such as individual schools or programs. In this model there may be a dotted-line relationship to the dean or program director, but the ultimate management responsibility rests with the central development organization. Funding for these arrangements is varied. In most cases of this model the central office covers the entire expense load; however, there are cases where the schools or programs are asked to underwrite some or all of the direct expenses for services performed on their behalf. This model is often found in public institutions that utilize institutionally related foundations for the management of fund raising. In some cases the development staffs are actually employed separately by the foundation. While this approach is an effective means of financing development operations, it runs the risk of fostering a "separatist mentality" on the part of those charged with raising money for the institution.

A second model has the *constituent-based programs* reporting directly to the dean or program director. In this model there may be a dotted-line or coordinating relationship with the central development office, but the key hiring and evaluation decisions are made by the unit rather than at the central level. Here, the total expense of the school or program development budget, including the salaries of the development professionals working on its behalf, are likely to be paid entirely by the divisional unit. The central organization in this model is usually responsible for managing the institution's largest donors and prospects, administering shared services and information such as the donor database, and carrying out more specialized development functions such as planned giving, corporate and foundation relations, and annual giving.

Still a third model is a more *hybrid* approach. In this increasingly popular model there may be a joint reporting relationship between the divisional development unit and the central development office. In these situations, the hiring and evaluation decisions usually are made jointly, and often the salary and fringe benefits of the chief school or program officer (and sometimes their entire budget) are shared in some proportion by the central office and the divisional unit.

THE CASE FOR THE HYBRID MODEL

What is the best approach? This question is most easily answered by considering the size and culture of the college or university. Where there is a tradition of strong centralized management and services, there stands the best opportunity to make a centralized development program—one in which development officers may be "assigned" to cover schools or programs and support deans, but maintain their reporting lines solely to the development hierarchy—work successfully. However, there are strong pressures to put at least some of the responsibility for managing and funding the school or program development operation into the hands of the divisional development unit and the deans. Why? First, because deans themselves are becoming much more active in fund raising—no longer are they hired merely as academic managers. Indeed, one commentator writing about the role of college administrators in fund raising described it as a dean's "most critical role."[2]

As staffs and programs have grown over the years—and more importantly, as the size and complexity of larger gifts to higher education have increased—it has become clear that donor affinity to schools, programs, and even to individual faculty members is crucial to the fund-raising program. Sheer numbers (of both major prospects and major donors) have necessitated the involvement of deans and more faculty members as well. While presidents and key volunteers can manage the most important (meaning: "having the largest potential dollar total") donor relationships, there are simply too many such relationships for a single president and lead volunteers to manage. Larger universities count their major gift prospects (which might be defined as potential donors of $50,000 or more) in the thousands. Staff members who are dedicated—as opposed to being assigned—to a given academic unit tend to identify with that unit more strongly and therefore tend to be more effective in motivating both themselves and their deans in the fund-raising enterprise. It should be pointed out that these staff also have an opportunity for greater job satisfaction, as they are charged with managing their own development programs and developing strategies specific to their own school or program.

"Better One Bad Master Than Two Good Ones"

The larger question is whether the development staff working on behalf of a given school or program should have a reporting relationship to the central development organization as well as to the dean or program director. Like the Chinese proverb above, organizational behavior theory has long held that dual reporting is less effective than having a clear and unitary reporting relationship.[3] However, there is a strong case that the organization of the development function within complicated colleges and universities serves as an exception to this management theorem. It is important that development staff have a strong connection to the school or program for which they are raising money. Moreover, it is the prerogative of the chief academic officer of a unit—in this case the dean or department chair—to set the fund-raising priorities. Conversely, the setting of academic priorities to be fulfilled through private support should never be viewed as being overly influenced by the development professionals within an academic organization.

While affinity—that of both donors and employees—and priorities argue in favor of school-based reporting, the importance of having a consistent and effective process should play a role in this organization dynamic as well. Chief among the process elements is the importance of prospect management and clearance. All complicated development environments require some system of ensuring that prospects will be "managed" in such a way that competing or conflicting interests are not placed before them. Having some strand of a reporting relationship with central development helps to contribute to the integrity of a prospect management system. Likewise, there are three important areas in which the participation of the development organization—as a genuine partner—can be enormously helpful: personnel hiring, evaluation, and the budget process.

The number of development officers employed throughout higher education has grown exponentially in recent years. The hiring process for these new staff members has grown more complicated as institutions have competed in an increasingly tight market for new development talent. Development professionals are now essential in evaluating prospective development colleagues and work best in tandem with academic deans and directors in this process. Likewise, the ambiguity of development staff evaluation, covered later in this chapter and in Chapter 26, is tempered by the involvement of campus development professionals *and* the establishment of standards that apply across the university or college. Finally, the assessment of the appropriate budget for school-based development is again better informed with the involvement of development professionals.

A hybrid model with joint reporting and some sharing of budget between the central development office and the school or department can provide the right balance between affinity and development expertise. In order for such a system to be effective, however, it is essential that the two parties—the dean/director and the central development office representative—agree on a number of issues. Together, they should set out a clean process for hiring and setting the initial compensation package of their joint supervisee, the school-based development professional. The two parties should agree on the broad objectives that will be presented to their joint employee, the evaluation process to which the employee will be subjected, and the structure and content of any work plans or performance standards that might be utilized in the evaluation process. Most importantly, the two should agree that they will not place their joint supervisee in an untenable situation, forcing him or her to have to choose between one master or the other. Indeed, they should identify a clear means of communication in order to deal with such a conflict should it arise.

Changing the Structure

Given that most academic institutions are not "top-down" management structures to begin with, it is difficult to make wholesale changes in the basic structure of development programs operating within them. Nevertheless, moving from a more centralized system, or even the most decentralized system, to the hybrid approach can be accomplished if there is a commitment from the president and consensus among the development leadership and the deans that such a change will provide long-term positive results. The question of how centralized or decentralized the operation should be is sometimes complicated when new resources are needed: for example, to effect a splitting of salaries between the central office and the schools or programs. While there may be sentiment to make the double-solid-line arrangement immediate and to postpone the splitting of salaries until such resources can be found, such a decision may render the new structure considerably less effective than if there was a complete sharing of expenses from the time of the change. (People really do respond to the issue of who "signs their paycheck.")

Public institutions with support foundations can sometimes facilitate a change in structure more easily. Often the foundation's resources can be used to help balance the salaries or expenses in a more flexible manner. Once these changes are made, the hiring of new deans and/or chief constituent development officers helps to solidify the acceptance of the new arrangement.

BUDGETING

Another important issue in the management of the development operation is the budget. Development vice presidents are often accused of thinking like IRS agents: "The more of us, the more money we will collect, and as long as we cover our salaries, the institution is ahead!" This thinking does not translate into unlimited development budgets, however, and it is critical for good development operations to conduct rigorous budgeting processes.

How much should be spent on development? There are at least seven factors to consider. In order to first approach this question, development leaders may stumble over the question of "What does it cost to raise a dollar at this institution?" While several surveys have purported to measure the cost of fund raising across a sampling of institutions, this concept remains one of the most elusive in higher education development. It has been particularly difficult for groups of institutions to agree on standards in the area of fund-raising expenses. Perhaps more challenging has been the effort to consistently track these expenses. This "apples and oranges" dilemma is always a factor when considering comparative descriptions. Nevertheless, *benchmarking* among like institutions remains critical, particularly related to a wide range of factors, including overall budget, size of staff, size of "professional" staff, and the cost per capita of such areas as annual giving.

Next, the *budgeting philosophy and culture* of a particular institution generally has an impact on the size and character of the development budget. One must first characterize the institution's budget at large: is it particularly tight (as they almost always are) or worse, desperate? (Ironically, tight budgets may produce across-the-board cutbacks whereas desperate financial times may argue for *more* spending on development.) And how is the development operation viewed? Is it seen as being successful? Efficient? Integral to serving the institution's mission? Does the development organization produce critical support to the institution— either in unrestricted money and/or in program or endowment support that helps provide a distinguishing edge? The answers to all of these questions help frame the context for the budget conversation within an institution.

Third, *priority setting*, both within the institution and within the development organization, has to be taken into account. If the institution's priorities are such that more fund raising is designated for particular objectives or programs, then the development budget needs to reflect these strategies. More unrestricted giving? Increase the support of the annual giving office. Specific projects? Assign a major gift officer or officers to focus on the prospect pool to support it. Increase the endowment over time? Strengthen the planned giving staff and charge them to solicit more endowment support. Institutional priorities indeed can and should influence budgeting priorities.

Likewise, the priorities of the development organization—almost always couched in a choice of short-term versus longer-term benefits—are important. All development leaders seek to invest in programs that will be most productive (read: "result in the largest gifts") over time. There is a balancing act before funding *major gift fund raising*, truly the most efficient way of raising money, with *annual giving*, which clearly serves to broaden the donor base and cultivate the next generation of donors, and *infrastructure* (for example, one does not want to overspend on gift processors and database management services, and yet, one does not want to have gifts being entered incorrectly or data being lost to future development officers).

Fourth, any sound budgeting process in development should include a *numbers analysis*. How much is being spent for each annual fund gift? How much is being spent to renew past donors? Do these expenses— and various other measures in the annual fund area—track with those of competitors? (Once again, benchmarking.) Still other numbers to review in the area of major gift fund raising include: How many prospects are being visited in a year? How many proposals are being given? How many prospects can a single major gift officer comfortably handle?

How many stewardship contacts are needed in a particular time frame? Are more major gift officers needed to handle additional prospects and proposals, or can some of the existing staff's responsibilities be delegated to specialists such as proposal writers and special event coordinators? Any number analysis requires good data, and the budgeting process—in particular building the case for additional budget—heavily depends on the data provided by accountability systems.

Campaign budgeting often presents both an opportunity and a challenge to development leaders. Campaigns can provide opportunities to enlarge the development staff and increase the budget for infrastructure and support. Additionally, there may be elements in a campaign that are not typically budgeted in the "normal" development budget, including special communications materials such as campaign videos and case statements, as well as campaign-specific special events such as kickoffs, screening sessions, and volunteer gatherings. While hiring additional fund-raising staff to meet higher annual and campaign goals seems logical as a part of a campaign plan, it is important to increase the size of the organization's infrastructure as well. Campaigns by definition generate more activity and gifts, and an increased number of data processors, gift processors, and researchers, for example, need to be factored into the overall campaign budget. Still another feature of campaign budgeting is the opportunity to set a budget over a multi-year period. This multi-year budget can be constructed in two ways: by applying the institution's cost per dollar raised against the overall campaign expected revenues, and by actually setting out a strategy of extra staff and expenses needed in order to raise more money. It is hoped that these two processes produce numbers that are somewhat alike! Committing to a four- or five-year budget is a challenge, however, as situations are often fluid; there must be enough flexibility to respond to opportunities along the campaign trail. Another more significant challenge is, what happens to the campaign budget at the end of the campaign? While it used to be that institutions "ramped up" for campaigns and then released staff once the campaign goals were achieved, it is more often the case today that institutions maintain much of their campaign staff and spending following the campaign in an effort to maintain the higher level of giving.

A sixth key issue in the development budget mix deals with *sources of development budget*. While early fund-raising budgets were almost always funded by a combination of general institution funds and unrestricted donations, the pressure on both of these sources has caused institutions to develop other resources for funding their development operations. These sources include:

- Myriad *taxes*, such as levies against current gifts, endowments, unendowed funds, and a variation: delaying the use of a gift for a specific period of time while the "float" is taken for development or other administrative expenses
- *Specific gifts* from trustees or other individuals or entities whose relationship with the institution is such that they respond to an appeal demonstrating that their gift would help leverage larger and more restricted giving to the institution
- *Windfalls*, such as unrestricted estate gifts
- *Unrestricted gifts* from the annual fund or other donor society recognitions, which are often used to underwrite general fund-raising expenses

It is important to stress that all of these arrangements must be established within the legal and cultural context of the institution, and furthermore, there must be adequate disclosure of them, both internally and externally.

Finally, all development budget conversations must acknowledge certain *expense sensitivities*. Given the nature of development work and its use of entertainment for cultivation purposes, development leaders must continuously be sensitive to how much of the development budget is spent for entertainment and recognition, that is, how lavish are the donor recognition events (and premiums), and what is the style in which development officers travel? All development professionals, regardless of the perceived wealth of their institution and the mandate they have to do things in a "first class" manner, must remember that they are raising money for what is in effect a charity. If, over time, a development office's entertainment and travel expenses are perceived as excessive—either internally or externally—the development budget and/or gift revenue will suffer.

RECRUITING

With the explosion of the market in higher education for fund raising and fund raisers, recruiting new talent has become an increasingly important function for the development organization. Almost all organizations have a formalized process for recruiting. Here are some features that are most important to achieving successful results.

Cast a wide net. Use all appropriate advertising sources including the *Chronicle of Philanthropy* and the *Chronicle of Higher Education* and their respective web sites; Council for Advancement and Support of Education (CASE) online; and other publications and web sites pertinent to the position, including in some cases discipline-specific academic journals.

Work the networks of all the development and alumni professionals in the organization. Referrals are an important source of candidates because they are both "pre-screened" by their contact person in the organization and, one would hope, predisposed to joining the organization because of the presence of the same contact person. All staff members should be made aware of professional openings within the organization and kept up-to-date on the process for filling them. Furthermore, some organizations have utilized referral bonuses in order to encourage staff to participate more actively in the search process.

Use in-depth interviews with a broad mixture of staff. While staff may complain because "here comes another candidate to interview," they should be reminded that, short of raising a major gift, their most important role in the organization is to find good people to work with them—and ultimately succeed them—in their roles. Prospective candidates should be interviewed both within the area for which they are applying (such as annual giving or arts and sciences), and by development staff in unrelated areas as well. The interview process should include meals, group presentations, and other activities to gauge candidates' stamina and versatility!

Check references dutifully. The checking of references often determines whether someone wins a new position or not. At the same time, how many times have you heard a manager say that a troubled employee has left to join another organization and "no one from the hiring institution even bothered to call"? There are significant ethical and legal issues to navigate in this area, and it is useful to know the institution's overall human resources policies. Finally, remember that ensuring a prospect's confidentiality is important, but be wary of candidates who are overly anxious—even after an offer is on the table—about a current employer discovering a job search. These candidates may be more trouble than they are worth.

Consider "related" experience. As experienced professionals become harder to find for certain types of positions, it is prudent to assess those who may have related experience, such as in sales or perhaps another part of the institution. In the case of these candidates, it is vital that the process account for their lack of experience. They should be questioned thoroughly about how they expect to fit with the type of work, and about their comfort level operating within an academic environment.

Use all available resources to recruit. These resources should include the president, dean, and/or key volunteers of the institution. It is important to provide literature to candidates about the community, including the housing market, schools, and other information, and to demonstrate an interest in the candidate and his or her family.

Consider using "headhunters." The use of search firms can be a helpful asset, particularly for upper-level or more targeted positions. These searches are expensive, however, and search professionals tend to be more responsive to clients who most closely track their progress.

RETAINING AND MOTIVATING DEVELOPMENT STAFF

It is costly and time consuming to find good development staff; it is costlier, more time consuming, and disheartening to replace them. While high salaries and bonuses are at the top of every list to help maintain staff morale, financial reward alone can never be high enough to guarantee every employee's satisfaction. Focusing on other issues affecting retention and motivation can help. Following are some ideas:

- Show *intentional* appreciation of staff through notes, awards, comments, and events.
- Emphasize staff development and training through a comprehensive program, which should include a standard staff orientation plan.
- Encourage staff to attend conferences and professional development seminars.[4]
- Institute a culture of promoting from within when feasible. Encourage staff members to discuss their career aspirations with supervisors and other senior development professionals within the organization.
- Encourage informal mentoring throughout the organization.
- Involve staff in organizational leadership opportunities, such as running training sessions and heading task forces, and thank them for their participation.
- Give additional or special time off (for good behavior!), and look for special opportunities to allow staff a combination of personal and professional time.

Now back to the issue of bonuses. Any decision to implement a bonus system must be made in the context of the culture of the institution. Are there other such programs in existence? If not, will setting one up segregate the development staff from the balance of the institution's employees? Both CASE and the Association of Fundraising Professionals have ethical standards that discourage compensation programs based on the percentage of money raised by a particular development officer. However, several creative models have been developed recently that include a mixture of subjective and objective standards such as dollars raised, prospects discovered, contacts made, proposals delivered, stewardship activities initiated, volunteers recruited, and so forth. It is important that consideration be given to all employees, including support staff and others who are not frontline development officers, as well as to have institutional and/or unit goals that must be met in addition to individual goals. The key to a successful bonus system is the establishment of clear criteria, well-understood definitions, and realistic goals, all set within the framework of a data system and accountability structure that supports the entire process.

OTHER ATTRIBUTES OF A WELL-MANAGED DEVELOPMENT OFFICE

In addition to having an appropriate structure, comprehensive budget process, effective recruitment, and successful motivation and retention strategies, well-managed development organizations generally have a number of other common attributes.

Leadership. The head of the organization is an outstanding leader and a "triple threat," that is, he or she possesses strengths as a fund raiser, manager, and an academic administrator.

Strategic direction. The organization has a strategic plan in place to both increase giving and protect the process over time.

Good communications. There exist open and clear communications—internally and externally.

Accountability. The organization is structured to both encourage accountability and measure outcomes. Such a program helps staff understand what is expected of them and of the organization, and provides a framework for either defending existing budget support or making the case for additional funding.

Ethical and other values. A focus on integrity with a strong system of ethical values is essential, both in the positive representation of a particular academic institution, and—more importantly—for the well-being of the entire organization. The dignity and integrity of each staff member, within and outside the development organization, and each donor and volunteer must be paramount in all institutional endeavors.

NOTES

1. For an interesting history of fund raising, see Scott M. Cutlip, *Fund Raising in the United States: Its Role in America's Philanthropy* (New Brunswick, NJ: Rutgers University Press, 1965), 3–26.

2. Ralph L. Lowenstein, *Pragmatic Fund Raising* (Gainesville, FL: University of Florida Press, 1997), 4.

3. For example, M. C. Rorty, President of the American Management Association, formulated "Ten Commandments of Good Organization" in 1934, which included: "(4.) No executive or employee, occupying a single position in the organization, should be subject to definite orders from more than one source." See Carl Heyel, ed., *The Encyclopedia of Management* (New York: Van Nostrand Reinhold Company, 1973), 654.

4. Encouraging staff to attend outside conferences and professional meetings, not only helps satisfy them professionally, it broadens their network and brings favorable attention to their organization—both useful components in the staff recruiting program.

CHAPTER 23

Prospect Research and Prospect Management

Eric Siegel

T he term "prospect research" used to conjure up an image of clerks laboriously copying biographical information out of reference books and alumni files because the development office thought it would be a good idea to know something about prospective donors. This stereotype has now been replaced by that of the amazing techno-wizard with the power to instantaneously find everything about everyone. Over the past decade, the field of prospect research has changed perhaps more than any other aspect of fund raising. Print resources have been almost entirely replaced by the Internet and a vast array of on-line databases and CD products. The challenge of unearthing a few tidbits of information on most prospects has been replaced by the daunting task of sifting through a mountain of data on the majority of prospects.

Prospect research at most educational institutions has progressed far beyond the simple task of compiling information. It is now a multifaceted process of information retrieval, analysis, maintenance, and dissemination that forms the foundation for identifying, cultivating, and soliciting major gift prospects.

WHAT IS PROSPECT RESEARCH?

The definition of prospect research, and the responsibilities of the researcher, varies with the fund-raising operation itself. Depending on the size and scope of development activity, prospect researchers frequently double as proposal writers, gift processors, administrative assistants, or frontline development officers. Fortunately, most educational institutions now realize that prospect research is an essential component of development and, as such, requires full-time staff. The prospect researcher is now a master of one discipline rather than a jack-of-all-trades.

Even with this understanding, the meaning of prospect research can vary. Many research offices still function entirely reactively. Development officers and volunteer leaders unearth new prospects or reactivate old ones and ask the research office for information on these prospects. The researcher's role begins and ends with this task.

Although this will always be a crucial element of the researcher's job, most progressive institutions realize there is much more to prospect research. Specifically, there is proactive research, in which individual researchers and the director of research play a key role. Proactive research includes identifying individuals, corporations, or foundations that appear to have the capacity for significant giving (called "suspects"); screening, or qualifying, these suspects to determine who among them may be bona fide "prospects" for major gifts; and then classifying them according to potential giving level and interest in the institution.[1] Proactive research ensures a constant influx of new prospects into the prospect pipeline and represents a vital aspect of continued fund-raising success. Prospect "tracking," the systematic monitoring of steps in the cultivation of a prospect, is also a part of the prospect information continuum, and as such is also a logical duty of the research office.

RESEARCH RESPONSIBILITIES

All these tasks—suspect identification, prospect screening, information development, prospect classification, and prospect tracking and management—are part of a collaborative effort between frontline development officers and the research office. Following is a detailed examined of these steps.

Suspect Identification and Qualification

The research staff should play a pivotal role in discovering suspects, both within and beyond an institution's identified constituency. Indeed, this is in many ways the key contribution to the fund-raising effort made by prospect research. Suspect names come from many sources, but the research office can contribute significantly by routinely running names of alumni and lower-level donors through Internet search engines and stock ownership services, as well as subscription-based real estate and private company ownership databases. Frequently, the information available is so plentiful that research beyond the identification stage may involve only asset monitoring. However, merely collecting information is not enough. The research office must develop procedures for maintaining data and tracking suspects, and research staff must routinely inform key development officers of potential prospects.

Electronic psycho-demographic screening has greatly enhanced the suspect identification process. Many fund-raising consultants offer services for ranking and analyzing an institution's constituency based not only on demographic data but also lifestyles, consumer habits, and prior giving history. At least one vendor has taken screening a step further, providing its clients with an asset-tracking database. It is essential to remember, however, that psycho-demographic screening can only predict people's giving capacity and behavior; until they are examined individually, they remain suspects.

Prospect Screening

As suspects are identified, their names often go to volunteer and staff screening committees who try to separate those who have major gift capacity and inclination from those who do not. The research office's role in the screening process can include preparing suspect lists and research profiles, supervising screening sessions, and tabulating accumulated data. The primary goal of the screening process is, however, finding key volunteers who are acquainted and comfortable with soliciting the prospects.

Information Development

Screening results yield rosters of major donor prospects. The qualifying data is augmented and identified assets are tracked, emphasizing a prospect's capacity to give, philanthropic interests, relationships with people affiliated with the institution, and attitudes toward the institution.

However, even the most sophisticated and well-equipped research staff cannot always accurately assess all prospects. The development officer can help by providing timely contact reports detailing information from personal visits with prospects and volunteers. This information often provides the hints researchers need to transform sketchy data into a comprehensive overview of a prospect's potential.

Prospect Classification

Thorough prospect research provides the criteria necessary for classifying prospects. Using accumulated data and input from staff and volunteers, research staff can rate major gift prospects according to their financial capacity, interests, and readiness to give. This classification information is then incorporated into a prospect tracking and management system that routinely charts and assesses progress regarding each prospect.

Prospect Management and Prospect Tracking

An effective prospect management system, designed ultimately to guarantee that the right prospect is asked for the right gift at the right time, is the glue that holds a major gifts effort together. Essential components of prospect management are regular prospect review sessions where cultivation/solicitation activity is discussed and new names are brought to the table and assigned to frontline development officers; a clearance system that gives development officers a specified amount of time to initiate cultivation and complete solicitation; regular dissemination of prospect activity through contact, or trip, reports; and stewardship activity designed to keep current major donors involved with the institution until it is time to resolicit them. Successful prospect management recognizes that the major gifts process, from identification to solicitation and stewardship, is cyclical. Even as the solicitation of top prospects comes to closure, other prospects are being classified, researched, screened, and identified. Major gift donor pools must continually grow. Routine identification of new prospects fuels the growth of development programs for years to come.

Prospect management requires a comprehensive prospect tracking system, and the research staff is the most logical place for this system to reside. This system, now provided more or less effectively by most alumni/donor software vendors, must allow for the maintenance of multiple donor ratings, levels or steps in the cultivation process, prospect manager and volunteer assignments, previous and scheduled contact with prospects, and so forth. The system must have the capability of providing a multitude of reports, such as individual prospect reports for each development officer, tickler reports, executive overviews of prospect activity, reports on recent contacts, as well as statistical reports assessing the activity of all major gifts staff. Many development offices employ a "moves management" system, which assists in evaluating development officers based on the number of significant contacts and solicitations they accomplish.

THE RESEARCH OFFICE AND THE ORGANIZATION

The question of where the research office fits in the organization's reporting structure bedevils advancement operations. At some institutions, research reports directly to a vice president for advancement, the development director, or the director of major gifts. At other, larger institutions, research reports to a director of development operations or the head of administrative and financial services. Logic, however, dictates that the head of research should report directly to the staff member chiefly responsible for cultivating and soliciting major gifts.

Reporting relationships notwithstanding, the primary emphasis of a prospect research program should be on major gifts. Contemporary educational fund raising, especially in the context of large, multi-year campaigns, places an enormous burden on the research staff. There are more than enough major donor prospects to be discovered and researched, and the research office can ill afford to be bogged down preparing profiles on potential alumni award recipients, honorary degree nominees, annual fund donors, and the like. Yet this often occurs. Since many of these special projects are high-volume and seasonal, large backlogs of pending major prospect research can develop. Thus, advancement leaders must ask themselves these questions: What is the most cost-effective use of the research staff's time? What advancement priorities are best served by the research office?

More important than the research office's position in the organizational hierarchy are issues of communication and access. When the research department does not report directly to the director of development, and even more so when it reports to a separate service department, there is significant potential for isolation. In the worst cases, the research office cranks out voluminous amounts of major prospect profiles only to see them disappear into the major gifts office. Research staff receives little or no feedback on how the information is used or whether their work is truly instrumental in major gift cultivation. They feel no sense of involvement in the development process.

Prospect research must be regarded as an integral part, rather than an adjunct, of the development process. The research director and staff are in fact development officers who possess considerable knowledge of an institution's prospect base, even though they are not involved in daily contact with donors. Indeed, prospect researchers, along with the development director and major gifts director, probably have the broadest knowledge of an institution's major gift potential and should be consulted every step of the way toward a major solicitation. Regular reliance on research expertise will enable the development office to maximize its major gift opportunities.

Regardless of reporting structure, the research staff should attend all meetings where major gift prospects are discussed and should be prepared to add new information to enhance cultivation and solicitation. The research director should be in routine contact with all development personnel with major gift portfolios. By emphasizing interaction between research and senior development personnel, an institution will be better able to take advantage of the knowledge and skills of prospect researchers and will be able to devote less time to organizational issues.

STAFFING AND TRAINING

Prospect research is a labor-intensive effort, particularly when an institution is launching a major campaign. Research will be conducted on many more prospects than the relative few who will actually become major donors. A well-designed screening program, however, will eliminate many prospects before research becomes too heavily involved in the process. Development planning, and especially campaign planning, must take into account how many major donors will be needed to ensure a program's success, how many prospects will be needed to guarantee the desired number of major donors, and how many researchers will be needed to provide adequate financial and biographical data on all of the identified prospects. One must also factor into this equation what responsibilities other than major donor identification and research are assigned to the research office.

There is no rule of thumb governing the size of the research staff. Some commonly repeated formulas are one full-time researcher for every $10 million of a campaign goal, one for every $10 million raised annually, or one for every four development officers with major gift responsibilities. These formulas are rarely put into effect. The ratio of research staff to major gifts officers is rarely 1:4; more often it is 1:8, or worse. To be sure, prospect research is a much speedier process than it used to be. The Internet and on-line databases have enabled the researcher to become far more productive and successful. Unfortunately, at most institutions, development planning rarely anticipates the vast quantities of research requests generated by a large major gifts operation.

Even if an ideal ratio is unattainable because of budgetary constraints or other factors, a commitment to a full-time professional research staff is essential. Institutions that rely heavily on students to do their prospect research run the risk of high turnover rate and lack of employee loyalty.

A commitment to full-time employees also necessitates a commitment to providing salaries that will attract and retain skilled researchers. The days when successful advancement offices could get by paying researchers an administrative assistant's salary are over. In the increasingly complex world of information, it takes a trained professional to sift through the myriad Internet resources and on-line databases that have become the working tools of the prospect research office. Competitive salaries will greatly reduce turnover—an important factor in developing staff loyalty and continuity—and boost recruitment potential, ensuring a choice among qualified candidates. The person assigned the responsibility of overseeing the identification and research of major donor prospects should be accorded the same status and salary as a senior development officer.

Researchers, like their development counterparts, come from a wide variety of educational and professional backgrounds. The best research-ers, however, share some common traits. Most are well read and have a tremendous amount of curiosity about the world around them. They are thorough and highly detail oriented. They are persistent; if information exists on a prospect, they will find it.

When hiring a new researcher, it is best to look for people with these traits and, whenever possible, to seek those with extensive, if not pro-fessional, computer-based research experience. An applicant with pro-fessional library and information science credentials is already well versed in information storage and retrieval and will be much easier to train in the intricacies of prospect research. Writing skills are also im-portant, but the ability to retrieve, analyze, synthesize, and disseminate information quickly is the chief hallmark of a good prospect researcher.

Hiring the right person makes training that much easier. A new re-searcher with the requisite information skills needs only be introduced to the fund-raising environment: the alumni/donor database and record systems, the confidential nature of development work, and some of the specialized resources used in prospect research. If a new researcher re-quires little or no training in research resources and methodologies, the training period can be as short as one month and certainly no more than three.

Training a director of research is another matter entirely. Assuming there are no internal candidates, emphasis should be placed on hiring an external candidate with prospect research experience. The candidate must be a self-starter, because there will rarely be anyone in-house with sufficient prospect research background to be of much assistance to the new director. If none of the candidates possesses adequate prospect research experience, it is advisable to opt for information experience over development experience. The transition will be easier for someone with professional information skills even if experience in a development setting is lacking.

The past decade has witnessed the dramatic growth of the Association of Professional Researchers for Advancement (APRA). APRA provides a wide variety of training and networking opportunities for both experienced and novice researchers. The national organization and regional chapters conduct conferences and workshops highlighted by presentations from the top researchers in the field. These provide the research background necessary for those institutions with limited in-house experience. Prospect-L, a list serve for prospect researchers, also is an invaluable discussion group, enabling researchers to keep abreast of current trends and new resources in the field.

RESEARCH RESOURCES

Developing a professional prospect research office requires not only a serious staffing commitment but also a commitment to provide the staff with the resources needed to do the job. Primarily, this means that every researcher must have a fast computer with Internet access. But, in addition, significant funds must be devoted toward building a state-of-the-art electronic prospect research library. The size and scope of a research library will vary greatly depending on an institution's major donor constituency. Those institutions with national or international constituencies will require different resources than an institution with a regional or local base of support.

Other factors are the relative proximity of the research office to an institution's library, the library's collection development policy, and the nature of the working relationship between the research office and development officers. If the research office is located near the campus library, the need for a comprehensive in-house library may be lessened; still, the most efficient and cost-effective research operations are self-sufficient ones where a minimum amount of staff time is lost to travel. Additionally, the libraries at many institutions, even some fairly large universities, do not satisfy some basic needs of prospect research. This is especially true of institutions not offering a business curriculum.

One must also consider the development-research relationship. Is there a frequent demand for immediate information? Is the research office in constant e-mail and telephone contact with field officers? If so, the need for comprehensive internal resources will be greater.

Budgeting for prospect research resources is a difficult exercise. The Internet is an essentially free treasure trove of prospect information. Biographical data for corporate officers, stockholdings and salary for officers and directors of public companies, and real estate ownership and assessment data for many counties nationwide are all at the researcher's fingertips. Internet equivalents of several expensive hard-copy publications are also available. Still, not all resources are free and some, especially on-line database services, can be quite expensive. A bare-bones resource budget might be in the neighborhood of $15,000 per year, but a budget of $40,000 to $50,000 would enable the research office to pull out all the stops in its search for prospect information.

Essential References

This chapter will not attempt to provide a detailed bibliography of the resources routinely used by prospect researchers, but some of the resources that should be part of every prospect research library deserve note here.

Internet Resources. The Internet has revolutionized prospect research. The amount of information available is astounding and it is growing every day. Internet search engines, each with differing and useful search options, are the essential tools to guide the user to specific prospect information. Some of the search engines of most value to researchers are Google (http://www.google.com), Fast Search (http://www.ussc.allthe web.com), Northern Light (http://www.northernlight.com), AltaVista (http://www.altavista.com), and HotBot (http://www.hotbot.lycos.com).

Other notable websites are the attorney and physician directories provided by Martindale-Hubbell (http://www.martindale.com) and the American Medical Association (http://www.ama-assn.org). Official corporate filings for public companies are available through the Securities and Exchange Commission website, EDGAR (http://www.sec.gov). Many prospect researchers prefer searching these filings using 10K Wizard (http://www.10kwizard.com). 10K Wizard allows the research to search by director or officer name and by institution name, an extremely valuable feature since most proxy statements report the educational background of directors.

A number of research offices around the country have constructed their own research websites, providing links to a wide variety of websites most frequently visited by researchers. Two of the more useful sites were created at Northwestern University (http://pubweb.acns.nwu.edu/~cap 440) and the University of Southern California (http://www.usc.edu/dept/source).

On-line Databases. Although no longer the revolutionary tools they were a decade ago, fee-based on-line database services are still an essential component of the prospect researcher's arsenal. While the Internet is a marvelous tool, it does not possess the archival depth of on-line databases. It is only with a comprehensive on-line database service that a researcher will have access to non-current, full-text newspaper and magazine articles. Additionally, many of these services provide the researcher with a vast array of biographical data, real estate ownership information, state corporate filings, and other information.

Once perceived as being inordinately expensive, database searching is now considered one of the most efficient, cost-effective ways of conducting prospect research. Many of the available databases are expensive to use, especially if researchers do not have proper and thorough training. They have, however, become much more user-friendly over the years. It is no longer necessary to have a strong library science background to be a proficient searcher.

The database service of choice for most prospect researchers is Lexis-Nexis. Lexis-Nexis is a gigantic family of databases covering almost every topic imaginable, many of which are of no use to the prospect researcher. The price tag is also very high. Any researcher considering subscribing to Lexis-Nexis would be well served to contact a company representative familiar with the non-profit world. If a researcher has a good idea of how much money is available, Lexis-Nexis will be able to put together a package of databases that will match the institution's needs and budget.

Two other on-line services are worthy of note. Dun & Bradstreet (D&B) publishes a Million Dollar+ directory, providing financial and ownership data on most American companies, both public and private, that have over $1 million in sales. D&B offers a print version, a CD version, and, best of all, an Internet version. For about $7,000 a year, it provides the researcher with a wealth of information on corporate America. D&B's corporate biography section contains educational data, so it is an easy process to search for any mention of a particular institution. If the price of Dun & Bradstreet is too steep, ReferenceUSA offers a completely searchable national yellow pages, complete with sales ranges and key personnel for about $900 a year.

DataQuick and First American Real Estate Solutions provide on-line real estate assessment services. The cost of the service varies, depending on the number of hours per month an institution opts for. Both have extensive nationwide coverage and, for some states, the capability of searching statewide, rather than county-by-county. Since the assessed value of real property is, in many states, much lower than market value, both services permit the researcher to search for comparable sales within a defined region. The value of these services cannot be overstated. The American dream is still to own a home, and, for many prospects, real estate data is the only asset information available.

Other Sources. There are also a number of CD products that researchers find very helpful. Marquis Who's Who has put its entire collection of *Who's Who* publications on two CDs. One contains all current *Who's Who* editions and the other is a historical disk containing citations from past editions. The Foundation Center puts out a CD called FC Search that gives comprehensive data on all U.S. foundations. It contains a complete index of all foundation trustees. A network version for up to eight users is available for around $1,400.

While reference books have largely disappeared from the shelves of prospect research libraries, there remain a few that are convenient to keep on hand. Walker's *The Corporate Directory of U.S. Public Companies* has a complete index of all officers, directors, and five percent owners of American public companies. And, if FC Search is too costly, the Foundation Center publishes *Guide to U.S. Foundations, Their Trustees, Officers, and Donors* with a complete index of all foundation trustees. Additionally, there are a number of state and regional business directories with no on-line or CD counterpart. Subscriptions to national and local business periodicals also should not be neglected. They are a vital source for keeping track of prominent alumni, prospect identification, and staying abreast of business trends.

Another important resource is the interview—either with the prospect him- or herself or volunteers who know the prospect well. Interviewing should be the responsibility of field officers, who should file contact reports after meeting with volunteers and prospects. However, it is advisable to recruit a few well-placed volunteers on whom researchers, or at least the director of research, can rely for additional prospect information.

The days of researchers prowling around county courthouses looking at wills, divorce settlements, and civil actions are over. These documents are still considered part of the public record, but, out of ethical considerations and recognizing a prospect's right to privacy, they are now taboo.

RESEARCH PRIORITIES

Even with the Internet and sophisticated databases, it is not always possible to find substantial information on all prospects. Even finding nothing takes time—about three or four hours of thorough searching. Conversely, information on some prospects is so plentiful that a researcher must be trained to recognize the point at which research becomes redundant. The researcher must keep in mind the essentials of prospect research (assets, philanthropic tendencies, connections with and attitudes toward the institution) in deciding when to press on or when to quit.

Still, the volume of research requests generated by a large development operation can overwhelm even a sizable research staff. Guidelines enabling development officers to best use researchers' skills and knowledge are essential. A simple and perhaps obvious notion is that not all prospects require the same amount of research. It makes no sense to devote as much time to a $1,000 prospect as a $1,000,000 prospect. First, the development office must define what it means by a major gift, a leadership gift, a special gift, and so on. It must also establish a bottom-line figure for prospects for which any research will be done. These figures will vary considerably from one institution to another, but once established, they help bring a coherent structure to the research process.

The continued growth of the Internet and the increased breadth of on-line database services has somewhat lessened the need to create a tiered structure of research. Formerly, quick research was done at the identification stage. More substantial work was done during the cultivation process. In-depth profiles were reserved for the best prospects as they neared solicitation. Now, in this increasingly automated world of information retrieval, the researcher can produce the same in-depth results in no more than one or two days.

Another integral part of the prospect research process is the maintenance of an accessible central file system. The rapid growth of database searching technology has caused some researchers to question the need for maintaining paper files at all. They argue that all pertinent research information can be stored on a computer and that additional information can be pulled up during a simple database search. This, however, deprives the institution of a valuable archival resource, a complete history of an institution's relationship with its donors. From the researcher's point of view, files with years of accumulated newspaper and magazine clippings may pose space and storage problems, but they significantly reduce the number of unnecessary research requests. If development officers have access to extensive donor and prospect files, some prospects may require little or no additional research. If there is a future for the paperless office (and for some offices the future is now), it will come not from eliminating aspects of a vital institutional resource, but rather from image processing systems capable of storing large quantities of file materials.

No matter how resource-rich and efficient a research office is, there are still times when even a large research staff faces conflicting priorities. One solution is to involve the director of development or the director of major gifts in setting priorities for research. When requesting research, development officers should be asked to indicate whether the request is of high, medium, or low priority. The director of development can then be asked to approve all high-priority requests in light of overall institutional priorities. When conflicts or competing deadlines arise, the director of research can consult with the development director to determine an appropriate course of action.

ETHICS AND CONFIDENTIALITY

In the summer of 1988, prospect research became a hot news item. The nation's press suddenly "discovered" research and began to call into question some of the profession's practices.[2] Since then, the ethics of contemporary fund raising, and prospect research in particular, have dominated much of the discussion at professional conferences and workshops. The concerns expressed both by the press and by researchers themselves revolve around the lengths to which one will go to collect prospect information and the idea that philanthropy is a noble calling and therefore does not merit prying into the lives of potential donors.

Reporters looking for a good story are capable of exaggerating certain aspects of prospect research; the idea of a "nonprofit CIA" is certainly more glamorous than that of researchers sitting at a computer terminal. Still, prospect researchers are at times overly aggressive in their pursuit of information, and data maintained in donor files may sometimes portray prospects in an unflattering light. Researchers and development professionals must learn how to police themselves. Indeed, APRA has published a very strongly worded code of ethics. In the ever-increasing competition for philanthropic dollars, the tendency to over-research must be avoided. Back in 1986, but even more valid today, Bobbie Strand wrote,

> Respect is at the heart of [prospect research]. Information that could
> damage a prospect's reputation or cause embarrassment to him or

her should not be recorded or shared indiscreetly. . . . Security for any personal information should be assured. . . . Respect for the institution and its needs and respect for possible donors will enable the researcher to produce information and suggest strategy to meet those needs with integrity and pride.[3]

Prospect researchers are very much caught up in the information explosion and the technological innovations that have made that explosion possible. Prospect data will become even more plentiful and accessible. Providing the essential information to fuel the development process is an enormous responsibility, one that must be undertaken with a clear understanding of an institution's mission and a respect for the privacy of donor prospects.

NOTES

1. Emily P. Henderson, "A Prospectus for Prospect Research," in *Prospect Research: A How-to Guide*, ed. Bobbie J. Strand and Susan Hunt (Washington, DC: Council for Advancement and Support of Education, 1986), 5–18.
2. Anne Lowrey Bailey, "Today's Fund-raising Detectives Hunt 'Suspects' Who Have Big Money to Give," *Chronicle of Higher Education*, June 22, 1988, A-1; Connie Leslie, "Prospecting for Alumni Gold," *Newsweek* (September 5, 1988): 66–67.
3. Strand and Hunt, *Prospect Research*, i–ii.

CHAPTER

Development Information Systems

Gail Ferris

I n the formulation of new strategies for educational fund raising, one
of the areas in which fund raisers have the greatest ambivalence is
the use of development information systems. Properly utilized, information systems can be one of the critical parts of the fund-raising
infrastructure. Unfortunately, too often they have instead become demanding masters in their own right rather than the servants that they
were intended to be, at best ignored, at worst consuming valuable time
and effort that should have been devoted to fund raising.

A development information system, in the broadest sense, is any
method used by fund raisers to gather and store data that may later be
of value either in reporting past gifts or in supporting efforts to secure
future gifts. Thus, the system could vary in scale from the development
officer's Day-Timer to the largest mainframe-based computer systems.
For purposes of this analysis, the discussion will be limited to computer-
based systems, regardless of their scale.

The importance of an effective development information system can
hardly be overstated. Over the last generation, fund raising has become
increasingly information-intensive. The scale of development efforts
thirty years ago could still be adequately supported by a largely paper
record system, but the fund-raising efforts of today rely so heavily on
being able to "slice and dice" information that this is no longer practical.
Fund raisers need to be able to view the data both on a macro and micro
level, easily accessing summary information on overall campaign progress
and then being able to drill down to the level of the individual prospect.

Fund raising has always been a business of "who knows whom." As the relationships of prospects have become increasingly complex, however, and as turnover in development staff continues to be rapid, systems are being called upon to serve as the "institutional memory." More correspondence is being produced than ever, be it in electronic or hardcopy form, and development information systems provide the necessary vehicle to ensure that this information is accessible when and where it is needed.

With this volume of information being necessary to support fundraising efforts, it becomes even more critical that the system assist the fund raiser in focusing on the information that is truly important to the task at hand. It is only with the help of an effective information system that the fund raiser can maximize productivity in garnering support for the institution.

HISTORY

Managers in educational fund raising are becoming more and more aware of the fact that, in order to manage their fund-raising operations effectively, they must manage the information on which fund-raising decisions are made. For them to be able to make the best use of the systems that store their information, they must be familiar with the strengths and limitations of their systems. An appreciation of the advances made in information systems over the last generation is a good starting point for understanding why systems are what they are today, how they can be used optimally to support educational fund raising, and what support to expect from information systems in the future.

A generation of fund raisers ago, fund-raising record keeping was largely a mechanical operation. Record keeping was largely divided into biographic records and giving records. The first significant advance in biographic records came with the advent of systems that had addresses stamped on metal plates. These could then be sorted in a variety of ways, using holes punched in particular locations on their perimeters, and they could be used to print envelopes for targeted mailings.

Advances in gift processing systems were much slower in coming, really not advancing beyond ledger sheets and adding machines until the very first electronic systems became available. These early electronic accounting systems were extremely dependent on paper for their inputs as well as their outputs. Information for such systems was entered on punch cards, mechanically punched by operators, and outputs equally were produced in voluminous reports that analyzed the information fed into the system via the cards.

It was not until well into the 1970s that development information systems had the capability of entering and viewing information on-line. At this point the private sector had not recognized the potential profit to be made from producing and licensing development information systems, so the institutions with adequate financial and technical resources began programming their own systems. It would be the better part of a decade before vendors would really enter the market.

The systems developed by institutions in the 1970s were limited by the technical platforms available at the time. This was the era of the mainframe computer, with large machines requiring strictly climate-controlled environments. End users began to get on-line access to their information, but since the graphical user interfaces that would become available in the 1990s were not yet available, users had to use complex series of keystrokes to navigate through the screens of data in these systems. The result was that systems remained mostly within the purview of the technical and "back office" staff.

In the 1980s, a number of companies saw the potential market for fund-raising information software. Initially, these systems vendors offered only the same platforms that the institutions already had, but they were able to offer software that provided regular enhancements as the fund-raising field changed. Institutions began increasingly to contract for vendor systems in order to externalize the cost and risk of their software enhancement and maintenance.

By the late 1980s, the trend was clearly for institutions to replace their aging, homegrown systems with vendor systems. The pace of this change accelerated as mainframes began to cost more and more to maintain, and vendors began producing their systems to run on the much smaller, less expensive minicomputers that were then becoming available. More and more fund raisers were accessing fund-raising information from their desktops, albeit still using keystrokes to navigate.

This all changed in the mid-1990s, as graphical user interfaces came to predominate on the desktop as the desktop hardware became increasingly powerful. One vendor package after another converted to point-and-click user interfaces, making navigation within the development information system truly intuitive to end-user staff. As the majority of end users began to access their own data, the demand for additional functionality in vendor systems grew. Vendors began more and more to partner with institutions to produce prospect and event management software. Scanning and accessing existing paper files followed, along with increased demand for remote access to data. The time is now very near when the fund raiser will expect and be able to have fund-raising information available on personal, handheld computers.

TYPES OF INFORMATION

The question of what information is needed to support educational fund raising can perhaps best be answered the same way that Samuel Gompers was reputed to have answered the question of what the three things were that organized labor wanted: he replied, "More, more, and more." Fund raisers are increasingly finding that, in order to succeed effectively in a world of more and more competition for the philanthropic dollar, they need information that will give them the edge over their competitors. Nevertheless, answering the six questions used to form the basis for newspaper stories can help categorize the information necessary to track who, what, when, where, why, and how.

"Who?" is the question that is often at the core of getting to the donor—who are the donor's family members, work colleagues, social friends, and who is the person who can most effectively solicit a gift from the donor (be it a staff member or volunteer)? Knowing who has key relationships with the donor can be essential to persuading that donor to increase the size of a commitment, or in some cases, to make the commitment at all. The fund-raising system of the twenty-first century must provide this data to the fund raiser.

The "what?" question deals more with the situation or status in which the donor finds himself or herself, or preferences that the donor has shown. What is the donor's occupation? Equally important, what are the donor's avocational interests, such as volunteer and recreational activities? At what point is the donor in his or her career? What are the assets that the donor has acquired? These data become an essential part of the overall profile of the donor.

To know "when?" best to ask a donor, while still the consummate art of fund raising, is becoming more and more of a science due to the data that can be brought to the timing strategy. Large amounts of data are now available to fund raisers regarding when donors may come into large sums of money. Required Securities Exchange Commission filings for inside traders is but one of the sources that can be incorporated into the development information system, helping the fund raiser to know what the donor's financial assets and liquidity may be. Knowing when a donor is going to stop paying college tuition also may indicate that he or she may suddenly have much more disposable income. Therefore, data as well as judgment can help determine the timing of a solicitation.

"Where?" is really the point at which automated development information systems began a generation ago. Then, as now, having correct information on how to contact a donor is pivotal to the fund-raising process, but the means by which this information is obtained and recorded are quite different. Thirty years ago, to find a lost donor one was at the mercy of directories (phone, social, or professional), tracer cards, or the post office. Now, credit reporting networks and various tools available on the Internet come as near as possible to ensuring that the diligent records department can find the vast majority of lost alumni and donors.

What will motivate a donor to give (the "why?" question) is an area for which the information system is expected to provide critical information. Fortunately, more sources are now available for information regarding a donor's charitable inclinations. Data available from external rating services will tell the institution the extent to which a donor can be expected to provide support, based on the donor's previous known gifts. This data, together with past giving history to the institution itself and perhaps other information—such as the donor's own answers to affinity questions on various surveys—combine to produce a powerful indicator of the likelihood of future support.

The issue of "how?" a donor may support an institution can have a critical impact on the timing and size of a solicitation. Tracking stock options in the development information system can be a very reliable predictor of when the donor may recognize an increase in his or her assets that might be shared with your institution. Tracking appreciated property can lead to the identification of scenarios in which both the donor and the institution can win through gift planning.

ACCESS TO INFORMATION

The revolution in development information systems has become largely focused on how staff members access the information necessary to their activities, and access it in such a way that they only get the information they really need. In one sense, the fund raiser had total access to fund-raising information when the information was stored exclusively in paper files. The problem was that with all of the information available in that form it became extremely cumbersome to focus only on the information that was really needed.

Enter the era of automated information systems. In the early days, in order to manage the increasing amounts of information, fund raisers gave up the "hands-on" access to the data. They came to rely on the their data-processing intermediaries to produce reports to meet their needs, but there was a constant tension between end users and technical staff over getting the data to the end user in the form and the time in which it was needed.

This loss of hands-on access was lamented for many years, but, fortunately, advances in technology have over time put the data directly in development officers' hands. The advent of the Internet has made remote access simple and dependable, so that even a non-technical user need not be separated by time or space from the information needed for fund raising. Fund raisers now access data from development information systems with software that has the same look and feel as other applications that they use on a daily basis in their work and personal lives.

In the last five years, there has been an explosion in the use of handheld computing devices. Originally designed as replacements for pocket appointment books, the power of these devices has exploded with improvements in electronic components. Technology is now being developed by a number of companies that will provide a fund raiser on the road with access through a handheld device to the same information that he or she now can obtain at the desk. This will again bring the availability of information up to the level of other management tools used by fund raisers.

GETTING THE INFORMATION OUT

One of the most common laments of the fund raiser with regard to development information systems is, "I've put all of this information in, now how do I get it out?" Many of the systems vendors readily admit that they do not provide a large number of reports with their baseline products because each institution is going to have its own specific information output requirements. That means that institutions, even when paying tens or hundreds of thousands of dollars for a system, need to be prepared to invest more internally in the production of reports. In the implementation of a new system, the issue of reports needs to be included in the initial phase of the implementation, not as an afterthought, or the system will not be effective regardless of the quality of the data.

When developing reports, the same three factors always need to be considered: what records are to be selected, how are the data to be sorted, and in what format are the data to be displayed? The same factors apply whether the fund raiser is running the report directly or whether a request for the report is being submitted to technical staff. These factors thus need to be addressed on the screens or forms on which the user submits the request.

With the many attractive options for end-user reporting tools now available, more and more development officers are creating their own reports. However, from a management point of view, the advantages of this new approach need to be considered against the disadvantage that the time the fund raiser spends producing reports is not time being spent in the field. The best middle ground is for technical staff to package a number of reports, giving fund raisers a number of options for record selection, sorting, and format. When the fund raiser's request is outside of these packaged reports, it is more efficient, as well as more likely to yield accurate information, if technical staff perform the data retrievals on behalf of the fund raiser.

How to deliver the output of reports, whether run by development officers or technical staff, is another area where all options should be explored to determine the optimal medium. Although hard-copy reports, printed centrally or distributed to printers in the fund raisers' offices, still serve a critical function, other media are supplanting paper reports. For reports that a number of staff in a large fund-raising operation need to view, posting reports on office-wide home pages is a very effective way to disseminate information, especially to fund raisers working far from the office. For data that may need to be combined with other data to produce mailings, electronic files of data allow for much easier manipulation of that data into the final format.

THE POWER OF INTERFACES

One of the most important maxims in the administration of development information systems is, "Shoot all duplicate databases." If parts of the organization are permitted to track their fund-raising efforts outside of the enterprise (or central) system, confusion ensues. Gift solicitations will not be optimized, and there is great potential for annoyance to donors due to uncoordinated contacts from the institution. With all data kept on the enterprise system, fund raisers making contact with the donor can be sure they have the "big picture" of the overall relationship with that individual.

This picture can be greatly enhanced by a variety of data sources beyond the institution's own development information system. Some of these sources can significantly improve the quality of the basic biographic information. For example, the National Change of Address file not only provides addresses for lost alumni, but also improves the format of existing addresses. The helps to make mail to donors more deliverable and qualifies the institution for postage discounts for meeting the postal service's address standards. Similar electronic updates are available for telephone numbers, useful for both mass solicitations through phonathon programs as well as individual calls by major gifts fund-raising staff. Several organizations provide electronic information on companies' matching gift policies, which are suitable for loading into the institution's information system.

Other external sources of electronic information are of even greater import to the major gifts effort. A number of firms provide ratings of individuals' capacity and willingness to give, as well as particular assets that they hold; most of this data lends itself easily to loading into the development information system. Also, institutions can purchase and incorporate electronic data on insider trading of securities, which can assist in both prospect identification and the creation of prospect solicitation strategies.

Some interfaced systems may either be internal or external to your institution. On-line alumni directories are now common. These systems allow alumni both to update their own information and to look up fellow graduates. Some of the development information systems include this directory/update as a feature of the system, but there are also several outside vendors who provide this service. Most of these vendors have historically been producers of print directories and now have entered the on-line directory field. Although having this feature as an integrated part of the institution's own system is clearly easier for acquiring data, the outside directory vendors have also worked very hard to make the transfer of data to and from external on-line directories as seamless as possible.

Another key interface to donors that has developed as a result of e-commerce applications is the ability of donors to make gifts via the Internet. As with on-line directories, a number of systems vendors offer this capacity within their software packages, but there are also service bureaus that offer such services. Donors can make a gift on these sites, and the information is sent electronically to both the institution's bank, for credit to its account, and directly to the institution for recording in the development information system.

BUY-IN

The biggest problem with most development information systems, however, is not technical at all, but rather human. "Tone at the top" is critical to the success of any system. If management does not believe in the system, it is highly unlikely that the rank and file will. At one institution, the vice president for development and the development staff were invited for a demonstration of the system that the institution had just purchased. Shortly after the lights dimmed, the vice president left the room. When the demonstration ended an hour later and the lights were turned on, only the demonstrator, the technical staff, and one or two fund raisers remained. The message received by the fund raising staff on the importance of the system was loud and clear.

In another situation, the vice president made the information system the backbone of measuring and rewarding performance by the fundraising staff. All contacts were required to be entered promptly in the system as an essential element to managing the campaign. Bonuses and raises were determined from information entered on the system, and the word went out that "if it wasn't on the system, it didn't happen." Nonparticipation was no longer an option.

A number of other factors can help to ensure that fund raisers accept the use of the system. Effective training is a key element in the successful implementation of any system. Development officers need to know the system's potential to assist them in doing their jobs and that it actually can reduce, not increase, their workload. Without proper instruction, the system will become an unmanageable burden, and staff will resort to virtually anything to avoid using it, especially keeping their own off-system records. Proper training makes certain that the data is entered according to the institution's standards, making it useful for the overall management of the fund-raising effort.

The result of proper training and support from top management is that fund raisers will come to "own" their data and the system. It will be their system, not the computer center's or the software vendor's. However, this will only occur with cooperation among all of the users. Development officers need to provide information so that the system can be a comprehensive source of fund-raising information. At the same time, the system needs to provide information in a way that supports development officers' own fund-raising efforts. In this way, properly maintained and utilized, the system will not become a burden to overworked development staff, but rather a servant making their jobs easier and their performance more successful.

Actually, the ultimate success in development information system implementation is that the fund raiser does not view the system as belonging to anyone. The data is the only issue, and that belongs to the institution. Everyone is entitled to easy information access to enable them to perform their fund-raising duties. Properly implemented and supported, a fund-raising information system thus will sell itself as an integral part of fund-raising management.

CHAPTER 25

Benchmarking, Accountability, and Measuring Performance

James M. Langley

My career has afforded me the honor of being present on many occasions when donors announced very generous gift commitments. My initial elation at such moments is always followed by a heavy tug of responsibility. I remind myself that the gift commitment was an outgrowth of a relationship nurtured over time. As the relationship deepened, the donor became more trusting. In making the commitment, the donor acted out of both trust and faith. In accepting the gift, I realize how important it is for us to secure that trust and perpetuate that faith by keeping our promises, by spending that money wisely and well, and by being conscientious stewards. In accepting a gift, we have moved from courtship to marriage. Now the real work begins and weight of real obligation is felt.

"If that is the case," some may say, "how can one measure success? How can one apply metrics to the building of relationships and intangibles like faith and trust? Doesn't that denigrate the nobility of philanthropy by trying to quantify how much it cost, how long it took, and who should get credit for it?" But, it is crucial that effectiveness be measured no matter how imperfectly, precisely because philanthropy is a part of a larger social contract.

Development officers need to keep the costs of raising and managing private dollars to a defensible level so donors can be assured that the largest possible portion of their gifts is being applied to the intended project or purpose. And, they need to account for and justify every cent that is not.

Development officers need to show that endowments are being well managed and that their institutions or foundations are constantly trying to improve performance while being guided by reasonable risk-reward strategies. By doing so, they can show donors that the value of their gifts will be preserved and directed toward their intended purposes, even after they have died. By the same token, they need to show donors that their investments are overseen by highly capable professionals and by trustworthy, accomplished trustees who will always seek to balance the needs of the university with the intentions of the donors. Discerning donors who are contemplating sharing sizable portions of their estate will gravitate toward those institutions that demonstrate the highest degree of efficiency in converting gifts to real and lasting value.

Development staff need to prove to the faculty and administrative colleagues that their slice of that limited budgetary pie will accrue to the institution's long-term benefit, albeit at their short-term expense. And, yes, they need to show their bosses that development is using precious resources for the greater good of the institution. For those reasons, and many more, it is crucial to attempt measuring success. The search for the right and reasonable metrics is the manifestation of accountability.

DETERMINING THE METRICS

So, what metrics should be applied, and how is it done without being arbitrary or mercenary? The cornerstone of accountability is the overall cost of raising private support. It must be shown that private funds are raised with an efficiency that approximates that of similarly situated institutions. To do that requires benchmarking. The key is determining, fairly and accurately, which other institutions are similarly situated.

In the past decade, this author has met with representatives of universities in Asia, Europe, and Scandinavia who are eager to learn how to raise private dollars. They are often well schooled in development technique but assume all they need do is transfer U.S. practices to their countries. It is important to caution that philanthropy in the United States is both an outgrowth of American culture and history and of the maturity of its universities and their fund-raising programs. Those things are decades, if not centuries, in the making.

Comparing the performance measures or development strategies of a 150-year-old urban institution with a long history in fund raising to a fifty-year-old rural institution with a decade-old development program will not yield much useful information. Young institutions have young alumni and are less rooted in tradition, including development traditions. They don't have the benefit of generations of alumni support. Having that well-developed cycle and the power of that example in place makes fund raising much easier.

Nor can the development prowess of a university with schools of medicine, engineering, management, and law be compared to that of a liberal arts college. Certain disciplines produce more wealth for their graduates and more gratitude returned in the form of generous gifts. Young institutions or young development programs need to spend significant amounts just to build a base of awareness and then convert it into a base of support. Their costs cannot be compared to the household-name university. In addition, it is essential to be attuned to regional differences. Prominent public institutions in the Midwest have enjoyed considerable private support for fifty years or more, while publics in the Northeast have to labor mightily to be seen as something other than lesser adjuncts to the famous private institutions in that region. Each development program has to determine which organizations are most similar, not mirror images, but as similar as possible. Only then can useful comparisons be made.

After they've determined their true cohort group, fund raisers can glean useful information by consulting the Council on Aid to Education (CAE) *Voluntary Support of Education* reports or, perhaps, by creating a data exchange peer group. Such peer groups can determine exactly what kind of data they want to assemble and share precisely the way the data is calculated. No matter how specific any survey may be in the questions it poses, questionnaire institutions will calculate the cost of fund raising in different ways. Some will be conscientious to a fault; others will fudge or just interpret different questions in different ways. But, any comparison of like institutions will provide at least a general idea of how a particular one is doing.

For young universities and immature development programs, the cost of doing business is probably toward the high end of the norm—14 to 16 percent. (And those norms are more anecdotal than authoritative. While various fund-raising consultants have done comparative analyses, no large studies on the topic have been conducted since the Council for Advancement and Support of Education [CASE]/National Association of College and University Business Officers [NACUBO] study of more than a decade ago.)[1] Mature development programs not in or anticipating a campaign should come in under 10 percent. Most colleges and universities shoot for 10 percent or less, but even higher degrees of efficiency can and should be achieved by universities that have staged successive successful campaigns. Remember, those percentages apply to the development program overall. There's an inverse proportion in effect for various fund-raising efforts in any given development program, that is, the smaller the gift the greater the percentage overhead. It is necessary to spend more proportionally to raise an annual gift than a major gift.

Return on investments in development operations cannot be measured in one-year increments. The reason for that can be found in donor behavior. The process of securing gifts, from the time a prospect is identified to the time a commitment is secured, generally takes eighteen months to two years. Larger gifts generally take even longer. Mega-gifts can be a decade or more in the making. Moreover, looking at most seven-figure donors to college or university campaigns, there is a history of annual giving over two decades in the vast majority of cases. Before development officers can determine if their investment in a major gifts effort has been productive, they must determine the strength of the annual fund and the depth of the prospect pool it can draw upon. And, they must be willing to wait at least two years before jumping to too many conclusions. Yes, revenues should be expected to total at least ten times the resources invested in mature programs at mature institutions. But, patience and perspective will be required for fledgling programs at emerging institutions.

By the same logic, it is unwise to expect individual development officers to show a one-year return on investment. Their productivity can be measured, but it must be done in a philanthropic context and over a reasonable period of time, so that they can demonstrate their ability to identify, inform, involve, cultivate, solicit, and steward. They should not be judged on their ability to induce one-time gifts but rather on their ability to secure support in such a way that donors become more committed to their organization's vision, mission, and goals—and, therefore, more likely to give again in the future. The philanthropic context needs to be communicated to and understood by the entire staff before performance measures can be agreed to by supervisors and development officers. It entails spelling out guiding principles, larger values, or the ethical framework for the development operation. For example, below are the "Development Values" for the University of California at San Diego.

DEVELOPMENT VALUES

The development "market" is shaped by donor interests and intentions, as well as by relationships that individual donors have with institutional representatives. The Development Office at UCSD, therefore, must be organized and act in a way that respects those market forces.

At UCSD, we must place the premium on doing what is best for the donors (current or prospective) including:

- Listening to the needs and interests of donors to make sure that our suggestions are consistent with their values and propensities.

- Stating our needs in a fair, accurate and ethical way to make sure that the credibility of the institution is not tarnished, and that no relationship with any donor is sullied by false, misleading, or self-serving information.

- Presenting a unified front in our words and deeds to demonstrate that we all represent one institution and the needs of the whole always exceed the interests of individual units, which entails sparing all donors and volunteers from internal squabbles, disputes and personality conflicts.

- Supporting our colleagues and working as a team to satisfy the interests and intentions of donors.

- Living steadfastly by the rule that "the donor decides."

- Being conscientious stewards of private funds and treating donors like "investors" in the institution, which should involve regular updates to donors on the use of their dollars or on the status of their endowment, trying to resolve any ambiguities in the use of private funds by first clarifying "donor intentions," and informing donors of all significant institutional developments, good or bad, before they are vetted in the popular press.

These precepts should guide collective decision-making and govern the conduct of individual development officers. They should also be used to evaluate staff performance in concert with individual unit or office goals and the general measures of development effectiveness.

MEASURING INDIVIDUAL PERFORMANCE

With an ethical framework soundly in place, it is possible to begin to measure the performance of individual development officers. Though it may sound counterintuitive, the most important thing to measure is each development officer's judgment. Asking the right questions can bring that judgment out and help establish a baseline of expectations from which performance can be monitored and measured. Those questions might include:

1. What was the state of the development operation or area of responsibility that you inherited?

A. Highly advanced
B. Reasonably sophisticated
C. Mediocre
D. Poor
E. Primitive
F. Non-existent

2. What were the greatest strengths of the operation or the major assets within your area of responsibility, if any; for example: the quality of the academic leadership, the availability of the academic leader, the strength of the case for support, the compelling nature of the unit's needs, the breadth and depth of the prospect and donor base, the adequacy of the fund-raising budget, and the quality of support from the academic unit and/or central development?

3. What were its greatest weaknesses, if any (could be related to the same factors above)?

4. What have you done, or what do you propose to do to amplify those strengths or mitigate those weaknesses?

5. How many donors are you stewarding (list by level, i.e., eight-figure, seven-figure, six-figure, etc.)?

6. How many prospects do you have (list by level)?

7. How many of those prospects at each level would be receptive to a well-crafted proposal or solicitation in the next six months? Is there a solicitation plan and timetable in place for each?

8. How many of those prospects would be ready for solicitation within twelve months? Is there a cultivation plan in place for each?

9. How many of those prospects would you classify as actively engaged, either through advisory boards, substantive and sustained volunteer activities, or regular and predictable interactions?

10. How many of those prospects would you classify as well informed but not engaged? What strategies, activities, and events will you employ to engage as many as possible?

11. How many of those prospects would you classify as only vaguely aware of the academic discipline or unit that you represent? What strategies, activities, events, or publications will you use to make them more aware? Have these prospects demonstrated any propensities to lead you to believe that, if properly informed, they would become more engaged and supportive?

12. What strategies are you employing to inform and engage recently identified prospects?

13. What strategies are you employing to identify new prospects?

14. What strategies are you employing to raise the visibility of your unit, operation, or area of responsibility in select prospect segments or communities?

Keep in mind that these questions will have to be tweaked according to the kind of development officer and his or her level of responsibility. However, sophisticated supervisors will ask these kinds of questions and listen, or review the written answers, with great care. They will spend enough time with the development officer to understand the nuances of each situation. These kinds of interviews allow the development officer to exercise his or her judgment and for the supervisor to track the exercise of that judgment over time. But what else is going on in these interviews? The supervisor is asking about the number of prospects and trying to determine if the development officer has the right prospect load, is focusing on all phases of the development cycle from identification to stewardship, and has thought through the next steps for various prospects at various phases. At this stage the negotiations between supervisor and development officer can move toward the application of more specific metrics, including:

- How many solicitations do you plan on conducting in each quarter of the next fiscal year?
- How many pre-solicitation cultivation moves will you make in the same time frame?
- How many initial cultivation moves will you make?
- How many new prospects do you intend to identify and qualify (visit face-to-face)?
- How many stewardship calls, contacts, or events can you schedule?

Again, these questions help to quantify performance measurements, but not by imposing unrealistic or arbitrary standards on the development officer. He or she is being asked to exercise judgment, to make best guesses, and to establish reasonable goals and targets. The supervisor will have to determine if the numbers represent modest, reasonable, or aggressive goals and will need to be candid about what levels of awards and incentives will be used if those goals are reached. For instance, if the stated goals are on the modest side, the supervisor may have to say that even if they were attained, they would not warrant a merit increase. By the same token, he or she may want to offer special incentives to those who are willing to stretch. What this all suggests is that metrics can and should be applied to the development process, but only after an ethical framework has been set and the development officer has been allowed to set goals based on the maturity and sophistication of the operation for which he or she is responsible.

INCENTIVES

A wide variety of incentives are available to managers and supervisors of development staff. Many of those options are spelled out in detail in a book published in July 2001 by CASE, entitled *Attracting and Retaining Good Staff.*[2] Again, rather than springing an incentive program on a development staff person, it is wise to ask development officers what kind of incentives they find most rewarding. Responses are likely to vary from development officer to development officer. Everyone likes money, and financial options can include, for example, such things as annual increases, spot awards, annual bonuses, extra vacation days, budget increases, or one-time money added to the office budget to experiment with innovative approaches. Rewards can include perquisites, such as car allowances, club memberships, and professional development opportunities.

In 1999, this author introduced a bonus program in the development office at his institution. This program offers annual incentives up to 15 percent of a development officer's base salary (in addition to normal merit increases). The bonus plan does not emphasize size of gifts received but gives credit for the number of contacts made, the efficacy of various initiatives, the number of solicitations undertaken, and teamwork. The program also is designed to accommodate the belief that the major gift process requires at least two years to result in a major gift. It is tailored to each development officer in terms of the length of his or her employment. For example, in an employee's first year, emphasis is placed upon identification and qualification of new prospects, the cultivation of existing prospects, and the stewardship of existing donors. In the second year, more purposeful cultivation and an upswing in the number of cultivations are expected.

At the time of this writing, the program is in the second year of its pilot phase. In retrospect, the biggest mistake was not spending enough time with individual development officers to get a better qualitative assessment of their plans and areas of responsibilities. In the absence of a strong qualitative base, some of the metrics attempted seemed too narrow and limiting. Indeed, most of the advice dispensed in this chapter has been learned from that experience.

CASE and other professional organizations frown on commissions as a form of compensation. A commission is any payment, salary, or bonus calculated as a percentage of the value of gifts raised. Commissions run counter to the spirit of philanthropy and the values that should underpin every development program. Innovative managers, however, can give generous bonuses for fund-raising success based on a number of variables besides dollars, including teamwork, effective and conscientious stewardship of donors, the number of prospect contacts completed, the number of well-crafted solicitations (whether or not they were successful), imaginative identification strategies, and the development of creative cultivation strategies and approaches. If these functions are performed well, it should be assumed that increasing gift support will result.

The key is to keep the bonus program from becoming so overweighted on the successful solicitation of major gifts that it becomes a de facto commission. Bonuses should be given to those who are mindful of, and productive in advancing the various phases of the development cycle while also adhering to institutional values.

BENCHMARKING FOR BEST PRACTICE

Development professionals operate in the higher interest of philanthropy when they recognize that benchmarking is a way to seek and find best practice. The field of philanthropy has attracted many fine practitioners. They are sprinkled throughout many educational and charitable organizations, large and small, and can sometimes be found in the most unlikely places. Development officers may want to pursue best practice in broad areas, for example, by determining which institutions are most proficient in securing gifts from corporations or foundations or friends. Such information can be gleaned from the CAE reports and is sometimes gathered by NACUBO.

It is vital to benchmark against the very best. For instance, when this author was at Georgia Tech, the director of advancement services was concerned that it was taking an average of eleven days to acknowledge a gift. When he benchmarked that against many other institutions, he learned the best were acknowledging gifts in two days. The comparison raised the obvious question, "How are they doing that in two days?" A review of the best practitioners' processes revealed that they did not worry about elaborate routing within the organization; they put the premium on getting the thank-you to the donor. Benchmarking is the practice of comparing data, but it is done best when underpinned by an attitude of continuous learning and finding best practice no matter where it exists.

CONCLUSION

Ronald Reagan was fond of espousing a doctrine of "trust but verify" when dealing with the former Soviet Union. But isn't that a false dichotomy? Isn't trust really built and maintained on constant verification? Shouldn't those who aspire to preserve the trust of the public and donors always be verifying results to make sure that they are highly efficient agents of philanthropy? Don't they raise their confidence and performance level and lend more credibility to the whole enterprise of philanthropy when they measure prudently and infuse their operations with a spirit of accountability? Those are not rhetorical questions. Time and experience have provided the right answer, and it is, "Of course."

NOTES

1. *Expenditures in Fund Raising, Alumni Relations and Other Constituent (Public) Relations* (Washington, DC: Council for Advancement and Support of Education, 1990).

2. James Langley, ed., *Attracting and Retaining Good Staff: Building an Efficient and Satisfied Advancement Team* (Washington, DC: Council for Advancement and Support of Education, 2001).

PART IX

Development and Other Fields

C hapter 1 identified educational fund raising as one component of the broader field of institutional advancement. The relationships among fund raising, communications (or public relations), and alumni relations should be mutually supportive, but they are often complex. On some campuses, there are tensions among professionals in the three areas, and they are not always encompassed within a single administrative unit. Indeed, some observers have noted a trend toward the organizational separation of communications from development and alumni relations, which may further complicate relationships among these functions.

Two chapters in this section describe these relationships from the fund-raising perspective. That is, fund raising is at the center of the discussion, and the chapters describe how the other advancement disciplines relate to *it*. This is not to imply that fund raising is more important than the others or that the other disciplines exist only to support fund-raising efforts. Indeed, both communications and alumni relations programs serve other critical institutional goals and needs. But, as the focus of this book is on fund raising, the relationships are approached from that perspective with the discussion focusing on how the other disciplines support the fund-raising effort. In Chapter 26, Roger Williams discusses the role of public relations in fund raising, and in Chapter 27, Charles Webb outlines the important role of alumni relations.

The development office also interacts with other administrative offices of the college or university, indeed, with most all of them in some manner. One relationship that is increasingly critical, and sometimes troubled, is between development and the business or financial office of the institution. Tensions between the chief development officer and the chief financial officer historically have been part of the lore on both sides, sometimes degenerating into unpleasantness and mild name calling ("car salesmen," "bean-counters")! This historic tension may reflect different professional cultures, even personality differences between individuals drawn to either type of work. But, it needs to end. In today's environment, it is essential that the development office and the business office work not only closely, but as partners. Fund-raising goals must be linked to the institution's financial plan. Management of the endowment and donor stewardship are linked. Many gifts involve a financial instrument or arrangement that require the expertise of financial officers to devise and administer.

Fortunately, at many institutions development and business officers are working together in close and productive partnerships. In the final chapter of this section, Karin George and Ruth Constantine, respectively the chief advancement officer and the chief financial officer of Smith College, describe why and how this important relationship can work.

CHAPTER 26

The Role of Public Relations in Fund Raising

Roger L. Williams

A chapter I wrote in *Educational Fund Raising: Principles and Practice*, published in 1993, I observed that the proliferation of major gift campaigns during the economic expansion of the 1980s had generated a valuable byproduct: Because of the new institutional working relationships these campaigns demanded, development and public relations officers had come to collaborate as never before, much to the benefit of their institutions.

Indeed, the collaboration between fund raisers and communicators helped to fuel the success of these campaigns. This was particularly true in the public sector of higher education, where serious fund raising was relatively new. Public institutions had to overcome initial reservations about both treading on the traditional preserve of their private counterparts and threatening their state appropriations. Such notions now seem antiquarian.

The extraordinary success of college and university fund raising in the red-hot economy of the 1990s has created an ironic problem for public relations practitioners in the first decade of the new century. At a time when billion dollar campaigns and multibillion dollar endowments have become commonplace, colleges and universities are encountering criticism on a variety of related fronts. Why are campaigns still needed when endowments have grown so large? Why is so little revenue from such robust endowments used to offset ever-increasing tuition? Why can't colleges and universities use endowment earnings to create a "living wage" for their lowest-paid employees? Why can't the endowment be used to help the struggling neighborhoods and cash-strapped cities that provide colleges and universities their home? The list goes on and on.[1]

As victims of their own success, public relations officers increasingly will be called upon to justify to a skeptical public why fundraising remains essential to the vitality of their institutions. At a time when colleges and universities increasingly are viewed as warehouses of wealth, public relations officers will need to focus more energy on communicating the social good such extraordinary philanthropy makes possible.

Development officers have come to rely more and more on their in-house colleagues for public relations support, and most campaign plans include a public relations component describing how the campaign will be communicated. During the 1990s, however, reporting lines between development and public relations began to change. Particularly at research universities, public relations positions were taken out of the traditional advancement matrix and placed in direct reporting lines to the institution's chief executive officer. Despite this separation, public relations officers must continue to regard fund raising and major gift campaigns as one of the most important initiatives their institutions undertake and respond accordingly. They must not only help structure institutional communications and marketing programs in ways that will create a climate for successful fund raising, but they need to provide their fund-raising colleagues with strategic and tactical support. And they must also become skilled in explaining the issues that arise from raising vast sums of private dollars and building stupendous endowments.

WHAT PUBLIC RELATIONS CAN DO FOR EDUCATIONAL FUND RAISING

Public relations can contribute to educational fund raising on three levels:

1. *Contextual*—creating visibility for the institution and enhancing its reputation with a variety of constituencies so that fund raising can succeed
2. *Strategic*—helping to resolve the "what" and "why" issues of educational fund raising (that is, "What are we going to do?" "Why are we going to do it?" and "How do we explain it for maximum effect?")
3. *Tactical*—determining how to fulfill fund-raising goals and objectives with specific events, communications vehicles, and other activities

An effective public relations plan will tie the strategic and tactical components together.

Before these contributions can become real, however, public relations professionals need to work with development leadership to secure the resources necessary for the communications operation. In the survey mentioned above, most of the institutions strengthened their public relations considerably as they launched their campaigns. They added new positions and reconfigured reporting relationships—not only to provide support for the campaign, but also to increase general visibility for the institution.

Institutional leaders must also address the larger question of formally integrating the three fundamental advancement functions: development, public relations, and alumni affairs. In a 1991 article, G. David Gearhart and Michael Bezilla wrote that a united structure under one senior administrative officer provides benefits not only in executing a campaign but in preparing for it as well.[2] Because of the need to coordinate all aspects of a campaign, a unified structure may be more important in a campaign situation than it might be in "normal" times. Despite these advantages, as mentioned above, the tendency over the last decade has been to place public relations in direct reporting lines to the chief executive officer rather than the chief advancement officer.

CONTEXTUAL ISSUES

Public relations' most valuable contribution to the educational fund-raising process is to help create the wide context for success. This is accomplished through activities that define, sharpen, and market the institution's identity; strengthen the institution's reputation and relationships generally and among key audiences; and heighten the institution's visibility in key geographic regions.

Public relations officials should keep development leadership informed about the public relations plan for the institution or the context of goals and objectives within which public relations operates. At the University of Arkansas, the strategic framework for public relations focuses on six objectives that support the vision statement and goals of the institution proper. The public relations objectives are as follows:

1. Position the University of Arkansas as a nationally competitive, student-centered research university, and support its goal of reaching $100 million in external research funding.
2. Enhance the position of the U of A as the state's flagship university and preeminent institution of higher learning. Build public understanding and support for its unique mission as Arkansas's state and

land-grant university and as an economic engine and cultural resource for the entire state.

3. Foster increased pride and morale among internal audiences, as well as external constituencies, for the University's history, role, and contributions to the state and for its growing stature nationally and internationally.

4. Support the University's efforts to raise substantially more private gift support, particularly through the Campaign for the Twenty-First Century.

5. Support the University's efforts to grow the size and quality of the student body, on both undergraduate and graduate levels. The goal is to move from 15,396 to 22,500 by 2010.

6. Support the University's efforts to enhance cultural diversity on the part of students, faculty, staff and administration.

Aside from strategic activities on behalf of larger institutional goals, public relations professionals can help by conducting opinion polls to assess the strengths and weaknesses of the institution's reputation. With that information, they can then devise communications strategies to market the institution as they wish the public to see it and to influence the public's behavior toward it.

This shaping of institutional identity and reputation is of extreme importance to fund raising. Study after study has shown that the single most important variable in fund-raising success is institutional prestige—in fact, one study found that prestige far overrode the institution's status as public or private.[3] A prime example is the significant fund-raising success public colleges and universities have enjoyed since the 1980s. As the academic prestige of public institutions has increased, so has their ability to raise funds from the private sector (particularly the corporate sector). For that reason, many colleges and universities strengthen their public relations staffs well before launching campaigns. For example, during the quiet phase of its Campaign for the Twenty-First Century, beginning in 1998, the University of Arkansas added four new positions to its University Relations staff, most of them focused on heightening the institution's reputation for research.

Another critical contextual issue is the institution's graphic identity. A perfect time to create a new institutional graphic identity, or to refine the existing one, is before the institution launches a major gifts campaign. In an age of increasing communications clutter, a college or university must have a compelling and consistently deployed graphic identity, which campaign or fund-raising communications must use consistently as well. If fund-raising officers deem it desirable to have a logo or campaign wordmark, it must be consistent with, or highly complementary to, the overarching institutional graphic identity system. If not, confusion will reign.[4]

PRELIMINARY STRATEGIC CONSIDERATIONS

For public relations to contribute directly to the fund-raising process, development must have easy access to public relations expertise. To increase this access, some institutions establish additional channels through which fund raisers can draw on the public relations function. One popular arrangement is to establish a special staff unit for development communications; another possibility is to form an advisory council.

Development Communications Units

A development communications unit offers a twofold advantage: It provides an exclusive focus on fund-raising communications, and it also precludes an "overload" situation that can overwhelm the public relations staff. An overload can impair communications support for development and dilute the effectiveness of institutional communications overall.

The chief obstruction to establishing a dedicated unit is cost. Some institutions are reluctant to build up staff for a limited activity because it is hard to reduce that staff after the campaign. Other institutions consider development communications to be an investment in success.

Reporting arrangements vary widely. At some institutions, members of the development communications unit report to the development office; at others, to public relations. In all cases this author found, however, the media relations activities spawned by development communications are funneled through the existing news bureau or public information department.

Campaign Communications Councils

Colleges and universities often hire external fund-raising counsel to help plan and execute their campaigns. Rarely, however, do they retain a professional public relations firm in a similar capacity to provide continual campaign public relations and communications, although public relations firms are often hired on a task-specific basis—for example, to mount a gala or to produce the case statement.

Many colleges and universities have turned instead to another resource for outside advice on the public relations aspect of educational fund raising: A council composed of alumni who have distinguished themselves as journalists, editors and writers, advertising and marketing executives, and public relations professionals. Such a council may help open doors for media visits in key markets, advise on the worthiness of campaign story ideas, and offer advice on the public relations plan, the campaign slide show, campaign publications, and website design.

In lieu of forming a formal campaign communications council, public relations officers can ask communications alumni to convene for a single day to review the campaign communications plan and related materials, and offer advice for improvement.

STRATEGIC ISSUES

Given reasonable communications between the development and public relations functions, public relations can contribute to the fund-raising process in additional strategic areas.

The Case Statement

The key strategic task that should significantly involve public relations is the creation of a case statement and the resulting lead brochure—whether for a large major gifts campaign, for a smaller focused campaign, or for the institution's educational fund-raising programs in general.

The case statement has been described as "the single most important document of a capital campaign"[5] and "the communications backbone of any capital campaign."[6] Indeed, it is all that and more. The case statement is the basic argument for philanthropic support of an institution. It also functions as the rhetorical primer and the "copy platform" for all campaign communications. Campaign speeches, publications, videos, and news stories should borrow heavily from the case statement. The case statement positions both the institution and the campaign by describing institutional goals and aspirations (ends) as well as strengths, specific institutional needs (barriers that must be surmounted in order to achieve the ends), and the specifics and "spirit" of the campaign (the means for achieving the ends).

One of the major considerations in writing the case is whether to employ outside experts or to do it in-house. The advantage of outsiders is the fresh perspective they provide as well as the considerable skill they can bring to the task. But going out-of-house does not mean less work for the in-house staff. Many hours and much energy will go into acquainting the outsider with your institution.

The chief arguments for staying in-house are that it costs less and that in-house staff are already familiar with the institution. If you do stay in-house, the key is to encourage your public relations writers to "step outside" the institution and view it from a fresh, unbiased perspective. It helps if they can look at the institution critically, adopting a "show me" skepticism, to ensure that the case is not polluted with vague generalizations and unsubstantiated claims.

As communications become more carefully targeted to smaller audiences, the idea of a single overarching case statement may become obsolete, to be replaced by a series of case statements designed to appeal to the differing needs, values, attitudes, and lifestyles of different target audiences. In addition, video case statements are growing in popularity, not so much as a replacement of the printed case statement but as a supplement to it.

The Public Relations Plan to Support Fund Raising

The heart and soul of communications support for educational fund raising—particularly a major gifts campaign—lie in the public relations plan, which combines strategy and tactics. Do not mistake the plan for holy writ, however; it will be subjected to revisions, additions, deletions, and improvisation over time. All good plans encourage continual correction.

The art and science of educational fund raising is a variant of the marketing process, and the public relations plan should also reflect a strong marketing orientation. Fund raising requires the identification of "suspects" and then "prospects." This calls for extensive market research. After identification and ranking of the prospects (the target market), the cultivation (sales) process begins, culminating in a successful solicitation. A public relations plan to support educational fund raising must harmonize with this process.

The first step is to set goals for the communications plan, taking into account the contextual issues addressed previously. The goals can be broad, such as "to increase awareness, understanding, and support for the institution and the campaign," but they are usually better when more pointed. For example, the overarching goals of a campaign communications plan might include:

- Creating messages and communications materials that help the institution meet its campaign goal of $10 million in five years
- Helping position the institution and forge a new identity through campaign communications
- Clarifying the institution's relationship, through campaign communications, with state government, a religious denomination, the surrounding community, or any other vital constituency
- Delivering key messages to key audiences. For example, it may be important to convey a message about "preserving the special sense of place" about the campus to alumni prospects.
- Providing a high level of visibility among the extended campus family for the campaign's volunteer leadership
- Demonstrating to faculty and staff a determination to move the institution to greater heights of achievement
- Introducing a new, or strengthening the institution's current, graphic identity system

The goals of the communications plan should be prioritized in accordance with institutional goals, strategic directions, and needs, and should be worked out with the institutional and advancement leadership.

Goals are only one element of the fund-raising or campaign communications plan. Other components will include the following.[7]

Target audiences. Fund raising is essentially a marketing process, particularly in audience segmentation. Prospects rated at the $100,000 mark and above may require, and respond to, different communications strategies than those rated under $10,000.

Timeline and geography. The campaign is a continuum of varied phases and activities: The planning and quiet stages, the public launch, the plateau, the climax, and the post-campaign environment. Communications strategies must vary in accordance with this lifespan. The planning and quiet stages might be the best time to attend to image-building and communications research; the public launch may require some high-end publications and news media activity. Campaign geographics should be treated similarly. Where are the alumni and prospects clustered? Within a 100-mile radius of campus? In a three-state region? In additional pockets around the nation? How do you reach them and when? If the campaign has a regional approach, and it's time for a high-profile volunteer push in, say, Chicago, it may be time to prepare letters, brochures, and even try for some media visibility.

Campaign themes. These generally reflect the institutional positioning statement, institutional strengths and indices of excellence, and campaign goals. They should be incorporated in all communications materials. As with any marketing or advertising campaign, frequency and repetition of message are the bywords here.

Tactics and methods. These are the "guts" of the communications plan (to be discussed shortly). These are the materials you'll produce and the activities you'll undertake to implement the strategy.

Evaluation. How do you measure the results of your fund-raising or campaign communications plan? Do you commission a follow-up attitude and opinion survey when the campaign concludes? Do you initiate readership surveys of campaign materials? Be wary of merely assuming a successful campaign communications effort just because the dollar goal has been met.

TACTICAL ISSUES

Given specific goals and a well-defined plan for supporting fund raising, public relations staff can then proceed to plan and carry out specific activities to accomplish those goals. Some typical examples follow.

News Media Visibility

Fund raising activity—especially during a campaign—produces many unique and newsworthy events. Pursued aggressively and handled wisely, these events can result not just in heightened visibility, but also in golden opportunities to help reposition the institution.

Gift stories carry many creative possibilities. News about gifts for minority scholarships, for educational partnerships, for novel ways of improving undergraduate education, and for special research programs (especially in the medical and health fields) are among those that carry strong potential for high media visibility. Unusual circumstances or an intriguing benefactor can also make for a compelling story.

Consider what you can persuade major gift donors to say about the institution in the news release or at the news conference. As a third party endorsement, a benefactor's statement has enormous credibility. The dramatic increase in the threshold for mega-gifts in recent years has made it somewhat more difficult to attract attention among national media for such stories. The anonymous gift of $360 million to Rensselaer and the $400 million gift to Stanford in the spring of 2001 have raised the bar considerably. By applying strategic thinking and creativity, however, public relations officers will still be able to draw media attention to major gifts.

And, as always, campaign progress reports provide other news possibilities, as they provide numbers, statistics, and quantifiable evidence of fund-raising achievement. The point to remember here is not to talk about dollars raised as an end in itself, but as a means to an end—to strengthen the institution and its capacity to serve society.

Periodicals and Publications

The alumni magazine should accord a measure of visibility to educational fund raising. Many alumni magazine editors are fiercely independent, and some are quite resistant to development stories. While the editorial judgment of alumni magazine editors deserves respect, most will also agree that their publications should work within a framework of institutional goals and objectives, and that there are clever ways to handle important development stories without making them appear as such.[8]

For some target audiences, the best vehicle is a separate fund-raising periodical. As Ann Waldron, editor of Princeton University's campaign bulletin, wrote, "A newsletter is as necessary to a fund-raising campaign as matches are to fire building."[9] A campaign newsletter keeps key people interested in the campaign. It can also relate fund raising to academic achievement in ways that might not be convenient or appropriate in regular communication channels. And it can establish links between donors and the programs they support, reinforcing overall campaign objectives.

Special Events

Although special events offices exist on many campuses, campaign events should also engage the expertise of the public relations staff. Indeed, such occasions should be viewed not just as "cultivation events," but as "communications events," because they communicate in an extraordinarily powerful way. Special events "put an institution on display," said April L. Harris, director of alumni relations at the University of Alabama in Huntsville. "They offer the opportunity for people to look at and, indeed, to scrutinize the institution and its programs. Powerful communicators, they send messages that make a far more lasting impression than the most expensive brochure or the slickest alumni magazine money can buy."[10]

The keys to staging a successful event, such as a campaign kickoff, are "planning and panache," said Heather Ricker Gilbert, a special events consultant. She advises that fund raisers:

- Know their purpose: Why are they having this event?
- Understand their audience and situation: Is a black tie gala appropriate for the culture of the institution?
- Promote a theme that plays up what is special about the institution and its aspirations
- Create clear and compelling invitations, and mail them at least eight weeks before the event
- Consider the aesthetics—the food, flowers, decor
- Analyze the program: What's the best way to showcase key volunteers? Is a celebrity needed or will a famous alumnus make a better emcee?
- Rehearse and prepare: Assume nothing, practice everything possible on site—musicians, sound, lighting, etc.[11]

Special events can inject excitement, spark enthusiasm, and generate momentum in a way that nothing else can approximate. They can introduce, recognize, thank, and motivate volunteers and major donors, communicate key messages about your institution, and dispel myths and misinformation. They exhilarate participants far more than most football games can, and they can be designed as creatively as the imagination will allow.

Video

The use of video in fund raising is now commonplace and, as a communications specialty, should fall within the purview of the public relations staff.

"The future of institutional advancement lies with increasingly sophisticated use of electronic systems (computer technology and database management) to integrate direct mail, telemarketing, and personal solicitations," wrote Robert Roehr. "Video will come to play a larger role in that mix, to some degree replacing but more often supplementing both print and people."[12]

But in the midst of what would seem to be a budding video mania, experts caution that such productions need to be carefully thought out, targeted to certain markets, and produced with the right set of expectations. In addition, keep in mind that video works much better in the realm of emotion than that of cognition. Video can enthuse, arouse, stir passions, and elicit warm feelings, but it is not the best tool for conveying facts and information; print works better for that purpose.

Basic marketing principles need to prevail when crafting a video. It should be targeted to the specific interests and attention spans of the intended viewers. For example, videos that offer nostalgia work better with older audiences. Younger audiences respond better to videos that show the school in a straightforward way, as it is now.[13]

The World Wide Web

The Internet and the World Wide Web have opened a new universe of development communications opportunities—and imperatives. Many print pieces can be reworked and posted on the institution's website. Information about the advancement operation and fund-raising program can be posted on a special website for viewing by alumni, faculty, staff, and students. E-mail campaign updates can be created and sent as needed to listservs of prospects, volunteers, and supporters. Passive annual fund solicitation sites can be set up. It is daunting and exciting to think of the as-yet-unimagined ways in which the web will be used for fund-raising communications in the years ahead, particularly as the generations turn.

A PLACE FOR PUBLIC RELATIONS

People outside public relations often view the profession as little more than publicity work and news release and article writing. Fortunately, the development leg of the institutional advancement triad has come to recognize the strategic value of public relations in the context of educational fund raising.

In today's climate of intensifying competition for resources, educational fund raisers cannot afford to wait for the next campaign to harness the contributions that public relations and marketing communications have to offer. The need for communications support is continuous. In the absence of a major gifts campaign, public relations expertise can help to sharpen baseline programs in annual giving, planned giving, corporate and foundation relations, and the other components of educational fund raising. Most important, public relations support can be vital to maintaining the levels of private gift support created by the previous campaign—and to building support inside and outside the institution in preparation for the next comprehensive campaign.

NOTES

1. Roger L. Williams, "Essay: PR and the Capital Campaign," in *Public Relations and the Presidency*, ed. John E. Ross and Carol P. Halstead (Washington, DC: CASE Books, 2001), 221–225.

2. G. David Gearhart and Michael Bezilla, "Fund-raising Success Takes Teamwork," *Fund Raising Management*, March 1991, 42–46.

3. Roger L. Williams and Robert M. Hendrickson, "In Fund Raising, Prestige Means More Than Public or Private," *AGB Reports* (November/December 1986): 20–23.

4. Carol Cheney, "Designing the Campaign," *Currents* (November/December 1995): 34–38.

5. Richard Chamberlain, "The Campaign Case Statement," in *The Successful Capital Campaign: From Planning to Victory Celebration*, ed. H. Gerald Quigg (Washington, DC: Council for Advancement and Support of Education, 1986), 87.

6. Roland King, "Stating Your Case: The Art, the Science, and the Future of the Quintessential Campaign Document," *Currents* (June 1989): 46.

7. Roger L. Williams, "Development Communications," in *CASE Handbook of Institutional Advancement* (Washington, DC: Council for Advancement and Support of Education, 2000), 203–208.

8. Robert J. Bliwise, "Detente with Development: Editors Can Give Fund Raisers the Support They Seek by Listening, Defending, and Innovating," *Currents* (November/December 1988): 48–52.

9. Ann Waldron, "News You Can Use: Publishing a Campaign Newsletter," *Currents* (May 1985): 34.

10. April L. Harris, "Special Events: Creative and Strategic Planning," in *Handbook of Institutional Advancement*, 3rd edition (Washington, DC: Council for Advancement and Support of Education, 2000), 209–213.

11. Heather Ricker Gilbert, "The Winning Combination: When You Put Together Planning and Panache, It Adds Up to a Successful Campaign Special Event," *Currents* (June 1989): 42–44.

12. Robert J. Roehr, ed., *Electronic Advancement Fund Raising* (Washington, DC: Council for Advancement and Support of Education, 1990), i.

13. Alan Dessoff, "Moving Pictures," *Currents* (November/December 1994): 30–33.

CHAPTER 27

The Role of Alumni Relations in Fund Raising

Charles H. Webb

The feeding frenzy for the dollar on many college and university campuses has created an unhealthy competition between development and alumni relations that, based on the current rules of the educational game, the alumni office cannot and is not winning. Why? In an educational climate in which there are short-term presidents, short-term officers, and short-term deans, these individuals often must seek short-term answers. The result: Presidential attention, power, money, staff, and prestige are vested to a significantly greater degree with the development office than with alumni relations. Too often an adversarial relationship develops between the alumni office and the development office. Alumni relations soon discovers that it is sharing the bed with a 900-pound gorilla and cannot control the brute's snoring or seemingly erratic movements.

The alumni office exists for two primary reasons—to provide diverse and quality programming for alumni, and to provide opportunities for alumni to engage in a lifetime of service to their alma mater. Alumni relations programs are inclusive, including all alumni who wish to participate in some manner, whether related to fund raising or of benefit to the institution in other ways. Every graduate can help in some way. Alumni may become donors, student recruiters, providers of jobs for fellow graduates, promoters of legislative programs, advisors, governing board directors, guest lecturers and adjunct professors, and institutional advocates. Through their involvement in such roles, alumni are encouraged to maintain a lifelong relationship with their alma mater.

The alumni office is every bit as important as the development office because a college or university has no greater single resource than its alumni. Higher education institutions cannot buy the support the alumni can provide. When that support is forthcoming, it represents a tremendous source of not only economic power and intellectual advocacy, but also service capacity. In this sense, one major function of the alumni office is to harness the institution's alumni resources in support of the basic mission of the institution.

The institution and the development office should value the alumni office because, among other reasons, it manages programs with long-term payoffs. As William Stone, former president of the Stanford Alumni Association, writes, "[Alumni relations professionals] . . . have a responsibility to shape our institutions' futures because they depend greatly on the business we do best: cementing a lifelong relationship between graduates and alma mater"[1] that fund raisers may not have time to undertake. Although there are sometimes tensions between them, it is imperative for alumni relations and development to have and act upon a shared vision that supports the institutional mission. Alumni expect such cooperation. They are interested in the welfare of the institution, not in turf wars between the alumni relations and development staffs.

ALUMNI INVOLVEMENT AND GIVING

If the alumni office went out of business, it would have to be reinvented by the development office. This is a truth most educational fund-raising professionals know—that involvement of alumni in their alma mater generates interest, and that interest often translates into the giving of time, advocacy, and money. Alumni who are interested, concerned, and involved not only are a good source for substantial dollars, but they also can be instrumental in securing dollars from corporations, foundations, friends of the institution, and other sources.

Studies confirm that the degree to which alumni are involved with college or university activities directly correlates with the level of their financial support to the institution. A study published by the Massachusetts Institute of Technology measured this relationship. The findings were stunning: Regardless of graduating class, department, or current geographic location, alumni who were "involved in MIT alumni activities" gave "much more frequently than their uninvolved peers." Overall, involved alumni gave more frequently than uninvolved alumni by a ratio of more than 3 to 1. That held true at each of the three giving levels examined: four-year giving totals in excess of $500, $1,250, and $5,000.

Interestingly, the study found that merely attending class reunions or centennial activities was as significant a factor as actual volunteer activity—if not more so.

Although the study did not determine whether alumni involvement caused superior fund support or vice versa, it concluded that the issue was moot: "To the extent that alumni activities—reunions, club events, departmental events—serve as gathering points for our very best supporters, they serve as the best possible means of cultivating those who are not contributing to the alumni fund or who are contributing at a nominal level. By supporting a broad spectrum of high-quality alumni activities, we are providing an atmosphere . . . where the norm is to support the alumni fund in a significant way. There could hardly be a more effective way to enhance the overall quality of alumni fund support." At the same time, the study added, universities do well to provide their best supporters with high-quality alumni activities to reinforce their commitment. In other words, it doesn't really matter what came first, the chicken or the egg. What matters is to "recognize chickens . . . in our own backyard!"[2]

An earlier study worth noting was conducted in 1985 by the University of North Carolina at Chapel Hill. That year, S. Philip Harris, president of the University of North Carolina's General Alumni Association and also acting director of development, reported to the board of trustees:

> The association's expanding membership efforts in recent years, which have seen membership move from 28,000 to 37,000 in just two years, have been essential in building the base for strong development efforts. Over 90 percent of all donors are General Alumni Association members. Those who are members of the General Alumni Association make gifts to the university that are three to four times greater than gifts from those who are not members. Thus, by continuing to increase our membership, the association provides the needed base from which to build an ever-expanding donor pool. . . .

In short, this "friend raising" by the General Alumni Association . . . is essential to a successful development effort. It can be argued that the basic identification and cultivation of donors is in large measure done by the General Alumni Association through its records, publications, chapter meetings, reunions, programs, seminars, tours and other activities. Furthermore, the officers and directors of the association who participate in our quarterly board meetings . . . have become some of the strongest leaders in the university's overall development efforts.[3]

Dr. Leland D. Patouillet, associate vice chancellor and executive director of the Pitt Alumni Association at the University of Pittsburgh, conducted a study in 1990 of 75 Council of Alumni Association Executives (CAAE) institutions, representing many of the nation's largest and most prestigious universities, to address the question of whether members of the alumni association were more or less apt to donate to the annual fund compared to nonmembers. The results of this study indicated that "on average 24 percent of CAAE alumni were members of the respective alumni associations. In addition, 47 percent of alumni association members donated to the annual fund compared to 16 percent of nonmembers. The study also revealed that alumni association members donated 25 percent more money than nonmembers."[4]

Laney Funderburk, associate vice president, alumni affairs and development, and director, alumni affairs for Duke University, reported that the class of 2001, the Half Century Club, and Duke's ten classes who took part in DAA-organized reunions in spring 2001 gave checks representing more that $70 million in total giving by members of these classes since their prior reunion just five years earlier. When planning alumni activities, Mr. Funderburk considers Duke's fund-raising plans. For example, during Duke's 1998–2003 $2 billion campaign, the alumni association assisted by running significant high-profile alumni educational events in major cities six to twelve months prior to regional campaign dinners. Many Duke alumni assume leading roles in their alma mater's capital campaigns; most of these leaders got their start working on clubs, reunions, and serving on alumni interviewing committees.

ALUMNI PROGRAMS AND DEVELOPMENT

These studies, and others conducted across the country, provide incontrovertible evidence that alumni involvement in meaningful alumni activities correlates directly with the size and frequency of gifts. Clearly, an institution of higher education cannot reach its fullest potential without actively engaging its alumni.

Offering a wide range of opportunities for alumni service not only involves alumni but also creates a climate more conducive for financial gifts from these individuals. The following types of alumni programming have proven effective in achieving both goals—that is, providing alumni with opportunities to serve their alma mater, and creating a positive climate that enhances their participation in fund raising.[5]

- Alumni involvement in student recruitment
- Student career assistance, including on-campus lectures by alumni or off-campus visits to alumni on the job
- Student-alumni programming to acquaint current students (future alumni) with the alumni and development programs
- Homecoming, Alumni Day, and other special events that bring alumni back to campus
- Class reunions. Many reunion programs are tied to a class gift program and hence directly support development efforts
- Awards recognizing alumni achievements and service
- Minority alumni programs
- Young alumni programs. Young graduates pose a special challenge to both fund-raising and alumni associations; alumni programs geared specifically to young alumni needs and interests can stimulate their involvement and, in turn, their giving participation.
- Senior alumni programs. With more time and more discretionary income, alumni over age 55 become an increasingly important market for alumni and development programming.
- Constituent alumni associations—special-interest groups affiliated with an academic program on campus
- Regional alumni clubs, which offer programs for alumni in a geographic area. Clubs also provide an existing network from which to launch a capital campaign regionally.
- Alumni magazines, tabloids, newsletters, or other publications. These serve as excellent vehicles to educate alumni on major gifts and givers, and honor rolls or donor club listings.
- Alumni family camps
- Alumni lifelong education, including classes as well as travel programs
- Alumni community service programs, such as literacy programs, assistance with food banks, senior citizen programs, or other projects. Many of these programs have high visibility and open new markets for development
- Alumni legislative programs—advocacy programs designed to influence legislation that would enhance philanthropic giving to institutions
- Outreach programs to reestablish relationships with alumni who have not maintained connections with the institution. This function also expands the prospect pool for development.

INVOLVING ALUMNI IN DEVELOPMENT

The alumni activities on the preceding list benefit development indirectly by helping create an environment that encourages alumni to give. However, alumni can help with fund raising directly as well.

Here are some ways alumni are directly involved with development efforts:

- Alumni are donors.
- Alumni help to secure gifts from other alumni and nonalumni friends.
- Alumni serve on development boards and on the institution's governing board.
- Alumni are instrumental in securing major corporate gifts.
- Alumni are instrumental in securing major foundation gifts.
- Alumni are the key component of a capital campaign.
- Alumni assist with capital campaign feasibility studies.
- Alumni assist in research.
- Alumni host meetings with potential donors.
- Alumni contribute their professional services.
- Alumni organize special events for fund raising.
- Alumni serve as professional consultants for clients interested in making planned gifts.
- Alumni are essential to the success of the major donor clubs.
- Alumni assist in local business community solicitations.

LINKING THE ALUMNI AND DEVELOPMENT OFFICES

It is common to refer to alumni relations staff as "friend raisers" and development staff as "fund raisers." But, such a distinction is too simple. Common to both roles is the need to build and sustain relationships between individuals and the institution.

When one takes a closer look at the development and alumni offices, it is clear that both perform similar steps in dealing with constituents, whether alumni or nonalumni friends. Both alumni and development offices carry out identification, research, cultivation, involvement, and stewardship. Only one step of the fund-raising process—solicitation—is arguably unique to development, and that, too, is sometimes shared. Development officers would do well to utilize alumni relations professionals in the solicitation of major gifts, in rating sessions, and in organizing special donor meetings.

An effective alumni relations program is the stewardship responsibility of the institution, whether or not a dime is ever raised. Alumni relations must not be measured by development standards—they are different. Likewise, the development program fulfills a basic and critical institutional need. But the development program can never reach its potential without an effective alumni program. Above all, the alumni and development staffs must have, *and act on*, a shared vision, fulfilling the institution's mission.

NOTES

1. William E. Stone, "Rethinking Our Craft," *Currents* 27, no. 6 (July/August, 2001), 26.

2. Jeffrey R. Solof, *Measuring the Impact of Alumni Activities on the Quality of Alumni Fund Support* (Cambridge, MA: Working Group of Alumni Activities Measurements, Massachusetts Institute of Technology, 1989).

3. S. Philip Harris, remarks to the trustees of the University of North Carolina at Chapel Hill, June 28, 1985.

4. Leland D. Patouillet, "Alumni Association Members: Attitudes Toward University Life and Giving at a Public AAU Institution," *The Case International Journal of Educational Advancement* (Washington, DC: Council for Advancement and Support of Education/Henry Stewart Publications) 2, no. 1 (2001): 53–66.

5. Stephen L. Barrett, "Basic Alumni Programming," in *A Handbook of Institutional Advancement*, 2nd ed., edited. A. Westley Rowland (San Francisco: Jossey-Bass, 1986), 416–425.

CHAPTER 28

The Development Office and the Business Office

Ruth Constantine and Karin Lee George

I t's one person's job to raise as much money as possible to fund the vision and mission of an institution. It's another person's job to manage and conserve the resources wisely in order to support the vision and mission of the organization. Similar sounding responsibilities to be sure, but when one is the development professional and the other is is the business officer, these areas can seem distinct, even conflicting. While it makes sense to understand why conflicts occur between the development office and the business office, the approach here focuses on bringing the two offices together for efficiency, enhanced bottom lines, greater communication, and a much more enjoyable work environment.

Sometimes it may seem that the development and business office views are diametrically opposed; for example when people say things like, "This gift should count in our totals so that the class gets recognition," or, "That gift has too many conditions to be considered unrestricted," or, "Let's add 10 percent to the goal to bring the budget in line," and so on. But, the relationship forged between these two offices can set the tone for staff and constituency members alike. Allies and advocates can be found in both offices; identifying and developing them is crucial.

WHY ARE THEY SO DIFFERENT? OR ARE THEY REALLY SO DIFFERENT?

A development officer most likely spends a great deal of time immersed in numbers—annual goals, weekly goals, monthly visit quotas, and the endless stream of contacts with donors about how and when their gift will count. It's no different for the business officer. She spends as much time or more studying goals and projections and the specific revenue streams. She, too, is immersed in how these numbers will affect the bottom line, accomplish goals, or lead to stasis, based on a careful analysis of trends. Development officers have allowed the notion of soft numbers (development) versus hard numbers (business office) to persist at their peril. They are really not so different. The two need to reconcile themselves to the fact that there may be differences in interpretation of numbers and goals, while still reaching a mutual understanding. The development profession suffers at times from its own self-critical sense of lacking knowledge or the formal professional certifications such as those found in a business office.

The business office has external guidelines that must govern its work—IRS regulations, American Institute of Certified Public Accountants (AICPA) audit guidelines, Financial (or Government) Accounting Standards Board (FASB and GASB), and so on. The very mention of these acronyms leads to scowls and consternation in the development office. But development has its own set of governing guidelines and policies that, when used appropriately, can bring balance to the relationship.

The Council for the Advancement and Support of Education provides guidelines for reporting philanthropy in an ongoing effort as well as in a campaign, and the Voluntary Support of Education report, submitted to the Council for Aid to Education, has become the standard by which we measure our success. Individual institutional policies also are becoming more formal in nature. If one were to take an inventory of the similarities in development and business operations right now, one would find that direct connections are much easier to forge as a result.

While there is no standard advanced degree in development comparable to an MBA, nor certification as in accounting's CPA, development officers do have a thorough understanding of the goals and numbers that they follow. This understanding is informed by the depth of knowledge of donors' interests and decisions and dealings with members of a shared community. If a development officer considers the business officer to be the chief stewardship professional, she will soon see the development officer as a savvy manager of complex budget concepts and a partner in working to achieve the institution's goals.

THE BASICS OF THE RELATIONSHIP

Any good relationship is based on communication, trust, and understanding. In the case of the business office and the development office, this could not be more true than it is today. After a sustained period of economic health, it may now be as challenging to meet institutional goals as it was in the early 1980s. Tuition increases are carefully scrutinized by governing boards, elected officials, the press, and the public. Meeting enrollment goals is a challenge for most institutions. Financial aid awards are more competitive than ever. Fluctuations in investment markets have become the norm. Intervals between capital or comprehensive campaigns are unpredictable. The management of campuses can seem more and more corporate, whether the institution is large or small, public or private. None of these trends spell doom, but if the basics are overlooked, the relationship between development and business offices quickly can become filled with doubt and mistrust—even become contentious.

Starting with Communication

While a wonderful benefit of working in advancement is forging relationships with various departments and their leaders, it is risky for a development officer to assume he or she will find friends. That may occur, but instead of looking for a buddy, it is important to look at all the ways the two offices communicate. In the case of the development office and the business office:

- Is there a direct communication pathway from the vice president for finance to the vice president for development?
- Are there communication points at all other levels in the organization?
  —gift records to gift accountant
  —controller to gift officer/unit director
  —securities officer to budget officer
- Is there a diverse mixture of communication practice?
  —e-mail
  —telephone
  —regularly scheduled and ad hoc meetings
  —memoranda

- Is communication routine or is it only employed in times of perceived or real conflict?

  —It's June 30 and the numbers wildly disagree.

  —Development is about to announce a campaign total, and the business office says that certain gifts can't count.

- Are the chief advancement officer and chief financial officer called in at the last moment, or are they informed along the way?

- Are the two viewed as arbiters of all disputes, or as another link in the chain of communication?

The systems used for communication will be as critical as the content of the communications in achieving balance in this important relationship.

Shared Goals and Timetables

It's obviously too simplistic to view one office as the one that brings in money and the other as the one that spends it. Development and business goals are more similar than not, since both work to secure the organization's financial underpinnings and to provide the flexibility and nimbleness to meet changing needs and achieve new initiatives. Both want the organization to thrive and to withstand challenges, otherwise they would not be there. It's a shared responsibility, then, to approach fiscal goals and deadlines with an appreciation for the other's priorities. It's up to the development officer to set a tone of respect with staff and colleagues as well. It is essential for development officers to be able to answer the following questions:

- Who are development's colleagues in the business office? What do they do?

- What are the reporting lines?

- What pressures do business officers face?

- Which questions are asked of them most frequently?

A development officer's goal is not to know business officers' jobs well enough to do them, but to understand the framework of their work.

Though the development officer is focused primarily on his or her own goals and operation, it doesn't mean that a colleague will share that level of attention. Common goals are shared, but each area's responsibilities are different and should be understood and respected by the other team. The director of the annual fund may need to know the interest accumulation on a particular account for a volunteer report, but that doesn't mean that the controller will understand the information need. The budget director may need gift revenue projections at the end of each quarter to inform his supervisors or for board review, but the chief advancement officer won't know that automatically. Individuals from both groups should sit down together to review schedules and establish the regular and critical communication needs.

The two offices need to synchronize their calendars. In a program that runs the fiscal year from July 1 to June 30, certain peak activity periods will run parallel to one another. The development office needs to know when the audit takes place, and when financial statements are developed and issued. The business office should be familiar with reunion cycles, campaign planning timetables, and key events. Schedules should be compared to see when both offices are experiencing similar crunch periods and divergent ones. Not all crunch periods are predictable in nature, but the predictable ones should be well known to both operations. Communications should improve and will certainly be more sensitive if both offices develop this awareness.

Knowledge

While it is not necessary for every development officer to understand all accounting principles nor for each business officer to know gift recognition rules inside and out, a common level of understanding must be established. In many organizations, the relationship between the planned giving staff and the business office staff can be held up as an example of effective cooperation. A great deal of that success stems from the way in which policies and plans (including budgets) are developed and followed. This is a good model for the rest of the organization, such as helping directors in academic and administrative areas understand each other's needs.

It is important for each development officer to know the following:

- What common practices and controls interest the controller and/or audit committee?
- What will the auditor want to review?
- What information do financial planners need, and when, for effective budgeting?

It is important for each business officer to know the following:

- What approach and timing works best for planning fund-raising goals?
- What makes for good donor relations?

- What are the key policies and procedures in areas such as planning and gift records?
- What gift recognition/counting policies are most and least appealing to donors?
- How are crediting policies set, and by whom?
- How are database reports created? Can a common report minimize confusion?

Both offices need to agree ahead of time on how gift announcements will be made and how this information will be expressed in donor reports, financial statements, annual reports, and reports to trustees. Touch points need to be established throughout the year to discuss budget assumptions and projections in order to avoid surprises and to develop shared strategies.

Systems and Procedures

There are some specific systemic aspects of the authors' programs that have allowed their offices to forge a strong relationship. These systems have been in place for a long while and have withstood transitions in leadership and personnel at all levels. A few examples are offered here that should be adaptable for other organizations, regardless of size or focus.

Regular Meetings. At Smith College, a group of business office professionals and development office professionals meets on a monthly basis to discuss issues related to gift recording, audit trails, counting and credit, donor intent, and much more. The current members include the director of advancement services, chief accountant, gift accountants, advancement systems personnel, and personnel in charge of gift reporting and programming. It's important for this group to meet without the oversight of the vice president for finance or the vice president for advancement. That keeps the group self-motivated, and the absence makes it easier for them to hash out issues and thoroughly discuss procedures that should be applied in particular cases.

The relationship forged between members of the two offices is stronger because trust has been developed by group members and not just as dictated from the top. A typical meeting agenda might include such matters as reconciling totals for a specific fund, calendars for year-end gift processing, and upcoming changes in gift tax legislation.

There are times when members agree to disagree, but the issues are put on the table in a regular way, and the group has the authority and ability to work through them. Knowing that this meeting is on their calendars each month, when tough issues arise, the members of the group are able to hold them for review in this cooperative, face-to-face setting.

Common Policies and Procedures. A recent lengthy project to document Smith College policies regarding gift documentation and policies related to restricted and unrestricted gifts at various levels brought out differences in stark relief. Transition in personnel and an active campaign provided motivation to establish clear written policies regarding the treatment of these gifts. We attempted to chart the pathway of each gift from the point of entry through stewardship, and established report forms and checkpoints for a variety of scenarios. The resulting gift policy manual helps each office understand the processes, information needs, and work flow necessary to make both operations successful. The system that we created ensures that gifts of $25,000 or more receive focused attention from both the business and development offices. Our shared, documented policies have made individual gift officers more accountable, have brought gift recorders in closer touch with their business office counterparts, and have ensured that the stewardship of all gifts at this level or higher is documented and monitored.

The year-long process of developing this manual also helped ensure that business office colleagues are as concerned about the stewardship and donor relations aspect of the gift as is the development office. In many cases, the business office knew more about particular donor patterns because staff turnover in that area has not been as high as in advancement. The group that drafted the procedures manual recently came together to review how this has affected work in the past year.

The group agreed that while some procedures have at times been cumbersome and problematic, it has been highly beneficial to have clearly delineated gift paths and report forms that support greater accountability and follow-up. The review revealed the weaknesses in the new systems that can be amended so the procedures work to everyone's advantage. In the discussion, particular aspects of the policy emerged as having been quite helpful to individuals in each office. The business office likes an identified contact for the donor and the gift agreement. The development office has more easily been able to determine, in advance of finalizing a gift, just how the gift will be used and will affect the institution. An added benefit is the additional knowledge that each office now has about the entire gift process, enhancing mutual respect for the intricacies of the other office's work.

Shared Reports. Another area of collaboration can be found in the way numbers are expressed in reports (internal or external). This area might appear to be one of high drama and conflict, but it is really a good place to focus. The reports that are used to generate the financial statements need to be examined and the gifts isolated by type. Those lines should resemble the reports in the development office in some way. Is it possible to use one report? The data logic that is driving the controller's report on outside trusts will have some excellent parameters for reports the development office may need to share with planned giving volunteers. It shouldn't automatically be assumed that a whole new set of criteria has to be created. If the reports don't match, why not? The times when figures must match (such as audit) and when it doesn't matter as much (gift announcements at reunion celebrations) need to be established. Taking a simple inventory of all the reports that exist in each office will reveal many similarities and opportunities for collaboration (not to mention happier computer programmers in the information technology area).

Cross Training

While it's not practical to send the chief gift recorder off to get an accounting degree or have the controller go on donor calls, there are some key opportunities for the business officer to be included in development planning, and in turn, the development officer can lend valuable insight to budget planning and priority sessions. Some institutions have these two positions combined, such that one senior officer oversees both development and business operations or business and planning.

Look at the schedule of on-campus activities and think of when the vice president for finance can speak to volunteers, describe the budget cycle, and answer questions about investment practice. Donors will be better informed and the development-finance relationship will be stronger. Is the chief development officer at the table when priorities are set and key budget decisions are made? Is he or she able to suggest strategies for particular initiatives? The chief development officer may not be the one who sets the priorities, but his or her influence in the planning stages will also lead to improved goals, better coordination, and clearer understanding between these two areas.

WHY DOES ANY OF THIS MATTER?

Will an organization achieve and surpass goals without harmony between the business office and development office? Sure, it's possible, but the long-term effect on an institution can be deleterious and divisive. The advantages of working through perceived and real difficulties far outweigh the disadvantages. Perpetuating the stereotype of the bean-counter business officer and the funny-money development officer leads to disrespect and distrust. An organization can ill afford that type of relationship, particularly because it draws energy and focus away from achieving institutional goals.

Establishing a positive working relationship between these two key areas is not only more efficient and productive, it will ensure better planning, improved donor relations, and hence more resources to meet the institution's needs. Maybe development officers won't be best friends with their colleague across the campus, but they are bound to find common areas of interest and responsibility. A healthy organization relies on trust, mutual respect, and positive working relationships.

PART X

The Development Profession

Throughout this book, there are numerous references to "the development profession." The question of whether fund raising is a profession, or even, as some have described it, "an emerging profession," is unresolved, although most say it does not yet meet the accepted definitions of a true "profession." Nevertheless, it is an important activity in this society, a critical endeavor of educational institutions, and the life's work of a large and increasing number of individuals who possess complex and sophisticated professional skills. Development has its own professional jargon and its own professional culture. Although they continue to emerge and evolve, development also has its own standards of excellence and ethics.

This part of the book includes three chapters that explore issues related to the "development profession." In Chapter 29, Eugene Tempel and Matthew Beem address the question of whether fund raising is a profession or a "field" and describe trends that are shaping its future. Tempel and Beem also discuss important questions of individual professional ethics. In Chapter 30, Jake Schrum also explores ethical concerns, but from the perspective of a university president and with sensitivity to the impact of ethical decisions on the values of higher education institutions. Concluding this section, in Chapter 31, Bruce Hopkins summarizes legal trends that will affect the practice of fund raising by colleges and universities as well as other types of organizations.

CHAPTER 29

The State of the Profession

Eugene R. Tempel and Matthew J. Beem

I t has been nearly 400 years since the first organized effort was made to seek philanthropic support for higher education in the United States. In 1643, two volunteers, with a case statement entitled "America's First Fruits" to give them courage, set out for England to raise funds for the fledgling Harvard College.[1] Nearly four centuries later, Harvard University raised $485 million in one year (2000)[2] with a professional staff of 80 fund raisers working university-wide.

Forty-three years ago, The Greenbrier Conference created the concept of university advancement, the overall umbrella under which many college and university fund raisers work today. The development of professional organizations like the Council for Advancement and Support of Education (CASE), the Association of Fundraising Professionals (AFP), and the Association of Healthcare Philanthropy (AHP) have worked to improve the professional level of fund-raising practice.

Today's university fund raisers take the legitimacy of their appointment for granted. Newcomers or senior practitioners are likely to be viewed as legitimate professionals in the institution. University presidents in the early 1990s and at the beginning of the current century viewed their fund-raising staffs with high levels of satisfaction.[3] The presidents' perceptions of their fund-raising staff and fund-raising productivity were strongly related to presidential satisfaction with the fundraising program itself. So fund raisers in higher education who are successful are viewed very positively by their institutions. This represents considerable progress from earlier decades, when their predecessors often were viewed with some disdain.

DEFINING A PROFESSION

Has fund raising become a profession? Maragaret Duronio and Eugene Tempel deliberately chose to call fund raising a field instead of a profession.[4] They concluded that fund-raising practitioners desired to do their work as professionals but that fund raising as a field had not developed into a true profession by the mid-1990s. The same holds true today.

If the six characteristics that Robert Carbone outlined in 1989 as defining a profession are examine clearly, fund raising does not yet qualify as a profession, although progress has been made in some areas.[5]

1. *Autonomy.* The only fund raisers likely to have some autonomy are those in senior positions. Lower level staff members have less autonomy. Things have not changed markedly from the time Carbone conducted the study.

2. *Systematic knowledge.* There has been significant progress on this front. College- and university-based research programs, The Aspen Institute, the Social Science Research Council, Independent Sector, and others have created a body of knowledge about philanthropy and fund raising in the past 12 years. The new CASE *International Journal of Educational Advancement* has provided a vehicle for the dissemination of fund-raising knowledge specifically related to colleges and universities.

3. *Self-regulation.* Fund raising is no closer to entry-level control than it was in 1989. There is an increase in those holding the Certified Fund Raising Executive certificate granted by the AFP, but entry into the field is still open. There is no formal body that controls membership in college and university fund raising. In fact, a recent story in the *Chronicle of Philanthropy* outlined a trend toward appointing individuals from the business world over those with careers in fund raising.[6]

4. *Commitment and identification.* Carbone said, "Little evidence exists that fund raisers are committed to fund raising as a career or that they identify with it as a unique subculture."[7] But fund raisers are likely more willing to identify with their colleagues today, especially in higher education.

The increase in AFP membership alone indicates level of commitment may be changing. One study shows that fund raisers do today identify with fund raising as a subculture, with 53 percent indicating a "professional" orientation, having made a commitment to both the institutions for which they worked and fund raising as a career.[8]

5. *Altruism and dedication to service.* Fund raisers are committed to their work, but they also value and consider their compensation. Duronio and Tempel found that fund raisers generally were more generous in both their giving and volunteering than the general population. Also, fund raisers talk about their work as missionaries; their commitment to the cause energizes them.

6. *Ethics and sanctions.* Fund raisers have well-developed codes of ethics that provide a floor of professional conduct. AFP has a well-developed code of ethics; CASE also has a code of ethics. But most fund raisers are unsure about how to enforce the codes. CASE has no sanctioning process, so fund raisers in higher education are left to monitor themselves. The inability to enforce ethical standards may be the most serious challenge to professionalization.

Paul Pribbenow has written about professionalism from the perspective of service to the public good, where service to others transforms work.[9] The commitment to serving a cause impacts the way in which work is done. Serving both the programs of colleges and universities and the needs and interests of donors creates an environment where college and university fund raisers can establish trust. From the perspective of several scholars on this topic, trust is at the heart of professional behavior. Development officers cannot become more professional without increasing the level of trust they engender as fund raisers.

COMPENSATION OF FUND RAISERS

Few in the nonprofit sector refute the notion that fund raisers are important human resources in today's competitive world. Studies have shown that fund raisers are among the highest paid staff members in the nonprofit sector, including higher education. Top-level advancement officers in colleges and universities have seen their salaries grow at higher rates than their mid-level colleagues' have, according to several recent measures. A 2000 report shows a 4.4 percent increase in high-level external affairs salaries in 2000.[10] This marks an increase over the 4 percent gain in 1999, following a 1998 increase of 4.5 percent. Mid-level external affairs salaries increased only 2.12 percent in 2000, according to the survey, following a significant drop from 4 percent growth in 1999 and 3.5 percent in 1998.

The survey also provided median salaries for high-level advancement posts: $93,000 for chief development officers, $61,706 for chief public relations officers, and $50,000 for alumni affairs and publications directors. Those who administer fund raising and other functions are paid higher salaries, $99,240 on average. There is anecdotal evidence that some institutions are paying well beyond this.

The study shows that salaries among institutions vary greatly depending on their overall budgets. For a chief development officer at an institution with an annual budget of $18.1 million or less, the median salary is $65,000; on a campus with a budget of $93.8 million or more, the same position pays $135,000. At the other end of the salary spectrum, a survey released in 2000 by the Association of Professional Researchers for Advancement found that the typical association member is a woman earning $30,000 to $35,000, with a college education and four to five years of research experience.[11]

The competition to cultivate and secure major gifts has caused organizations to explore what it takes to hire and retain good fund raisers. This exploration has resulted in a trend toward performance-based or incentive-based pay.

Performance pay in professional fund raising is uncharted territory. A *Currents* article reported that organizations that compete for top fund raisers were adding incentive-based bonuses to pay packages.[12] And educational fund raisers were thinking about incentive-based pay plans to help them retain, reward, and motivate talented development staff members in light of the tight salary scales common at colleges and universities. At that time, only three out of 330 development offices that responded to the survey offered cash bonuses for outstanding performance. By 1999, a study by Matthew Beem reported that seven of 21 respondents were compensated for performance, with the remainder reporting a preference for such an arrangement.[13] And a 1998 metaanalysis quantitatively analyzed the results of 39 surveys and found a positive correlation between financial incentives and performance quantity.[14]

Until recently, fund raisers joined their profession and higher education institutions because they believed in the causes they represented. In his 1966 fund-raising classic, *Designs for Fund Raising*, Harold J. Seymour clearly states the traditional view that fund raisers should be paid for service, not performance.[15] The intangible but significant personal satisfaction that came from association with a favorite university was more than enough to offset the below-average salaries. Such an approach to fund raising led professionals to perform their duties in exchange for standard cost-of-living raises and the significant pleasure of advancing a meaningful cause.[16]

In recent decades, however, a new organizational model has emerged. Colleges and universities have seen the environments in which they operate become increasingly competitive. They have been forced to compete for scarce resources—including human resources. Many organizations, in an effort to attract, hire, and retain the best development professionals, have created compensation plans that pay fund raisers cost-of-living and performance-based increases. The positions that result are often among the highest paying throughout the entire institution.

Institutions are struggling with the competing priorities of an institutional commitment to traditional modes of operation and a resource-dependent commitment to new ways of doing business. A recent survey aimed at measuring fund raisers' conceptions of their compensation, while not generalizable or conclusive, did reveal two distinct perspectives.[17] One group of fund raisers clearly work for the causes they represent. They believe mission is of primary and compensation of secondary importance. Although not all members of this group overtly oppose performance-based pay, each member said serving the cause he or she represents is paramount. The other group is motivated by money. For them, performance-based rewards are a potent incentive, and their reliance on such motivations is central to their success and happiness.

THE IMPACT OF SUPPLY-SIDE PHILANTHROPY

Changes in donor behavior have implications for the way in which fund raisers do their work. In 1998, Paul Schervish and John Havens estimated that the total transfer of wealth from one generation to the next in the next 55 years would between $41 trillion and $136 trillion, depending on how the economy grows.[18] Even using conservative figures for the larger amount, the total is considerably larger than the $10 trillion estimated by Robert Avery and Michael Rendall in 1989.[19] The estimate is that $6 billion to $25 billion will be dedicated to philanthropy, much of it to America's colleges and universities. Big gifts go predominately to higher education. During the second quarter of 2001, the Center on Philanthropy's Million-Dollar List found 673 gifts of $1 million or more, with 422 gifts totaling $2.51 billion given to colleges and universities. There were 106 gifts of $10 million or more; 62 went to colleges and universities.[20]

The challenge for nonprofit organizations, including colleges and universities, and their fund raisers is to increase the share of wealth dedicated to philanthropy. With concepts like "venture philanthropy" and "social investing" in ascendancy, adhering to the traditional fund-raising model may be inadequate to create this larger share for philanthropy. Schervish believes that this new approach to giving represents "supply-side philanthropy," driven by donors rather than institutions and their fund raisers.[21]

Fund raisers have traditionally worked from a "demand-side" model, based on organizational needs, described in the form of the case statement and increasing involvement to increase donor contributions. This model was given a theoretical framework by Schervish in his description of the philanthropic identification model, with communities of participation the key factor in success.[22] But, college and university fund raisers have always modified the demand-side model as the gift solicitation moved into major and planned gifts, recognizing that donor interests in specific projects might result in larger gifts if the institution were willing to be flexible.

The supply-side model concept suggests an even more open approach. Those with the most wealth to give to philanthropy often want to be a force for major change in society. Many want to fund programs and operating projects instead of facilities and endowments. And many want to fund multiple projects through a single source. The increase in private foundations and donor-advised funds in community foundations is part of this phenomenon. So is the huge growth of funds at investment banking firms like the Fidelity Charitable Gift Fund. This growing trend has led some colleges and universities to create donor-advised funds and accept gifts that are partially designated for other institutions. Many believe that only by accepting the supply-side model will philanthropy be expanded.

To work in this supply-side world, fund raisers must use a "discernment model" instead of the "scolding model" traditionally employed in demand-side philanthropy.[23] For example, rather than pointing to an obligation to give (the scolding model), fund raisers can help donors through a process of discovery about philanthropy and discernment about the use of their wealth. With this approach, institutions have an opportunity to help increase the amount of philanthropy and enhance the quality of gifts at the same time. College and university fund raisers are in an excellent position to adopt this model because they have programs and activities that relate to almost any topic or problem that might be of interest to a donor. They are often in a position to involve faculty, students, and alumni in solving problems and taking on projects when partnerships outside the institution are required. And, their fund-raising infrastructures are usually larger, providing the professional guidance and expertise that the donor may need and the time the donor may require.

Tension is created when the fund raiser works with a potential donor in the discernment process. As the donor discovers the values that motivate his or her philanthropy and begins thinking of larger commitments to philanthropy, gifts might go to other organizations in addition to the fund raiser's organization, or totally to other organizations. How will colleges and universities respond in this environment? If one takes the supply-side model to its extreme, fund raisers would be employed by donors instead of institutions. Fund raisers can avoid this extreme by creating understanding of this phenomenon at their institutions and seeking to be recognized and rewarded for service to the general philanthropic sector as well as their own institutions. Fund raisers must adopt a perspective of abundance rather than scarcity. There is reasonable certainty that an increase in the share of wealth committed to philanthropy will result in an increase in philanthropy for their own institutions.

ETHICS AND THE PROFESSION

The complex environment in which fund raising takes place today requires a strong commitment to personal ethics on the part of the fund raiser. Rosso says, "fund raising is the servant of philanthropy."[24] Others talk about fund raising and the public trust. Fund raisers recognize that the work they do has both a technical and an ethical component. The ethical component of fund raising has two sides: a personal-professional side and an organizational side. In Chapter 30, Jake Schrum, a university president, considers ethical issues from the perspective of the institution. In this chapter, the focus is on the personal-professional side, that is, the issues of concern to fund-raising professionals as individual practitioners.

Independent Sector reports that those who presume to work for the public good must assume the public trust.[25] "A profession is built upon the notion of service to others and the trust that comes from a commitment to place the interests of clients above self-interest. This trust results from the practitioner's performance with both technical and ethical proficiency."[26] Each fund raiser has a personal responsibility to ensure the public trust. The CASE, AFP, and AHP codes of ethics provide a floor of ethical principles that can inform personal and professional decision-making. These codes assign fund raisers the responsibility for educating organizations about ethical behavior. If fund raisers are to uphold the public trust, they must accept the responsibility for the ethical behavior of the college or university for which they work. For example, one action fund raisers take in this regard would be to encourage their colleges and universities to formally adopt the Donor Bill of Rights.

Fund raisers must work to build public trust. Ethical behavior is based on values their constituents expect them to demonstrate. When Michael Josephson asked more than 10,000 individuals what values they attributed to an ethical person, the following ten values topped the list: honesty, integrity, promise-keeping, loyalty/fidelity, fairness, concern for others, respect for others, law-abidingness/civic duty, pursuit of excellence, and personal accountability.[27]

These ten values reflect the nine beliefs Independent Sector asks each fund-raising professional to incorporate:

1. Commitment beyond self is at the core of a civil society.

2. Obedience to the laws, including those governing tax-exempt philanthropic and voluntary organizations, is a fundamental responsibility of stewardship.

3. Commitment beyond the law, to obedience to the unenforceable, is the higher obligation of leaders of philanthropic and voluntary organizations.

4. Commitment to the public good requires those who presume to serve the public good to assume a public trust.

5. Respect for the worth and dignity of individuals is a special leadership responsibility of philanthropic and voluntary organizations.

6. Tolerance, diversity, and social justice reflect the independent sector's rich heritage and the essential protections afforded it.

7. Accountability to the public is a fundamental responsibility of public benefit organizations.

8. Openness and honesty in reporting, fund raising, and relationships with all constituencies are essential behaviors for organizations that seek and use public or private funds and that purport to serve public purposes.

9. Prudent application of resources is a concomitant of public trust.[28]

Both the list of values and the Independent Sector commitments relate to fund-raising work. An article in *U.S. News & World Report* discusses the "dance of deceit" between funders and fund-seekers.[29] Adopting the values of honesty, integrity, loyalty, and promise-keeping will help make certain that we are not involved in that dance.

Fund raisers must keep the promises they make to donors (and not overcommit the institution). They must be loyal to both the donor and the institution. They must be fair to both the donor and the individual. They need to demonstrate concern for donors as individuals and respect them rather than view them as sources of funds to be manipulated for gain. They have a responsibility to be the best that they can be and prepare themselves technically and ethically to carry out their work and hold themselves personally accountable for what they do.

It is important for fund raisers to be grounded in values that help guide their work. The philanthropic world is more complex today than it was two decades, even a decade, ago. For example, the question of "who is the client?" has become much more difficult to answer as major gift work has increased and new types of donors have emerged. The development officer can no longer simply see his or her institution as the client when donor interests drive the planned and major gifts that have been the most rapidly growing category of higher education philanthropy.

To build and preserve the public trust it is essential to act with transparency. Development officers must decide ethical dilemmas in ways that their key constituents would see as most beneficial to most stakeholders. And they must be willing to explain their decisions to the stakeholders, often a complex task when faculty, students, alumni, parents, employers, funders, and the public have different expectations.

CONCLUSION

Fund raising has evolved significantly and is today regarded positively by the leadership of American colleges and universities. Fund raisers are comparatively well paid. But, fund raising has not yet achieved the status of a full profession. Fund raising at American colleges and universities requires a renewed commitment on the part of professionals in the field to be active in service to the institution. The major increase in wealth and the amounts of wealth held by single individuals create "supply-side" philanthropy that changes the nature of development. Competition for the best fund raisers and increased use of bonus plans and other compensation systems challenge the focus on mission. Fund raisers must define themselves and their work in ways that create public trust if they are to realize the potential growth in philanthropy that will help colleges and universities serve the public good.

NOTES

1. David Hammack, *Making the Nonprofit Sector in the United States: A Reader* (Bloomington: Indiana University Press, 1998), 30.

2. Council for Aid to Education website (http://www.cae.org.dataminer21/ dm/user/rankings/rankingdisplay.cfm), viewed July 10, 2001.

3. Gary A. Bouse, "Factors Related to Levels of Presidential Satisfaction with Fund Raising at Selected Colleges and Universities" (Ph.D. diss., Indiana University, 2001); and "University Presidents: Satisfaction with Fundraising Efforts as their University," The Center on Philanthropy at Indiana University (Indianapolis, IN, 2000), ix.

4. Margaret A. Duronio and Eugene R. Tempel, *Fund Raisers: Their Careers, Stories, Concerns, and Accomplishments* (San Francisco: Jossey-Bass Publishers, 1997), 2.

5. Robert F. Carbone, *Fundraising As a Profession* (College Park, MD: Clearinghouse for Research on Fund Raising, 1989), 13–14.

6. Elizabeth Schwinn, "Banking on Corporate Experience," *The Chronicle of Philanthropy* (http://wwwphilanthropy.com/free/articles/v13/i18/18003901. htm), viewed July 9, 2001.

7. Carbone, 36–37.

8. Duronio and Temple, 98.

9. Paul Pribbenow, *Serving the Public Trust: Insights into Fundraising Research and Practice*. New Directions in Philanthropic Fundraising, vol. 26 (San Francisco: Jossey-Bass, 1999), 29–50.

10. College and University Professional Association for Human Resources, *2000–2001 Administrative Compensation Survey* (February 2001), 9–28.

11. Association of Professional Researchers for Advancement, *Searchable Salary Results* (Westmont, IL: Association of Professional Researchers for Advancement, 2000), 3.

12. Mike McNamee, "Scaling the Salary Heights," *Currents* 12 (October, 1986), 6.

13. Matthew J. Beem, "Fundraising in the Balance: An Analysis of Job Performance, Appraisals and Rewards," *International Journal of Nonprofit and Voluntary Sector Marketing* 6, No. 2 (May 2001), 164–71.

14. Douglas G. Jenkins et al., "Are Financial Incentives Related to Performance? A Meta-Analytic Review of Empirical Research," *Journal of Applied Psychology* 83, no. 5 (1998), 777–87.

15. Harold J. Seymour, *Designs for Fund Raising: Principles, Patterns, Techniques* (Rockville, MD: Fund Raising Institute, 1988), 171–78.

16. Stewart R. Clegg and Cynthia Hardy, *Studying Organization: Theory and Method* (London: Sage Publications Ltd., 1999).

17. Association of Fundraising Professionals, *Compensation and Benefits Survey* (Alexandria, VA: Association of Fundraising Professionals, 2000).

18. Paul Schervish and John Havens, "Money and Magnanimity: New Find-

ings on the Distribution of Income, Wealth, and Philanthropy," *Nonprofit Management and Leadership* 8 (1998), 421–34.

19. Paul G. Schervish, "The Material Horizons of Philanthropy: New Directions for Money and Motives," in *Understanding the Needs of Donors: The Supply Side of Charitable Giving*, New Directions for Philanthropic Fundraising, vol. 29 (San Francisco: Jossey-Bass, 2001), 10.

20. Million-Dollar List, The Center on Philanthropy at Indiana University, 2001.

21. Schervish, "The Material Horizons of Philanthropy," 13.

22. Paul G. Schervish, "Inclination, Obligation, and Association: What We Know and What We Need to Learn about Donor Motivation," in *Critical Issues in Fund Raising*, ed. Dwight F. Burlingame (New York: John Wiley & Sons, 1997).

23. Paul G. Schervish, "The Spiritual Horizons of Philanthropy: New Directions for Money and Motives," in *Understanding the Needs of Donors: The Supply Side of Charitable Giving*, New Directions for Philanthropic Fundraising, vol. 29 (San Francisco: Jossey-Bass, 2001), 23–26.

24. Henry A. Rosso, *Achieving Excellence in Fund Raising* (San Francisco: Jossey-Bass, 1991) 7.

25. INDEPENDENT SECTOR, *Ethics and the Nation's Voluntary and Philanthropic Community: Obedience to the Unenforceable* (Washington, DC: INDEPENDENT SECTOR, 1991), 12–13.

26. Eugene Tempel, "Ethical Frameworks for Fundraising," in *Principles and Techniques of Fund Raising*, ed. The Fund Raising School (Indianapolis, IN: The Fund Raising School, 2001), 101.

27. Michael Josephson, *Ethics in Grantmaking and Grantseeking: Making Philanthropy Better* (Marina Del Ray, CA: Joseph & Edna Josephson Institute on Ethics, 1992), 9–17.

28. INDEPENDENT SECTOR, 12–13.

29. Betty Streisand, "The New Philanthropy; The Tech Economy May Have Collapsed, But Tech Millionaires Are Still Giving," *U.S. News & World Report* (http://www.usnews.com/usnews/issue/010611/biztech/philanthropy.htm), viewed August 2, 2001.

CHAPTER 30

Ethical Issues in Educational Fund Raising

Jake B. Schrum

T hose engaged in educational fund raising face an important task. In addition to striving toward monetary goals, they must work to preserve their personal integrity and the integrity of both institutions and their donors. Meeting this challenge requires that they make ethical decision making a fundamental component of the philanthropic process.

During the last three decades, there has been an increasing discussion and a growing literature on the subject of fund-raising ethics. This chapter will explore fund raising from three different perspectives—the institution, the fund raiser, and the donor—and attempt to grapple with the ethical issues often faced in the process of ensuring the honor and integrity of educational fund raising.

In looking at these three perspectives, the situations chosen are ones that a host of institutions and individuals have faced through the years and that are common to almost all fund-raising organizations: (1) ethical issues linked with institutional mission, (2) issues of personal integrity for fund raisers, and (3) donors and the opportunity for enlightenment.

ETHICS AND INSTITUTIONAL MISSION

Institutions whose missions are poorly defined or that lack a comprehensive statement of purpose are most susceptible to recurring ethical dilemmas in their pursuit of gift resources. Conversely, institutions with well-defined comprehensive mission statements will find it easier to understand and answer ethical questions regarding fund raising.

Following is a brief case study that helps to make the point. A major donor who wants to give away $20 million wants a law school named for her. The first female law graduate from her alma mater, a large public institution, she desires a legacy tied to her chosen field. The law school at her alma mater is named for someone else, so she turns to the fine small private university, located in the city where she has made her reputation as a federal judge. She asks the president if she will take her $20 million to build and endow a new law school that would bear her name.

This small university is just ending the fourth year of a five-year, $50-million capital campaign. The campaign is at a standstill with $25 million raised. Most of the goals related to support of facilities and students have not been fulfilled. The university is in a relatively small city, and the largest public university in the state—which has educated most of the state's lawyers—is thirty minutes away.

A broad mission statement for this president's institution might read as follows: "The mission of our university is to educate students to live fuller lives and gain a lifelong appreciation for the pursuit of knowledge." On the other hand, a better defined statement might read: "We are committed to providing a superb undergraduate education in the context of a residential community that values the intellectual, spiritual, and physical growth of the whole person."

Does the president have an ethical dilemma? If so, how do these two mission statements help or hinder finding a solution to that dilemma?

This case study is basic to the ethical issues faced in fund raising. A mission statement as loosely defined—and therefore almost meaningless—as the one in the first scenario gives the president much flexibility, and yet it seldom aids the institution in defining priorities for securing charitable gifts. The president might take the gift in good faith, build the law school, cause irreparable damage to the faculty in arts and sciences, and have trouble securing law students due to the strong and established competition from the nearby public university. If the president refuses the gift, she might be declining the opportunity for the university to explore new academic frontiers and achieve the campaign's financial goal.

In the second scenario, the president's decision is simple. The mission statement is very clear about the central educational purpose of the institution. It is an undergraduate institution, exclusively. This does not mean that the president should not be open to new opportunities, even those that might change the purpose and priorities of the institution. However, it would be evident to all of the university's constituents that establishing a professional faculty and curriculum alongside a comprehensive undergraduate program would alter the university's educational direction significantly. In almost all instances the president in scenario two would refuse the gift. Moreover, since trustees have the final fund-raising responsibility for the institutions, a clearly defined mission statement helps to inform their perspective regarding why a president might have kindly refused a $20-million gift.

Presently, more institutions are taking a step beyond their mission statements and now publish their core values too. Often, these core values give even more clarity to ethical decisions regarding gift acceptance and solicitation. For instance, if the core purpose of the undergraduate institution in the case study had been stated as "Fostering an undergraduate liberal arts institution whose values and actions contribute to the betterment of humankind," then the word "undergraduate" more clearly makes the argument for the refusal of a gift that changes the type or category of the institution into one that also awards professional degrees.

If an institution is clearly committed to its mission as well as its core purpose and values, and that clarity and commitment are shared by all of its constituents, then ethical dilemmas concerning the solicitation, acceptance, and use of gifts are easier to solve.

THE FUND RAISER'S PERSONAL INTEGRITY

The nature of their work often places educational fund raisers in situations involving personal ethics. At the risk of oversimplification, there is one question that fund raisers should ask in such situations: "If my decision were open to public scrutiny, would I or others have cause to believe that I had jeopardized my personal integrity or the integrity of the institution?"

Chief development officers repeatedly emphasize cost-effectiveness in their fund-raising programs, especially in direct-mail programs. They have suggested no program should cost more than 25 percent of dollars raised—a reasonable and generally accepted percentage. However, they increasingly need to acquire new donors by direct mail, and they have been told that to do this they might have to spend as much as 50 cents on the dollar to acquire these new donors. Do they approve the program and hope it is so successful that no one questions the cost? Do they quietly get the president's approval and not mention it to others important to the institution? Or, do they inform their constituents of the need to acquire new donors and tell them that they are considering the possibility of spending a larger-than-average amount of money to accomplish this goal?

The answer is obvious. They should proceed with number three, make their case, and keep their credibility intact. They avoid having to answer embarrassing questions that would make others wonder about their personal and professional integrity while also raising concerns about the institution's investment in fund-raising costs.

Another example might involve the ethics of confidentiality in fund-raising research. How much should fund raisers seek to know about their donors, and how should they use information to formulate their approach for funds? The guideline is simple. Fund raisers should not preserve, transmit, or otherwise use any information about their donors unless that information comes from public sources or has been provided by the donor.

Suppose an institution's financial aid director tells a development officer that the parents of a freshman student have just sent family financial information to determine if their child is eligible for any type of scholarship or financial aid. The parents, who also seem to be good prospects for future major gifts, assume that this information will be held in a confidential file in the admissions and financial aid office. Should it be available to development or any other office in the university? The answer is clearly "No." The information does not come from a public source, and the parents did not intend for it to be shared with other offices within the university.

Each development professional must protect his or her own personal integrity and self-worth. The continuous questioning of the motives of minds and hearts enhances the professional's ability to know when his or her own integrity is in jeopardy. Moreover, if fund raisers' decisions and actions can withstand public scrutiny as well as their personal test of moral responsibility, then they will find themselves in fewer ethical compromises. It is important to remember that an educational fund raiser not only represents his or her ethical beliefs but should also mirror the core values of the institution.

ETHICS AND POTENTIAL DONORS

Most donors want to be helpful to the charity they support. However, without adequate precautions on the part of fund raisers, the donors' zeal to contribute funds sometimes can create more harm than good.

Derek Bok, former president of Harvard, reminds us that some gifts perhaps should be refused:

> In some situations, donors seek to attach conditions to their gifts that invade Justice Frankfurter's "four essential freedoms of the university"—"To determine for itself on academic grounds, who may teach, what may be taught, how it shall be taught, and who may be admitted to study." Since these freedoms are central to the university, a president or dean must constantly work to protect them against encroachments, whether the incursions come in the form of government regulations or in the more seductive guise of restricted gifts. Accordingly, an institution must reject donations that would require it to deviate from the normal standards of admissions, or give a donor the power to appoint a professor, or restrict a chair to persons advocating a particular set of values or beliefs.[1]

Do instances such as those described by Bok have to be unsavory, compromising, or confrontational? more than likely, these instances provide those in educational fund raising one of the most significant opportunities they might ever have to stretch beyond the ivy-covered walls to enlighten those who say they want to support education.

How often does one hear an educational administrator, dean, president, department chair, or development officer say to a colleague, "That donor just does not understand academic freedom or, for that matter, higher education"? Often, in frustration, institutions accept gifts that raise questions of ethical compromise, or refuse gifts believing that the donor intended to compromise the integrity of the institution from the beginning.

Many of these instances offer what can be described as "an opportunity for enlightenment." It is possible that some educators do not understand the intricacies of the nation's economic system. Likewise it is also possible that some businesspeople might not fully understand the philosophy and reasoning behind the importance of academic freedom in the nation's colleges and universities.

Educators should welcome the opportunity to interact with donors in a way that allows the latter to teach the former about their needs and desires while enabling educators to enhance donors' understanding of the intricacies of the academic community. If educators reject this opportunity, then one could wonder about their commitment to the use of education as a means to enlighten and possibly inspire others.

If a donor wants to give a gift that may compromise the mission of the institution or the integrity of those in the academic community, educators have an obligation to explain to their donors why such gifts would harm the institution. Donors have reasons, important to them, for directing their financial resources to one cause or another. Fund raisers should be sensitive to the history, philosophy, and emotional reasons that lead them to suggest sharing their resources in a certain restricted manner. As fund raisers learn, so too can donors. Willingness to understand the needs of donors will, in many cases, encourage them to understand academia. If fund raisers handle these situations sensitively and openly, the result might be greater understanding on the part of both parties.

Unfortunately, sometimes neither the educators nor the donors are willing to strive to understand the other. Or, in some cases, after much discussion and explanation, deeply held values and reasons still prevent either side from budging. The fact remains that educators must refuse some gifts, and some donors must recognize that the academic community cannot fulfill their philanthropic needs or their desire for a certain kind of recognition. However, both donors and educators should welcome "opportunities for enlightenment." Such interaction should be a valued part of the fund-raising process.

CONCLUSION

Educational fund raisers, their colleagues, their institutions, and their donors continue to face ethical questions. Often there are no easy answers to these dilemmas. All parties should and must answer difficult questions before making decisions that affect—sometimes for several generations—individual lives and the institutions they care about.

In making these decisions, however, fund raisers should always bear in mind three fundamental questions: Is the proposal in keeping with the mission of their institution as well as its core values? Will it jeopardize their personal integrity as well as the integrity of the institution? And, finally, can the situation benefit both parties by providing an "opportunity for enlightenment?"

NOTE

1. Derek Bok, *Beyond the Ivory Tower: Social Responsibilities of the Modern University* (Cambridge, MA: Harvard University Press, 1982), 266–267.

CHAPTER 31

Legal Trends Affecting Philanthropy

Bruce R. Hopkins

P hilanthropy—the transfer of revenue and property for charitable purposes—is a major activity of the nonprofit sector, including its educational component, of the United States. By any conceivable measure (other than volunteering), this sector is experiencing immense growth. No end to this phenomenon is in sight; the sector will continue to expand. This trend is informing all of the legal trends affecting philanthropy, of which there are 20.

GROWTH OF THE PHILANTHROPIC SECTOR

A few statistics sustain the point, derived from IRS, congressional, and charitable sector data. There are, officially, over 1.5 million tax-exempt organizations (the actual number is probably higher). The revenue being generated by exempt organizations is in excess of $900 billion; their assets have a total value of about $2 trillion. Charitable giving in 2000 totaled $203 billion. The sixth largest tax expenditure is the charitable contribution deduction, predicted to be $181.7 billion for the federal government's fiscal years 2000–2004.

The matter is, in fact, more dramatic. One of the byproducts of the recent reorganization of the IRS, and specifically the establishment within the agency of its Tax Exempt and Government Entities Division, is the marshaling of even more tax-exempt income and assets. Now, in addition to what has been traditionally regarded as the tax-exempt sector, there have been added about 900,000 retirement plans and 86,000 state and local governmental entities. Public retirement plans control about $3 trillion in assets, while private retirement plans have about $2.4 trillion in assets. The concept of the nonprofit sector is further expanded if the total value of $1.3 trillion in tax-exempt bonds is taken into account.

INTENSIFIED GOVERNMENT REGULATION

This spectacular and ongoing growth of the charitable sector is spawning the most overarching of the legal trends affecting philanthropy. The first of these trends in the law, then, is intensifying government regulation of philanthropic organizations and those who raise funds for them. It is a trend that will be shaping the development and direction of the law concerning philanthropic organizations.

Not everyone is cheered by this seemingly endless expansion of the charitable realm. There are policymakers—more than a few—who are of the view that the sector is too large and that its growth should be curtailed (see the 20th trend). These policymakers—including members of Congress and their staff, representatives of the Treasury Department and the IRS, and judges—may be heard muttering that "there are too many tax-exempt organizations." Some of this reflects the never-ending battle over what functions belong in which sector. That is, there are those who believe that certain functions now underway in the charitable sector should be the province of the governmental sector (federal, state, or local), and there are those who advocate that certain charitable sector functions belong in the commercial business sector.

Unhappy policymakers vent their frustrations in many ways. One of them is by stepping up regulation. This phenomenon, then, leads to the principal legal trend affecting philanthropy. This is, as noted, an overarching trend, one that supplies the framework for the other 19 legal trends. This trend is driven by, in part, the sheer growth of philanthropy. The fact that policymakers are decidedly disturbed about all of this is reflected in increasing reference to the sector, or elements of it, as an industry.

USE OF THE INTERNET

The hottest legal issue of the day affecting the philanthropic world is use by charitable (including educational) organizations of the Internet. Philanthropic organizations are daily using this mode of communication to solicit contributions and to engage in related and unrelated business activities, not to mention pursue forms of advocacy, including attempts to influence legislation and participate in political affairs.

Government is being quick to respond, although affirmative guidance in this area will be slow in coming. The IRS is making it clear that Internet use does not entail some special exception; rather, all the usual requirements apply. This includes the panoply of intermediate sanctions, private inurement, private benefit, charitable gift substantiation, the quid pro quo contribution rules, and the appraisal rules. The states see Internet fund raising as forms of gift solicitation requiring state law regulation, principally by means of their charitable solicitation acts. Not uncommonly, localities (counties, cities, towns) are picking up the pace of assuming jurisdiction over, and regulating, charitable gift solicitations.

Government will be reacting to charitable organizations' Internet practices, which include email and Website gift solicitations, ongoing auctions, corporately sponsored Websites, clicks to commercial business, charity malls, online advertising, virtual trade shows, and all the rest this technology is rapidly bringing.

Tax law specialists at the IRS surf the 'Net; it is an easy way for the agency to monitor what philanthropic organizations are doing. This practice is not confined to the IRS; other governmental agencies do it, such as congressional staff and committee members.

Thus, the second of the legal trends affecting philanthropy: use of the Internet by philanthropic organizations will engender much new law and considerable application of existing law principles. For the short run at least, Internet communications by philanthropic organizations, and the law they will engender, promise to trigger a—perhaps the most—significant legal trend affecting philanthropy.

ENTREPRENURIAL SPIRIT

The legal trend concerning the Internet nicely leads to another principal manifestation stimulating the trend of more government regulation—actions by philanthropic organizations themselves.

Just as increased use of the Internet by philanthropic organizations is bringing greater scrutiny of that use, to be followed by pronouncements and regulation, more aggressive entrepreneurship is bringing more applicability of the unrelated business rules (see the 13th trend). The entrepreneurial spirit certainly can be found in the field of education. There, educational institutions are broadening the scope of their reach to areas such as adult education, publications, distance learning, fitness facilities, and seminars to name a few. Other activities by educational institutions are spawning more law and regulation, such as the emerging rules pertaining to corporate sponsorships and travel tours. Indeed, many of these fields are no longer the principal domain of education; they are now discrete areas of inquiry and law expansion.

This, then, is the third of the legal trends affecting philanthropy: the law that is coming in response to the upsurge in entrepreneurship by philanthropic organizations.

INTERMEDIATE SANCTIONS

Another major issue of the day is the matter of the intermediate sanctions rules. Much enforcement and litigation in this arena lies ahead. This is the fourth of the legal trends affecting philanthropy: expansion and enforcement of the intermediate sanctions rules in ways that will directly and indirectly affect fund raising for philanthropy.

A brief history of the intermediate sanctions rules illustrates how quickly these trends can develop (see the 20th trend). Just a few years ago, if the IRS found a philanthropic organization to have engaged in an inappropriate transaction (such as the payment of excessive compensation or the sale of an asset for less than fair market value), its only formal recourse would be invocation of the doctrine of private inurement or private benefit. In either instance, the sanction is revocation of tax-exempt status (see the 13th trend). Today, however, the considerations are quite different.

The intermediate sanctions body of law was enacted in 1996. It constitutes the most important package of rules concerning philanthropic organizations since the basic statutory scheme in the field of public charities was established in 1969. Proposed regulations emerged in 1998; temporary regulations were issued in 2001. Final regulations were issued in early 2002, thereby launching this area of the law as one propelled by major IRS guidance and enforcement.

In the case of the intermediate sanctions rules, the penalties fall on the person or persons involved in the transaction. As part of this trend, the IRS will be concentrating on enforcement of these rules. This focus will entail the emergence of private letter rulings on the subject, as well as considerable litigation. Philanthropic organizations will be endeavoring to comply with these rules, for instance by reconfiguring the composition of their boards of directors and relying more heavily on the analyses provided by consulting firms. Two of the aspects of this law that will be relied on are the rebuttable presumption as to reasonableness and the initial contract exception.

Greater emphasis on the intermediate sanctions law means more concentration on the matter of compensation arrangements and compensation amounts involving philanthropic organizations. This is particularly a problem for the larger institutions, such as colleges, universities, and health care entities. But, far more is at stake than compensation issues; greater attention will also be given other transactions with insiders, particularly lending, rentals, and assets sale deals.

Also a concern will be contractual arrangements involving philanthropic organizations and companies that organize and operate special events. Under certain circumstances, these companies will be considered disqualified persons. This means that not only will the amount of fees paid be scrutinized but also the structure of the contractual arrangement. The intermediate sanctions rules include the concept of the revenue-sharing arrangement, which can cause the entire amount involved to be a prohibited excess benefit transaction.

As to insiders, a fifth trend will be extension of the concept of the persons that are considered insiders or disqualified persons with respect to philanthropic organizations. Traditionally, these persons are trustees, directors, officers, and key employees, coupled with their family members and controlled entities. This trend will see the concept of the insider/disqualified person deepened and expanded.

The matter of the insider will be deepened by the definition of the term in such a way as to reach more deeply into the ranks of the institutions. Again, this problem will be of the greatest concern for colleges, universities, and health care entities.

REPORTING AND DISCLOSURE

The sixth legal trend affecting philanthropy will be additional emphasis on reporting and disclosure. The principal form of reporting today is by means of the annual information return (Form 990). This return will be revised and expanded.

Those in philanthropy know that, today, other forms of federally mandated reports must be faced: appraisal summaries, gift substantiation, the quid pro quo contribution disclosure rules, and reporting of the sale of contributed property, just to name a few. More of this kind of thing is on the way. And these are only federal tax forms; other government agencies may join in.

Disclosure requirements will also be increasing apace. Not too long ago, the philanthropic sector had to comply with document disclosure rules. This law required (and still does) charitable and other tax-exempt organizations to make their annual information returns and applications for recognition of exemption available for public inspection. Not content with that, Congress subsequently required public dissemination of these documents. Many of these returns and applications are now available on the Internet.

Fund-raising professionals are only beginning to cope in an environment in which prospective donors, the media, and others have immediate access to sensitive information about educational and other philanthropic institutions. Gift decisions are being made on the basis of data the fund-raising professional never hears about.

All of this activity should start another trend, but it probably will not. This preferred trend would be greater involvement in the preparation of annual information returns by fund-raising executives. Much is said in those documents that pertain directly or indirectly to charitable fund raising—statements that are made without any consultation with the development professional.

ABUSES IN PLANNED GIVING

The seventh of the emerging legal trends affecting philanthropy is ongoing, and perhaps increasing, abuse of planned giving techniques. The planned giving vehicles, particularly the charitable remainder trust and the charitable gift annuity, are wondrous and amply beneficial to donors and donees—particularly when coupled with the full charitable contribution deduction for gifts of appreciated property. Nothing is ever static: being so marvelous, it is not surprising that these vehicles are starting to be manipulated and abused for wrongful ends. Given the fact that the statutory law in this area was written over 30 years ago, the sector can be thankful that this trend did not commence earlier.

Unfortunately, this trend is already well underway. Congress has had to revise rules in this area. The IRS has promulgated regulations in an effort to stop egregious exploitation of the charitable remainder trust and charitable lead trust rules. More noncharitable uses of planned giving vehicles by crafty tax planners are on the way.

PRIVATE FOUNDATION LAW AND PUBLIC CHARITIES

The eighth legal trend affecting philanthropy will be extension of some of the private foundation rules to public charities. This trend also is well underway, as seen in the development of the intermediate sanctions rules. Those rules, applicable to educational institutions and other public charities, are based largely on the self-dealing rules applicable with respect to private foundations.

Congress may decide that some public charities are not expending sufficient funds for charitable purposes. If it comes to that, perhaps some form of mandatory payout rule will be enacted, modeled on the present rules applicable to private foundations and based on the concepts of minimum investment return and qualifying distributions. This trend is likely to begin with imposition of this type of rule on only some philanthropic organizations, such as supporting organizations (see the 11th trend).

The taxable expenditures rules are another fertile area for expansion. This could come about if Congress decides to crack down on lobbying, political activities, and other forms of advocacy by philanthropic organizations. Many of these limitations are in the private foundation law, ready to be plucked out and imposed on public charities.

There are two sleepers here. One involves the private foundation jeopardy investment rules. If Congress ever decides to take a look at investment practices by some public charities, imposition of the jeopardy investment rules on public charities could be the consequence.

The other sleeper is the tax on private foundations' investment income. A time will come when the federal government is looking for additional tax revenue (see the 19th trend). The massive amount of accumulated tax-exempt income and capital gain stored up within philanthropic institutions and other tax-exempt organizations (see above) may suddenly appear quite attractive to the government's revenue-seekers. Should that happen, the statute taxing private foundation net investment income and capital gain would likely emerge as an attractive model.

INVOLVEMENT IN JOINT VENTURES

The ninth legal trend affecting philanthropy will be greater use by educational and other philanthropic organizations of joint ventures, including partnerships and limited liability companies. Many charitable programs are being housed in these vehicles; this practice will increase.

In the past, a philanthropic organization became involved in a partnership solely as a financing vehicle. Sometimes, joint ventures with exempt or for-profit companies were used to advance limited program goals. Today, charitable organizations are using joint ventures and limited liability companies to conduct substantial exempt functions. Indeed, the law is evolving quickly to the point where some of these ventures will themselves be able to qualify as tax-exempt, charitable organizations.

This trend will have immense consequences for philanthropy. Most donors and grantors do not understand joint ventures and limited liability companies, or at least have trouble fathoming the use of them in the philanthropic setting. They are finding these separations of activities confusing. Even if some donors and grantors find these ventures understandable, they may not support them with their largesse. The law will be wrestling with the question as to the deductibility of gifts to these entities. Likewise, the law will grapple with the matter of the appropriateness of grants by private foundations to these entities and, if they are to be permitted, the circumstances in which that will be the case.

OTHER ALTERNATIVE ENTITIES

Use of alternative vehicles will not be confined to limited liability companies and other joint venture vehicles. The tenth legal trend affecting philanthropy will be greater use of appendages such as supporting organizations and title-holding companies. The increased use of donor-advised funds (see the 12th trend) is part of this trend. Once again, this greater emphasis on bifurcation will stimulate additional uncertainty, if not more confusion, among donors and grantors. Also stimulating more tax-exempt organizations, it will generate more government regulation.

Two other trends will emanate from all this. The 11th trend will be greater federal government examination of supporting organizations. The IRS is finding instances of control by disqualified persons of these organizations, in contravention of law. This may well cause Congress to extend some of the private foundation rules to supporting organizations (see the seventh trend).

The 12th trend will be increasing government scrutiny of donor-advised funds. The IRS does not like them, and the agency may persuade Congress to dislike them as well. The IRS is of the view that, at least in some cases, organizations that maintain these programs are not engaged in philanthropic activities, that transfers to them are not gifts, and/or that contributions to them do not qualify as public support. A consequence of all this festering may be legislation governing the ability of philanthropic organizations to maintain these funds.

PRIVATE BENEFIT DOCTRINE

The 13th legal trend affecting philanthropy will be the emergence of the private benefit doctrine as a major force in the law concerning philanthropic organizations. While this doctrine has been around for years, it has been rarely applied and has been almost always overshadowed by the private inurement doctrine and the intermediate sanctions rules (as to the latter, see the fourth trend). Like the private inurement doctrine, the sanction for violation of the private benefit doctrine is revocation of tax exemption. Unlike the private inurement doctrine, however, the private benefit doctrine does not require the involvement of an insider, which makes its application so potentially pervasive.

This trend that will be emerging is application of the private benefit doctrine to relationships between philanthropic organizations and for-profit businesses. These businesses will include fund-raising companies and corporate sponsors. They may also include management companies and landlords—perhaps even accountants and lawyers. The IRS will be looking for ways to assert that the ostensible philanthropic organization has become merely an instrument of the for-profit organization. The philanthropic organization's "affiliation" with a for-profit entity or a "system" involving one or more for-profit entities can taint the philanthropic organization with a substantial commercial purpose (see the 15th trend). The result: private benefit that causes the philanthropic organization to lose or be denied tax-exempt status.

UNRELATED BUSINESS RULES

Just as increased use of the Internet by tax-exempt organizations is bringing greater regulation of that use (the second trend), more aggressive entrepreneurship (the third trend) will be bringing more application of the unrelated business rules. Thus, the 14th trend (and the second easiest of them to predict): the development of more law as to what constitutes an unrelated business. This will be true generally and in the philanthropic context.

Fund raising and the unrelated business rules long have had an awkward coexistence. This trend will transform the relationship from awkwardness to hostility. The fact is (and many fund-raising professionals deny this) that fund-raising is not *program* activity of philanthropic organizations. Most fund-raising activities (aside from the seeking of gifts and grants) are, in the tax law setting, businesses. That is, they are efforts to sell goods or services for the production of income. This is a particularly vulnerable area for special events.

Historically, fund-raising activities have been sheltered from taxation either by a specific statutory exemption (such as businesses conducted by volunteers) or by the rationale that they are not regularly carried on.

The 14th trend will see this shelter weaken. The more philanthropic organizations engage in entrepreneurial efforts to generate funds and overall diversify their approaches to fund development, the more the unrelated business income rules will intrude.

COMMERCIALITY DOCTRINE

The third and 14th trends in turn will lead to more extensive application of the commerciality doctrine. This doctrine, the development of which is the 15th trend, causes loss or denial of tax-exempt status where the philanthropic organization is operating in a commercial manner, that is, in a manner comparable to that of for-profit business. Evidence of commerciality is found in audience selection, profit margins, and advertising. Functions that are particularly vulnerable are restaurants, grocery stores, gift shops, consulting, and publishing.

To date, the commerciality doctrine has been largely created and sustained by the courts. This will continue and intensify. This trend, however, is likely to see Congress engraft the commerciality doctrine into the statutory law. Also, the trend will see the IRS utilize the commerciality doctrine in assessing whether activities are unrelated businesses.

DEFINITION OF "CHARITABLE"

Other trends portend the emergence of the 16th trend: redefinition of the term "charitable" for purposes of tax exemption. This trend can manifest itself in many ways. One could be by more aggressive application of the unrelated business income rules (see the 14th trend). Another possibility could be more pervasive application of the commerciality doctrine (see the 15th trend).

More likely, however, will be developments at the state and local level. There, some jurisdictions are striving to narrowly interpret the law as to what is "charitable" for real property tax exemption purposes. This is most apparent in the realm of health care, but the approach is spreading. If it catches on at the state and local level, it would be an incentive and a precedent for those who want to narrow the scope of federal law tax exemptions (see the 19th trend).

WATCHDOG AGENCIES

The 17th trend—really a quasi-legal trend but with some bearing on legal aspects of philanthropy—will be the demise of the watchdog agencies. They are being marginalized because of the access to vast amounts of information due to recent changes in the disclosure laws (see the sixth trend). Prospective donors, for example, can obtain ample information about charities without having to contact these agencies. The same is true for the media. Thus, the need for the watchdogs is declining, and they will decline in number and perhaps disappear altogether. The recent merger of the National Charities Information Bureau with the Philanthropic Advisory Service of the Better Business Bureau is a manifestation of this trend.

Unlike most of the other legal trends, this one actually embodies good news for the philanthropic sector. The watchdog agencies, fancying themselves to be "voluntary" in nature when in fact they are *coercive*, too often establish and enforce standards that are arbitrary and nonsensical. These groups frequently and openly display an anti-philanthropy perspective. For reasons that remain mysterious, their pronouncements often are passively accepted as objective information, when in fact the materials they disseminate are subjective in nature and obtained by processes that are decidedly at odds with principles of fairness and due process. Their passage as mere filters will be good for the philanthropic sector.

COMPLEXITY OF THE LAW

The 18th trend is, in the light of the foregoing, somewhat obvious (and thus the easiest to predict): greater complexity in the law affecting philanthropic organizations. It is one thing for law enforcement and regulation to increase (the first trend); however, it is another thing altogether for the sheer complexity of the law to intensify.

The complexity will come in response to the growing sophistication of philanthropic organizations. Areas of particular applicability in this regard will be use of the Internet (see the second trend), corporate sponsorships, creative uses of planned giving vehicles (see the seventh trend), and greater attempts to regulate the fund-raising process.

Most of the complexity in the law pertaining to philanthropic organizations will be generated by the Department of the Treasury and the IRS. This will come in the form of more regulations and rulings, which in turn will spawn more litigation and court opinions. Seeking to refine, revise, or reverse some of these rules and court decisions, Congress will create more statutory law. As the Internal Revenue Code grows, the process of rulings, regulations, and court opinions will be occasioned again. This cyclical process will continue and intensify.

Other federal agencies will similarly be active. Likely candidates are the Federal Election Commission, the Federal Trade Commission, the U.S. Postal Service, and the Departments of Education and Health and Human Services. Not to be overlooked, however, are the state governments. Somehow, these governments are going to have to coordinate their regulation of charitable fund raising or face an effort to preempt the field by federal law. Also, the emergence of local government regulation of fund raising will add to the complexity in this field.

RATIONALE FOR TAX EXEMPTION AND CHARITABLE DEDUCTIONS

The 19th trend that seems to be developing, although it is too soon to be certain, is loss (or denial) of the true rationale underlying tax exemption for philanthropic entities and the income, gift, and estate tax charitable contribution deductions. These features of the federal tax law are mainstays of what has come to be known as a "civil society" or a "democratic state." They are the essence of "pluralism" of institutions— the structure of society by which there are the nonprofit, business, and governmental sectors. The principle is that a civil society needs all three sectors; these sectors must thrive and, by definition, operate in some tension with respect to the others. This means that there will always be rivalries and disputes about what functions properly belong in which sector.

Tax exemption of most nonprofit organizations has traditionally been seen as a necessary and inevitable consequence of this philosophical construct. It is an unavoidable aspect of pluralism, in that taxation of philanthropic organizations amounts to hindering and interfering with them. Tax exemption is thus not simply tax policy; it is a natural reflection and component of what is essentially a political philosophical doctrine. Therefore, tax exemption and the charitable contribution deductions are not *benefits* conferred by governments. The revenue generated by philanthropic and other tax-exempt organizations is not that of governments to begin with. This is a regime of coexistence; it is not (nor should it be) a situation where one sector dominates another and designs to confer benefits on the other sector.

Yet, evidence is emerging that this philosophical rationale for exemptions and deductions is being forgotten or discarded. More and more, these tax features are viewed as *subsidies* bestowed by government. These elements of the tax law are being rationalized in stark economic terms, their philosophical underpinnings ignored or reconstructed. The pressure for more disclosure of the funding and operations of philanthropic organizations—the sixth trend—is based in large part on the thought that an entity that is tax-exempt lacks privacy rights and is free to be pummeled by government.

The 19th trend—coupled with the first trend—spells trouble for the philanthropic sector. There are those—and their number may be growing—who want to shrink the role of the charitable sector, treat tax exemptions and deductions as merely forms of "federal financial assistance," and tax (if only because of their size and growth) philanthropic and other nonprofit organizations. There are enough signs to regard this as a trend, thus warning the philanthropic sector to be prepared to combat it.

SURPRISE ATTACK

The 20th legal trend affecting philanthropy is a continuation of policy developments in the recent past involving the "surprise attack": the sudden emergence of a body of law affecting philanthropic organizations created by statute or by regulations. The rules come out of nowhere. In recent years, the philanthropic community experienced this phenomenon with the advent of law concerning charitable gift substantiation rules, the quid pro quo gift rules, the law concerning charitable split-dollar insurance arrangements, and incremental repeal of the estate tax.

While this trend will continue, it cannot be known at this time how it will be manifested nor how frequently. One possibility is an IRS rewrite of the charitable remainder trust and other planned giving vehicle prototype documents. Another is a significant change in the definition of the terms "income" and "principal" for charitable and other trust purposes. Still another may be a significant federal law initiative in the area of regulation of charitable solicitations.

CONCLUSION

Philanthropy in the United States does not seem to be abating, although the assessment of trends outside the law must be left to others. What is clear from the 20 legal trends affecting philanthropic organizations is that development professionals are going to have to learn to ply their trade in an environment of ever-increasing government regulation and legal constraints. This regulation is not coming solely from the tax and fund-raising regulation authorities; a telling example is the impact of the privacy regulations, developed in response to enactment of the Health

Insurance Portability and Accountability Act, is having on those who are raising funds in the health care context. Emerging government regulation certainly will not strangle philanthropy, but those who administer and raise funds for the philanthropic sector are going to have to develop and deploy sophisticated coping mechanisms to effectively function in the emerging era of more vigorous government regulation and oversight.

Conclusion: Issues and Perspectives

Michael J. Worth

I n this conclusion, I will review themes that emerge from the chapters in the book, offer some speculation about the future, and exercise the prerogative of an editor to be "editorial," that is, to express some opinions.

NEW RELATIONSHIPS WITH DONORS

In the years ahead, colleges and universities will face donors and prospects who are different from those of the past, requiring new ways of communicating, organizing, and thinking about relationships. These individuals will be of diverse backgrounds and experiences and will hold different attitudes toward higher education and their own institutions than did alumni in the past. This change will require new strategies to keep higher education among their top priorities for philanthropy.

Fund raisers in other types of charitable organizations were earlier than those in higher education to recognize the shifting realities of demographic change and adopt the sophisticated techniques of marketing to address their constituencies. Higher education fund raising has enjoyed a somewhat "protected" environment in decades past. Few other types of organizations have addressed constituencies that were relatively homogenous, affluent, and "captive," having spent four or more years of their lives physically present at the institution—in a sense, an intensive and prolonged opportunity for "cultivation" that other types of organizations could only envy.

But, as Judith Nichols points out in Chapter 14, we may already be experiencing the subtle effects of the approaching storm. Well-publicized mega-gifts and planned gifts from older donors have played a major part in pushing fund-raising totals higher, somewhat masking the reality that overall alumni participation rates have remained essentially unchanged for twenty years and that participation by young alumni remains below the average of the past. Something is happening. Indeed, many things. In addition to the forces of change described in the Introduction to this book, there has been a dramatic shift over the past thirty years in the relationship of students to their colleges and universities as a result of changing attitudes and public policy.

First, since a large portion of young people now attend college, higher education has lost some of its mystique. Being visibly associated with an institution of higher education once demonstrated to others the extent of one's exceptional educational achievement and subsequent financial success. Such pride of association is still important for alumni of the most prestigious colleges and, in years when the team is doing well, for alumni of institutions that are athletic powers. But, for many alumni of many institutions, just being a college graduate is no longer an unusual distinction and, indeed, no longer a guarantee of financial success. It may be taken for granted.

In addition, our system of financing higher education has changed dramatically in the decades since the 1970s. Expanding student assistance programs, including loans as well as grants, have shifted the locus of public support of higher education from institutions to students. Thus "empowered" by their control of funds designated for them as individuals, students have indeed become "consumers." Colleges and universities have responded effectively to the change—increasing tuition, strengthening student recruitment efforts, and improving student (or customer) service. But, it is important to remember that few former "customers" make voluntary gifts to Wal-Mart! The full fund-raising impact of this changed relationship between students and their institutions still lies ahead.

Today's donors have convenient access to multiple options for their giving. At websites such as America Online's helping.org, donors can "shop" for organizations whose purposes coincide with their own interests and make a gift with a click of the mouse. Such options offer primarily an alternative to the annual fund, but higher education institutions cannot assume that they have a "lock" on major gifts either. Indeed, many of the largest gifts of the 1990s were made to other types of organizations and causes. Although Bill Gates has made substantial gifts to universities, most of his philanthropy has been directed to international issues of particular interest to him and his wife. In his largest gift to education, he chose to work through an organization, the United Negro College Fund, rather than directly through individual institutions. In recent years, headline-generating gifts even have been directed to national and international governmental agencies; for example, the Library of Congress and the United Nations. In nearly all of these instances, the donors were alumni of some college or university that did not receive the money.

In some regards, individual donors are now undergoing a transition in their approach to giving analogous to the shift in foundation giving over the past thirty years. They are moving away from support of specific institutions to giving based on their own predefined interests and priorities. They are selecting for support those institutions and organizations that appear to possess the "capacity" to have an impact in an area of concern to them. When they do focus on supporting organizations, they increasingly take the approach of the "venture philanthropists," preferring to give their funds where they can give their time and have influence as well.

In addition to donors' changing perspectives regarding the objects of their support, they also are increasingly responsive to their own life stages and financial cycles rather than the institution's calendar. This trend does not doom the future of the campaign, for reasons discussed in the introduction to Part IV of this book, although it may redefine it. But, it does suggest that fund raising in the future likely will be more "donor-centered," a reality noted by a number of observers.

In Chapter 29, Eugene Temple and Matthew Beem explain the concept of "supply-side philanthropy," which is related to this new donor-driven environment. They argue that "College and university fund raisers are in an excellent position to adopt this model because they have programs and activities that relate to almost any topic or problem that might be of interest to a donor." But, this reassurance does not fully acknowledge the potential inconsistency of this approach with higher education's culture and its most cherished values of academic freedom and autonomy. Indeed, to an extent, colleges and universities and their donors may be moving in opposite directions, with more institutions basing their campaigns on their strategic plans and more donors preferring to set their own agendas.

NEW APPROACHES TO FUND-RAISING PRACTICE

Higher education development officers can learn much from their colleagues in other types of charitable organizations who have developed effective strategies for addressing their more diverse constituencies. There is likely to be more commonality in fund-raising practice in the years ahead, as higher education adopts more of the techniques of the broader nonprofit sector while, at the same time, a growing number of nonprofit organizations adopt "university-style" fund-raising models and refine their own pursuit of major gifts. This is not to suggest that charity auctions will soon become a mainstay of university fund raising, nor that local food banks will be launching billion-dollar campaigns. But, the adoption of more similar techniques is already occurring in some fund-raising specialties, fostered, for example, by the growth of professional organizations like the Association of Professional Researchers for Advancement (APRA) and the National Committee on Planned Giving (NCPG), which include professionals from a variety of institutional and organizational types.

For higher education development officers, this "professional convergence" offers the promise of increased effectiveness in confronting the changing realities of their work. But, it also carries the risk that a growing identity with the "fund-raising profession" will exacerbate their historic isolation from their academic colleagues on the campus and further complicate their relationships with colleagues in other disciplines of institutional advancement. The trend toward incentive-based compensation of development officers provides an illustration. The practice has been common in other types of nonprofit organizations for a long time and has been adopted by colleges and universities increasingly over the past decade. It reflects not only the professional convergence mentioned above, but also a movement toward a business culture quite different from the traditional values of academe.

NEW STANDARDS FOR ACCOUNTABILITY

Increased demands for accountability reflect growing competition and the dominance of market thinking described in the Introduction to this book. It applies at two levels, to institutions and to individual development officers. Colleges and universities now compete for public resources with other state and national priorities and for private philanthropy with a growing array of good causes. They are required, by legislators and donors, to demonstrate measurable results for the dollars invested in them. At the same time, development officers are being held accountable for meeting specific performance targets, and their compensation is increasingly "at risk" if they fail to do so.

Insistence on performance by development officers is not exactly a new concept. Indeed, development programs always have been driven by demanding goals, often publicly known and with deadlines for their achievement. That is the essence of campaigns. But, campaigns are collective enterprises, and what has changed is the focus on the performance of the individual development officer against quantitative targets specific to that individual. Several trends have converged to create this new environment.

Traditionally, fund raising has been a shared responsibility of the trustees, the president, and the development professional. In reality, however, volunteer participation has been declining even as the need to raise more major gifts has been increasing in order to meet larger goals. As Jon Dellandrea and Adel Sedra note in Chapter 5, the length of time and number of contacts required to obtain major gifts simply exceeds the time available from volunteers. Nor do volunteers necessarily possess the technical knowledge to close gifts that may involve complex gift planning. This means that more and more of an institution's gift revenue results from staff solicitations, shining the spotlight on the individual development officer's performance. Increasing development salaries also have sharpened the focus on what relationship exists between performance and reward.

By delineating what is expected and what must be accomplished to be successful, specific performance targets for individual development officers can be helpful to them. This is a far better environment than one in which judgments and salary increases are determined subjectively, perhaps based on such irrelevant criteria as style or even personal characteristics rather than objective data. But, there is a need for caution.

Many incentive programs today employ a variety of indicators to measure and evaluate a development officer's level of productive activity but stop short of basing compensation on the amount of dollars raised by that individual. Some formulas consider the achievement of dollar goals, but give credit to an entire staff or unit rather than a specific individual. It is important to keep a close eye on the line that always has been drawn between good practice and the payment of commissions, even if de facto.

Leaving aside ethical concerns, the *practical* risks in crossing that line are at least four in number. First, it could encourage fund raisers to focus on short-term results, quite possibly at the expense of the long-term "nurturing" fund raising that produces the largest gifts. Second, it could erode the relationship of trust between the fund raiser and the prospective donor and cause the solicitor's representation of the case to carry less credibility. Third, it could create tensions between volunteer leaders and the institution's staff. As Sara Patton explains in Chapter 6, a partnership including volunteers is an important ingredient of success. But, if a development officer's income depends on closing a gift, one could imagine his or her impatience over the inattention or unavailability of a trustee leader needed for a call. The temptation could be to proceed in a less than ideal manner in the interest of expediency, with the result a less than ideal response. Fourth, and most significantly, commissions could, over time, erode the distinction between philanthropy and simply doing business.

It is important to remember that fund raising is not just sales. Even allowing for research findings that donors may have mixed motives, as Kathleen Kelly reports in Chapter 4, giving still implies a substantial element of altruism and the individual's identification with the common good. The job of a salesperson is to convince somebody that he or she needs something. The job of a fund raiser is to convince that person that others need it more. To place the solicitor's personal financial interest too much at stake could make the argument less persuasive, disingenuous, even cynical. An important element in persuasion is the advocate's commitment to the cause, and research on human motivation suggests that commitment is a more powerful motivator than money. The concern that compensation might come to replace commitment as the primary incentive to development officers' best efforts does not reflect a disregard for tangible results. Rather, it is a practical concern, based on what we know *works*.

In concluding this discussion, however, I emphasize that I favor performance-based compensation of development officers as a way to clarify expectations, reward good work, and bring the incentives offered individuals into congruence with institutional priorities. But this enthusiasm remains only so long as the primary considerations in devising such plans are always the *long-run* best interests of the institution and philanthropy.

Professionals associations such as CASE and AFP may face continuing opportunities to redefine the lines, and the task will not always be an easy one, because some lines can be subtly drawn. Like freedom, good fund-raising practice may require eternal vigilance as its price.

NEW PATTERNS OF COOPERATION

Francis Pray's book, *Handbook of Educational Fund Raising*,[1] was published in 1981, more than twenty years ago and just seven years after the movement toward the institutional advancement model had culminated in the establishment of CASE. In one of his concluding essays, Pray advocates a new concept: "the integration of advancement and development functions into the institution's general administrative structure, in accord with what might be called a philosophy of 'total resource development.' "[2] Today, more than twenty years later, Pray's concept is receiving some discussion.

As Pray envisioned it, implementation of total resource development would involve appointing a senior vice president or executive vice president for institutional resources who "would direct and coordinate financial and business management, university development, public relations and alumni affairs, physical plant, and other appropriate support offices."[3] Noting that academic programs gain synergy by reporting to a single academic officer, for example, a provost, Pray argues that similar benefits might accrue by placing advancement and business functions under a single executive:

> most college and university managements and boards of trustees take a very circumscribed view of the resources of their institutions. And the ways in which resources are conceptualized unquestionably affect the possibilities of devising new strategies for better management and higher return. The almost universal habit of managing endowment as one project, cash flow as another, fund raising and solicitation of trusts as another, and plant and auxiliary enterprises as yet another, tends to prevent the development of larger and more productive resource management strategies because each small policy group or management group never conceives of the true magnitude of the enterprise subject to control and exploitation.[4]

Pray suggests that CASE and the National Association of College and University Business Officers should explore "further cooperative endeavors," and he adds that it might be chief advancement officers as well as chief financial officers who would ascend to the new senior vice presidencies he proposes.[5]

In the two decades following Pray's proposal, institutionally related foundations at public universities have achieved some elements of the integration that he envisioned. While not responsible for their institution's physical plant or budget, full-service foundations such as Curtis Simic describes in Chapter 18 do bring together the raising of funds, the management of endowments and other accounts, and even real estate and entrepreneurial ventures under one umbrella.

Reconsideration of "total resource development" in today's environment coincides with the emergence of the "integrated marketing" concept, under which many functions today associated with institutional advancement also could be subsumed. As Roger Williams observes in Chapter 26, the communications function now has been separated from development and alumni relations at a number of larger institutions. Concurrently, as noted in Part V of this book, some universities have established new reporting relationships for corporate and foundation relations professionals, often involving a dual responsibility to the vice president for development or advancement and the chief academic officer. Some companies even have appointed vice presidents for corporate relations to manage the institution's multiple relationships with the corporate world across the campus.

One imaginable scenario for the future, then, could encompass a reshuffling of the institutional advancement organization along three lines—communications becoming a part of integrated marketing, corporate and foundation relations becoming integrated with offices of sponsored research under the management of the academic officer, and the development office becoming subsumed with business and financial affairs under the banner of "total resource development."

First, there remain solid arguments for the institutional advancement model that places alumni relations, communications, and development under one executive officer. The close relationships among these disciplines are discussed by Roger Williams and Charles Webb in their chapters in this volume. Since this book focuses on educational fund raising, a full discussion of the benefits of the institutional advancement model is beyond its scope. With regard to fund raising, however, new relationships consistent with Pray's concept of total resource development pose their own problems.

For example, it is clear that closer relationships between development and the business functions of the institution are increasingly important as more gifts involve financial planning, donors require competent stewardship and more reporting, and philanthropy comes to play an ever-larger role in the financial well-being and growth of colleges and universities. But, among other concerns about the "total resource development" structure that Pray proposes would be the fear that fund raising might not retain its proper place in the priorities of the institution's leadership. Particularly at large institutions, would one executive with the wide span of responsibility that Pray describes have the time and attention to devote to fund-raising matters, or would he or she be distracted by other financial and management demands? Would the budget for planned giving be traded off against the need for a new roof on a dormitory—the former "deferred" in its impact, the latter an immediate necessity? If fund raising becomes the responsibility of a second-line officer of the institution reporting to a senior executive with competing responsibilities, then can it achieve its proper place at the board table and make the case for long-term investment in philanthropy directly to the highest levels of leadership? If not, then there is the risk that the short term will be favored over the more distant horizon, and that donors will develop relationships with other organizations that have been more patient and sustained in their attention to them.

A NEW BUT NOT SO DIFFERENT WORLD

Prior to the current volume, I served as the editor of *Educational Fund Raising: Principles and Practice*, published in 1993. It takes a long time to publish a book, especially one that includes contributions by multiple authors. The process involves enlisting the authors, sharing ideas, transmitting various drafts back and forth, then considerable additional time while the publisher accomplishes the actual production of the book. It is thus risky to make much reference to contemporary events; the use of words like "recent," and "now" introduces the possibility that the writing will seem dated by the time it appears in print. The chapters for the 1993 book were written in 1991 and 1992, and the chapters for this volume were written in 2001 and 2002, a decade later. In preparation for working on this volume, I reviewed the 1993 book with an eye to what has changed and what has not, finding both irony and reassurance in the comparison.

Several authors in the former volume (writing in 1991 and 1992) mention the then weak condition of the American economy, some even speculating that the era of mega-goal campaigns may have ended. The writings include expressions of concern over the magnitude of campaigns and the credibility of goals, suggesting the possibility that colleges and universities may alienate their donors with images of greed unless fund-raising ambitions soon return to more "realistic" proportions. How ironic that those words were written at the beginning of a decade that encompassed the longest and most robust economic boom in history and philanthropy on an unprecedented scale. Ironic, too, that as I write this conclusion to the present volume (in early 2002), the nation finds itself again gripped by recession and doubts about the future of philanthropy, references to which are scattered throughout this book. Perhaps by the time this book is published, the economic cycle will have turned positive once again. In any event, surely better days lie ahead, as they did in 1993, and as they always have.

In the conclusion to the 1993 book, I reflected on the then recent demise of communism and the possibilities for a "new world order" (a popular concept at the time), based on cooperation among nations rather than superpower stalemate. I also expressed the concern that the world might see a retreat to ancient ethnic, religious, and tribal rivalries, in which the definition of who is "us" and who is "them" might contract, weakening the concern for others that is the basis of philanthropy. The following decade provided disheartening evidence of such a retreat in the Balkans, in Afghanistan, and, still, in the Middle East. But, the 1990s also saw an expansion of philanthropy around the world and, in the United States, continuation and renewal of the tradition by a new generation of entrepreneurs. That final decade of the twentieth century and the opening years of the twenty-first have provided heartening evidence that giving is based on more than tradition—or even tax law. Instead, it reflects something more basic about human nature.

At the time of this writing, shock at the terrorist attacks of September 11, 2001, continues to affect the national spirit and concern about the future is widespread. Much of my work on this book, in late 2001 and early 2002, has been accompanied by the sounds of fighter jet aircraft flying over my home in Washington, D.C., a constant reminder of unsettled times. By the time this book is published, those events will be farther in the past and hopefully less vivid. Perhaps the world will have returned to greater tranquility. But, the events of 2001 will not be forgotten and, I hope, some positive lessons will be remembered as well. Amidst the horror and the fear, we learned that people are by nature giving, that they respond to the pain of others, that when the need is clear and lives are at stake, people are heroic and unselfish and good. In this there is reason for continued optimism about the future of society, philanthropy, and the important institutions it sustains.

RENEWING THE CASE FOR HIGHER EDUCATION

Fund raising begins with a case for support. For higher education to retain its place as the most favored recipient of philanthropy (after religion), it will need to renew its case in a way that resonates in this new age. As Seymour reminds us, "The heart has to prompt the mind to go where logic points the way."[6] In today's world, appeals to loyalty and obligation will not stir hearts. Neither will resorting to clichés, slogans, or proposals that read like business plans. People are unlikely to be moved by institutions' self-serving ambitions to be more prestigious than the one down the street or across the state or the one ranked just a notch higher in *U.S. News & World Report.*

It is true that donors wish to be assured that their gifts are used effectively, that the institutions they support are well managed and accountable for performance. But, many of the individuals who support our institutions and serve on their boards are business people who manage their own companies and have many opportunities to fully exercise their interest in business matters. What draws them to be associated with a college or university is not the chance to participate in just another corporation, but rather a search for something different—an experience that broadens their horizons, that enables them to remain in touch with the world of ideas, that provides them an opportunity to devote their abilities to something beyond self interest. If we speak to them about our institutions in purely business terms, they may understand, they may appreciate and admire our own good management skills, and they may even find it interesting. But, it will not inspire their commitment to our cause.

As David Dunlop in Chapter 8 and Frank Schubert in Chapter 9 remind us, exceptional support is forthcoming when the individual's most important values and those of the institution coincide. And yet, too many institutions state their goals in lifeless terms like "continuing the tradition" or "the pursuit of excellence." Why are a new building and additional scholarships needed? The question is often answered in terms of competition with other institutions, an approach likely to arouse only the most faithful, and without reference to the purposes— or values—of education.

Most of all, today's and tomorrow's donors want to make their gifts relevant, to have an impact, and to solve real problems. If it will refocus on the basics of its mission and role, higher education can renew its case for support and persuasively claim to fulfill all three of those criteria. In a world in which peace is threatened by hatred based on ideological and religious animosities, colleges and universities are institutions committed to reason. In a world with widening gaps between rich and poor, colleges and universities offer the opportunity for individual advancement based on merit. In a world still filled with ignorance and misunderstanding, colleges and universities stand for the creation and perpetuation of knowledge and enlightenment. In renewing the case for higher education with new donors in a new world, development officers can play a key role by keeping their donors—and their institutions— focused on these important truths.

RENEWING COMMITMENT TO OUR WORK

In the summer of 2000, I found myself driving in the vicinity of a college where I once had worked as a development officer and which I had not revisited—nor even followed closely—in the nearly twenty-five years since I had left. I had some time to spare that day, so I took a detour, parked my car, and walked alone around the campus. The experience brought back memories, but it also made me think about the meaning of a development career.

I passed students walking across a small quadrangle under tall trees. I remembered that we had raised the money to renovate this area of the campus and plant the trees. It happened before the students walking there that day had been born, and they likely were taking the beauty of the campus for granted. But, I knew how it had happened and remembered the donors who had made it possible.

There were new buildings on the campus and some bore names of individuals who were familiar to me, although I had not seen any of them in many years. I smiled, remembering one of them as a young prospect whom I had visited on behalf of the college for the first time almost three decades before. Obviously, others had successfully continued and developed the relationship begun then, culminating in major support and a major addition to the campus. I knew my own small role, played so long ago, had been forgotten by everyone except me, but I looked at the building with considerable pleasure. After that trip I returned to my own campus at The George Washington University and looked around with a similar perspective. These experiences increased my appreciation for the most important rewards in a development career.

The daily preoccupations of development officers are goals and dollars and visits and mailings and reports, and the work inevitably includes frustrations, disappointments, and failures. It is difficult to know the ultimate impact of each small step—each visit, each phone call, the endless events, and often exhausting travel. But, the small steps add up and successes occur—scholarships are created, professorships are endowed, buildings are constructed, and an institution changes over time. The greatest reward for our work in development comes not from our paychecks, not from any recognition we will receive, indeed not from anything that can be measured day-to-day or even be stated in quantitative terms. It comes from the private satisfaction of knowing that we have helped to make a lasting difference in the lives of our institutions and the people they serve. There are few careers I can imagine that offer such an opportunity to connect one's professional work to an important larger purpose. Despite the changes and challenges of this new age, educational fund raising remains a life's work worth pursuing, with commitment and with pride.

NOTES

1. Francis C. Pray, ed., *Handbook for Educational Fund Raising* (San Francisco: Jossey-Bass, 1981).

2. Ibid., 389.

3. Ibid., 395.

4. Ibid., 392.

5. Ibid., 400.

6. Harold J. Seymour, *Designs for Fund Raising* (New York: McGraw-Hill, 1966), 29.

Glossary

Advancement services. A term encompassing the "back office" operations in support of fund raising and other *institutional advancement programs*. Advancement services include such functions as prospect research and management, gift accounting and acknowledgment, and the management of information systems.

American Alumni Council (AAC). An organization of professionals in development and alumni relations, established in 1913. The AAC merged with the *American College Public Relations Association (ACPRA)* in 1974 to create the *Council for Advancement and Support of Education (CASE)*.

American Association of Fund-Raising Counsel (AAFRC). An organization of fund-raising consulting firms. Member firms subscribe to a code of ethics.

American College Public Relations Association (ACPRA). An organization of college and university communications professionals. ACPRA merged with the *American Alumni Council (AAC)* in 1974 to create the *Council for Advancement and Support of Education (CASE)*.

Annual gift. Gifts donors make in response to yearly requests to support the institution's current operating needs. Annual gifts are usually solicited through an organized program involving *direct mail*, organized telephone campaigns, the Internet, and personal solicitation.

Ask. The point in a *solicitation* at which the solicitor explicitly requests a gift.

Association of Fundraising Professionals (AFP). A professional association comprising individual members who are employed in higher education institutions as well as other types of nonprofit organizations (formerly known as the National Society of Fund-Raising Executives).

Association of Professional Researchers for Advancement (APRA). An organization of professionals engaged in prospect research, prospect management, and advancement information systems, established in 1987.

Benchmarking. A technique by which a college or university studies the programs of identified "peer institutions" in order to identify best practices with the goal of improving the efficiency and performance of its own comparable efforts.

Bequest. A gift made through the donor's will, becoming effective on the death of the donor.

Capacity. An individual's financial ability to make a gift, based on income and wealth, without regard to the likelihood that the individual will be motivated to do so.

Capital campaign. An intensive, organized fund-raising effort to secure *major gifts* and pledges toward specific capital needs or projects within a finite time period, usually one or more years.

Capital gift. A gift that adds to the institution's long-term assets, designated for a facility or equipment (physical capital) or for addition to *endowment* funds (financial capital).

Case statement. A thorough and definitive written description of the institution and its plans, including the justifications for needs addressed in a *campaign*. The case statement is a master document from which various other campaign communications, including brochures and proposals, ultimately derive.

Cause-related marketing. Activities undertaken by companies for profit with some financial benefit going to a nonprofit institution or organization. For example, a company may promise to "contribute" a certain percentage of every sale of a product.

Centralized development program. A pattern of organization in which all development staff in an institution report, through channels, to a single chief development officer. The central office maintains authority over all fund-raising policy decisions, approves fund-raising priorities, and coordinates prospect assignments. *See* Decentralized development program.

Charitable gift annuity. A contract between an individual and an institution whereby the individual makes a gift and the institution agrees to pays a life income to the donor or other beneficiary.

Charitable gift planning. The process of determining effective methods for an individual donor to make a gift, generally in connection with that individual's overall financial and estate planning. The term is preferred to "planned giving" by many professionals because it focuses on the donor and encompasses a collaboration among the donor, the donor's financial advisers, and the development professional, rather than emphasizing specific gift vehicles as "products." Most charitable gift planners are employed by institutions, but some work independently as advisers to individual donors.

Charitable remainder trust. A fund created through a gift and invested by a trustee, with income to be paid to one or more beneficiary/ies until death. After the death of the final beneficiary, the remaining principal becomes the property of the specified institution to be used as designated by the donor.

Class agents. Alumni volunteers who take responsibility for soliciting gifts from the members of their graduating classes.

Combined ask. A strategy whereby a prospective donor to a campaign is solicited for an overall campaign commitment that encompasses the annual fund as well as some capital objective. *See* Dual ask.

Community foundation. A foundation that limits its grantmaking to its local community. Community foundations generally receive their assets through contributions from donors in the community and are governed by boards representing local constituencies and interests. Many community foundations administer *donor-advised funds*.

Comprehensive campaign. An intensive, organized fund-raising effort similar to a *capital campaign* but encompassing a broader range of needs, often including annual giving as well as facilities and endowment. Comprehensive campaigns usually have larger overall goals than capital campaigns, encompassing various types of support, and usually extend over a longer period of years.

Constituent alumni associations. Organizations for alumni who attended a particular school or college within a university or who have a particular interest in a specific area (for example, the performing arts). Constituent alumni associations often are subgroups of the institution's general alumni association and are frequently represented on the larger association's governing board.

Constituent-based fund raising. A form of development program in which donors are solicited for support according to the priorities of specific schools or programs with which they are associated. This approach usually is found in programs that are *decentralized*.

Continuous campaign. A term coined to describe the reality that the interval between *campaigns* has become shorter and shorter, such that many institutions are nearly always engaged in some stage of a campaign.

Corporate foundation. A foundation that receives its funding from a parent corporation and whose grants reflect the interests and priorities of that corporation in its giving.

Council for Advancement and Support of Education (CASE). An organization of professionals in all institutional advancement disciplines, created in 1974 through the merger of the *American Alumni Council (AAC)* and the *American College Public Relations Association (ACPRA)*.

Cultivation. The process by which an institution develops a relationship with a prospective donor by providing information and involving the individual in the institution's planning and life, with the goal of engendering that person's commitment and support.

Decentralized development program. A pattern of organization in which individual schools, colleges, and other units of a large university directly employ and supervise development officers. These units have considerable autonomy in setting fund-raising policies and priorities. *See* Centralized development program.

Deferred gift. A gift made by bequest, insurance, or a life-income arrangement or trust, with the institution's access to the principal being "deferred" until the death of the donor or another beneficiary. The term "deferred gift" has for the most part been replaced by the broader term *planned gift*. *See also* Charitable gift planning.

Development. A process that includes the identification of institutional needs and priorities; the identification, *cultivation*, and involvement of prospective donors; the solicitation of gifts; and *stewardship* intended to continue the donor's interest and involvement. The term is generally used synonymously with *fund raising* today but has been used more broadly in the past to mean the activities now encompassed by the term *institutional advancement*.

Direct mail. The solicitation of gifts with a mailed "package," usually including a letter, brochure, and response device designed to encourage the recipient to send a gift by return mail.

Donor-advised fund. A charitable fund created by an individual donor and held in trust by a *community foundation*, a commercial investment firm, or another organization. The donor makes recommendations to the trustee regarding gifts to be made from the fund, but the trustee retains the ultimate discretion.

Donor-driven. A fund-raising campaign or program that is primarily responsive to the interests of prospective donors. *See* Need-driven.

Donor relations. Activities undertaken with the purpose of maintaining and enhancing relationships with donors, but not including solicitations. Donor relations encompasses such functions as donor communications, recognition, and *stewardship*, and has emerged as a specialty within the development profession.

Donor research. *See* Prospect research.

Dual ask. A strategy whereby a prospective donor to a *campaign* is solicited for a pledge toward some capital purpose, then continues to be solicited for a gift to the annual fund each year throughout the pledge period, with the hope that he or she will provide both types of support. *See* Combined ask.

Electronic screening. The electronic analysis of an institution's database of donors and prospective donors against various criteria in order to identify individuals most capable and likely of supporting the institution's fund-raising efforts. *See* Peer screening.

Endowment. Funds invested for the long term, with principal remaining intact and only income being available for expenditure. Income from endowment funds may be earmarked for specific programs or activities or may support general institutional needs.

Family foundation. A foundation established and controlled by the members of a family as a vehicle for their philanthropy. Family foundations are typically small, and their grants reflect the personal interests of family members.

Feasibility study. A market survey to determine the potential level of support for the institution and its needs from among its identified constituency. Feasibility studies are usually conducted prior to a campaign as a guide to goal-setting and campaign planning, and usually involve confidential interviews conducted by an outside consultant.

Fund raising. Programs and activities involving the solicitation of gifts to the institution. The term is generally used synonymously with *development.*

Fund-raising pyramid. A graphic device used to illustrate the way in which *annual gifts, major gifts,* and *ultimate gifts* relate to each other. A large base of donors, giving relatively small gifts, form the bottom of the pyramid, and the largest portion of total gift revenue comes from a much smaller group of donors at the top.

Gift club. A technique for recognizing donors by granting them membership in various club levels according to the size of their annual or capital gifts.

Gift-in-kind. A gift of physical property intended for use by the institution in its educational or research programs (for example, books, equipment, or artworks).

Institutional advancement. Defined by A. Westley Rowland as "All activities and programs undertaken by an institution to develop understanding and support from all its constituencies in order to achieve its goals in securing such resources as students, faculty, and dollars." *CASE* uses the term to include the professional disciplines of educational fund raising, alumni relations, communications, and related specialties.

Institutionally related foundation. A foundation that exists solely for the purpose of raising, managing, and disbursing funds to support the programs of a specific (usually public) college or university.

Integrated marketing. An approach that includes coordination of communications strategies and messages across the entire institution.

Kickoff. The point at which a *campaign* and its goal are made public. The kickoff usually includes an announcement of the *nucleus fund* total and is typically marked by a highly visible public event.

Life-income gift. A gift made to the institution with the provision that the donor and/or other beneficiaries receive income for their lives.

Major gift. A gift larger than an annual gift, often paid in installments over a period of years, and usually designated for a capital purpose. The dollar level at which a gift is considered "major" depends upon the needs and fund-raising history of the institution.

Mega-campaign. A term coined to describe college and university comprehensive campaigns with very large goals, typically in the hundreds of millions or billions of dollars.

Metrics. Numerical indicators selected to measure the efficiency and effectiveness of a fund-raising program. Metrics may include dollars raised as well as many other variables; for example, the length of time needed to mail a receipt, the number of major gift solicitations completed, and others deemed relevant by the institution's management.

National Association of College and University Business Officers (NACUBO). A professional organization that, along with *CASE*, developed reporting standards for the accounting of voluntary support.

National Committee on Planned Giving (NCPG). A professional association of individuals engaged in the field of *planned giving* (or *charitable gift planning*), established in 1988.

Need-driven. A fund-raising campaign or program whose primary focus is to raise gifts for specific, predetermined needs of the institution. *See* Donor-driven.

Nucleus fund. The total of gifts and pledges made during the initial *quiet period* of a campaign, after the institution's internal approval of a campaign but before the public announcement or *kickoff*. A nucleus fund totaling at least 40 percent of the campaign goal is generally recommended as the minimum necessary for campaign success.

Operating foundation. A foundation that develops, supports, and manages its own programs or activities and generally does not accept outside proposals.

Peer screening (or rating). A technique whereby staff and volunteers review lists of potential donors and offer judgments, based on personal knowledge, as to the prospects' ability and inclination to support the institution. Many institutions now use computerized screening programs to tentatively rate prospects' financial capacity. *See* Electronic screening.

Philanthropy. A tradition in which individuals contribute, for reasons of altruism, their time and financial resources to nonprofit institutions, with the goal of improving society.

Phonathon. An organized program of telephoning, either by volunteer callers or paid professionals, to solicit gifts from a large number of donors. Phonathons are commonly used in annual giving programs.

Planned gift. A gift made in the context of the donor's total financial and estate planning. Planned gifts often involve a bequest, trust, or annuity arrangement and usually provide tax benefits or other financial advantages to the donor as well as benefiting the institution. *See* Deferred gift, Charitable gift planning.

Principal gift. A major gift of substantial magnitude. The amount qualified as a principal gift is relative to the institution and is often defined in the context of a campaign; for example, some apply the term to gifts of $5 million, $10 million, or more. Principal gifts often are *ultimate gifts* from the perspective of the donor.

Proposal. A formal, written solicitation for a gift or grant, typically used when approaching corporate or foundation donors.

Prospect. An individual or organization confirmed as having the capacity to make a gift to the institution and some existing or potential interest in doing so. *See* Suspect.

Prospect management and tracking. An ongoing process including the matching of prospect interests to institutional needs, the development of *cultivation* and *solicitation* strategies, the assignment of responsibility for the prospect to staff and volunteers, and the systematic monitoring of activity undertaken with the prospect.

Prospect research (sometimes called *donor research*). The identification of potential donors, the gathering of background information on their interests and giving capacity, and the development of cultivation and solicitation strategies tailored specifically to the individual prospects.

Quiet period. The phase of a campaign in which the *nucleus fund* is solicited, but preceding any formal announcement of the campaign or its goal.

Regional campaign. An intensive effort to secure gifts and pledges from donors in a specific region or city, usually as a component of a larger overall campaign.

Resident management. An arrangement through which a consultant works at the institution full-time for a finite period to direct a specific campaign. Once common, the use of resident managers by higher education institutions is now rare.

Rule of thirds. A long-held and widely accepted axiom, originated by Harold J. Seymour, that states that for any campaign, the ten largest gifts will account for one-third of the goal, the next 100 gifts will account for another third of the goal, and the rest of the gifts will account for the final third. Many writers contend that these proportions have changed over time, as an ever-higher proportion of campaign funds come from a smaller number of top donors.

Sequential fund raising. A term attributed to fund-raising consultant George A. Brakeley, Jr., describing the practice of soliciting *prospects* "from the top down and the inside out." This means that prospects with the greatest *capacity* to give and those closest to the institution (e.g., board members) should be solicited before gifts are solicited from prospects of lesser capacity or whose relationships with the institution are more remote.

Solicitation. The process of asking a donor to make a gift. The solicitation visit, or "call," includes various elements of communication or conversation leading up to, or following after, the *ask* itself.

Special gift. A gift made toward some specific, nonrecurring need of the institution. In a formal campaign, the term "special gift" is sometimes used to distinguish capital gifts at some arbitrary intermediate level (for example, $10,000 to $99,999) from "major gifts" at a higher level (for example, $100,000 and up).

Sponsored research. Specific research studies undertaken by faculty or staff and paid for by a donor (or "sponsor") who often has an interest in the results.

Stewardship. Activities designed to keep donors informed and involved regarding the use and benefits of their past gifts. Stewardship is often seen as an aspect of cultivation for donors' future support. The term also is used more broadly to include the institution's careful management of the gift and the activities it supports in order to keep faith with the donor's intentions and confidence.

Suspect. An individual or organization identified as a potential donor for the institution but whose financial capacity or interest remains undetermined. *See* Prospect.

Total resource development. A concept that encompasses all efforts to secure financial resources for the institution from varied activities, including fund raising, business ventures, partnerships, sponsorships, and others.

Ultimate gift. A term coined by David Dunlop to describe the largest gift a donor is capable of making. *See* Capacity. Ultimate gifts are often, but not always, given through a planned giving device such as a trust or bequest.

Unrelated business income tax. A federal tax on income that colleges, universities, alumni associations, and other nonprofit organizations receive from activities not directly related to the educational, research, or charitable purposes of the organization.

Venture philanthropy. An approach to giving that emphasizes sustained commitment to a select number of institutions or organizations and that is accompanied by the close personal interest and involvement of the donor/s. Venture philanthropists consider charitable gifts to be "investments" and insist on measurable performance against agreed-upon targets by the organizations that they support.

Voluntary support. All gifts and noncontractual grants to colleges and universities, defined according to standards established by *CASE* and reported annually to the Council for Aid to Education in connection with the *Voluntary Support of Education* survey.

Further Reading

GENERAL BOOKS ON FUND RAISING AND INSTITUTIONAL ADVANCEMENT

Brakeley, George A., Jr., *Tested Ways to Successful Fund Raising*. New York: AMACOM, 1980.

Broce, Thomas E., *Fund Raising: The Guide to Raising Money from Private Sources*. Norman: University of Oklahoma Press, 1979.

Buchanan, Peter McE., ed., *Handbook of Institutional Advancement*, 3rd edition. Washington, DC: Council for Advancement and Support of Education, 2000.

Dove, Kent E., *Conducting a Successful Fundraising Program: A Comprehensive Guide and Resource*. San Francisco: Jossey-Bass, 2001.

Kelly, Kathleen S., *Effective Fund-Raising Management*. Mahwah, NJ: Lawrence Erlbaum Associates, 1998.

Rhodes, Frank H.T., ed., *Successful Fund Raising for Higher Education*. Phoenix, AZ: Oryx Press/American Council on Education, 1997.

Rosso, Henry A., and Associates, *Achieving Excellence in Fund Raising*. San Francisco: Jossey-Bass, 1991.

Rowland, R. Westley, ed., *Handbook of Institutional Advancement*, 2nd edition. San Francisco: Jossey-Bass, 1986.

Seymour, Harold J., *Designs for Fund Raising: Principles, Patterns, Techniques*. New York: McGraw-Hill, 1966.

Worth, Michael J., ed., *Educational Fund Raising: Principles and Practice*. Phoenix, AZ: Oryx Press/American Council on Education, 1993.

ACADEMIC JOURNALS THAT REPORT RESEARCH ON FUND RAISING AND PHILANTHROPY

CASE *International Journal of Educational Advancement* (Council for Advancement and Support of Education, Washington, DC, and Henry Stewart Publications, London).

Nonprofit and Voluntary Sector Quarterly (Association for Research on Nonprofit Organizations and Voluntary Action, Indianapolis, IN).

Nonprofit Management & Leadership (Mandel Center for Nonprofit Organizations, Case Western Reserve University, and the Centre for Voluntary Organisation, London School of Economics and Political Science).

PERIODICALS ON FUND RAISING AND PHILANTHROPY

Advancing Philanthropy, bimonthly magazine (Association of Fundraising Professionals, Alexandria, VA).

Currents, monthly magazine (Council for Advancement and Support of Education, Washington, DC).

Chronicle of Philanthropy, newspaper (Washington, DC).

Fund Raising Management, monthly magazine (Hoke Communications, Garden City, NY).

Giving USA, annual report on philanthropy (AAFRC Trust for Philanthropy, Indianapolis, IN).

New Directions for Philanthropic Fundraising, quarterly journal (Jossey-Bass, San Francisco, CA).

Philanthropy Matters, semi-annual magazine (Center on Philanthropy at Indiana University, Indianapolis, IN).

WEBSITES RELATED TO FUND RAISING AND PHILANTHROPY

The following recommendations are limited to major organizations. They provide links to other sites.

Association of Fundraising Professionals (http://www.afpnet.org).

Association of Professional Researchers for Advancement (http://www.aprahome.org).

Association for Research on Nonprofit Organizations and Voluntary Action (http://www.arnova.org).

Council for Advancement and Support of Education (http://www.case.org).

Indiana University Center on Philanthropy (http://www.philanthropy.iupui.edu).

National Committee on Planned Giving (http://www.ncpg.org).

SOURCES ON SPECIFIC TOPICS

Advancement Services and Information Systems

Burlingame, Dwight F., and Michael J. Poston, eds., *The Impact of Technology on Fund Raising* (New Directions for Philanthropic Fundraising, No. 25). San Francisco: Jossey-Bass, 1999.

Dove, Kent E., *Conducting a Successful Development Services Program*. San Francisco: Jossey-Bass, 2001.

Taylor, John H., ed., *Advancement Services: Research and Technology Support for Fund Raising*. Washington, DC: Council for Advancement and Support of Education, 1999.

Weiner, Robert L., "Buying and Implementing a Development System," in *Handbook of Institutional Advancement*, 3rd edition, ed. Peter McE. Buchanan. Washington, DC: Council for Advancement and Support of Education, 2000, 461–472.

Annual Giving

Burdenski, Robert A., "Proceed According to Plan: Why and How to Create a Strategic Plan for the Annual Fund," *Currents* 26, no. 5 (May/June 2000): 19–21.

Cardillo, Charlie, "The Unexamined Donor: For Better Planning and Greater Returns, Segment the Annual Fund by Giving Behavior," *Currents* 26, no. 5 (May/June 2000): 25–27, 29–30.

Carter, Lindy Keane, comp., *Classic Currents: Annual Giving*. Washington, DC: Council for Advancement and Support of Education, 1998.

Dove, Kent E., Jeffrey A. Lindauer, and Carolyn P. Madvig, *Conducting a Successful Annual Giving Program: A Comprehensive Guide and Resource*. San Francisco: Jossey-Bass, 2001.

Schroeder, Fritz W., *Annual Giving: A Practical Approach*. Washington, DC: Council for Advancement and Support of Education, 2000.

Schroeder, Fritz W., "Making Peace Between Annual and Major Gifts: Create a Culture That Values and Solicits Both Types of Commitment—From the Same Donor," *Currents* 27, no. 4 (April 2001): 26–30.

Wylie, Peter B., "Model Behavior," *Currents* 25, no. 4 (April 1999): 16–23.

Campaigns

Dove, Kent E., *Conducting a Successful Capital Campaign*, 2nd edition. San Francisco: Jossey-Bass, 2000.

Flessner, Bruce, "The Next Generation: How Economic and Philanthropic Trends Will Affect Your Next Campaign's Goal, Length, and Focus," *Currents* 23, no. 10 (November/December 1997): 15–20.

Gearhart, G. David, *The Capital Campaign in Higher Education: A Practical Guide*

for College and University Advancement. Washington, DC: National Association of College and University Business Officers, 1995.

Hall, Holly, "Venture Capitalists Are Changing the Capital-Campaign Rules,
Fund Raisers Told," *Chronicle of Philanthropy* 12, no. 12 (April 6, 2000):
23.

Holcombe, Terry H., "Capital Campaigns: Working Within the Goal and
Working Within the Total Fund-Raising Effort," in *Handbook of Institutional Advancement*, 3rd edition, ed. Peter McE. Buchanan. Washington, DC: Council for Advancement and Support of Education, 2000,
331–336.

O'Shea, Catherine L., "Up, Up, and Away: With Careful Piloting, Mega Campaigns Can Help Campuses Reach New Heights of Fund-Raising Success," *Currents* 25, no. 10 (November/December 1999): 21–25.

Polizzotto, Salvatore F., "A Steady Ascent: How Institutions Can Avoid the
Peaks and Valleys of Constant Campaigning," *Currents* 26, no. 9 (No-
vember/December 2000): 20–24.

Pollack, Rachel H., "Starting on the Right Foot: Answers to Campaign Questions That May Have You Stopped in Your Tracks," *Currents* 23, no.
10 (November/December 1997): 31–36.

Quigg, H. Gerald, ed., *The Successful Campaign: From Planning to Victory Celebration*. Washington, DC: Council for Advancement and Support of
Education, 1986.

Walton, Christopher R., "Rethinking Feasibility Studies," *Fund Raising Management* 28, no. 7 (September 1997): 14–19.

Corporations and Foundations

Burlingame, Dwight F., and Dennis R. Young, *Corporate Philanthropy at the
Crossroads*. Bloomington: Indiana University Press, 1996.

Glass, Sandra A., ed., *Approaching Foundations: Suggestions and Insights for Fundraisers* (New Directions for Philanthropic Fundraising, no. 28). San
Francisco: Jossey-Bass, 2001.

Gregory, Patricia, "Seeking Foundation Support," in *Handbook of Institutional
Advancement*, 3rd edition, ed. Peter McE. Buchanan. Washington, DC:
Council for Advancement and Support of Education, 2000, 325–330.

Murphy, Mary Kay, ed., *Corporate and Foundation Support: Funding Strategies for
the 21st Century*. Washington, DC: Council for Advancement and Support of Education, 2000.

Pollack, Rachel H., "Which Way Is the Wind Blowing? Trends in Corporate
and Foundation Giving and How Fund Raisers Can Stay on Top of
Them," *Currents* 26, no. 4 (April 2000): 42–48.

Sanzone, Carolyn S., "Securing Corporate Support: The Business of Corporate
Relations," in *Handbook of Institutional Advancement*, 3rd edition, ed.
Peter McE. Buchanan. Washington, DC: Council for Advancement and
Support of Education, 2000, 321–324.

Demographics and Traditions of Giving

Abbe, M. Ann, "The Roots of Minority Giving," *Currents* 26, no. 6 (July/ August 2000).

Brooks, David, *Bobos in Paradise: The New Upper Class and How They Got There.* New York: Simon & Schuster, 2000.

Gow Pettey, Janice, *Cultivating Diversity in Fundraising.* New York: John Wiley & Sons, 2002.

Nanji, Azim, "Charitable Giving in Islam," *Alliance* 5, no. 1 (March 2000): 12–15.

Philanthropy Among Business Women of Achievement: A Summary of Key Findings. Washington, DC: National Foundation for Women Business Owners, 1999.

Scanlan, Joanne, ed., *Cultures of Caring: Philanthropy in Diverse American Communities.* Washington, DC: Council on Foundations, 1999.

Smith, Bradford, Sylvia Shue, Jennifer L. Vest, and Joseph Villarreal, *Philanthropy in Communities of Color.* Bloomington: Indiana University Press, 1999.

Donor Relations and Stewardship

Barden, Dennis, "The Rationale for Donor Relations," *Currents* 27, no. 2 (February 2001): 30–34.

Davis, Judith T., "Charting a Course for Donor Stewardship: Virginia Tech Used Triangulation to Map Out a Process for Recognizing Institutional Supporters," *Currents* 27, no. 2 (February 2001): 36–41.

Donor Relations: The Essential Guide to Stewardship Policies, Procedures and Protocol. Washington, DC: Council for Advancement and Support of Education, 1998.

McLelland, R. Jane, "Essentials of Endowment Stewardship: Meet Campus and Donor Endowment Needs with Good Agreements, Well-Managed Money, and Regular Reporting," *Currents* 23, no. 8 (September 1997): 28–33.

Savage, Tracy G., "Donor Relations: Achieving Effective Donor-Centered Stewardship," in *Handbook of Institutional Advancement*, 3rd edition, ed. Peter McE. Buchanan. Washington, DC: Council for Advancement and Support of Education, 2000, 341–346.

International Fund Raising

Burg, Robert, "Finding Funds Abroad: Some Charities Are Soliciting Donors Beyond Canada's Borders," *Front and Centre* 6, no. 2 (March 1999): 1–3, 5.

Currents, Special Issue: *Advancement's Global Reach* 27, no. 8 (October 2001). Washington, DC: Council for Advancement and Support of Education.

Currents, Special Issue: *Advancement's Global Marketplace* 25, no. 9 (October 1999). Washington, DC: Council for Advancement and Support of Education.

Hayter, Scott, "Stranger in a Strange Land: A North American Learns Advancement in the UK," *Currents* 26, no. 8 (October 2000): 15.

Pollack, Rachel H., "A View From Across the Pond," *Currents* 25, no. 5 (May 1999): 32–35.

Major Gifts, Principal Gifts, and Planned Gifts

Abrams, Deborah Blackmore, and Linus Travers, "Making the Ask: A Step-by-Step Description of How to Prepare for and Solicit Major Gifts," *Currents* 26, no. 7 (September 2000): 51–59.

Burlingame, Dwight F., and James M. Hodge, eds., *Developing Major Gifts* (New Directions for Philanthropic Fundraising, No. 16). San Francisco: Jossey-Bass, 1997.

Heintzelman, Jonathan R., "Major Gifts: Up Close and Personal," in *Handbook of Institutional Advancement*, 3rd edition, ed. Peter McE. Buchanan. Washington, DC: Council for Advancement and Support of Education, 2000, 315–320.

Jordan, Ronald R., and Katelyn L. Quynn, *Planned Giving: Management, Marketing, and Law*, 2nd edition. New York: John Wiley & Sons, 2000.

Matheny, Richard E., *Major Gifts: Solicitation Strategies*, 2nd edition. Washington, DC: Council for Advancement and Support of Education, 1999.

Panas, Jerold. *Finders Keepers*. Chicago: Bonus Books, 1999.

Sharpe, Robert F., Sr., *Planned Giving Simplified: The Gift, the Giver and the Gift Planner*. New York: John Wiley & Sons, 1999.

Managing Development Programs

Asp, James W. II, "Pay for Performance," *Currents*, 25, no. 7 (July/August, 1999): 28–33.

CASE Management Reporting Standards. Washington, DC: Council for Advancement and Support of Education, 1996.

Clark, Virginia B., "Staff Management: Strategies for Success," in *Handbook for Institutional Advancement*, 3rd edition, ed. Peter McE. Buchanan. Washington, DC: Council for Advancement and Support of Education, 2000, 103–106.

Currents, Special Issue: *Managing Advancement* 27, no. 3 (March 2001). Washington, DC: Council for Advancement and Support of Education.

Greenfield, James M., *Fund Raising: Evaluating and Managing the Fund Development Process*, 2nd edition. New York: John Wiley & Sons, 1999.

Langley, James, ed., *Attracting and Retaining Good Staff: Building an Efficient and*

Satisfied Advancement Team. Washington, DC: Council for Advancement and Support of Education, 2001.

Phair, Judith T., and Roland King, *Sample File: Organizational Charts and Job Descriptions for the Advancement Office.* Washington, DC: Council for Advancement and Support of Education, 1998.

Rooney, Patrick M., "A Better Method for Analyzing the Costs and Benefits of Fundraising at Universities," *Nonprofit Management & Leadership*, 10, no. 1 (1999): 39–56.

Taylor, Barbara E., and William F. Massey, *Strategic Indicators for Higher Education.* Princeton, NJ: Peterson's, 1996.

Online Fund Raising

Currents (Special Issue: *Advancement Online*), 27, no. 5 (May/June 2001). Washington, DC: Council for Advancement and Support of Education.

Davis, Derek, "The Future of Planned Giving: Seniors and the Online Revolution," *Fund Raising Management* 32, no. 2 (April 2001): 6, 20, 33.

Grobman, Gary M., "Charleston Principles: An Important First Step," *Contributions* 14, no. 6 (November/December 2000): 26–27.

Hawthorne, Jeff, "Creating Effective Strategies for Online Fundraising," *DM News*, 23, no. 13 (April 2, 2001): 21–25.

Professional Issues, Laws, and Ethics

Bok, Derek, *Beyond the Ivory Tower.* Cambridge, MA: Harvard University Press, 1982.

Burlingame, Dwight F., ed., *Critical Issues in Fund Raising.* New York: John Wiley & Sons, 1997.

Duronio, Margaret A., and Eugene R. Tempel, *Fund Raisers: Their Careers, Stories, Concerns, and Accomplishments.* San Francisco: Jossey-Bass, 1996.

Elliott, Deni, ed., *The Ethics of Asking.* Baltimore, MD: John Hopkins University Press, 1995.

Hopkins, Bruce R., *The First Legal Answer Book for Fund-Raisers.* New York: John Wiley & Sons, 2000.

Hopkins, Bruce R., *The Law of Fund-Raising*, 3rd edition. San Francisco: Jossey-Bass, 2002.

Prospect Management and Research

Carnie, Christopher, "Finding Sunken Treasure: Uncovering the Pearls of Information in the Murky Sea of European Prospect Research," *Currents* 26, no. 8 (October 2000): 38–43.

Lindsey, Jonathan A., "Prospect Research: An Introduction," in *Handbook of*

Institutional Advancement, 3rd edition, ed. Peter McE. Buchanan. Washington, DC: Council for Advancement and Support of Education, 2000, 439–444.

Sommerfield, Meg, "Prospecting the Web for Donors: Up-to-the-minute News Delivered to Fund Raisers Automatically," *Chronicle of Philanthropy* 12, no. 20 (August 9, 2001): 27–29.

Tess, Samuel, "Coming Attractions: Five Trends That Will Affect Prospect Research on the World Wide Web," *Currents* 22, no. 6 (June, 1997): 24.

Verrette, Claire, "Get the Picture," *Currents* 25, no. 8 (September 1999): 38–43.

Williams, Karla, "No More Hit or Miss: The Role of Donor Research in Annual Giving," *Contributions* 12, no. 4 (July/August 1998): 6, 19.

Related Advancement Disciplines

Lauer, Larry D., "Marketing Across the Board," *Currents* 25, no. 1 (January 1999): 18–24.

Sevier, Robert A., and Robert Johnson, *Integrated Marketing Communication: A Guide to Comprehensive Strategies*. Washington, DC: Council for Advancement and Support of Education, 2001.

Todd, Jeffrey S., "Alumni Involvement in Fund Raising," in *Handbook of Institutional Advancement*, 3rd edition, ed. Peter McE. Buchanan. Washington, DC: Council for Advancement and Support of Education, 2000, 271–272.

Williams, Roger L., "Essay: PR and the Capital Campaign," in *Public Relations and the Presidency*, ed. J. E. Ross and C. P. Halstead. Washington, DC: CASE Books, 2001, 221–225.

Williams, Roger L., "Development Communications," in *Handbook of Institutional Advancement*, 3rd edition, ed. Peter McE. Buchanan, ed. Washington, DC: Council for Advancement and Support of Education, 2000, 203–208.

Roles of Key Individuals

Fisher, James L., and Gary H. Quehl, *The President and Fund Raising*. New York: American Council on Education/Macmillan, 1989.

Hall, Margarete Rooney, *The Dean's Role in Fund Raising*. Baltimore, MD: Johns Hopkins University Press, 1993.

Murphy, Mary Kay, *The Advancement Presidency and the Academy: Profiles in Institutional Leadership*. Phoenix, AZ: American Council on Education/Oryx Press, 1997.

Smith, G. T., "CEOs and Trustees: The Key Forces in Securing Major Gifts," in *Developing Major Gifts* (New Directions for Philanthropic Fundraising,

No. 16), ed. Dwight F. Burlingame and James M. Hodge. San Francisco: Jossey-Bass, 1997.

Worth, Michael J., and James W. Asp II, *The Development Officer in Higher Education: Toward an Understanding of the Role* (ASHE-ERIC Higher Education Report No. 4). Washington, DC: The George Washington University Graduate School of Education and Human Development, 1994.

Special Institutional Settings

Colson, Helen A., *Philanthropy at Independent Schools*. Washington, DC: National Association of Independent Schools, 1996.

Hedgepeth, Royster C., *How Public College and University Foundations Pay for Fund Raising*. Washington, DC: Association of Governing Boards of Universities and Colleges, and the Council for Advancement and Support of Education, 2000.

MacArthur, Karen M., "Advancement in Community Colleges," in *Handbook of Institutional Advancement*, 3rd edition, ed. Peter McE. Buchanan. Washington, DC: Council for Advancement and Support of Education, 2000, 487–490.

Manzo, Kathleen Kennedy, "Comprehensive Fundraising Programs Breathe New Life Into Community College Coffers," *Community College Week* 8, no. 47 (September 25, 1995): 8, 11.

Phelan, Joseph F., and Associates, *College & University Foundations: Serving America's Public Higher Education*. Washington, DC: Association of Governing Boards of Universities and Colleges, 1997.

Smith, Nanette J., "Raising Funds for Community Colleges," in *Educational Fund Raising: Principles and Practice*, ed. Michael J. Worth. Phoenix, AZ: American Council on Education/Oryx Press, 1993.

Index